ODD TRIBES

ODD

JOHN HARTIGAN JR.

TRIBES

TOWARD A

CULTURAL ANALYSIS

OF WHITE PEOPLE

DUKE UNIVERSITY PRESS

DURHAM AND LONDON

2005

© 2005 DUKE UNIVERSITY PRESS

ALL RIGHTS RESERVED

PRINTED IN THE UNITED STATES

OF AMERICA ON ACID-FREE PAPER ∞

DESIGNED BY AMY RUTH BUCHANAN

TYPESET IN MINION BY

KEYSTONE TYPESETTING, INC.

LIBRARY OF CONGRESS CATALOGING-

IN-PUBLICATION DATA APPEAR ON THE

LAST PRINTED PAGE OF THIS BOOK.

For Zia and Teague

CONTENTS

ACKNOWLEDGMENTS

This book is the outcome of roughly fifteen years of sustained research across a variety of disciplinary boundaries, so I owe thanks to many people. For reading drafts and offering excellent suggestions, I thank my colleagues in anthropology at the University of Texas, Katie Stewart, Richard Flores, Ward Keeler, and Polly Strong; I also am grateful to Jason Mellard, Chris Labuski, Beth Bruinsma, Amanda Morrison, Matt Archer, Jerry Lord, Scott Webel, George Baca, Mathangi Krishnamurthy, Andria Shively, and David Isaacson for their comments on various drafts. I have many debts, direct and indirect, to those I have tapped for their expertise or guidance in research areas with which I was unfamiliar—many thanks to Pete Daniel, Marvette Perez, Tom Sugrue, Tony Kaye, Ruth Frankenburg, and Ellen Crowell. For inspiration and direction in this project's earliest stages, I thank Donna Haraway, Susan Harding, Jim Clifford, Lorraine Kenny, and (again) Katie Stewart. I am particularly grateful to Matt Wray, who has been exceedingly generous with his time and thoughts on material and topics that we share in common. In some of my tightest binds, I've relied on his input to work through the difficulties of formulating such odd subjects of study. I also deeply appreciate Ken Wissoker for his remarkable patience in letting this project come painfully slowly to fruition. Additionally, I want to thank all the librarians who contributed generous efforts to this project, especially Jim Roan and Stephanie Thomas (at the National Museum of American History), Polly Lasker (Smithsonian Institution Central Reference and Loans), Sharon Clayton and Laurie Sauer (Knox College), and the Interlibrary Loans people at ucsc, who never cut me off, and Carolyn Herbst and Bethany Berlejung. This work was made possible by a great deal of generous support from the Social Science Research Council, the Harry Frank Guggenheim Foundation, and the National Museum of American History, Smithsonian Institution. In the end, I am most grateful to Rebecca Lyle for her enduring love and patience. Thank you all very much!

What is it about white people? This deceptively simple question cuts to the core of racial matters, but answering it requires more than an attention to race. Whites are increasingly the focus of debates about the significance of race, reversing the previous tendency to equate "racial" solely with the actions and interests of peoples of color. *Odd Tribes* also takes whites as its subject of study, but it does so without making race the singular basis for analysis. Instead, this book examines the cultural dynamics that underlie and shape racial identities.[1] This involves critically assessing assumptions that shape our understandings of race in the course of using cultural analysis to objectify whites as racially interested social subjects.[2] *Odd Tribes* is a sustained argument for the need to simultaneously critique notions about what counts as race while also analyzing the behaviors and beliefs of whites in the United States.

Odd Tribes works at making sense of white people from two angles; one focuses on the powers and privileges associated with whiteness as the other keys in on uses of "white trash" to police color lines in this country. Whiteness and white trash are hardly equivalent or entirely adequate means for examining white cultural identity. But they are useful starting points because they each bring some degree of specificity to generalization about white people. Whiteness, as a concept honed by academics and activists, asserts the obvious but consistently overlooked fact that whites are racially interested and motivated.[3] Whiteness both names and critiques hegemonic beliefs and practices that designate white people as "normal" and racially "unmarked." White trash, a lurid stereotype and debasing racial epithet, applies to poor whites whose subordination by class is extreme. This charged label is a reminder that there are important class dimensions to whiteness and that whites are not uniformly privileged and powerful.[4] These two terms are at once disjunctive, yet clearly related, making them odd subjects for cultural analysis.

"Odd" denotes one of a pair that is missing or a remainder left over after others are paired, as well as quirky, awkward, mismatched, unexpected or not easily placed, irregular, and hard to name. The key oddity of these two concepts is that they are difficult to hold equally in view: whiteness is associated with domination and hegemony; white trash applies to poor whites who are far from dominant. White trash is also a remainder of prevailing academic discussions of whiteness and blackness, a pairing that assumes these terms are sufficient for explaining race, leaving the degraded status of poor whites to fall from view (see Wray and Newitz 1997). These terms are also odd cultural subjects because the collective order each projects is as much rhetorical as it is objectively given. White trash is a degrading insult; in a sense, no one *is* white trash unless he or she is so labeled. Whiteness, in contrast, is an academic or activist term used to name a range of hegemonic practices and images. But how do generalizations about whiteness relate to the experiences and perceptions of collective identity by white people in diverse locales throughout the United States or around the world? Both labels project collective orders without examining whether or how such categories relate to actual social groups.

Undeniably, white trash and whiteness categorize collective orders in the United States, but beyond that certainty, tricky questions follow. What are the contours or characteristics of these collectives? Are they comprehensive social identities or ideological constructs; do they overlap or are they mutually exclusive? Is there a form of solidarity that links members of these collectives? Do they recognize in each other some basis of sameness, or are they negatively constructed through social exclusions and projections of difference? Is either label appropriate, given that many people are unwilling to be so characterized, whether by the degrading epithet of white trash or linked to the connotation of white supremacy inherent in whiteness?

These questions concerning their status as social collectives are framed by another suspect term, "tribes." This circumscribed concept is an artifact of colonial administrations and the pragmatic but usually distorting projection of collective orders onto heterogeneous populations. Tribes as a concept bears a sordid history and serves as a reminder of the misrepresentations that arise from efforts to objectify social collectives.[5] The perils and pitfalls entailed by such objectifications are most evident in the task of analyzing collective dynamics in relation to race.[6] Rather than rejecting the term, though, its improprieties help keep in view the difficulties of fixing the cultural contents of loose, fluid social orders. Collectives certainly exist, but are their discontinuities greater than their forms of coherence? The awkwardness of "tribes" keeps this question in view, while also asserting the importance of recognizing and analyzing the collective dimensions of social life.

"Tribes" also keeps in view the perhaps irreducible urge to objectify *those people.* Despite copious assertions about the socially constructed basis of race and numerous critiques of racial stereotypes, people still project collective forms of social difference with ease.[7] Questions about *those people* condense anxiety over how to speak properly about social groups and a desire for certainty about the character of cultural collectives in the midst of profound social, demographic, and political transformation. They also reflect a yearning for a confident high ground above the fray of accusations of prejudice, comfortably removed from the appearance of impropriety or name-calling. Arising out of the charged and contradictory expectations in contemporary public discourse that people simultaneously be knowledgeable about "cultural differences" and yet not project perceptions of difference in collective terms, *those people* encodes the selective, exclusionary strategy of projecting a delimited form of difference—whether in terms of race, class, or gender—that allows a normative center to operate. Questions about *those people* also emanate in response to assertions of political correctness, which encompass a range of efforts to police public discourse for disparaging objectifications of difference. "White trash" is an instance of this projection of *those people,* one that has received scarcely any scrutiny even in this era of highly critical attention to social stereotyping.

One means for analyzing the tangle of anxiety and uncertainty behind perceptions of *those people* is through critiques of representation that analyze projected images of Otherness (see Todorov 1984; hooks 1992). But the charged cultural work of white trash is not sufficiently encompassed by a critical attention to representational dynamics alone. Critiques will tell us nothing about how features of these representations relate to the real, daily circumstances of such whites, historically or contemporarily, or about how and why poor whites actively traffic in white trash as a means of self-identification. Deconstructions of stereotypes also too often ignore the critical role such degraded images play in the relational processes of group formation. Critical assessments of representations of poor whites need to account additionally for the way these depictions participate in and derive from the social processes that shape white middle- and working-class identities. Finally, demystifying stereotyped representations accomplishes little if this effort does not also engage the curious and steadfastly maintained disinterest in the problems of poor whites among academics and political activists who are concerned about links between poverty and racism. In stark contrast to the plethora of references to white trash in popular culture, social scientists and cultural critics appear completely disinterested in what the social predicament of poor whites, who constitute the majority of the poor population in the United States, reveals about how and why race matters in this country.[8] *Odd Tribes* thus engages white trash varyingly as a stigmatizing representation to be critiqued, as a crucial figure in the processes of class and racial formations, and also as a referent for a group that is important but difficult to depict and analyze.[9]

This book's overarching project is to analyze the relationship of phantasmic cultural forms, such as the racial stereotype white trash, to the actual social conditions of poor whites in order to generate new insights about the complex interrelation of race, class, and gender.[10] *Odd Tribes* thus deploys two alternating forms of cultural analysis, one that is empirically grounded and attentive to social processes that shape collective identity broadly, and one that critically examines the representational forms that people use and reuse to make sense of subjects like race.[11] These forms of analysis reflect the necessity of treating racial objectifications in their literal and figural dimensions, as well as examining the relevance of these objectifications to daily situations and learning from the actual uses people make of them.[12] Indeed, what is essential now to the task of making sense of race is an ability to both critique the constructed nature of representation but to also account for the way such racial objectifications operate, with an ear toward the way people work with and make sense of them.[13] It is not enough to disprove or dismiss racial stereotypes such as white trash; instead, we have to engage their figurative power. This involves examining the breadth of cultural sources for racial identities and delineating the copious forms of reinforcement these social constructs receive from the culture at large.

MORE THAN RACE?

The approach I am suggesting veers away from the theoretical and methodological choices made by cultural critics and social analysts who try to make sense of race by linking disparate phenomena to a core ideological function of racism.[14] In the face of the rapidly changing meanings and uses of race, these critics and analysts strive to reveal implicit or covert forms of racist thought and sentiment. This stance is perhaps best illustrated by the work of Eduardo Bonilla-Silva. In *White Supremacy and Racism in the Post–Civil Rights Era* (2001), Bonilla-Silva presents a thorough empirical and theoretical analysis of the covert ways racist ideology continues to maintain the manifest forms of racial inequality in the United States. He contrasts whites' general rejection of openly racialist discourse with the huge racial discrepancies in life chances among Americans. He explains that whites generally "avoid using direct racial references and traditionally 'racist' language and rely on covert, indirect, and apparently nonracial language to state their racial views" (153). Bonilla-Silva's conceptualization of the "new racism" specifies that it works via "the increasingly covert nature of racial discourse and racial practices; the avoidance of racial terminology in racial conflicts by whites; and the elaboration of a racial agenda about political matters (state intervention, individual rights, responsibility, etc.) that eschew any direct racial reference" (94). Basically, he sketches a dynamic whereby whites think racially but manage to avoid talking about race. As does any dominant group, Bonilla-Silva argues, whites still rely on "very complex ideological formations that provide them rhetorical ammunition to account for social inequality. They also cultivate a moral framework to deal with dilemmas arising from maintaining domination" (137). Whereas in the past, "white privilege was achieved through overt and usually explicitly racial practices, today . . . it is accomplished through institutional, subtle, and apparently nonracial means" (12). This complicated matter of distinguishing "racial" from "nonracial means" is the point that concerns me most and forms the basis for the cultural perspective on race sketched in this introduction (see Goldberg 1993).

Though race continues to affect discrepant life chances and to alternately limit or open access to social resources, it is increasingly difficult to find an explicitly racist component in much of what whites say and do.[15] Instead, there is a profusion of "nonracial" discourse that seemingly strives to obscure the real racist sentiments, perceptions, and interests of whites, who now cautiously and conscientiously police their public comments to efface any mention of race. Using concepts like new racism or whiteness, analysts of race work to make the implicit racial aspects apparent by linking the nonracial discourses to racist ideological constructs. My concern, though, is that this approach skews as much as it reveals in regard to the copious, often novel ways race matters in our current circumstances. I also wonder whether it is the best way to engage whites who have grown inured to charges or discussions of racism. Bifurcating racial and nonracial strikes me as an indication that the terms of racial analysis need to be either revamped or significantly broadened.[16] Rather than confidently subordinate the nonracial to an ideological obfuscation of the truly racial interests at work in contemporary society, I think it is important to examine how racial subjects, interests, and identities derive from fundamental cultural dynamics that also shape class and gendered social terrains. Cultural processes of classification and categorization can explain a great deal about how race keeps changing and the way racial identities play into and are supported by other social dynamics (see chapter 10).

Bonilla-Silva's delineation of nonracial and racial, in relation to the analytical contrast I am sketching here, suggests two distinct stances on race. One assumes we know with certainty what race is: how it works and matters, or how its effects can be recognized and ameliorated. This approach draws on both a vast knowledge base and a wealth of critical, political practice to update and demonstrate the enduring relevance of *racism* as an explanatory principle to novel contexts.[17] The other stance considers that what counts as race today is perhaps far less certain and more negotiable than it has been in the past. This perspective is easy to glimpse but somewhat hard to hold in view, especially for people who confront the inequalities of race on a daily basis. But it is an important view because it is oriented toward the onrushing future and the current tumultuous moment when, whether you consider popular culture or immigration trends, the significance of race is growing more fluid and dynamic (see Nobles 2000; Rodriguez 2000; Skerry 2000). The fact that nearly 7 million Americans classified themselves in the new "multiracial" category of the 2000 Census suggest that the meaning of race is hardly stable or uniquely defined by the polarized frame of "black and white." This speaks to the need for circumspection as much as certainty about the significance of race today.

Not too long ago demographers predicted with great confidence that whites were becoming a minority in the United States.[18] Immigration trends and birthrates reported in the 1990 Census seemed to point conclusively to the denouement of white majority status. But just a decade later that picture has been turned on its head, due partly to the number of immigrants who identify as white. Solomon Moor and Robin Fields (2002, 1A), reporting on this trend in the *Los Angeles Times*, relate that "the latest arrivals are upsetting conventional wisdom, which held that the percentage of white Americans would inevitably dwindle over time. About 75% of the U.S. populace defines itself today as wholly or partly white. Many demographers expect the same will be true in 50 years, despite continued immigration from Latin

America, Asia and elsewhere." This reflects the fact that so many immigrants are able and choose to be white. Immigrants identifying as white on the Census include Iranians, North Africans, Russians, and Armenians, as well as Central and South Americans. As Dowell Myers, a demographer from the University of Southern California, observes, "White is the most polyglot category, and it's morphing" (1A; see also Ware and Black 2002).

Another factor is that almost half of all Latino respondents to the Census racially identified as white. This choice is heavily influenced by class. Latinos living in affluent, suburban zones of the Los Angeles area tended to label themselves white, whereas Latinos living in the region's urban barrios racially identified as "Other" on the 2000 Census. This divergence in responses indicates that class is crucial, but it also shows the importance of regional dynamics and the enduring relevance of place in how people make sense of identity.[19] Moor and Fields (2002, 1A) report that "a growing number [of immigrants], influenced heavily by Latino culture, say they see race as fluid and whiteness as an unbounded territory they can enter and exit at will." This sense of fluidity turns on complex cultural dynamics that have yet to be rendered subjects of study by scholars grappling with whiteness, dynamics that are best rendered through some larger sense of culture than that entailed by racial formulations.

Two points are critical here: one is obviously that race, and whiteness in particular, still matters a great deal; but, as well, "whites" is a fluid and malleable category, encompassing a relentlessly heterogeneous population. The former point speaks to the enduring effects of racism and the need to bring it continually into view for those who are socialized to not recognize it at all. But the latter fact suggests that we be somewhat less certain and more inquisitive about analyzing and characterizing "white people." *Odd Tribes* works from a number of angles at raising the question of what counts as white, then takes the position that answers are best generated through cultural analysis, which comes in two basic forms. The first involves engagements in the field to learn from and study how people actually work at making sense of race in their daily lives. The second involves analyzing cultural representations without a predetermined certainty as to how they link back to or reveal ideological operations such as racism. To be sure, racism exists among whites and its impacts are profound. But the fact of racism does not explain everything about how and why race matters. Indeed, an overreliance on racism as an explanatory principle can obscure the ambivalence and ambiguity that characterize many whites' understandings of race. And these forms of ambiguity and ambivalence, along with the contradictory and conflicted beliefs and impulses and the often unstable, fluid forms of perceptions and comments that articulate racial matters, are best understood via cultural analysis.[20]

The central problem or challenge in this approach, though, is that the concept of culture has been subject to intense criticism over the past two decades and is regarded as highly suspect, particularly in anthropology, the discipline that has done the most to hone it conceptually. Culture has also been accused of participating in unsavory ways in reproducing racial thinking. Activists and academics who grapple with racial problems recognize that references to different cultures operate as a more polite way of imputing invidious racial distinctions. Gestures toward multiculturalism promote a view whereby peoples of color continue to be marked as cultural, while whites are allowed to stand as normal, unmarked subjects. How can culture, then, offer a means of thinking through the treacherous dynamics of racial objectification?

Odd Tribes presents an array of answers to this question, but they all stem from a basic assertion that we cannot effectively think through the processes of racial identification and disidentification without a cultural perspective.[21] An inability to grasp culture and its dynamics is central to why many whites are unable to think critically about race or to grasp its various manifestations and operations. Without some understanding that our experience of the world is culturally contoured, it is difficult to regard racism as more than just an individual failing or a vaguely perceived "institutional" byproduct. Without a recognition of the interlocking aspects of cultural perceptions and categorical identities, race appears as just another isolated topic of concern. But by starting with basic cultural dynamics, it is easy to show how race both inflects and is shaped by judgments Americans make about whether or not certain people appear to be "nice" or "friendly" or "hardworking"—each reflecting crucial categorical demarcations that ostensibly make no mention of race but that certainly operate at times in racial registers. A cultural perspective allows us to place race simultaneously in the mix of everyday life, shaping perceptions that do not appear racial, but without reductively asserting that "everything" is about race.

In the context of the United States, it is critical to engage the processes of socialization that lead whites to see each other as individuals and, in contrast, people of color as representatives of vaguely comprehended groups. At the same time, we must critically frame and analyze the collective forms that benefit whites as a group, regardless of individuals' personal sentiments about the significance of race. Historian George Lipsitz (1995, 381), in objectifying the "possessive investment in whiteness" that forms the economic, political, and social basis for white dominance, contends:

> The stark contrast between black experiences and white opinions during the past two decades cannot be attributed solely to ignorance or intolerance on the part of individuals but stems instead from the overdetermined inadequacy of the language of liberal individualism to describe collective behavior. As long as we define social life as the sum total of conscious and deliberate individual activities, then only *individual* manifestations of personal prejudice and hostility will be seen as racist. Systemic, collective, and coordinated behavior disappears from sight. Collective exercises of group power relentlessly channeling rewards, resources, and opportunities from one group to another will not appear to be "racist" from this perspective because they rarely announce their intentions to discriminate against individuals. But they work to construct racial identities by giving people of different races vastly different life chances.

The cultural perspective, as I formulate it here, addresses both this inability to grasp the distinctive social conditioning that individualism entails and the attendant ignorance of how collective processes shape our experiences and the very ground of the social order.[22] The power of this view is that it has the potential to engage whites' racial thinking by initially shifting discussions away from the charged accusations of racism and onto a ground—the subject of socialization—that may be more conducive to thinking about race and recognizing its intersection with other critical categories of social identity.[23]

A cultural perspective on racial matters has several additional advantages.[24] The first relates to the enduring contentious debates over the relative priority of the three critical registers of social identity: race, class, and gender. Analysts who feature one of these terms in their research often end up asserting the centrality or singular importance of, say, race over class, or gender over either class or race. A cultural perspective, in contrast, renders these registers simultaneously active and mutually informing, rather than disputing whether one is more fundamental than the others. In a cultural analysis, the signifiers of race, class, and gender are a series of interlocking codes by which patterns of inequality are maintained and reproduced in perceptions of similarity and difference.[25] No individual is ever only raced, or classed, or gendered, so it is a fundamental distortion of social situations to singularly analyze them as if only one of these is the primary basis for forms of disadvantage. A cultural analysis posits, instead, a range of basic processes of classification by which collective life is organized and that are at root an assignment and assertion of racial, class, and gendered identities.

Second, a cultural view offers a way of destabilizing the analytical tendency to overdraw or unwittingly reinscribe and reproduce the racial distinctions that should, rather, be subject to critique. Critical deployments of whiteness or blackness tend to reify differences between whites and blacks, rendering them as Difference on a grand scale. The concept of whiteness was honed to forefront the racially interested actions and motives of white-identified populations. But whiteness ends up being used to characterize conditions, ways of acting, forms of perception and consciousness that are allegedly unique to whites, instead of providing a way of regarding racial dynamics in some of their generic aspects. Consider the advantage of mobilizing instead an attention to cultural dynamics that shows how identification with racial matters works commonly across the color line. Despite the radical distinctions between whiteness and blackness as social positions, whites and people of color in the United States experience and perceive aspects of their daily lives in remarkably common terms—as individuals experiencing democracy, friendliness, or freedom, key tropes in American culture (see chapter 10). Highlighting these commonalities is a powerful way to assail racial thinking at large, and this is part of the promise of a cultural perspective.

Third, and perhaps most important, a cultural perspective widens the frame of reference and compels us to grapple with the way race works throughout the world. As a concept, whiteness gestures toward a broad view of the world and certainly has the potential to help us discern and analyze linkages in the ways race operates in diverse locales. But this potential largely goes unrecognized because whiteness studies are overwhelmingly focused on the United States and draw very little insight from racial dynamics in other countries (Hartigan 2000). Cultural analysis, in its basic orientation, is geared to comparative perspectives, and nowhere is such an approach more necessary than in regard to discussions of race in the United States, which are overwhelmingly concentrated on the black-white paradigm. Analyzing race in terms of culture lets us address race in a more global framework, both for the insights of a comparative perspective and in terms of assessing what, at root, commonly constitutes racial experiences, perceptions, and conditions.[26]

Cultural analysis, of course, is hardly a self-evident concept or approach. There are copious competing and often conflicting definitions of culture and varying degrees of commitment to its explanatory principles across the disciplines of anthropology, sociology, and history, not to mention the range of interdisciplinary work of cultural studies. This is not the place to resolve ongoing, animated debates over what counts as culture, but it is the place to offer a provisional sketch of what I mean by cultural analysis. This involves framing points of overlap and contrast between prevailing, competing forms of cultural studies and social sciences approaches. In broadest terms, culture, as an analytical perspective, treats collective dynamics of belonging and differentiation, the assignment of social meaning to arbitrary biological traits, the naturalization of certain orders of inequality or dominance, the forms of etiquette or decorum that discipline bodies and behaviors, the expressive styles that organize each of these into tangible forms of meaning that people encounter in a multitude of reinforcing or challenging circumstances, and the forms of performance in which categorical identities and more fluid constructions of self are reproduced or revised.[27] Each of these dynamics informs the interpretive work of cultural subjects in making sense of their world and negotiating the uneven social terrains that shape their individual and collective identities.

This last point is, arguably, the central focus in a cultural analysis and what differentiates it from ideological forms of analysis.[28] Conceiving of subjects in terms of culture highlights the performative, relational, and situated dynamics that shape and are often recast by people's interpretation of their personal and collective circumstances. These situated circumstances—as they reflect and combine local and global economic, political, and social flows—often involve ambiguous, even contradictory constructions of meaning. Taken in concert, these elements of cultural analysis cohere into a distinctive take on race, one that, interestingly, is lacking in current approaches to studying whiteness and has yet to be adequately applied to questions of white trash.

In contrast to the approach I am sketching here, whiteness studies instead is dominated by the enormously influential model of Otherness, which prioritizes an attention to representation and ideological explanations. This model, best evidenced in the work of Edward Said but also, importantly, Toni Morrison, has been very effective at describing in general terms how racial representations are formulated and circulated. But it brackets off attention to the social processes that are encompassed by cultural analysis: the work of sorting out matters of belonging through the recognition and replication of sameness and similarities, the construction of affinities and the contests over common depictions of collective identity, which each typically bears the convoluted traces of the site where that work is done (Sokefeld 1999). The social dynamics of establishing, comparing, and ranking similarities is as fundamental to the operation of racial identities as is the projection of Otherness. But these dynamics are usually left unexamined in racial analyses that forefront the contentious matters of establishing and drawing boundaries around forms of difference (see Rahier 1999).

David Cannadine (2001) develops a critique of this analytical attention to Otherness in his work, *Ornamentalism: How the British Saw Their Empire*. He examines how upper-class Britons' perceptions of the urban poor derived from a complex dynamic by which forms of equivalence, rather than projected forms of difference, were fashioned between the "dangerous classes" and the colonized "natives." That is, the Other was not the singular basis for construction of British identity. Cannadine explains, "The mode of imperial ranking and imaging was not just based on the Enlightenment view of the intrinsic inferiority of dark-skinned people: it was also based on notions of metropolitan-peripheral analogy and sameness. For as the British contemplated the unprecedented numbers massed together in their new industrial cities, they tended to compare these great towns at home with the 'dark continents' overseas and equate the workers in factories with the coloured peoples abroad" (5–6). Cannadine explains how such "domestic-imperial analogies," fixated on forms of similarities between the metropolitan "dangerous classes" and the " 'negroes' of Empire," relate to contemporary debates over the urban underclass and its racial characteristics. The critical point from Cannadine's argument that I draw on here is that "the British Empire was at least as much (perhaps more?) about the replication of sameness and similarities originating from home as it was about the insistence on difference and dissimilarities originating from overseas" (xix). The "replication of sameness and similarities" is at the core of the cultural dynamics of belonging, and it opens onto a far more heterogeneous and conflicted subject than is typically rendered in discussions of projected forms of Otherness (see also Porter 2004).

Cannadine (2001, xix) makes this point explicit, arguing that, "pace Edward Said and his 'Orientalist' followers, the British Empire was not exclusively (or even preponderantly) concerned with the creation of 'otherness' on the presumption that the imperial periphery was different from, and inferior to, the imperial metropolis: it was at least as much (perhaps more?) concerned with what was recently called the 'construction of affinities' on the presumption that society on the periphery was the same as, or even on occasions, superior to, society in the metropolis." Undoubtedly, the critical concepts of Orientalism and the Other profoundly alters the way race is comprehended by making apparent a host of representational dynamics around race that are evident and active today in many realms of popular culture. But Cannadine's attention to an entirely different set of social dynamics at work in British constructions of identity—featuring practices that purposefully racialized, demonized, and excluded ostensibly white urban poor, much like white trash—suggests that Otherness as an analytical model also has its limits.

Another problem with a focus on Otherness is that it promotes a view of the world privileging psychoanalytic accounts that emphasizes psychological diagnostics over social processes as explanatory principles. This view projects a uniform collective consciousness, in contrast to a cultural view that comprehends subjects as composed by multiple (at times discrepant) discourses and responding to diverse, shifting sets of concerns, rather than being wholly oriented by an ideological disposition. Whites, via the Otherness model, are overdrawn as uniform ideological subjects all operating under a shared perception of Difference. The psychoanalytic dynamics assumed by the Otherness model may well apply at the individual level, and it has some insight to offer into how individuals are socialized to recognize social patterns, but it is not clear that psychoanalysis has any effective insight into collective processes, especially the intense contests over belonging that are constitutive of cultural orders.

The limits of the Otherness model are becoming apparent as a variety of new research projects challenge its relevance to explaining collective aspects of racial identity.[29] Studies engaging in closer examinations of the operations of racial domination from the perspective of the dominant have found that "it" is not simply a unified subject, but rather is a collective order riven with numerous social distinctions. Rather than representing a uniform social position, whiteness is constituted and reproduced by distinct political, economic, and social forces, operating with differing impacts at local, regional, national, and international levels. These conditions produce social subjects more intricately assembled and far more difficult to assail than is perhaps imagined by scholars and activists who advocate the abolition of whiteness (see chapter 7). I am not arguing simply for a more nuanced and "human" view of the dominant, but rather for the value of a different analytical orientation for assailing forms of racial thought and their reproduction (Limon 1998; Stoler 1995).

A cultural view of whites in the United States as a distended collective shaped by disparate circumstance—as a group constituted by distinct processes but that is also indistinguishable in aspects of its identity from other collectives within American culture—emerges from recent ethnographies that offer critical insight into the complexities of white racial identification and modes of differentiation, globally and in the United States (see Kenny 2000; Perry 2002; Sanjeck 1998; Byrne forthcoming). These works reveal the intensely local nature of social dynamics that shape whites' racial judgments and perceptions; they also underscore a critical disconnect between characterizations of whiteness as a nationally hegemonic force and white racialness as it manifests in particular places. The overarching finding of these ethnographies is that local circumstances—racial demographics, popular cultures, political orders, and economic conditions—deeply inflect the significance of race and the processes by which racial matters are perceived and engaged.

Rather than simple conveyors of racism or as automatons dominated by a racial ideology, whites' engagement with race involves interpretive work, as with any cultural dynamic. This work is made more or less precarious depending on the types of reinforcements provided by particular social settings. One key to understanding whiteness, then, is recognizing that racial interpretations are always competing with other interpretive repertoires such as class and gender and neighborhood and nation. Chapters in the second half of this book investigate how a racial reading is at times outweighed or reinforced by competing options for interpreting social circumstances. They offer up reminders that instances of white attitudes and behavior that have racial consequences often are not only about race. Instead, they result from multiple, overlapping, and at times mutually reinforcing or contradictory frames of reference that inform social judgments and actions.

Once we recognize the cultural dimension of racial analysis, many subsequent points follow. First is the need to recognize the vast disparities of power and privilege among whites. Intense intraracial contests constantly shape and regulate participation in whiteness. Though "white skin privilege" is a profound and telling concept, it has limits and can be severely curtailed through such debasing boundary-marking terms as white trash (McIntosh 1989). We also must recognize the rapidly changing demographic and political circumstances that are reconfiguring racial formations in the

United States. It is simply not the case that whites, particularly in the lower classes, in Detroit or Los Angeles, Miami or Houston, participate in a uniform order of racial dominance. The powers and privileges attributed to whites nationally are severely attenuated by certain local contexts, particularly circumstances of local minority group status and access to limited social and economic resources or opportunities. Though exceptional now, such situations will become far more common given the changing demographics of the United States.

Acknowledging the significance and diversity of these local circumstances leads to another point. We need to recognize that whites, too, are racial subjects. They are not subject to the same forms of racial domination or subordination as people of color. However, in certain contexts and social situations, they are confronted by the humiliations, hostilities, ambiguities, and charged discrepancies that constitute racial subjectivity. The advantage of this shift—from regarding whiteness as uniformly unmarked to examining the racialization of whites in specific situations—is that it undercuts the emerging focus on whiteness studies and the enshrinement of whiteness as a unique subject of study. Each of these points—the intraracial contests that constitute whiteness, the critical role of place in determining the significance of race, and the various circumstances through which whites are racialized— addresses, first, the need for a mode of analysis that distinguishes between racial dynamics at the national and local levels (while acknowledging their interrelations), and, second, the fundamental role culture plays in these matters.

KEY CONCEPTS FROM CULTURAL STUDIES
AND THE SOCIAL SCIENCES

The following chapters tack back and forth between cultural studies approaches and those characteristic of the social sciences.[30] I use the strengths of these alternative perspectives to analyze the convoluted dynamics of racial matters. In moving between cultural studies and social science methods, addressing different audiences and deploying distinct theories and methods, several concepts remained constant in my inquiries. These concepts— figuration, etiquette, and boundary work—have distinct histories and uses, but they are currently deployed in ways that move them beyond a singular association with either of the two broad perspectives I delineate here. Taken in concert, these concepts open a powerful perspective on the cultural dynamics shaping racial identity.

The concept of figures emerged from early hermeneutical endeavors in understanding the interrelation of biblical characters, and it represents an analytical model that is currently migrating from literary criticism to the social sciences (see Frei 1974; White 1999). Figures call attention to the way people come to consider their identities in relation to potent images that circulate within a culture. Figuration is a drastic improvement over stereotype in that it captures the active way people subjected to certain debasing images are able to inhabit them in complex ways that involve critique and elaboration. Stereotype tends to imply a static form of representation, one that can only be deconstructed or demystified. But, as Donna Haraway (1997, 11) explains, "Figurations are performative images that can be inhabited." There is more to the work of understanding white trash than disabusing people of the conceptions that come to mind when they hear the term or to convince them to no longer use or tolerate this racial epithet. As well, figures also "make explicit and inescapable the tropic quality of all material-semiotic processes," as Haraway further observes (11). This tropic dimension is too often dismissed or discounted in social science research endeavors that insist on the literal realism of their objects of study.[31] If we cannot catch the figural play of images in the lives of racial subjects, then the vast reservoirs of signification that animate a figure like white trash will remain inaccessible to critical study and thus retain all of its insidious power that is mobilized in its common usage.

An excellent example of how the concept of figures is informing more powerful social science approaches to race is anthropologist Mary Weismantel's (2001) *Cholas and Pishtacos: Stories of Race and Sex in the Andes.* Weismantel deploys a deft analytical attention to race by tracing three cultural dynamics: first, naming practices (stereotypes) that distance people by asserting racial distance and boundaries; second, social exchanges that bring people together and enact racial identities as both fluid and negotiated; and third, forms of economic accumulation that make these fluid identities fixed again. The first process involves a series of rhetorical gestures and mythic images that provide the signifying structures for the social landscape. The second reveals that racial identities are not the property of bodies but the result of certain acts and behaviors—roles that reflect or respond to structural inequalities. The third shows how, despite not being a property of bodies, race still becomes identified with particular bodies; it accumulates there through individuals' social history.

In all this, Weismantel's attention is grounded by the cultural figures of *cholas*, a racialization of market women, and *pishtacos*, a mythic white vampire figure. "Each represents the dynamic tension between Indian and white, women and men—and between myth and reality" (2001, xxiv). The primary dilemma Weismantel confronts is that, as a social scientist, using these labels to describe collective dynamics risks reinscribing "the distorting set of racial and sexual myths" that these terms embody. Such usage also risks reproducing objectifying practices that sexually and racially stigmatize these subjects. Yet, Weismantel argues, "if foreign scientists and native romantics enjoyed looking at cholas too much, and for all the wrong reasons, we do not rectify their errors by refusing to look at all. The market women's anomalous location on the social map might seem to be a projection on the part of elites and outsiders, but it is also a product of what the women themselves say and do" (103). Eschewing such terms entirely misses the important work, particularly of self-designation, that these labels perform. "Cholas and pishtacos—both in story and in fact—reveal the relentless movement of people and things across social boundaries, driven by processes of unequal exchange that link together metropolis and periphery, commodity exchange and domestic consumption. These interconnections are as structurally integral to the geography of race as is the phenomenon of estrangement" (80). Here Weismantel confronts "the inadequacy of social scientific descriptions" (106). She addresses this conundrum effectively by construing these rhetorical identities as figures. Unlike stereotypes, figures do not beg for deconstruction but impel an attention to the imaginative ways people draw on charged identifying representational forms in negotiating complex, mutable social settings.

Weismantel's critical assessment of social science approaches to such charged racial identities as cholas is worth quoting at length:

> Rather than unambiguous descriptions, they are multivocal instruments of social intercourse. In one context, cholo expresses contempt; in another, it establishes intimacy; in a third, it promises violence. This language pulls people towards one another and pushes them apart; gender and sexual tensions detach the words themselves, so that chola and cholo no longer mean the same thing. This volatility makes these terms singularly inappropriate as fixed categories for social science. But the same qualities make them perfect tools for the women of the produce market, who inhabit a social world just as mobile—and just as unequal—as the linguistic universe mapped out by the words cholo and chola. (2001, 98)

Weismantel's treatment of these rhetorical identities as figures holds at arm's length the competing, false assumptions that they are either external impositions or simply accurate, literal designators for collective orders: "Despite its power to insult, the use of the word chola to describe women who work as produce vendors, chiceras, butchers, and cooks is not an imposition by foreign anthropologists, nor the fancy of literary writers; all Cuzco knows them as cholas. But neither does this word have the absolute definitional power with which social scientists sought to invest it . . . it is too freighted a term to serve as an objective description of anyone. What is needed is an analytical framework that encompasses all these insights" (2001, 103). For cholas, pishtacos, and white trash, "what makes these words matter is not their utility in social science, but their use in the give-and-take of everyday life" (101). The value of figures as an analytical concept, then, is in directing our view to the representational dynamics involved with invoking collective forms of identity without reductively asserting that these collectives are "real" or "unreal" in an empirical sense.

Etiquette is a related concept in that it, too, centers on labeling practices, but it involves a rather different set of dynamics, that of disciplining social bodies and speech (see Elias 1994). As anthropologist T. O. Beidelman (1986, 60–61) relates in his study, *Moral Imagination in Kaguru Modes of Thought*, "The word etiquette derives from a term for label, for the attributes we stick upon others and hope they stick upon ourselves. Yet this sounds misleadingly limiting, for etiquette also has roots in terms for embroider, as in stitch, and, true enough, it provides means not merely for labeling but for a wealth of elaboration and shading, depending upon the protagonists' means and training." In its most basic function, "etiquette creates culture through bodily discipline, through modulation and repression of our impulses" (61). Etiquette is a mode of naturalizing social classifications, schemes, and hierarchies, making their importance tangible through the series of restrictions on what can be said or done and linking transgressions of these prohibitions to the viability of the social order. The implication with any form of etiquette is that horrible things will happen if its strictures are not adhered to studiously. The disciplining of bodies and speech through etiquette involves the most basic process of establishing cultural identity: instilling habits that are policed by concepts of disgust and embellished through ideas about pollution and dirt.[32] This process of viscerally encoding perceptions and sentiments via disgust is fundamental to the process of naturalizing a view that unequal relations between groups are immutable.

This concept is central in *Odd Tribes* for a variety of reasons. Foremost, it highlights the dynamic that makes white trash a cultural object and identity in the first place. Counter to a generalized perception that white trash is simply a given, obvious condition and problem, we have to grasp that it is the forms of etiquette—and importantly, their transgression—that maintain and reproduce the unmarked status of white identity that constitutes white trash. Just as important, etiquette as an analytical focus brings into view an important dimension of the coconstruction of race, class, and gender identities (Rapp 1999, 74–77; Tapper 1999, 104). Social hierarchies rest on the perception that unshakeable rules for behavior both derive from and support a "natural" order of relations. Such social strictures for proper and improper behavior are multiply inflected by received notions of what is normative in terms of racial, class, and gender behaviors. Furthermore, the ritual forms of etiquette that guide routine forms of socializing are profoundly charged with notions of how racial, class, and gender identities are to be recognized and respected. This assures their reproduction in these most unconscious dimensions of social relations.

Etiquette has a special charge in discussions of race because the practice of segregation was articulated in terms of proper and improper forms of interactions: the social control function of etiquette was explicit in terms of race (see Doyle 1937; E. Anderson 1990). Interestingly, the various efforts at integration following in the wake of the civil rights movement, which have largely failed to undermine either the social significance of race or forms of inequality based on race, are also critically illuminated via an attention to etiquette. As Elisabeth Lasch-Quinn (2001, 2) asserts, "An exploration of racial rituals broadly conceived—our unwritten expectations, our taboos, our notions of proper etiquette—helps to pinpoint the ways in which we have failed thus far in some of the most important tests of integration."[33] Lasch-Quinn argues that integration has had little effect on the most invasive forms of discrimination because it generated instead a heightened attention to very stylized forms of what racial subjects could properly speak about or do. "Attempting to address the conundrum of race under integration in significant part through etiquette, Americans became deeply mired in a set of assumptions and practices from which it was increasingly difficult to extricate themselves." This development "helped ensure that the civil rights movement would be reoriented away from the realm of politics, civic, and business life, where it began and where the worst inequalities remain. Casting interracial problems as issues of etiquette put a premium on superficial symbols of good intentions and good motivations as well as on style and appearance rather than on the substance of change" (6). In order both to objectify this thoroughgoing investment in etiquette and to undermine its powerful influence on how race is imagined and discussed, it is necessary to place this cultural dynamic in the analytical foreground.

Perhaps the most valuable aspect of an attention to etiquette is the way it brings into view the visceral, bodily dimension of the reproduction of class and gender identities. As Pierre Bourdieu (1984) asserted, classes have distinct bodily images and forms of comportment. The way these materialize and are performed is revealed in forms of etiquette and bodily discipline, as much as in consumption practices. Etiquette, in this regard, is not a singular concept but a nexus of concerns that range from hygiene to decorum, each of which is a critical dimension of class formation. The crucial point in deploying this conceptual nexus either in field settings or in relation to representations is that it brings into view the relational dynamics of group formation in processes seemingly as disparate and mundane as civic code battles over public and private space to discourses about "comfort" or "comfort levels" in the face of racial integration.[34]

The concept of boundary work, like that of figuration and etiquette, combines attention to both material and symbolic forms and highlights their interplay in the labels that construct social identities. This concept probably has the most salience across the divide between disciplinary and interdisciplinary approaches to cultural subjects. Cultural studies approaches boundaries with an emphasis on representations, analyzing how these are established, contested, and transgressed in various media of popular culture. Social science perspectives on boundaries primarily examine their symbolic role in the process of group formation, specifically in terms of the relational dynamics that influence how collectives cohere and establish their forms of integration. The social science perspective is best encapsulated by sociologist Michele Lamont's (1992, 2000) work on the dynamics of class and racial identity formation. Lamont examines how symbolic boundaries bring into view the role of culture in creating and reproducing social inequality. The conceptual power of boundaries, in this perspective, is that it represents a "pervasive phenomenon" rather than a unique dynamic specific only to issues of race, class, or gender. Most important for a topic like white trash and a difficult subject like racism, the cultural dynamic of boundary maintenance allows us "to view prejudices and stereotypes as the supraindividual by-products of basic social processes that are shaped by the cultural resources people have at their disposal and by the structural situations they live in" (1992, 2). These "basic social processes" simultaneously crosscut and contour the forms of inequality defined by class, race, and gender.

This perspective on generic social dynamics has the advantage of offering a view of race that does not entail reinscribing essentialized terms of racial identification, such as whiteness and blackness. As well, attention to boundaries engages the realm of the everyday and does not imply that operations of domination are the only significant function of a cultural order. The power here lies in the ability to move from a seemingly mundane dynamic to an insight into how culture reproduces inequality. Lamont (1992, 6) explains: "Through our necessary involvement in a wide range of groups, we are all constantly participating in the production and reenactment of competing boundaries, both as we label others and as we participate in communities whose shared beliefs make a specific definition of reality intersubjectively true. Indeed, we often carry out boundary work through our membership in professional groups, social classes, and ethnic racial groups, or as residents of a community." This characterization does not preclude an attention to racism; in fact, it allows her to then analyze how "workers come to adopt racist positions given the cultural and material worlds they inhabit" (2000, 5), which are constructed as symbolic communities defined by boundaries drawn according to ostensibly nonracial criteria. The key recognition here is that social boundaries are asserted and contested in multiple registers simultaneously, sometimes stressing class over gender or race and sometimes, with a provocative epithet like white trash, condensing all three registers into a charged representation of *those people*. Instead of looking solely for direct articulations of racial sentiments—or, with concepts like the new racism, ideological signs of active repression of any mention of race—we can engage the slew of categorical perceptions, discursive objectifications, and cultural assessments of belonging and difference that shape all projections of "community." This broader view then offers a vantage point onto the daily forms of reinforcement that racial thinking receives from the overlapping registers of popular culture, political discourse, and institutional practices.

An equally important dimension of this analytic perspective is that it maintains an attention to similar dynamics that crosscut racial lines. Lamont (2000, 4) observes, "For black and white workers alike, moral boundaries on the one hand, and class and racial boundaries on the other, often work together to provide them with a space in which to affirm their worth and preserve their dignity, a space for expressing their own identity and competence." She discerns "that whites and blacks alike subtly move from drawing moral boundaries to drawing racial boundaries" and that an " 'us' versus 'them' dynamic animated by two different conceptions of morality is closely associated with the collective identities of the two groups" (93). I stress two points in discussing such similarities in the following chapters, which I hope will have bearing on the way antiracist interventions operate. The first underscores that some social processes transcend racial lines, making it possible to talk about race without insisting on or unintentionally reproducing essentialized notions of difference between racial groups. Second, it is necessary to engage racial thinking not as an abstract function of ideology but as a more convoluted and complex product of socialization. In terms of antiracism, these perspectives hopefully offer an effective purchase on the attention of whites who have grown inured to discussions that singularly focus on racism.

The issue of racism and how to best analyze its relevance and operation in relation to race is central to the issues addressed in *Odd Tribes*. In this regard, Lamont's work offers another strong example. She sees her comparative research on workers in the United States and France as in dialogue with efforts by social scientists over the previous two decades to characterize basic transformations in the way racial identities and differences are articulated. These include "symbolic racism," "aversive racism," "modern racism," "subtle racism," and "new racism." Her findings complement aspects of this research, but she also goes well beyond it by considering the diversity of interests, concerns, and perceptions expressed by workers, rather than trying to render their nuanced sentiments reductively and singularly in terms of racism. Lamont develops a frame of reference from the commentaries, stories, and assessments of the world by these workers, then asserts, "By using as a point of departure the general moral worldview of workers, rather than racism itself, we can get at the very framework through which they think about racial differences instead of predefining the issue for them with questions that speak to racism as we understand it" (2000, 72). This perspective is fundamental to the form of cultural analysis I am arguing for in relation to race, which entails the ability to grasp the multiple categorical operations (not just race, but class and gender as well) that inform and inflect perceptions of sameness and difference as people negotiate the terms of belonging in particular neighborhoods, cities, regions, and the nation at large.

STRUCTURE OF THE BOOK

The first half of *Odd Tribes* grapples with understanding what the predicament of poor whites can tell us about the significance of race. This task involves critically reassessing social science efforts to depict and analyze urban poverty, but it also entails unpacking the historical and contemporary role of images of white trash in grounding a variety of popular discourses on racial and class identity. This half of the book opens and closes with a series of critical reflections on the production of social knowledge about the urban poor, examining confusions over race and class both in the minds of researchers and in the subjects they attempt to analyze. This discussion brackets an account of the historical emergence of white trash, tracing the work this cultural figure has performed in ratifying white middle-class identity up to the current moment, when this term's usage for disparagement is being supplanted with counterforms of self-ascription. These discussions confront the challenge of taking a degrading stereotype and making it a basis for comprehending important aspects of how racial and class distinctions operate, without reproducing its stigmatizing assumptions. This involves objectifying the interests and uses that animate the debased figure as well as depicting and analyzing the social conditions associated with the stereotype.

Poor whites have not been of much interest to social scientists investigating the links between race and social disadvantage; nor do they fit easily into current social science frameworks for analyzing poverty (Moss 2003). Making poor whites the focus of such inquiries requires two initial efforts: first, assailing social commentators' tendency to stress the singular and distinct importance of *either* race or class and, second, challenging the assumptions built into concepts like the "urban underclass" that practically preclude an attention to impoverished whites living in inner cities. The first of these tasks is undertaken in chapter 1, "Picturing the Underclass." Drawing on founding work by Charles Booth in studying urban poverty in London in the 1880s and 1890s, and juxtaposed with recent efforts to study "concentrated poverty" in the United States, this chapter frames the difficulties social analysts encounter as they try to make sense of both race and class simultaneously. This chapter compares an era when it was hard to keep the analytical registers of class and race distinct with our current moment, when, due to academic specialization, it is difficult to analyze both in concert. By attending to the relentless conflation of race and class, rather than striving to keep these analytical registers distinct, we can begin to grasp the role of culture in shaping and reproducing these fundamental registers of social identity. Culture provides the basis by which these identities are interpreted, performed, and recognized as significant, and, as such, it provides the vantage point from which these forms can be critically analyzed.

This view of the conflation of race and class hinges, in part, on an ability to grasp the bodily dimension of class identity and distinctions, a perspective that is second nature with race but not often analytically addressed in relation to class. Here the historical and contemporary uses of white trash are of great interest. White trash highlights dynamics critical to reproducing class identities that are typically overlooked in sociological and economic analyses of class. The perception and ascription of white trash hinges on bodily sensibilities; it involves a reaction to bodily conditions and behaviors that offend certain class decorums. In this regard, white trash captures some of the dirty work—the active forms of disparagement, insult, condemnation, and stigmatization—that constitute much of the relational aspects of class identification (i.e., techniques of distancing and boundary maintenance). Class is not simply determined in a sociological or economic sense; rather, it is actively produced and performed by individuals, often in charged, emotional interactions that can be characterized succinctly as efforts to put people "in their place" (see Ortner 2003; Rebel 1989a, 1989b). Uses of white trash keenly illustrate these dynamics, but they also reveal an important aspect of how racial identification works. White trash calls attention to the charged intraracial contests over belonging and difference that are a crucial dimension of racial identification. This dynamic draws on class distinctions that operate within a variety of racial groups and is not simply an aspect of whiteness.[35]

Despite these compelling theoretical reasons for thinking critically about white trash, this cultural figure is no easy object of analysis. Understanding white trash requires a view of this racial epithet's long career, which is examined in chapters 2 through 4. These chapters trace the emergence of a perception of white trash as representing a distinct kind of people, a social collective whose coherence hinged on its particular threatening relation to whiteness. This social perception was formulated in response to complexly shifting racial and class conditions in the United States from the 1850s through the 1930s (see chapter 2). Images of poor whites in these tumultuous decades played a fundamental role in the way middle-class whites articulated their sense of self in relation to "the race" and to the shifting dynamics of class distinction. From the 1940s through the 1980s, popular cultural depictions of white trash continued to serve this function, with characters in novels, movies, television shows, and music performing the debasement of problematic whites who transgressed the class etiquette maintaining whiteness as an unmarked identity (see chapters 3 and 4). In analyzing these representations, I regard white trash alternately as a rhetorical identity, as an unpopular cultural figure, and as generated by a distinctive cultural poetics;

each of these formulations gets at the relational dynamics that inform usage of this racial epithet.

But it is not the case that white trash exists only as a cultural representation in the minds of middle-class whites. The term has been applied with consistency over the years to a distinctive social condition of white poverty, one that is typically delimited or contrasted with less abject situations. "White trash" is not applied to poor whites generically; rather, it is one of several terms for designating marked forms of whiteness (Storrs 1999). The range of conditions in the "social bottom" of whiteness and the variety of cultural objectifications used to interpret the significance of this stratum, such as "redneck" and "hillbilly," are critical for comprehending how racial discourses in this country have developed and continue today to mutate into novel forms. Chapter 5, "Talking Trash," examines the diverse circumstances of poor whites, the textured rhetorical terrain for objectifying their social position, and the situation by which a few poor whites have produced self-representations in popular cultural media. The cultural role of white trash began transforming in the 1990s and today is far more ambiguous and convoluted than it has been before. Major entertainers like Eminem and Roseanne Barr both reflect and have themselves played active roles in the changing social and economic relations that shape productions of popular culture. In this shift from projections of Otherness to circumscribed self-representations, current uses of white trash, in contrast to redneck and hillbilly, reveal a great deal about the nuances of white racial identity and are critical to effective antiracist interventions. But, as cultural representations, they offer a limited purchase onto the ways white experiences and perceptions of race and class are shaped. To comprehend fully what it is about poor whites that disturbs and confuses received notions about race and class, we must additionally be able to formulate an empirical perspective on the cultural predicament of *those people* as well.

Returning, then, to the challenges raised in chapter 1 concerning the presuppositions informing social research on urban poverty, informed now with a sense of the tradition of stereotyping poor whites and the important role the figure of white trash played in ratifying white middle-class racial sensibilities, chapter 6, "Green Ghettos and the White Underclass," addresses the difficulties of using contemporary analytical constructs such as the urban underclass for examining the predicaments of inner-city whites. There are two major obstacles to constituting urban poor whites as an object of social knowledge: first, the overdetermined, stigmatizing aspects of any representation of such whites and, second, assumptions about the significance of race operating in discourses on the urban underclass. Given the history of representing poor whites, can any objectification of this social group not reproduce its prefigured role in the relational dynamics of class reproduction? And can any analysis of the significance of race—in this case, examining whites who are far from advantaged and dominant—develop a view of the changing dynamics informing racial identification that are radically altering a cultural landscape that for centuries has been singularly defined by the equations between whiteness and domination and blackness and subordination? Answers to both these questions lie in the ability to transform an attention to race via the framework of cultural analysis, which is the focus of the second half of *Odd Tribes.*

Part 2 of the book is based on fieldwork, my own and that of other anthropologists engaged in ethnographic studies of race, and shifts from the focus on popular cultural representation to compiling and analyzing accounts of whites in their daily lives in particular locales. These chapters draw widely from contemporary anthropological attention to racial matters to generate a thorough assessment of what a cultural perspective has to contribute to understanding race. In contrast to theoretical and political statements about whiteness, these chapters struggle to articulate the basis for generating social knowledge about white racial identity through observation-based studies that emphasize rather than reduce the complexity and nuance of site-specific cultural dynamics. This second half of *Odd Tribes* raises a host of epistemological issues about understanding racial matters, but it also links these to a range of political interventions that strive to subvert the reproduction of white domination and privilege. In assessing the basis for making knowledge claims about racial matters, these chapters also suggest means for thinking differently about race that are both drawn from and respond to everyday life circumstances.

"Establishing the Fact of Whiteness" (chapter 7) frames the difficulties and the necessity of moving from abstract pronouncements about whiteness as equivalent with domination to honing an objectification of white racialness that can be usefully deployed in ambiguous fieldwork settings. The power and problem of whiteness as a subject of cultural critique lie in the treatment of white racial identity as a uniform social construct and a coherent, historically determined ideology of dominance. But treating whiteness in generic terms disregards the most basic insights about racial identity that have been generated by studies of black racial identity, which demonstrate that (in contrast to many white assumptions) blackness is heterogeneous and complex. A cursory review of ethnographic approaches to race makes it obvious that this characterization holds true for whiteness as well; more important, it also underscores the analytical, methodological, and political need to establish some form of equivalence regarding these racial orders. The recognition of similar racial dynamics shaping whiteness and blackness becomes the basis for subverting the tendency to reproduce racial identities even as we assert that they are socially constructed. I argue that we must recognize that the continuum of racial dynamics—from plastic and negotiated to emphatically inscribed and enforced—evident in forms of blackness is also pertinent to how whiteness matters. Undeniably, it is important to pursue what Faye Harrison (1995, 63) characterizes as "a cultural critique of whiteness as the key site of racial domination." But insights gained from this critique will be skewed if in the process whiteness is considered a homogeneous order or identity—a generic "white culture" (Frankenberg 1993) or even the "absence of culture" (Roediger 1994)—and not, additionally, a conflicted and heterogeneous social position. The contribution that anthropologists can make to studies of whiteness lies in striking a balance between the critical power of *whiteness* and the often contradictory, muddled effects of race in everyday life as encountered in ethnographic contexts.

"Locating White Detroit" (chapter 8) draws directly on my ethnographic work to frame and discuss differences in scale from global and national to regional and local perspectives on racial formations. I approach this theoretical matter via an account of the kinship dynamics among two poor white families in Detroit's inner city. Although whiteness may be fixed as a unified or unifying phenomenon when regarded ideologically at the national level, on the ground that unity quickly becomes illusory. Instead of one firm ground, there is a shifting series of domains (local, regional, national, transnational) across which whiteness materializes according to distinct centers of significance, assimilating or effacing a varying array of internal differences, and projecting or excluding a host of corporal others. The intervals and gaps between domains create an irregular and unpredictable basis for the cultural reproduction of this racial category, white. In the case of these poor white families, the idioms of kinship do not reproduce uniform modes of racial identification; rather, they are a generative basis by which diverse white subjects emerge within particular families. This subject is important because it offers a positive view of cultural dynamics that disrupt the reproduction of racial categories and orders.

"Object Lessons in Whiteness" (chapter 9) draws on recent ethnographic studies of antiracist training seminars and political organizing efforts to offer some practical insights on how to better engage whites on the subject of race. These studies reveal that antiracists deploy a "hermeneutics of suspicion" when compelling whites to talk about their racial experiences. This stance, though useful in reading whites' comments and opinions against the grain, potentially displaying unintended or unconscious racial sentiments and beliefs, is deaf to efforts by white participants to make sense of situations that are more ambiguous or complicated than antiracists either realize or admit. I suggest that if antiracists are able to listen a bit more attentively to what whites are actually saying, and do more than simply regard their responses as smoke screens hiding racist intentions and beliefs, they can gain a critical purchase on whites' real-life situations and thereby more effectively engage whites' racial perceptions and judgments. The listening stance assumed by ethnographers can be a useful tool for antiracists, allowing them to better grasp the particular racialized predicaments encountered by whites, the density and specificity of how power works in daily circumstances (recognizing, for instance, that people of color can be both powerful actors and racially motivated in certain situations), and then orient these to broader understandings about race and racism rather than reducing whites to generic ciphers of racist ideology.

The final chapter, "Cultural Analysis: The Case of Race," brings together these various strands of inquiry and discussion in an assessment of how cultural analysis can contribute to current debates about whiteness. I argue that the power of cultural analysis lies in provoking people to recognize the dimensions of their lives that both exceed and inform their individuality: the idioms we speak, the ideas we express, the encounters that shape our biographies, all are socially contoured. This type of perception is crucial to the task of making sense of the enduring yet evolving significance of race because of its capacity to link seemingly disparate cultural domains, revealing similar dynamics constituting boundaries of belonging and difference operating in the fashioning of multiple dimensions of social identity simultaneously (e.g., nationality, class, gender, region, as well as race). Cultural analysis places race amid these additional social dimensions, demonstrating how the coconstruction of race, class, and gender distinctions operates according to place-specific dynamics that ground and facilitate the concurrent production and reproduction of multiple overlapping and mutually reinforcing identities.

The attention to culture that I am promoting can powerfully impact how people think about race. But it can be grasped only by taking seriously this dimension of human collective behavior and belief. The prevailing critical forms for analyzing race, such as whiteness studies and critical race theory, generally do not. These analytic approaches regard culture, at least for the analyst, as a transparent order, one that makes the operations of entrenched, fundamental forms of racial inequality commonsensical and natural to its subjects.[36] In contrast, I am arguing that culture comprises the signifying forms and expressive mediums by which the material and symbolic practices constituting racial, class, and gendered identities are performed and become meaningful. Though powerfully alluring, an ideological analysis that regards these forms and mediums as merely obfuscating or distorting of the "real" operations of social inequality will achieve only a limited explanatory purchase on the enduring significance of race. To challenge more profoundly people's experiences of race, we must mobilize a deeper attention to the mediums by which people make sense of and reproduce cultural categories, boundaries, and practices. This is why culture is necessary to the task of critically analyzing racial matters.

PART I

CHAPTER 1

PICTURING THE UNDERCLASS:

MYTH MAKING IN THE

INNER CITY

East London lay hidden from view behind a curtain on which were painted terrible pictures: starving children, suffering women, overworked men; horrors of drunkenness and vice; monsters and demons of inhumanity; giants of disease and despair. Did these pictures truly represent what lay behind, or did they bear to the facts a relation similar to that which the pictures outside a booth at some country fair bear to the performance or show within?

—Charles Booth, *Life and Labour of the People in London*

The starting point for the construction of the underclass is a willingness to believe, an a priori receptiveness to journalistic, anecdotal claims that could, after all, provoke skepticism just as easily as reflexive acceptance.

—Adolph Reed Jr., *Stirrings in the Jug*

Monsters and cities go hand in hand, as inextricably intertwined as fact and fiction. From the Sphinx to King Kong, Godzilla to RoboCop, monsters have terrorized cities. But cities, as well, have spawned monsters. These creatures, such as Jack the Ripper and Jeffrey Dahmer, are of a different order, ostensibly human and part of a routinized violence, which jars the comfortable view of monsters as fiction. All of these figures, imagined and real, depict a line along which certainty about monstrosities waxes and wanes. Judged more real, the connotations of fantastic inhumanity recede into vague after-image; regarded as imaginary, the real-life associations and conditions similarly fade from view. This alteration between fictive and factual is active today in depictions of another form of urban monstrosity: the "underclass." Representations of this population as alternately real subjects and imagined grotesque terrors, rendered in depictions that purposefully resist making clear distinctions between one or the other, are fundamental to the popularity of inner-city scenes in newscasts, reality shows, and fictive media such as films and novels.

Overarching concerns of this book—to critique representations of poverty while also producing social science knowledge claims about "the poor," and to grapple with the conflation of race and class in the realms of theory and of everyday life—are all broached in debates about the urban underclass. Obviously real in some sense, the underclass is also a statistical artifact of political interests in demonizing the urban poor and of the public's insatiable desire for images of contemptible yet threatening figures of debased humanity. This chapter thus pursues two distinct but related tasks. As it undertakes to deconstruct representations of the inner city it also presents a critical reassessment of how race and class are conceived in social science research in relation to objectifications of the urban underclass. In this chapter I build on powerful cultural critiques of representations of the urban underclass and suggest ways to reimagine the forces that constitute both the representational economy of the inner city and the real conditions of those who reside in such zones.

The problems with depictions of the underclass stem from the failure of social scientists to grasp the relational dynamics by which class identities are culturally constructed.[1] As Michael Katz (1993, 442) argues, the social forces that created inner cities, "structural transformations of the economy; the working out of racism in time and space; the consequences of institutional developments; the reshaping of urban space; and the activities of the state," have transfigured the basis of class identity broadly in this country. But social scientists ignore these larger connections when they isolate the underclass as a subject of study. The fundamental distortion, Katz explains, is that in pursuing a class analysis based entirely on one class, social science "uses the language of class but misses or ignores its relational dimension. Indeed, it defines the underclass as outside of, beyond, or not part of the class structure" when it characterizes this population as distinctive based on behavioral rather than economic characteristics. Robin Kelley (1997, 18) expands this critique, noting that "most interpreters of the 'underclass' treat behavior as not only a symptom for culture but also as the determinant for class. In simple terms, what makes the 'underclass' as a class is members' common behavior—not their income, their poverty level, or the kind of work they do. It is a definition of class driven more by moral panic than by systematic analysis."

The problems with this behavioral focus are threefold. First, these behaviors permeate society: *all classes* produce teenage parents, female-headed households, and drug users; the sharp contrast lies in the resources (cultural and economic capital) that members of the respective classes can draw on to meet such contingencies. Second, the behaviors keyed on by social scientists are dynamic and situational, individual responses to specific circumstances rather than all-encompassing moral categories (see Reed 2000a). The urban poor are no more instinctual or predetermined in their responses to certain situations than are members of any other class, though their "choices" are often far more constrained by their economic and social conditions. Third, emphasizing "bad" behavior relies on and reinforces the notion that a natural form of etiquette governs all human behaviors, making transgressions seem an obvious basis for concern. Appeals to a neutral, generic register of behavior turn attention from the contested aspects of class identity and reinforces a fundamental misrecognition of the bodily dimension of class relations.

These critiques render knowledge claims about the underclass suspect and raise a larger concern: that class analysis fails to recognize that class, like race, is culturally constructed.[2] These problems are compounded by both the excessive realness of the underclass and by middle-class audiences' credulity concerning depictions of the inner city. The extreme condition depicted by massive documentary and quantitative projects deployed in inner-city zones—and the way such objectifications are informed by and sanction popular cultural representations of the underclass—makes it unusually difficult to deconstruct such representations. So here I take a different tack, working instead to exploit the monstrous potential of the urban underclass (see Haraway 1992). Turning from the objectifying apparatuses deployed in documenting the underclass, I focus on the reservoir of anxiety that colors these representations. This view reveals urban monstrosities emerging from a voyeuristic middle-class Self that consumes such images. Instead of fearfully animating a sharp divide between "us and them," this view recognizes and depicts the intimate relations otherwise fundamentally distorted by representational techniques that place monsters in the city on parade. Simply put, the monsters *there* are of our own making, but recognizing this requires a bit of reflection and imagination.

To better imagine these relations, I turn to three powerful stories illustrating how the boundary maintenance work of class self-construction produces monstrosity effects in decimated urban spaces. I draw these stories from two periods when urban life underwent similar drastic transformations, which bracket the epoch of formal social science poverty research. The first centers on London in the 1880s and 1890s, the second features cities in the United States in their radical transformation during the 1980s and 1990s. Linking these periods and stories is the monstrous figure of the underclass. These stories both figure and critique the monstrosity of the underclass and, in the process, provoke a rethinking of the cultural construction of middle-class self-identity.[3] Robert Louis Stevenson's drama *Dr. Jekyll and Mr. Hyde* (1886/1985) is a mythic account of how the social and geographic distances between classes become internalized, with images of the underclass playing a crucial role in materializing the boundaries of middle-class identity. Oscar Wilde's *The Picture of Dorian Gray* (1891/1974) depicts a dream of urban spectatorship where a respectable gentleman can traverse the nether world of the underclass, seeking pleasure and raw experience without bearing any contaminating physical traces as a result.[4] Each of these tales has been told and retold in a variety of entertainment media because they compellingly figure nightmarish possibilities of losing self-control, which is a particularly potent problem for middle-class formation; each also titillates audiences with haunting images of the underclass.[5] These tales, in turn, are referenced and revised in a fascinating drama from our recent era, the Wes Craven movie *Candyman* (1992), a thrilling, vampyric tale that unfolds across the class and racially segregated landscape of Chicago's inner city.

These stories all feature a Self turned monstrous that allows us to think imaginatively about how class identities are produced and experienced in relation to race. Each story dramatizes mythic dimensions of representations of poverty and relational dimensions of class and racial identities that are too often distorted to monstrous effects. I use these narratives as a means of framing the classed Imaginary that animates representations of poverty, even those of staid, detached social scientists.[6] Ultimately, social scientific images of the poor are generated and consumed as part of the cultural construction of class identities, particularly the self-identity of the middle class. These tales offer an opportunity to reflect on the past hundred years of social science studies of poverty, asking What, if anything, have we learned from such work? Have such depictions ever not drawn from or played to popular anxieties and fascinations? and Is there a way we can represent inner-city conditions without feeding this appetite for monsters?

INNER-CITY LONDON OF THE 1890s

The critical link binding these tales is that they each respond to and dramatize similar drastic transformations of urban space. To grasp the striking correspondences between the transformations in these two periods—and the similarities in how social scientists tried to represent these conditions—I turn first to Charles Booth's (1902) mammoth social survey, *The Life and Labour of the People in London*, published between 1889 and 1902. Booth's study, especially the *Poverty Series* portion, offers a detailed view of the streets that Mr. Hyde and Dorian Gray haunted (see also Eckardt 1987). More important, his novel approach to analyzing the city, which initiated our current era of social research on poverty, provides an early incarnation of recent figurings of the underclass. As researchers do today, confronting an eerily similar decimation of city centers, Booth produced a delimited view of the possible threats posed by the poor. In place of the nebulous, spreading image of the "dangerous classes," he portrayed a smaller population, the "low class," as the source of danger in the city. The *Poverty Series* frames dynamics by which racialized populations in two periods of urban turmoil were scientifically objectified and moralized as monstrous threats.

As a foundational figure in sociology, Booth occupies an ambiguous position in the history of depicting and analyzing urban poverty (see Bales 1999; Marriott 1999; O'Day 1989; J. Walkowitz 1992). His lack of theoretical sophistication leaves him on the fringes of sociology's intellectual history, but his ability to spatially objectify and statistically represent the sprawling metropolis in an objective fashion ensured his enduring influence on urban researchers.[7] Booth portrayed London in the first systematic, street-by-street account of the city, drawing on census data and school board visitors' reports, correlated with the impressions of teachers and his own ethnographic observations. As with previous researchers, such as Friedrich Engels and Henry Mayhew, Booth presented a combination of quantitative and firsthand accounts of the alien streets and humanity of London's interior. But his sophistication in fashioning a totalized view of the city—by deploying spatial, temporal, and attitudinal registers to detail the boundaries of class formations—distinguishes his depictions from earlier representations and resonates strongly with current efforts to conceptualize the inner city.

Through the course of the 1800s, an "inner city" was gradually hollowed out in central London through a combination of processes, including the decline of key industries, the vast exodus of the upper and middle classes from the city's center, and the general depopulation of the central city through a series of "slum removal" efforts which had the unintended effect of crowding the poor and the working classes into "degenerate" zones. The result is described by Gareth Stedman Jones (1984, 154) in *Outcast London*: "The inner industrial perimeter developed into an area of chronic male underemployment, female sweated labor, and low-paid, irregular artisan work in declining trades; an area associated with small dealing, petty criminality and social desolation so graphically portrayed by Booth in his *Poverty Survey*." As in the United States, the development of such an area was a lengthy process, which only gradually came to represent a threat of a completely different order to the nation at large. The central city of London emerged as the product of residential segregation by class, as an "immense geographic gulf" developed between rich and poor. "There had been increasing expression of anxiety about this phenomenon in the manufacturing towns ever since the early years of the industrial revolution. But nowhere had the process of segregation been carried further than in London" (247). As this social distance increased, "the old methods of social control based on the model of the squire, the parson, face to face relations, deference and paternalism, found less and less reflection in the urban reality. Vast tracts of working class housing were left to themselves, virtually bereft of any contact with authority except in the form of the policeman and the bailiff. The poor districts became an immense terra incognita, periodically mapped out by intrepid missionaries and explorers who catered to an insatiable middle-class demand for travelers' tales" (14). In the 1980s, William Julius Wilson (1987, 8) recapitulated both this argument and anxiety when he asserted that the underclass today is characterized by "social isolation," leading to a series of "concentration effects," which combine to generate "aberrant behaviors" in a group that is "collectively different" from mainstream society (Wilson's argument is critically examined in detail in chapter 5).

Prior to the drastic transformation of industrial cities, the urban poor were considered to be simply "demoralized," the result of individually hedonistic drives and sinful lifestyle choices, no longer countered by the "good example" set by the pious upper classes. As anxieties sharpened attention to this class, its character was imagined increasingly in terms of "degeneration." The middle class came to believe that "the savage and brutalizing conditions of the casual poor were the result of long exposure to the degenerating conditions of city life" (G. Jones 1984, 286). The effect of such conditions was construed as a threat to the imperial race of England; a weakened or contaminated racial stock would undermine the strength of English armies abroad.[8] Descriptions of London laborers emphasized the constitutional weakness and an increasing loss of physical stature and stamina. Biologistic interpretations, rather than structural accounts of the economic transformation in the central city, found that urban existence was generating a lazy, obstinate, and perverse labor force. In a similar vein today, analyses and descriptions of the urban underclass key almost entirely on the questionable subject of behavior, while generally downplaying or ignoring the structural dynamics that have created this economic predicament.[9]

Racialized versions of the urban poor, descriptions that found the poor to be a distinct race apart from the national population, stretch back at least to Engels, who noted, along with other contemporary commentators, that the worst conditions always seemed to correlate with the presence of Irish migrants.[10] Booth's powerful empirical rendering of the city was important in that it countered and undermined, to some extent, this racialized view of the poor.[11] In place of a stark division of East and West London, one wretchedly impoverished and the other opulent, he produced a detailed, nuanced map of the city's social geography, supplanting unbounded images of physically degenerate, filthy masses with detailed renditions of working life in London.[12] Indeed, Booth invented the concept of the poverty line and scrupulously recorded the tenuous circumstances of those who straddled it, tossed to one side or the other capriciously by changing economic circumstances. Booth's humanistic rendering of impoverished workers, however, did not assail the basic racial logic that operated on the inner city; rather, he refined its application and directed it toward a more limited population.[13] This is a key commonality between Booth and contemporary researchers, who also strive to depict the underclass as analytically distinct from the larger, less specialized population, the poor.[14]

Booth (1902, 1: 38) labeled the social bottom-dwellers the low class:

From these come the battered figures who slouch through the streets, and play the beggar or the bully, or who help to foul the record of the unemployed; these are the worst class of corner men who hang round the doors of public-houses, the young men who spring forward on any chance to earn a copper, the ready materials for disorder when occasion serves. They degrade whatever they touch, and as individuals perhaps incapable of improvement; they may be to some extent a necessary evil in every large city, but their numbers will be affected by the economical condition of the classes above them, and the discretion of the "charitable world"; their way of life by the pressure of police supervision.

As this description suggests, the conceptual linkage between this initial objectification of the low class and today's underclass is the overarching attention to behavior and comportment, over against an acknowledgment of the economic, political, and social forces shaping such forms of poverty. Rather than suggesting that current depictions of the urban poor are compromised because they reproduce the representational logic of this earlier era, the point I pursue here is that this correspondence offers an interesting basis to consider what possibilities the earlier conflation of race and class offer us for thinking differently about representations of the inner city today.

In the 1890s, when systematic poverty research was initiated, race and class were conceptually and perceptually entwined, distinctly legible in a welter of physiognomic features—stature, "carriage," and posture, to name a few—and interchangeably addressed in a range of technical discourses (discussed in detail in chapter 2). Today representations of the underclass replicate this conflation. As Adolph Reed Jr. (2000a, 96) observes, "The underclass image proceeds from a view of class in general that strikingly resembles Victorian convention. Victorians often used 'class' and 'race' interchangeably; each category was seen as innate. Class and race essences generally were thought to include—in addition to distinctive physiognomy—values, attitudes, and behavior." William Julius Wilson boldly sought to downplay the significance of race in analyzing the formation of the underclass, but he reinscribed a racialized perception of the urban poor by asserting that they are behaviorally and constitutively distinct from unmarked Americans. Instead of faulting Wilson for a tendency that is widespread among social scientists, another insight can be gleaned here. Perhaps the racialization of today's underclass is not simply a function of the predominant blackness of these zones; perhaps this tendency to racialize the poor is reflective of a greater problem: the tendency to imagine their threatening difference in bodily and behavioral terms rather than as linked to economics. This predisposition is heightened by an apparent inability of some social scientists and cultural critics to think effectively about and describe the conflations of race and class.

One way out of this predicament, as illustrated by these parallels from Booth's approach to the inner city and the following narratives, is to imaginatively reconsider and rework the modes for analyzing race and class until they reveal the underlying cultural processes of classification that make these registers mutually reinforcing. To fully develop this perspective, we need to draw one more insight from Booth's work, and that concerns the problems entailed in objectifying a social collective or condition. Booth stood as a paragon of the possibility of systematic knowledge about the poor generated through neutral fact production, yet he was curiously attuned to problems of representation that continue to haunt poverty research today. If anything, he was far more attentive to these problems than are current researchers who are quite confident in their abilities to objectify the poor and the underclass. As Kevin Bales (1999, 157) notes, "Booth must have been one of the first social scientists to have the opportunity to observe his simply and factually stated research results twisted to the many editorial slants of various journals." Indeed, Booth offered the following caution in the first volume of his study:

> The special difficulty of making an accurate picture of so shifting a scene as the low-class streets in East London present is very evident, and may be easily exaggerated. As in photographing a crowd, the details of the picture change continually, but the general effect is much the same, whatever moment is chosen. I have attempted to produce an instantaneous picture, fixing the facts on my negative as they appear at a given moment, the constant changes, the whirl and turmoil of life. In many districts the people are always on the move; they shift from one part of it to another like "fish in a river." (1902, 1: 26–27)

The challenge of representing such a fluid, nebulous collective was further accentuated by Booth's recognition that such objectifications did not truly stand apart from the interpretive dispositions audiences brought to his depictions of the inner city.

Booth accomplished an unparalleled feat in his positivist rendering of the city, but he remained dubious about the power of such an account to break through the preconceptions about the poor held by his readers. The *Poverty Series* was heralded for its objectivist stance, but even Booth realized that fact production comes down to matters of interpretation. He observed that "two mental attitudes continually recur in considering poverty," and he cautioned: "There are two ways of looking at even mere figures, by which very different impressions may be produced by the same facts" (1902, 2: 18, 1:

178). Some readers, he realized, would not be stirred or troubled by his tally of some 100,000 poverty-stricken individuals residing in London, whereas others would "shrink aghast from this picture. The divergence between these two points of view, between relative and absolute, is in itself enough to cause the whole difference between pessimism and optimism. To judge rightly we need to bear both in mind, never to forget the numbers when thinking of the percentages, nor the percentages when thinking of the numbers. This last is most difficult to those whose daily experience or whose imagination brings vividly before them the trials and sorrows of individual lives" (1: 178). "To judge rightly" is the charge Booth offers as an accompaniment to his account, and this challenge shifts the focus briefly but critically from inner-city settings to the mind-set of the audience.

These two fundamental dispositions toward facts produced through poverty research are only the starting point for questions of representation, as Booth recognized. "Nor have we yet exhausted the complicated relativities which are crowded into the phrase 'point of view'; for we have to take into account the condition of the on-looker's mind and of public sentiment generally, and the changes of feeling that occur, in this or that direction, by which it becomes more sensitive or more callous. On these three points— (1) the relation to past experience; (2) the relation to expectations; (3) the degree of sensitiveness of the public mind—we have room for great gulfs of difference in considering the same facts" (1902, 1: 173). As with his techniques of survey research and statistical analysis, Booth's rendition of representational issues may strike us as rudimentary. Certainly, attention to representation is regarded in far more complex and sophisticated terms today (Spivak 1988). But these passages underscore Booth's recognition of the need to direct attention to the interpretive dispositions that people bring to bear in regarding the poor. Revisiting Booth's work reminds us that the task of fashioning effective representations of the inner city is not simply a problem of refining modes of fact production and honing analytical concepts. Rather, it involves engaging how people interpret factual accounts and their predisposition toward perceiving certain projected social collectives. Quite simply, we need to find ways to transform the interpretive stances for understanding and representing poverty; in particular, we need to assail the confident, often smug detachment that most people bring to bear in thinking about or observing poor people, and we must devise ways to de-essentialize views of the poor as a group apart from society as a whole. By way of addressing these interpretive stances, and of imagining ways to differently engage audiences— objectifying the relational dynamics of class self-construction instead of producing essentialized portraits of the poor—I turn now to the strange tale of Dr. Jekyll and Mr. Hyde.

WHOSE MONSTER IS LOOSE?

This tale, a dream turned nightmare, of emphatically segregated, physically distinct, and morally opposite class orders, offers a critical vantage point for grasping the relational dynamics of class identities and their grounding in projections of distinct bodily conditions. *Dr. Jekyll and Mr. Hyde* depicts the enduring desire that separate class orders should reflect distinct moral characteristics, representing qualitatively different orders of humanity, a desire animating current depictions of the urban underclass.[15] This dream of segregation receives certain affirmations from the extreme transformation of urban spaces and is nourished through depictions of the poor as morally debased and degenerate. Tracing the inevitable collapse of this segregated order and of the respectable class Self that is predicated on it underscores the monstrous impossibility of such desire, for it seeks to deny, distort, or circumvent the interrelatedness of class identities.[16] The monstrosity at the core of Stevenson's tale is generated by contradictory impulses: a recognition of the interrelatedness of two seemingly opposed moral orders and the concomitant desire to render these two conditions into distinct, segregated class registers.[17] Class contrasts provide the tension and momentum for this drama, as is well evidenced in the clash of distinct titles, Doctor versus Mister. Yet here the clearly class-coded terrains of bodily, urban, and psychological orders that propel the tale and generate its enduring dynamism are thoroughly conflated with what we regard today as the distinct analytic category of race.[18]

Dr. Jekyll represents privilege and professional status; he describes himself as born "to a large fortune, endowed besides with excellent parts, inclined by nature to industry, fond of respect of the wise and good among my fellowmen, and thus, as might have been supposed, with every guarantee of an honourable and distinguished future" (1886/1985, 78). An excellent beginning, but one that goes horribly awry. The trappings of respectability wear heavily on Dr. Jekyll, suppressing his "impatient gaiety" and other temperamental "irregularities," the pleasures of which he is forced to conceal so that he might rise in the esteem of distinguished members of society.[19] Here the forms of etiquette that solidify class identity are posed in tension with a conflicted, emergent "nature" within the heart of this class changeling. "It was thus rather the exacting nature of my aspirations than any particular degradation in my faults, that made me what I was, and, with even a deeper trench than in the majority of men, severed in me those provinces of good and ill which divide and compound man's dual nature" (79). The stress from upward striving both reflects the premium placed on proper conduct in achieving and maintaining bourgeois identity and makes the contingent tenuousness of etiquette a key feature of this drama.[20]

Dr. Jekyll dreams that this division can be accommodated through an elaborate process of segregation, one that unfolds in bodily and urban realms scored by class distinctions. Dabbling in "transcendental medicine" and various scientific experiments, he stumbles upon a chemical concoction that can temporarily dethrone the supremacy of his respectable identity, allowing, in its place, an unbridled, indecorous Self to run riot. The effects of this transition are made legible on Dr. Jekyll's body, which transmogrifies into the body of a ravenous, low-class criminal male, Mr. Hyde. As Dr. Jekyll's evil side emerges, bearing all the physiognomic traits of the low-class male, he describes his transformation: "I stretched out my hands, exulting in the freshness of these sensations; and in the act, I was suddenly aware that I had lost in stature. . . . The evil side of my nature, to which I had now transferred the stamping efficacy, was less robust and less developed than the good which I had just deposed. . . . Even as good shone upon the countenance of the one, evil was broadly written and plainly on the face of the other. Evil besides (which I must still believe to be the lethal side of man) had left on that body an imprint of deformity and decay" (83). The transformation of Jekyll's proper body and Self incorporates the process of degeneration, which social commentators in this era warned was reconfiguring the physiognomy of urban dwellers, and prefigures the interest in eugenics that began sweeping Britain and the United States at the close of the nineteenth century (see chapter 2).[21]

The signs of degeneration coded in Hyde's much reduced stature are accentuated further by a variety of sartorial contrasts: Jekyll's respectable attire appears ill-suited for Hyde's apparent social standing. Among the cultured observers of Hyde's monstrosity (those good friends of Dr. Jekyll), the descriptions are quite detailed and telling. When Jekyll's associate, Dr. Lanyon, first encounters Hyde, his attention is fixated on the mutant's wardrobe, which appears comical as well as horrible. That Jekyll's clothes do not fit Hyde's frame reveals the utter social distance between the two classed selves.

This person (who had thus, from the first moment of his entrance, struck me in what I can only describe as a disgustful curiosity) was dressed in a fashion that would have made an ordinary person laughable; his clothes, that is to say, although they were of rich and sober fabric, were enormously too large for him in every measurement—the trousers hanging on his legs and rolled up to keep them from the ground, the waist of the coat below his haunches, and the collar sprawling wide upon his shoulders. Strange to relate, this ludicrous accouterment was far from moving me to laughter. Rather, as there was something abnormal and misbegotten in the very essence of the creature that now faced me—something seizing, surprising and revolting—this fresh disparity seemed but to fit in with and to reinforce it; so that to my interest in the man's nature and character, there was added a curiosity to his origins, his life, fortune and status in the world. (73)

Jekyll's bodily and psychosocial transformations are related throughout the tale with an emphasis on the ill-fitting way his clothes hang on Hyde's greatly reduced frame, underscoring the class and racial coding of his reduced stature.

Hyde's physical carriage, though, allows Jekyll to escape the censuring gaze of respectable society and to roam the streets of dark London in search of pleasure, engaging in heedless, unrestrained, and immoral acts.[22] But it is hardly Hyde's body alone that depicts this class transformation; his haunts also clearly code his identity as low class. *Dr. Jekyll and Mr. Hyde* is a foundational text in a genre that features an enduring dream of certain members of the upper classes—that they might escape the strictures of class conventions and consort among the "lowlifes" in the inner city.[23] Hyde's place of lodging is described by Jekyll's close companion and the tale's most consistent narrator, the lawyer Mr. Utterson, who ventures to Hyde's quarters and is disturbed by the character of this inner-city zone. "The dismal quarter of Soho . . . , with its muddy ways and slatternly passengers, and its lamps, which had never been extinguished or had been kindled afresh to combat this mournful reinvasion of darkness, seemed, in the lawyer's eyes, like the district of some city in a nightmare" (29). This myth turns not just on the desire to segregate class/moral orders, but on the privileged ability of a member of the respectable classes to transgress without social costs this divide. Stevenson's depictions make the poverty-stricken setting obvious:

As the cab drew up before the address indicated, the fog lifted a little and showed him a dingy street, a gin palace, a low French eating house, a shop for the retail of penny numbers and twopenny salads, many ragged children huddled in the doorways, and many women of many different nationalities passing out, key in hand, to have a morning glass; and the next moment the fog settled down again upon that part, as brown as umber, and cut him off from his blackguardly surroundings. This was the home of Henry Jekyll's favourite; of a man who was heir to a quarter of a million sterling. (30)

This financial arrangement that so galls Lanyon reflects one of Hyde's most disturbing features: he is sufficiently ensconced in upper-class conventions and arrangements, yet he openly flaunts the forms of etiquette and decorum designed to keep the low class in their place.

Gradually, Dr. Jekyll loses his ability to control his alternating identities. Hyde's physique comes unbidden over the respectable body, evidencing the dreaded loss of self-control that threatened middle-class self-identity, dramatizing the dense ways class belonging and difference are bodily coded. Drowsing one morning in his bedchamber, Jekyll stirs groggily awake: "My eyes fell upon my hand. Now the hand of Henry Jekyll (as you have often remarked) was professional in shape and size; it was large, firm, white and comely. But the hand which I now saw, clearly enough, in the yellow light of a mid-London morning, lying half shut on the bedclothes, was lean, corded, knuckly, of a dusky pallor and thickly shaded with a swart growth of hair. It was the hand of Edward Hyde" (88). In this semiotic of bodily/class orders, "professional" is viscerally contrasted with the "lean, corded, knuckly" hand of a member of the low class, a difference underscored and paralleled by the colored distinction of "white and comely" with Hyde's "dusky pallor."[24] This visceral contrast underscores the importance of bodily registers in figuring class identities and it offers a glimpse of the overlapping symbolic basis that makes race and class mutually reinforcing.

The narrative act that proves irrevocably Hyde's monstrosity is at root an act of class loathing and conflict, but one that is embellished with racialized inscriptions of difference: he brutally beats to death a respected elder citizen "of high position" on a desolate city street. In this scene, racial and class codes are thoroughly intertwined in terms of the perpetrator's sense of provocation and his following actions. A maid who witnesses the murder describes the older man as "beautiful, polite, and his face seemed to breathe such an innocent and old-world kindness, yet with something high too, as of a well-founded self-content" (25). This composure and "civility" offends Hyde to the point of blind fury. When the respectable gentleman's presence requires a decorous rejoinder, "Mr. Hyde broke out of all bounds and club-bed him to the earth. And next moment, with ape-like fury, he was trampling his victim under foot and hailing down a storm of blows, under which the bones were audibly shattered and the body jumped upon the roadway" (27). This is one of several occasions when Hyde's actions are simianized as "ape-like," a trope that codes both racial and class difference.[25] I highlight these scenes not as evidence in an *argument* that race and class are always conflated, or that class distinctions are as crucial as racial ones in the constitution of white subjectivity or the operations of whiteness. These points are well established.[26] Rather, my interest lies in the opportunity these scenes present for imagining how such conflations were once a given dimension of urban observations and to consider imaginatively how we might once again see and think through this conflation of analytical registers that too often are kept apart in specialized academic discourse.

In the subsequent search for Hyde, efforts are hampered in part because of the searchers' inability to picture him. "He had never been photographed; and the few who could describe him differed widely, as common observers will. Only on one point were they agreed; and that was the haunting sense of unexpressed deformity with which the fugitive impressed his beholders" (32). The haunting impression conveyed by Hyde uniformly provokes disgust in those who see him. From the emergence of class culture, bodily disgust has been deployed to figure a social and economic divide (Stallybras and White 1981). As with racist reactions, impressions of Hyde are rooted in physical misgivings and nausea. Racist responses combine superficial readings (the ambiguous descriptions of physicality) with visceral reactions (the sense of disgust; see W. Miller 1997). This is a key aspect of Jekyll's narration of the difference embodied by Hyde. The story's first narrator, Mr. Utterson, describes him thus: "Mr. Hyde was pale and dwarfish, he gave an impression of deformity without any nameable malformation, he had a displeasing smile, he had borne himself to the lawyer with a sort of murderous mixture of timidity and boldness, and he spoke with a husky, whispering and somewhat broken voice; all these were points against him, but not all of these together could explain the hitherto unknown disgust, loathing, and fear with which Mr. Utterson regarded him" (16; see W. Miller 1997, 18–19, 96). This description captures well the sense of physical contempt that Pierre Bourdieu (1984, 174–175) describes as "class racism," the loathing, derived from "taste" operating as a habituated system of classificatory schemes, for the bodily form, foods, and speech styles one class holds for another.

Hyde succinctly describes the reactions to his classed Otherness: "None could come near me at first without misgivings of the flesh" (83). But Jekyll himself feels no sense of disgust or loathing when he regards Hyde's visage:

"Evil . . . had left an imprint of deformity and decay. And yet when I looked upon that ugly idol in the glass, I was conscious of no repugnance, rather of a leap of welcome. This, too, was myself" (83). As with the monsters that follow, Hyde's terribleness is suspended in a moment of self-recognition. Jekyll recognizes this monster for what it is: a physical effect of his desire to both maintain and transgress the social propriety and decorum that are constitutive of respectable class identity. In his confession, Jekyll acknowledges that "both sides of me were in dead earnest; I was no more myself when I laid aside restraint and plunged in shame, than when I laboured, in the eye of day, at the furtherance of knowledge or the relief of sorrow and suffering" (79). The lesson of Hyde's monstrosity is the terrible cost of such segregations and the fundamental distortions that result from the inability to recognize the common humanity of class identities.[27] What creates Hyde is, first, the distortion of fundamental forms of relatedness of these orders and, second, the dream that classed registers of moral difference can be wholly, physically segregated. The monstrosity of Hyde reflects the perversity of trying to replicate the segregation of urban space in the interior space of middle-class identity.

AESTHETICIZING URBAN DECAY

Another version of volatile distortions of the relational basis of class identities is provided by the figure of Dorian Gray, whose portrait materializes Jekyll's dream that class/moral identities can be physically separated.[28] *The Picture of Dorian Gray* more elaborately objectifies the manners and mentality of bourgeois social realms, but both dramas have at their root the division of a seemingly respectable social identity into two incommensurable creatures whose contrasts are depicted via codes of racial and class distinctions. As Dorian Gray's physical appearance gradually becomes the apotheosis of the aesthetic strivings of bourgeois manners, his inner, monstrous Self devours illicit pursuits on the inner-city streets of London. The trope of degeneration figures his inner Self's descent through East London's drug dens and alleys, while his social identity grows firmly ensconced in the realms of respectability.[29] In the end, this utter division destroys the entire creature, as with the divided Self of Jekyll/Hyde.

In Wilde's narrative, Dorian appears first as an oblivious, good-willed subject of a portrait in progress, with desires only for philanthropic work among the lower classes. Later, as his social background emerges, he is revealed as the product of a union of class extremes. His mother, Lady

Devereux, elopes with "a penniless young fellow; a mere nobody, a subaltern in a foot regiment, or something of that kind" (1891/1974, 39). Both parents die tragically after Dorian is spawned. As his portrait is finished, he utters "a mad wish . . . that his own beauty might be untarnished, and the face on the canvas bear the burden of his passions and his sins; that the painted image might be seared with the lines of suffering and thought, and that he might keep all the delicate bloom and loveliness of his then just conscious boyhood" (95). Following this wish, Dorian quickly falls under the tutorship of Lord Henry, who schools him in the pursuit of social observations: "Human life—that appeared to him the one thing worth investigating. Compared to it there was nothing else of any value. It was true that as one watched life in its curious crucible of pain and pleasure, one could not wear over one's face a mask of glass, not keep the sulphurous fumes from troubling the brain, and making the imagination turbid with monstrous fancies and misshapen dreams" (63). Lord Henry bestows upon Dorian a dream of unfettered powers of social observation and the ability to float effortlessly through the most refined social circles of London.[30]

The further Dorian rises to the heights of social adulation and development, the deeper he sinks simultaneously into the darkened streets of "degenerate" London. His adventure begins with a directionless journey into the city's depths: "I felt that this gray, monstrous London of ours, with its myriads of people, its sordid sinners and its splendid sins, as you once phrased it, must have something more in store for me. The mere danger gave me a sense of delight. . . . I don't know what I expected, but I went out and wandered eastward, soon losing my way in a labyrinth of grimy streets and black, grassless squares" (54). In these travels, he meets and falls in love with an actress, Sybil Vane, in a "cheap" and "tawdry" theater. The social distance that both opposes such a union and mirrors that which produced Dorian makes the attraction potent. When he suddenly and ferociously dismisses her affections, she takes her own life in despair. He sinks back into the streets. "Where he went he hardly knew. He remembered wandering through dimly lit streets, past gaunt black-shadowed archways and evil-looking houses. Women with hoarse voices and harsh laughter had called after him. Drunkards had reeled by, cursing and chattering to themselves like monstrous apes. He had seen grotesque children huddled upon doorsteps, and heard shrieks and oaths from gloomy courts" (93).

The role of such sites gradually shifts to the tale's background, but they remain the subject of incessant murmurings as his life and actions in the inner city are pushed to the edges of public knowledge and representation.

The painter of his portrait, Basil Hallward, laments: "Then there are the stories—stories that you have been seen creeping at dawn out of dreadful houses and slinking in disguise into the foulest dens in London. Are they true? Can they be true? When I first heard them, I laughed. I hear them now and they make me shudder" (154). Dorian's "mad wish" allows him to traverse rigorously segregated class zones without a trace on his body, and "these whispered scandals only increased, in the eyes of many, his strange and dangerous charm" (142). But his associates are far less fortunate in their efforts to crisscross class lines: "Why is your friendship so fatal to young men," Basil asks. "There was that wretched boy in the Guards who committed suicide. You were his great friend. What about Adrian Singleton, and his dreadful end? What about Lord Kent's only son, and his career? I met his father yesterday in St. James's Street. He seemed broken with shame and sorrow. What about the young Duke of Perth? What sort of life has he got now? What gentlemen would associate with him now?" (152). This string of sons of the well-to-do reduced to human wreckage bears testimony to the exorbitant costs of such transgressive social sojourns. "They have gone down into the depth. You led them there. Yes; you led them there, and yet you can smile, as you are smiling now" (154), Basil charges.

As the tale progresses, the brother of the dead actress, James Vane, returning from years at sea, seeks out Dorian Gray to avenge her death. The class connotations of his hatred are apparent. Dorian "was a gentleman and he [James Vane] hated him for that, hated him through some curious *race instinct* for which he could not account, and which for that reason was all the more dominant within him" (72; emphasis added). Two chapters starkly juxtapose their distinct class realms; the narrative shifts from Dorian's excursion in an opium den, where he and James first cross paths, to a fox hunt on the grounds of a country estate. James meets his accidental death in the wealthy realm of the estates where he seeks out Dorian to kill him. But this transgression of class zones, the first reversal of Dorian's ease of passage to lower-class locales, creates a panic state that drives him to destroy the portrait. This act, in turns, ends his life, as the impossibly separated elements of his own constitution converge in a molten, decaying mass, a representational meltdown on the upper floor of his house, where the picture has been carefully closeted for years.

Oscar Wilde is at his best in detailing the world of high society and its philosophy of manners, yet the poetic that emerges through Dorian's fragmented consciousness relies on an aestheticization of the inner city. As the allure of Art fades into banality and boredom, as the luster of high society appears finally superficial and mundane, the opium dens of the inner city beckon because they represent the Real for this class-constructed self-identity. Indeed, Dorian opts for the dens of East London even though he keeps opium in a gilded box in his room. *The Picture of Dorian Gray* marvelously depicts middle-class cravings and obsessions for glimpses of the underclass, as these figures represent reality over and against the social realms dominated by manners and decorum, evident today in numerous reality TV shows, such as *Cops*, featuring debased poor people being arrested in their trailers or their beat-up cars. In an opium den, "Dorian winced, and looked around at the grotesque things that lay in such fantastic postures on the ragged mattresses. The twisted limbs, the gaping mouths, the staring, lusterless eyes, fascinated him" (189). In such sites, in such dispositions, bourgeois decorum is shamelessly transgressed; hence the fascination of these figures. But "society's" fascination depends on the ability of spectators of such scenes to thoroughly aestheticize these subjects.[31] Wilde's character, searching after exquisite forms of experience, depicts this dynamic well. The more aesthetic his sensibility of the underclass becomes, the more monstrously detached he grows from the degeneration devouring his soul: "Ugliness that had once been hateful to him because it made things real, became dear to him now for that very reason. Ugliness was the one reality. The coarse brawl, the loathsome den, the crude violence of disordered life, the very vileness of the thief and outcast, were more vivid, in their intense actuality of impression, than all the gracious shapes of Art, the dreamy shadow of Songs" (187). Dorian's aesthetic detachment is further underscored in this scene as he surveys the debris of one of the young gentlemen, Adrian, whom he led to this den previously. Adrian's "grotesque posture" inscribes the effects of degeneration that has spread to him from lingering too long in these lower-class zones, but to which Dorian remains magically immune.

Two key connections between Dr. Jekyll and Dorian Gray are their internal monsters and their common dream that class/moral orders might be transformed into a bodily form of segregation. Dorian's wish allows the portrait, his "misshapen shadow," to bear the burdens of his class transgressions while his outward visage remains elegant and refined. Both characters dream of a physical realization of moral divisions between good and evil, beauty and decay; both dreams become nightmares when the artificial segregation inevitably collapses. The result for Dorian is a division of Self similar to Dr. Jekyll's: two bodies emerge to characterize the distinct "natures" embedded within one class being. Like Jekyll's chemical cocktail, Dorian's portrait promotes a division of class orders that is truly monstrous because of its effects on the Self and its distortions of reality. Feeling the surface of the portrait carefully, Dorian finds it "quite undisturbed and as he had left it. It was from within, apparently, that foulness and horror had come. Through some strange quickening of inner life the leprosies of sin were slowly eating the thing away. The rotting of a corpse in a watery grave was not so fearful" (160). But Dorian Gray takes us one step further than Dr. Jekyll in understanding the representational economy and the certain constitution of middle-class self-identity that, respectively, generate and consume images of the underclass and the inner city. Dorian Gray additionally figures the role of the spectator in these class realms, the purveyor of experiences both "sordid and sensual" in the distinct class spheres of "civilization and corruption." Understanding the role of urban spectatorship, then and now, is critical for grasping the monstrosity of the underclass and the persistent production of this terrifying figure.[32]

INNER CITY USA

Monsters may be destroyed, but seemingly not the reservoir from which they arise. Linking this reservoir to the present moment is the movie *Candyman*, which also features the inner city and the class-coded practices of urban spectatorship.[33] Monsters from both eras are spawned from similar conditions of heightened class segregation and increased concentration and desperation of poverty; as well, they arise out of similar processes of class self-construction.[34] As with the previous stories, this narrative is valuable for its attention to the crossings and transformations of the bounded class identities. The monster in this movie haunts the Chicago housing project Cabrini-Green. The terror there is, of course, completely real—a realness so excessive that it becomes fantastical as well.[35] Beyond the nightmares represented in contemporary housing projects, the character Candyman is also a historical creation; he became transfigured from human to monster in 1890 as a victim of racial violence. He was an artist, "a painter of portraits," and "was much sought after when it came to documenting one's wealth and position in society." The son of a former slave who amassed a great fortune in manufacturing, "he had grown up in polite society" and "was sent to all the best schools." His "crime" was seducing the virgin daughter of a wealthy, white patron. For this racial transgression he was brutally murdered and burned on a pyre at Cabrini-Green, where his ashes were then scattered. Over one hundred years later he is still haunting this site, home to perhaps the most notorious public housing project in the country.[36]

The movie unfolds in a collapsing distinction between fact and fiction. The drama features two graduate student researchers, Helen (white) and Bernadette (black), who are studying urban legends. Though racially distinct, their class commonalities are accentuated by contrasts with the subjects of their study, the black residents of Cabrini-Green. Their study, we are told, involves "modern un-selfconscious reflections of the fears of urban society"; their thesis is that "a community is attributing the horrors of their daily lives to a mythic being": Candyman. Such "modern oral folklore" seems, at first, merely a vain attempt by "urban peasants" to come to terms with the increasingly incomprehensible scale of violence that is their daily lives. But the specter really materializes, first in a number of killings, and then in pursuit of Helen, who doubted his existence and was "not content with the stories."[37]

Candyman marvelously figures several critical dimensions of the tradition of observing and recording the haunting worlds of the urban poor. Helen depicts the modern urban researcher, enthusiastically snapping pictures to document conditions in Cabrini-Green while she intrepidly travels into the interiors of a place few whites would willingly tread. Indeed, the movie's drama is generated by her repeated crossings of material and symbolic boundaries designed to isolate poor blacks in the inner city.[38] Helen makes contact with the "natives"—particularly one black woman, Anne-Marie—and uses them to pursue her inquiries concerning the monster terrorizing these subjects. Along the way she recognizes a series of connections that personally relate her to this setting and its violence. First, she finds that her apartment building was originally designed to be public housing. City planners belatedly realized that, if constructed as such, there would be no barriers between these proposed projects and Chicago's Gold Coast neighborhood along Lake Michigan, so they decide to convert the building into high-rent condominiums. Helen succinctly relates this strategy of urban planning, one that was deployed in cities throughout the Midwest to insulate white neighborhoods from public housing units, illustrating this suddenly legible design for Bernadette from the window of her high-rise apartment. Whites, she demonstrates, are profoundly implicated in the construction of such terrifying sites, and her interior space, the apartment, is a product of segregation.

Candyman further highlights the racial textures of urban spectatorship with Helen repeatedly marked as being out of place in Cabrini-Green. Viewers cannot easily assume the detached observer position because the exploitive contours of this position are repeatedly emphasized. "You don't belong here, lady," Anne-Marie snarls, informing her that "white folks don't never come here 'cept to cause us a problem." These and other comments make palpable the overdetermined and sordid history of white spectatorship of ghetto life as generated by well-intentioned researchers (see Kelley 1997). The film highlights Helen's awkward interactions with the residents of Cabrini-Green, who seem to know all too well what the conclusions of her thesis will be. "So you say you're doing a study," Anne-Marie says. "What you gonna say? That we bad? That we steal? We gang-bangers? We're all on drugs?" Helen hands out her card in each confrontational instance and tries to convince residents that she is not a cop. But there seems to be little she can report that will escape the predetermined modes for representing poor blacks.

In addition to its history lesson and critique of the class and racial dynamics of poverty research, *Candyman* viscerally figures the mythic dimensions of whites' responsibilities for the violent conditions facing poor blacks today.[39] The film takes two key scenes from black-white racial history and resoundingly amplifies their features until they color every dimension of this story. "Be my victim," the menacing black male with the gore-dripping, phallic hook commands of Helen, who is positioned as victim in the enduring scene of white males' sexual nightmares, one used to initiate and justify so many lynchings and beatings. Then, following her first encounter with Candyman, Helen wakes in Anne-Marie's apartment, covered in blood and linked to a heinous crime resonating back to the evils of slavery: the black woman's baby has been stolen, and Helen seems to be responsible. These two scenes condense the simultaneously mythic and real scales that figure heavily in black-white relations. Helen's sojourn as researcher has transformed her into a paraclete for whites' racial past (see Girard 1977).

The monster that emerges in this setting is an interesting fusion of the figures that roam the inner city. Candyman's appearance requires a self-reflective moment, not unlike Dorian's meditations on his portrait; he appears when somebody gazes into a mirror long enough to repeat his name five times. This raises the eerie possibility that the source of this monster is some repressed, lethal libido, suggesting that Helen has committed these crimes. Helen is charged with the murder of her friend, Bernadette, butchered by Candyman in Helen's apartment as the violence escapes its zone of containment in Cabrini-Green. Everyone seems convinced that some hideous aspect of her inner Self has been unleashed in these crimes. Strapped in a wheelchair and explaining herself to a psychiatrist, she insists, "I know this. No matter what's going wrong, no part of me, no matter how hidden, is capable of that." Yet, the monster appears and kills the psychiatrist when she summons him by looking into a mirror and chanting his name. The sharp contrast in this narrative from the earlier two is that the Id and the Ego have become accepted explanations for such muddled acts of violence. Hyde has become real. But Candyman is the product of a more geographically distended Self. The constitutively repressed inner Self is located in the inner city, as well as within the middle-class subject. Thus, the monstrosity of Candyman is of a larger order than a simple emergence of a repressed Self, one that is legible in the material and symbolic dimensions of the city.

Helen is held responsible for unaccountable black deaths and acts of inner-city violence, but the monster she is grappling with materializes a different order of responsibility. Candyman finally links her to the original act of racial violence that has been unfolding in the Cabrini-Green housing project. Escaping from police custody, she slips again into the walls of the project and comes upon a mural of portraits that confirm both the realness of Candyman and Helen's mythic status. She finds a depiction of the 1890 murder; the white woman at the scene resembles her. The writing on the wall announces, "It was always Helen." Her connection to this century-old violence succinctly condenses a tangle of complex realities that require accounting in the tabulation of racial debts and culminate with her self-sacrifice. But these are elusive realizations, more tangible in the mythic dimension of pictures than in the objectivist realm of rational assessments of the significance of racial differences. Candyman wants to make Helen part of the "writing on the walls." He promises her immortality if she dies in the place of Anne-Marie's stolen baby. "Our names will be written on a thousand walls," he offers. "Our crimes told and retold by our faithful believers. We shall die together in front of their very eyes and give them something to be haunted by." Helen initially refuses this offer, but then meets Candyman in the center of a massive bonfire/funeral pyre assembled by the residents of the housing project, where he has secreted the stolen black baby. She kills Candyman but exchanges her life for that of the child, gaining the promised immortality by achieving her own form of haunting monstrosity.

Candyman, viewed in the frame of an epoch of social science research and fictional narratives that have represented the inner city to middle-class audiences, provocatively poses the central questions in this essay: How do we imaginatively recognize and consider the mythic and real dynamics that inform poverty research? How do we assess the way their symbolic and overdetermined dimensions shape studies of the poor? Then, how do we represent these relations to students and a wider audience? How do we bridge the gap between fact and fiction in a manner that makes people aware of their complicity in these "social problems," which they've been trained to assume concern only a distant and alien, not-quite-human, tribe: "the poor"? Statistical research on poverty overwhelmingly convinces lay people and experts alike of the fundamentally alien and distant nature of the problem of poverty. Even the best efforts of urban ethnographers to demonstrate that the people who occupy inner-city zones are representative of American culture—exhibiting behaviors that can be found across the class spectrum, from corporate boardrooms to car dealership floors—have little overall impact on monstrous representations of the underclass (see Lassalle and O'Dougherty 1997; Torres 1998). Perhaps because, as Booth suggested, more humanistic accounts of the poor do not significantly challenge the predispositions of middle-class viewers who consume such imagery.[40] My suggestion is that if more humanistic accounts of the poor do not make an impact, then we need to engage the mythic dimensions of poverty research, to objectify the symbolic operations and make ledgible the traces of our ties to *those people.* In so doing, the focus has to encompass and challenge the sensibilities and anxieties of the consumers of these representations of the poor.

CONCLUSION

The monsters in the city are our own, produced by systems of class and racial segregation. Even the most sober and stolid contemporary work of social science is inflected by the dynamics of desire and loathing, fear and fascination depicted through these tales and images of monsters. Proceeding through this charged terrain does not depend on first purging these imaginary tendencies; they are irreducible and will remain active on the part of audiences for reports from the inner city. Instead, I use these tales to suggest ways to think more imaginatively about the fusion of racial and classed forms of inequality, particularly how they are produced and maintained in multiple, visceral, overlapping registers simultaneously. We collectively construct them and contribute to their power to terrify. We bear responsibility for them and an intimate connection to their creation. This relation is not easily grasped and it is almost entirely overwhelmed by the imagery and reporting generated on life in the inner city. The monsters reviewed here arise and are created out of the effort to keep class and racial realms distinct and to align these spheres with opposed moral orders. But in their horrible visitations they also hold out the promise or offer contorted glimpses of ways to cross and recross these culturally constructed boundaries, of ways to destabilize the rigorous insistence that class orders represent contrasting moral dispositions (Haraway 1992; Gordon 1997; Brogan 1998). Grasping this potential requires imaginative effort, applied to and in conjunction with empirical modes of socially analyzing and representing urban poverty. Fundamentally, to represent poverty effectively we must grasp the relational dynamics of class identity; this means rejecting the truncated deployments of culture in relation to class that promote the view that classes are insular social realms (Valentine 1968). We have a responsibility to deploy culture in a manner that catches us all in its meshes, figuring both "their" commonality and "our" complicity in these situations. Unless we feel an eerie presentiment of this basic relationship, we will not be able to assail the smug, confident sense of detachment and social distance from *those people* that perpetuates the monstrous depictions of the underclass. This clammy shudder of self-recognition is necessary if we are to short-circuit the process of myth making in social science accounts and dispel some of the terror of these monstrous figures.

CHAPTER 2

BLOOD WILL TELL:

THE NATIONALIZATION

OF WHITE TRASH

The Jooks and the Kelly-Cooks have been milking turnkeys and sucking the
blood out of the marshalsea since the act of First Offender.

—James Joyce, *Finnegans Wake*

Who counts as white and what basis of solidarity ties such whites together?
Current interest in the problem of whiteness increasingly focuses on how
such cultural judgments about belonging are made in relation to this racial
construct. The basis for answering such questions, though, begins with the
recognition that whiteness is not simply a racial identity and that race is not
an absolute social condition. No single cultural figure makes this clearer than
"white trash." Understanding how whiteness works requires grasping how
the visage, speech, and actions of certain whites can so disturb notions of belonging and difference that they are simultaneously marked as white yet expelled from the privileged social domain of whiteness. This dynamic obviously turns on matters of class and sexuality, but this is not to assert that class
and gender are more fundamental for understanding such judgments.
Rather, white trash demonstrates that decisions about belonging and difference are made in multiple registers concurrently and that cultural dynamics
fundamentally shape the way race, class, and sexuality are experienced and
perceived. Tracing the emergence of white trash in the United States in its

gradual shift from a regional folk epithet to a nationally recognized stereotype opens a vista onto these complex and muddled dimensions of whiteness.[1]

How did "white trash" spread from its place of origin, the southern slave states, to become a familiar term used throughout the country? More important, how did the image of white trash, a distinct figure of degraded and contemptible poor whites, become widely discernible as a social collective, a "kind" of people that threatened the stability and future of the white race at large? The answers lie in the period from the 1840s to the 1920s, an era that featured a notable "fracturing of whiteness," according to historian Mathew Jacobson (1998, 38, 41): "Whereas the salient feature of whiteness before the 1840s had been its powerful political and cultural contrasts to nonwhiteness, now its internal divisions, too, took on a new and pressing significance." Comprehending the dynamics of whiteness in this era, Jacobson cautions, requires breaking from current literalist assumptions about how race matters. In listening carefully to these distant sources, "we must admit of a system of 'difference' by which one might be both white *and* racially distinct from other whites" (6). This system of difference becomes audible in the rhetorical tactics and representational strategies that crafted white trash as a distinct cultural figure in the mid-nineteenth century and continue operating to this day.[2] Listening to the way scholars, social commentators, and lay people talked about white trash makes tangible the immense cultural work— of constituting and maintaining boundaries, policing through forms of etiquette, and judgments about identity and difference—this notorious figure performs in relation to race, sexuality, and class. Though "white trash" first appears as a form of otherness, its most troubling aspect is its dimension of sameness; its profoundest effects relate to the self-constitution of whites. White trash induces an intense self-anxiety in relation to explicit forms of white racial consciousness expressed toward the end of this era with the rise of the eugenics movement.[3]

The following historical account of "white trash" renders this unusual cultural object neither as simply a term nor as a distinct social group. Rather, uses of this epithet are read here as recording important cultural dynamics shaping class, gender, and racial identities in the United States. With class, it highlights bodily and rhetorical aspects of class identities that are typically overlooked in sociological and economic analyses of class.[4] With sexuality, it delimits the bounds of admissible physical relations and reflects state interest in controling reproduction, all in support of gendered notions of "domesticity." With race, white trash calls attention to the charged intraracial contests over belonging, typically drawing on class distinctions, which are a crucial dimension of racial identification. This intraracial aspect encompasses cultural dynamics that often are left unexamined by explanations that prioritize notions of Otherness. The following analysis of the uses of white trash opens onto a broader understanding of how racial identity is constituted and reproduced.

This speculative history examines popular writings from two eras. The first features travelogues and northern abolitionists' descriptions of white trash in the South during the 1850s and 1860s; the second peruses popular writing on eugenics that appeared in magazines such as *Good Housekeeping, Ladies' Home Journal,* and the *Saturday Evening Post* in the early 1900s. These genres feature distinct concerns: in the earlier period, primarily, over the negative effects of slavery on the "white race," and in the later time frame over wellsprings of "racial poisons" within the white race. But both discursive orders are grounded in and animated by a vivid and disturbing image of poor whites. Class, sex, and race clearly matter in each era's focus on poor whites, but their relevance is distinctly construed via particular discourses shaping representations of white trash in these two periods. In this narrative of the emergence and development of nationally circulated representations of white trash in the United States, it becomes apparent that notions of projected images of otherness are insufficient to the task of explaining how racial and class identities are formulated and experienced.

"WORSE THAN A NIGGER"

The term white trash appears to have entered into circulation in the popular literature of the North in the 1850s and 1860s, accompanied by a slew of synonyms such as "poor whites," "mean whites," "crackers," "sandhillers," "clayeaters," and "bobtails."[5] Newspaper correspondents fed a steady stream of firsthand accounts of southern life to northern audiences, who ranged from indifferent to animated in their attitudes concerning the effects of slavery. A series of travelogues and autobiographies, novels, scholarly treatises, and tracts on the South introduced these terms to northerners and depicted a racially distinctive, degraded people. Works published in 1857 offer several examples of usage of this charged epithet. James Stirling (1857, 221) explained in his travelogue, *Letters from the Slave States,* that the inhabitants of the slave states "constitute but two classes—the planters or rich class, and the poor class, variously denominated 'crackers,' 'white trash,' 'poor whites,' 'mean whites.' This social characteristic I consider the most remarkable and important feature of Southern civilization." Frederick Douglass

(1857, 344), in *My Bondage and My Freedom*, expanded on the lower portion of this bifurcated view of southern whites: "A free white man, holding no slaves, in the country, I had known to be the most ignorant and poverty-stricken of men, and the laughing stock even of slaves themselves—called generally by them, in derision, '*poor white trash*'" (original emphasis). But use of the epithet was hardly restricted to slaves, for, as Frederick Law Olmsted (1857, 439–440) relates in his travelogue, *A Journey through Texas*, the Germans there "are accustomed to regard all neighbors out of their own class as White Trash." Additionally, in a work that profoundly shaped debates about the status of poor whites, the southern abolitionist Hinton Helper (1860, 32–33) charged: "The liberation of five millions of 'poor white trash' from the second degree of slavery, and of three millions of miserable kidnapped Negroes from the first degree, cannot be accomplished too soon."

White trash in these usages ranges from the contemptible to the sympathetic, reflecting uncertainty both about the propriety of the term and the moral and social characteristics of the group to which it was applied. This range of sentiments regarding poor whites hinged, in part, on the crucial role they played in the "free labor" ideology of northern abolitionists, who regarded their predicament as another indictment of the institution of slavery (see Foner 1995). The image of white trash also raised a host of unsettling anxieties about the stability and content of racial identities. The volatility of the term combined with the fluid contours of the population to which it was applied, along with the anxiety and concern their image generated, resulted in a highly unstable labeling practice.

Northern writers were initially hesitant about using the term *white trash*, preferring labels such as *mean white* or *poor white*. Each of these was typically placed in quotes, conveying their charged rhetorical nature. This usage of *trash* stemmed from an American revival of a then archaic English term, and perhaps the connotations of pollution sat uneasily with essayists and scholars who felt links of sympathy with these unusual southern whites (see Mencken 1919/2000). *Mean*, too, was a word revived in the U.S. context, an Americanism for "cheap" and "shameful," but it seemed to present less degrading connotations than more contemptuous terms like poor white or white trash.[6] Key to these epithets was their emphatic association with the South and its charged racial landscape; they each designated a distinct boundary marker in the continuum of racial identities defined by whiteness and blackness. Certainly, there was poverty throughout the New England and midwestern states, but this condition was surprisingly easily racialized as a function of immigration and ethnic groups crowding into East Coast cities (Ward 1989). In contrast to this racialized population in their midst, when many northerners looked southward they were unnerved to recognize the pitiable visage of their own "kith and kin" debased by southern planters.

The use of "poor white" prevailed early on among sympathetic northern writers who saw the degradation of this population as another in the long list of slavery's infamies. George Weston (1856, 7), in an influential tract titled *The Poor Whites of the South*, depicted a people "deprived of all that constitutes civilization, and thrust down into barbarism" by the institution of slavery. Weston's tract is intriguing on a number of counts, but mostly for his entwined efforts at definition and quantification of this uncertain collective; his work marks perhaps the first effort to objectively depict poor whites as a social collective in economic and political terms. Citing census figures pertaining to literacy rates and property holding, he broadly equated debased poor whites with all nonslaveholding whites, which he estimated as constituting approximately 70 percent of the South's white population. Such a large group, he argued, "would seem to be entitled to some inquiry into their actual condition; and especially, as they have real political weight or consideration in the country, and little opportunity to speak for themselves" (1). Weston compiled accounts of the economic and social predicaments of these whites into a picture that

> is distressing and discouraging, in that it exhibits three fourths of the whites of the South substantially destitute of property, driven upon soils so sterile that only a scanty subsistence is obtainable from them, depressed in moral energies, finding the pathway to respectability so difficult that they decline the hopeless pursuit, ceasing to struggle, and becoming the passive subjects of the consequences of idleness; discouraging, in that it exhibits this great bulk of the white population growing worse instead of better, evidently deteriorating, and its younger portion, less industrious, and in every point of view less respectable, than their ancestors. (2)

The condition of poor whites—"degraded, half-fed, half-clothed, without mental or moral instruction, and destitute of self-respect and of any just appreciation of character" (3)—was construed as a product of southern planters' arrogance and callous self-interest as a class.

Weston's focused attention on this group, somewhat similar to Charles Booth's depiction of the London poor, cast them as both an object of sympathy to stir popular sentiment and, in political terms, a group that could perhaps be turned into allies of the North or at least neutralized in their support of slave owners. While Weston wrote to awaken northerners to this potential, others wrote directly addressing this unfixed population. Hinton Helper (1860, 23–24) of North Carolina dedicated *The Impending Crisis of the South* to "non-slaveholding whites, like myself," and stated as one of his goals "to open the eyes of the non-slaveholders of the South, to the system of deception, that has been so long practiced upon them. . . . How little the 'poor white trash,' the great majority of the Southern people, know of the real condition of the country, is, indeed, sadly astonishing." John Abbott in 1860 championed Helper's call for liberation, making the racial stakes of this interest in white trash or poor whites quite clear: "Shall we pass, unnoticed, the thousands of poor ignorant, degraded white people among us, who, in this land of plenty, live in comparative nakedness and starvation!" (148). Abbott, too, insisted that poor whites must "begin to get their eyes open, and to claim their rights" to defeat a system that "drags the whites with the blacks down into the gulf of ignorance and penury. And it is impossible to rescue the poor white man without, at the same time, liberating the negro, whose Ethiopian skin is becoming so rapidly bleached by the infusion of the blood of his master" (150–151). Abbott explicitly addressed the planters' racial sensibilities: "Gentlemen slaveholders, does it pay to practice all this vigilance and despotism, and to crush, actually, millions of your own white brethren, merely that you may be able to compel four millions of Negroes to work without wages?" (151–152). For these abolitionists, the key feature of this troubled collective was its whiteness and the bonds of racial solidarity so entailed. This racial sensibility, though, was largely absent from southern aristocrats' worldview, perhaps because they had accomplished a more rigorous policing of racial identity in terms of class boundaries.

These social observers each struggled to fix a clear image of a group whose size and defining feature were fluid and open to debate. The core features of this group were still in flux and the moral charge attributed to their condition was uncertain but profoundly inflected by whether anxiety or sympathy animated the particular observer (see chapter 1). The criteria selected by Weston—their displacement from power and their debased position in relation to the color line—were recognized by others, but not in a manner that suggested consensus. Indeed, these three writers did not even agree on the same label for *those people*, with Weston and Abbott relying on "poor white" and Helper alternating between the rhetorical identity "white trash" and the generic economic descriptor "non-slaveholding whites." Other writers agreed on these broad contours of size and scope but perceived a distinctly different moral charge to this collective. John Cairnes (1862, 54–55), in his book, *Slave Power: Its Character, Career, and Probably Design*, used Weston's population estimate but depicted a far less valorous people:

> In the Southern States no less than five million human beings are now said to exist in this manner in a condition little removed from savage life, eking out a wretched subsistence by hunting, by fishing, by hiring themselves out for occasional jobs, by plunder. Combining the restlessness and contempt for regular industry peculiar to the savage with the vices of the *proletaire* [original emphasis] of civilized communities, *these people make up a class* [emphasis added] at once degraded and dangerous, and constantly reinforced as they are by all that is idle, worthless, and lawless among the population of the neighbouring States, form an inexhaustible preserve of ruffianism, ready at hand for all the worst purposes of Southern ambition. The planters complain of these people for their idleness, for corrupting their slaves, for their thievish propensities; but they cannot dispense with them; for, in truth, they perform an indispensable function in the economy of slave societies, of which they are at once the victims and the principal supports.

The moral tenor of Cairnes's depiction keys on their proximity to the "savage life" and their contempt for physical labor. Notably, Cairnes overlays an interpretive frame of otherness on the visage of white trash, making a more ominous figure emerge.

Cairnes's account provoked a harsh rebuke from James Gilmore, using the pseudonym Edmund Kirke (1864), who, in his travelogue, *Down in Tennessee*, challenged such commentators: "Having read of, or seen, the wretched specimens of humanity who loiter about the railway stations, or hover around the large plantations on the great Southern thoroughfares, they have jumped to the conclusion that they represent 'seven-tenths of the whole white population' of the South!" (182–183). This is "a great error," Gilmore wrote, because such ill-informed accounts misrepresent a debased portion of this unfixed collective for the whole:

> The great mass of "poor whites" are superior (and I say this with due deliberation, and after sixteen years' acquaintance with them) to every other class of un-cultivated men, save our Northern farmers, on the globe. They all were born in this country, and have imbibed from our institutions—distorted and perverted as they are at the South—a sturdy

independence, and an honest regard for each other's rights, which make them, though of Scotch, Scotch-Irish, or English descent, better soldiers, better citizens, and better *men* than the over-worked, ignorant, half-starved, turbulent, and degraded peasantry whom England vomits upon the North to create riots. (183)

However, in a representational tactic that would often be repeated in subsequent descriptions of white trash, he grants that there is some basis for the perception these commentators have formed of a debased and vicious people: "There is at the South such *a class* as Mr. Cairnes speaks of. They are appropriately called 'mean trash,' and 'eke out a wretched subsistence by hunting, by fishing, by hiring themselves out for occasional jobs, and by plunder,' but they are a comparatively small class. The census shows that they cannot number above half a million" (183; emphasis added).

Following this concession, Gilmore slips into a quasi-ethnographic mode and develops a firsthand account of this degraded group's condition: "To give the reader an idea of what these 'mean whites' are, I will glance for a moment at their habits and ways of living." As Gilmore describes, "Often their houses are the rude pole wigwams of the Indian" or "small huts of rough logs . . . floored with nothing but the ground . . . and their one apartment is furnished with rickety chairs, a pine log . . . a cracked skillet, a dirty frying-pan, an old-fashioned rifle, two or three sleepy dogs, and a baker's dozen of half-clad children, *with skins and hair colored like a tallow candle dipped in tobacco juice*" (1864, 184; emphasis added). Gilmore's depiction is worth quoting and examining at length because he mobilizes central assumptions that informed most assessments of white trash: that they had no ability to labor, that they were closer to "Indians" than to "civilization," that they were intemperate, licentious, and prone to incest, resulting in a distinct physique that indelibly marked them as trash. "The character of the inmates of these hovels is suited to their surroundings. They are indolent, shiftless, and thieving; given to whiskey-drinking, snuff-dipping, clay-eating, and all manner of social vices. Brothers intermarry with sisters, fathers cohabit with daughters, and husbands sell, or barter away, their wives, as freely as they would their hounds, or as the planter would his slaves. I have myself met a number of these *white* women who had been sold into prostitution by their natural protectors, for a few dollars or a good rifle" (184). Gilmore read the physical ravages of poverty and disease via the trope of degeneration, as reflecting a moral state rather than an economic predicament: "Many of them—owing, no doubt, to their custom of intermarrying—were deformed and apparently idiotic, and they all had stunted, ague-distorted bodies, *untanned*-leather skins, small heads, round as bullets, and coarse, wiry hair, which looked like shreds of oakum gathered into mops, and dyed with lamp-black" (187; emphasis added). An interesting aspect of Gilmore's rendering of white trash is that these bodies are simultaneously marked as colored, "with skins and hair colored like a tallow candle dipped in tobacco juice," and as "white." But of all these representational dimensions, perhaps the most noteworthy is that this account is composed by an itemized mode of perception that heaps up details as a means of both describing and confirming the implicit problem *those people* present. Gilmore presents a series of excessive elements (physical conditions and social problems or "vices") that gesture toward confirming and explaining the character of *those people* without actually analyzing their predicament, but only naturalizing their condition. This representational tactic remains a basic starting point for characterizing white trash.

Cairnes and Gilmore agreed on one point that amounts to a consensus view among all these writers: that white trash was a uniquely southern phenomenon and a byproduct of slavery. Cairnes's disparaging view of this group stems from their derivative or dependent status in relation to the slave system: "Such are the 'mean whites' or 'white trash' of the Southern States. They comprise several local subdivisions, the 'crackers,' the 'sandhillers,' the 'clay-eaters,' and many more. The class is not peculiar to any one locality, but is the invariable outgrowth of Negro slavery wherever it has raised its head in modern times" (1862, 55). Gilmore largely concurred, claiming, "Nowhere but in the Slave States is there a class of whites so ignorant and so degraded as are these people" (1864, 188). The relation of poor whites to slavery degraded their very constitutions. "In every other country the peasantry labor are the principal producers, the really indispensable part of the community; but the 'mean white' of the South does not *know how* to labor; he produces nothing; he is a fungous growth on the body of society, absorbing the strength and life of its other parts, and he would not exist if the Southern system were in a healthy system" (188). Those designated white trash are defined here as fundamentally lacking crucial moral characteristics (i.e., the ability and willingness to labor) because of their racial status. Gilmore concluded: "The great mass of poor whites, as I have said, are a very different people. The *poor* white man labors, the *mean* white man does not labor; and labor makes the distinction between them" (188–189). The fundamental basis for objectifications of this group arose from this moral categorization of those who will and will not work.[7]

Gilmore's work succinctly deploys a strategic disassociation of poor white and white trash, one valorized and worthy of liberation, the other debased and deteriorating; this is an initial instance of a tactic that informs representations of whites in the lower social strata throughout the twentieth century (see chapter 3). But this distinction was unstable and perhaps unsustainable. As these writers strove to objectify this unique social collective, they tried to establish the boundaries between white trash and other class and racial identities. Despite their efforts to make the contrasts correspond to distinct boundaries between the hard-laboring, respectable poor white and the "indolent, shiftless, and thieving" white trash, the division could not be rendered permanent. The instability of this boundary derives from the lack of fixed, distinguishing criteria and the intense concerns generated by the need to keep whiteness and blackness distinct. Thus, depictions of poor whites are continually inflected by the anxieties and disgust that white trash provokes. A good example is Weston's sympathetic account of poor whites. As much as he invested this group with hope and valor, he also was anxious about the unnerving prospect that *those people* would leave the slave states and move north.[8] In addition to raising alarm about the plight of poor whites in the South, Weston was perhaps the first to call attention to the migration of these whites to the Midwest. Noting that the southern states had sent 105,755 people to Illinois and Indiana and another 69,918 to Missouri, Weston (1856, 6) lamented, "It is not wonderful that they seek escape from the nightmare which broods over them, and fly by the thousands to the refuge of the free States." Weston feared that the poor whites carried with them specifically the characteristics that commentators like Cairnes had placed in the foreground of their characterization of *those people*: "It is unquestionable that the immigration from the South has brought into the free States more ignorance, poverty, and thriftlessness, than an equal amount of the immigration from Europe. Where it forms a marked feature of the population, as in Southern Illinois, a long time must elapse before it is brought up to the general standard of intelligence and enterprise in the free State" (7). In anticipation of a key distinction eugenicists would make in constituting poor white families as a subject of investigation and scientific objectification, Weston negatively compares the import of "ignorance, poverty, and thriftlessness" into the North from poor whites to that of immigrants from Europe.

Whether the image of white trash invoked sympathy or anxiety depended on how this collective was used to figure the terrain of racial and class identity. Writers like Helper, Abbott, and Weston stressed bonds of racial solidarity with this group, emphasizing their whiteness as a basis for sympathy. The opening editorial epigraph to *The Poor Whites of the South* made this point explicit: "A careful perusal of the following is commended to all who feel an interest in the elevation of the white as well as the colored race. It is a very clear exhibition of the condition of the mass of the white population in the Slave States" (Weston 1856, 1). Against the pro-slavery argument that slavery was good because it introduced Africans to the benefits of civilization, Weston retorted: "Even if this be true, even if three million and a half of the peoples of African blood have been raised in the scale of civilization, the price paid for it is too costly. An equal number of people of Caucasian stock have been deprived of all that constitutes civilization, and thrust down into barbarism; thus reversing the order of Providence, and sacrificing the superior to the inferior race" (7). Against arguments for the extension of slavery, he warned that it would instead bring down the white race: "Our first and highest duty is to our own race; and it will be a most flagrant and inexcusable folly to permit such a sacrifice of it as we now witness in the Southern states, to be enacted over again upon the vast areas of the West" (7). This recognition of the vulnerability of whiteness to such a "sacrifice" undercuts the basis for sympathy and opens onto a greater anxiety over the possible futures portended by such whites.

These racial bonds that could be so passionately defended were also sources for anxiety because they threatened to be conduits for a contamination that could bring down the race. Weston (1856, 7) qualified the comments cited above by allowing, "This remark is made in no spirit of unkindness. The whites of the South are nearly all of the Revolutionary stock. They are a fine, manly race. Their valor, attested upon a hundred battle-fields, shone unvarnished and still resplendent in the last conflict of the Republic. I feel for that unhappy people all the ties of kith and kin. God forbid that any avenue should be closed by which they may escape out of the horrible pit of their bondage." The whiteness of his kith and kin in the South represented a confusing mix of sameness and difference, making for an unstable cultural figure. The multivalent moral charges to this figure and the distinct futures with which it was associated is rendered more sharply by contrasting these depictions to that of southern planters who disassociated themselves from the racial predicament presented by white trash (Genovese 1971 and 1976).

Northern writers' ambivalence over the predicament of white trash is entirely absent from the most developed southern account of white trash in this period, offered by D. R. Hundley (1860) in his tome, *Social Relations in Our Southern States.* Hundley wrote in response to many of the works cited above and "the persistent misrepresentations of the South by the rancorous journals and unscrupulous demagogues of the Free States," blasting northerners for their ignorance of the nuances of the slave states' class system. "As a general thing, the honey-tongued libellers of the Southern half of our Confederacy, appear to be totally unconscious that her citizens were ever divided into other than three classes—Cavaliers, Poor Whites, and Slaves" (8, 10). In a chapter titled "Poor White Trash," Hundley set out to correct this misperception by mobilizing a distinction similar to that employed by Gilmore, delineating a base, degraded social collective beneath that of more respectable poor whites. But he also wrote to discredit the idea that white trash was an outgrowth of slavery, thus dismissing the racial relevance of this people.

In striking contrast to northern writers' accounts of white trash, Hundley located their origins neither in the institutions of slavery nor in any ostensible relation to racial matters, but rather in the slums of London (see chapter 1). Stressing the classed aspect of their identity, he also disputed their unique connection to the South. White trash derive directly from "those paupers and convicts whom Great Britain sent over to her faithful Colony of Virginia . . . , those outcasts and paupers, picked up in the black slums and cellars of London, and transported at the public charge to Virginia, and there sold in the market-house to the highest bidder" (1860, 255–256). And what ensured the consistency of this collective through the many decades since their emigration? Anticipating a response that would form the basis of eugenical thought, Hundley replied, "Without presuming to solve this great social problem, still, and with all due deference to those of our readers who may be of a contrary mind, we contend there is a great deal in *blood*" (251). This status was hereditary, passed down "more in blood than people in the United States are generally inclined to believe" (258). Where northerners perceived a people debased by an economic institution and a social system, southern aristocrats insisted instead that *those people* were simply born that way. Hundley also challenged the association of white trash with the South and slavery by pointing to similarly degenerate whites in the North. In doing so, he prefigured another crucial dimension of the eugenics movement by delineating well in advance the areas in the North where poor white families would be found fermenting "racial poisons" and threatening "the future of the race" with their breeding practices and loose morals.

In sharp retort to northern accounts of white trash that assigned this collective strictly to the South, Hundley (1860, 257) stated:

To form any proper conception of the condition of the Poor White Trash, one should see them as they are. We do not remember ever to have seen in the New England States a similar case; though, if what a citizen of Maine has told us to be true, in portions of that State the Poor Whites are to be found in large number. In the State of New York, however, in the rural districts, we will venture to assert that more of this class of paupers are to be met with than you will find in any single Southern state. . . . They are also found in Ohio, Pennsylvania, Indiana, and all the States of the North-West, though in most of these last they came originally from the South.

In this passage, Hundley's sketch of the trajectory of white trash identifies the states where eugenics family field studies were to be undertaken in the early 1900s. The notorious poor white families featured in these studies were encountered exactly where Hundley first discerned them: the "Jukes" family in New York State, "the Tribe of Ishmael" in Indiana, "the Family of Sam Sixty" in Ohio, "the Dack Family" in Pennsylvania, as well as Minnesota's "Dwellers in the Vale of Siddem" and "the Smokey Pilgrims" of Kansas (discussed below). His larger point, though, was to trace an origin for poor whites that did not derive from the institution of slavery: "But every where, North and South, in Maine or Texas, in Virginia or New York, *they are one and the same*; and have undoubtedly had one and the same origin, namely the poor-houses and prison-cells of Great Britain. Hence we again affirm, what we asserted only a moment ago, that there is a great deal more in blood than people in the United States are generally inclined to believe" (258; emphasis added). In place of economic and political explanations, and countering the need for any anxiety over racial commonality, Hundley placed the origins of these whites in the "black slums" of London and located the root of the problem in their distinct physical constitutions, in their blood.

Despite an antithetical understanding of the origins of this collective and a disavowal of interest in the racial dimensions of this subject, the core features of Hundley's depiction resonate clearly with other accounts of white trash, finding them distinctive for their "laziness" and great fecundity, as well as their unique physique. Hundley (1860, 262–263) claimed, "They are about the laziest two-legged animals that walk erect on the face of the Earth. Even their motions are slow, and their speech is a sickening drawl . . . while their thoughts and ideas seem likewise to creep along at a snail's pace. All they seem to care for is, to live from hand to mouth; to get drunk, provided they can do so without having to trudge too far after their liquor." Hundley also found their physical appearance to be distinctive and telling: "Lank, lean, angular, and bony, with flaming red, or flaxen, or sandy, carroty-colored hair, sallow complexion, awkward manners, and a natural stupidity or dullness of intellect that almost surpasses belief; they present in the main a very pitiable sight to the truly benevolent, as well as a ludicrous one to those who are mirthfully disposed" (264). And as later eugenics fieldworkers would also claim, "They are quite prolific, and every house is filled with its half-dozen of dirty, squalling, white-headed little brats, who are familiarly known as Tow-Heads—on account of the color of their hair, as well as its texture and generally unkempt and matted condition" (265). The point to underscore here is that this composite perception of the collective identity of white trash as physically and behaviorally distinctive is articulated in class terms, specifically over and against an attention to racial commonality or solidarity. Class is as viscerally perceived and experienced as profoundly Other as are projections of racial difference.

Not surprisingly, Hundley did not consider white trash worthy of much sympathy; nor did he regard their fate as in any way tied into the "future of the race." Instead, he envisioned these clans trudging "further and further westward and southward, until they will eventually become absorbed and lost among the half-civilized mongrels who inhabit the plains of Mexico. . . . We are inclined to think their ultimate absorption by Mexico will prove a happy riddance to us; for they are of so little account at present, that, could every one of them be blotted out of existence to-morrow, neither the South or the North, nor the commercial world would be any the poorer for their loss" (1860, 272). This class of "pure, unadulterated pauper blood" would pass from the "civilized" realms without a trace—a far more benign ending than northern observers at the time were imagining, or than awaited white trash who stayed behind in the Deep South, where, following Reconstruction, white planters were, at times, more than willing to starve out poor whites rather than hire them.[9]

"I WAS PURER BLOODED THAN THE WHITE TRASH HERE"

White trash made the leap from a regional epithet to a nationally circulated cultural figure during the 1850s and 1860s. The core image of white trash and the cultural narrative explaining its migration to the North became an aspect of midwestern literature following the Civil War. But there were substantive changes to this image as another generation of social commentators and researchers reformulated the significance of poor whites in this new geographic context, against the backdrop of a rather different set of economic and social dynamics and concerns. Strikingly, northern observers, too, eventually acquired Hundley's disregard for the fate of white trash. These commentators adopted aristocratic southerners' contempt for poor whites when they began to recognize them residing in their midst. The basis for favorably regarding southern white trash as either potential allies or "kith and kin" crumbled along with the institution of slavery. The new ground for making sense of white trash was keyed instead to the dramatic economic changes that transformed the United States between the 1870s and the 1920s.

The nexus of concerns for interpreting the meaning of poor white families in the North initially focused on issues of sex and class. Along with white male anxieties over their sexual identities and their abilities to control women, the problems of "idleness" became newly tangible for northern middle-class whites amid the economic turmoil resulting from the rise of corporate capitalism (Stanley 1998; Montgomery 1993; Cohen 2002; Barker-Benfield 1976). The significance of poor whites as a threatening social collective was further fleshed out in relation to the dramatic social transformations produced by massive increases in immigration, industrialization, and urbanization as well as the rise of consumer culture in the United States from the 1870s through the 1920s (Kammen 1999; Lears 1994; Rabinowitz 1994; Jacobson 1998; Gerstel 2001). Manifold concerns over these economic and social developments were incorporated into depictions of the threat posed by poor whites, notably reconstituting some connotations of "white trash," but also generating new meanings as the problems posed by this troubling figure were formulated in a medicalized register through the eugenics movement. These new meanings somewhat fitfully coexisted alongside earlier representations of white trash, signaling the enduring relevance of this figure but also its reconfiguration in a broader landscape of charged racial, sexual, and class relations.

Following the Civil War, the term *white trash* entered common parlance in the Midwest, perhaps in conjunction with the southern white migratory populations first discerned by Weston, appearing in literature set in the states of Illinois and Missouri.[10] Edgar Lee Masters (1915/1962, 45), in his incisive depiction of small-town midwestern life at the turn of the previous century, *Spoon River Anthology*, recorded the scowling contempt of this label in the epitaph of "Indignation Jones":

You would not believe, would you
That I came from good Welsh stock?
That I was purer blooded than the white trash here?
And of more direct lineage than the New Englanders
And Virginians of Spoon River?

Sherwood Anderson also dramatized the appearance and influence of white trash in midwestern life. Anderson's (1966 [1920], 3) novel *Poor White* chronicled the adventures of Hugh McVey as he emerged from a "poor white trash" tribe in Missouri, "a race of long gaunt men who seemed as exhausted and no-account as the land on which they lived," all "of Southern origin."[11] Hugh's childhood days are spent lying in a quasi-reptilian state; his blood too cold to allow much movement, he lies "half asleep in the shade of a bush on the river bank" (4–5). His father lived in a "habitual stupor," from which he was driven only occasionally "by hunger and the craving for drink" (6–7). But Hugh is awakened from this degraded state by the missionary zeal of Sarah Shepard, a newcomer on the prairie, "in whose veins flowed the blood of the pioneers." She "worked upon the problem of rooting the stupidity and dullness out of his mind as her father had worked at the problem of rooting the stumps out of the Michigan land," and she chastised him: " 'Look at your own people—poor white trash—how lazy and shiftless they are. You can't be like them. It's a sin to be so dreamy and worthless.' " Gradually, "he became convinced that his own people were really of inferior stock, that they were to be kept away from and not to be taken into account." Inculcating a sense of shame for his own people and the disgust that animated his savior, Hugh undertakes his personal reclamation and moves east to Ohio to a life of industry and labor, being transformed in the process from white trash to poor white (259).

The distance between degraded white trash and redeemable poor white is underscored by the southern origin of his family and his sojourn eastward to the rapidly industrializing cities of Ohio:

In the South their fathers, having no money to buy slaves and being unwilling to compete with slave labor, had tried to live without labor. For the most part they lived in the mountains and the hill country of Kentucky and Tennessee, on land too poor and unproductive to be thought worth cultivating by their rich slave-owning neighbors of the valleys and the plains. The food was meager and of an enervating sameness and their bodies degenerate. Children grew up long and gaunt and yellow like badly nourished plants. Vague indefinite hungers took hold of them and they gave themselves over to dreams. The more energetic among them, sensing dimly the unfairness of their position in life, became vicious and dangerous. (1920, 18)

But how was this reinvocation of southern origins related to midwestern life?

Anderson proffers a narrative that links back to Weston's efforts to explain their location in the Midwest. "When, in the years preceding the Civil War, a few of them pushed north along the rivers and settled in Southern Indiana and Illinois and in Eastern Missouri and Arkansas, they seem to have exhausted their energy in making the voyage and slipped quickly back into their old slothful way of life" (1920, 18–19). This narrative, suggested also by Hundley, was further advanced and promoted in scholarly trappings by Madison Grant, one of the nation's foremost eugenicists. In Grant's development of this characterization, though, the trappings of a rather different explanatory framework materialize, one that would come to dominate discussions of poor whites in the North.

Grant's writings on white trash reveal the interest in and the difficulty of making stereotypes of poor whites adequately respond to the new set of anxieties with which they were being associated in the early 1900s. Grant attempts to explicitly link this charged label for poor whites to the new "science" of eugenics, with all of its concerns over urbanization, immigration, and questionable breeding practices among whites. But his effort is just as notable for the poor fit that "white trash," with its lingering connotations of southern origins and associations with slavery, makes with eugenics discourses fixated on northern metropolitan concerns. In mobilizing the narrative of white trash migration to buttress eugenicists' interest in poor whites, he was unable to fully orient "white trash" to the host of concerns animating northern middle-class whites, who were increasingly drawn to eugenical interpretations of the significance of race, class, and gender. Hence, Grant's commentary on white trash reveals points of continuity and disjuncture in representations of poor whites at the close of the nineteenth century that reflect both the enduring and the malleable dimensions of this charged cultural figure as it was used to make sense of emergent social and economic conditions in a different region.

Grant was disturbed by the way poor whites had spread across the United States and sought to explain their enduring presence in the burgeoning republic. In his most influential work, *Passing of the Great Race, or The Racial Basis of European History*, Grant (1916, 35–36) wrote, "This type played a very large part in the settlement of the Middle West, by way of Kentucky, Tennessee and Missouri. Thence they passed both up the Missouri River and down the Santa Fe Trail, and contributed rather more than their share of train robbers, horse thieves, and bad men of the West." In *Conquest of a Continent, or The Expansion of Races in America*, Grant elaborated this narrative, choosing, like Hundley, to strictly locate the origins of these troublesome whites in "pure" Anglo-Saxon cradles rather than as an outgrowth of slavery or even miscegenation. Following periods of indentured servitude, he surmised,

> the freed bondsmen therefore had to go to the frontier or drift down into North Carolina or some other region where they were not handicapped by their lack of funds. The most shiftless and least intelligent of them tended to collect in the least valuable lands at the fringe of civilization, or to drift along to other similar settlements farther west and south. In this way originated one of the peculiar elements of the Southern population, the "*poor white trash.*" Their numbers were recruited generation after generation by others of the same sort while the able, enterprising, and imaginative members were continually drained off to the cities or sought better land elsewhere. These "poor whites" in the Alleghanies and through the swamp lands of North and South Carolina have been an interesting feature of the population for three centuries. Largely of *pure Nordic stock*, they are a striking example of isolation and undesirable selection. (1933, 120–121; emphasis added)

This narrative of white trash migration linked instances of poor whites appearing in the Midwest to southern origins. But this gesture was hardly adequate to the task of accounting for the presence of poor whites in the many places they were now being recognized in the North, particularly in the older, eastern states pointed to by Hundley. Grant gestured toward addressing the limits of this narrative by additionally locating the significance of white trash within the framework of concerns addressed by the eugenics movement.

In Grant's hands, elements of Hundley's account (origins in the "black slums" of London) fused with eugenical interpretations that stressed hereditary sources for social problems and notions of "natural habitats" for the world's races. In so doing, Grant reframed the racial significance of white trash in the post-Emancipation era, recasting it in relation to intensifying debates and concerns over sexuality, citizenship, and the color line (see Bederman 1995; Hale 1998; Jacobson 1998). In this schema, the racially superior Nordic stock encountered problems when it strayed too far south from its "natural habitats." Grant (1916, 33) warned, "In the lower classes the increasing proportion of poor whites and 'crackers' are symptoms of lack of climatic adjustment. The whites of Georgia, the Bahamas, and above all the Barbadoes are excellent examples of the deleterious effects of residence outside the natural habitat of the Nordic race." But the notion of natural habitats hardly encompassed the problem, as Grant acknowledged: "The poor whites of the Cumberland Mountains in Kentucky and Tennessee present a more difficult problem, because here the altitude, even though small, should modify the effects of latitude, and the climate of these mountains cannot be particularly unfavorable to men of Nordic breed. There are probably other hereditary forces at work here as yet little understood" (35–36). In this reference to "hereditary forces . . . as yet little understood," Grant parses a host of emergent anxieties that exceed the initial explanatory framework for white trash as offered by Hundley's reference to "blood."

Grant's invocation of a hereditary interpretation reflects confidence that the figure of white trash is relevant to a host of new concerns facing white middle-class Americans, but also reveals that the exact dynamics at work were yet to be clearly explicated. As Grant noted:

> No doubt bad food and economic conditions, prolonged inbreeding, and the loss through emigration of the best elements have played a large part in the degeneration of these poor whites. They represent to a large extent the offspring of bond servants brought over by the rich planters in Colonial times. Their names indicate that many of them are descendants of the old borders along the Scotch and English frontier, and the persistence with which family feuds are maintained certainly points to such an origin. The physical type is typically Nordic, for the most part *pure Saxon* or Anglian [*sic*], and the whole mountain population show somewhat aberrant but very pronounced physical, moral, and mental characteristics which would repay scientific investigation. The problem is too complex to be disposed of by reference to the hookworm, illiteracy, or competition with the negroes. (1916, 35–36; emphasis added)

In confronting the disturbing "degeneration of these poor whites," Grant's account expresses a deep interest in extending the scope and relevance of the label *white trash*, but conditions in the North disrupt a seamless transfer of southern stereotypes and lore to explain the emergence of northern poor whites. This is evident as Grant admits that the explanatory tools at hand— "reference to the hookworm, illiteracy, or competition with the negroes"—

are insufficient in accounting for the presence of poor whites throughout the Midwest.

For commentators like Grant, the key registers continued to be poor whites' distinctive physiognomy as well as their degraded class, sexual, and racial status. But the interpretive repertoires by which their significance was assessed exceeded the set of concerns linked to slavery that initially made white trash interesting to northerners. In each of these eras' discursive construction of white trash, their racial identity remains similar; as Grant stresses, *those people* are "typically Nordic, for the most part *pure Saxon*," that is, members of the race Grant avowed to be superior to all others. What is notably different about the dynamics associated with the developing eugenical accounts of poor whites is that the form of whiteness imperiled by their debased condition was not solely formulated through, nor did it entirely hinge on, sharp contrasts to blackness. The uses of poor whites by the eugenics movement featured more complex assessments of what counted as racial and class boundaries. The eugenical threat posed by such degenerated whites reflects an era of radically altered racial dynamics (see Gerstel 2001; Carlson 2001). The source of the threat is depicted as arising from the allegedly purest of Anglo-Saxon strains, rather than through transgression of the color line. This in a world where the solidarity and solidity of whiteness was far less assured, given the fractious competition between the "white races," as noted earlier by Jacobson. The nature of the threat posed by such whites subtly changes from a sense of Otherness to an image of Self imperiled, where the ground of anxiety is that of the Same.

Indeed, though the cultural figure of poor whites was widely discerned now in New England and the Midwest, "white trash" increasingly seemed to be an inadequate descriptor, perhaps because narratives like Grant's and Anderson's, though indicating a far greater national range of application for the term, still fundamentally linked it to the South.[12] Northern whites' uncertainty over how to label and characterize *those people* instead came to be addressed via a novel investigative and narrative form that more effectively accounted for their presence outside of the South, without reference to the institution of slavery. The eugenic family field studies—quasi-ethnographic observations and description of poor whites in their "natural habitats"— became the dominant means of objectifying poor whites from the 1870s through the 1920s (see E. Larson 1995; Wray 2000). Given the instability of explanatory frameworks for sorting out racial and class forms of belonging and difference evident in Grant's account, this genre generated a new set of terms, draped in the trappings of scientific discourse, that more adequately labeled the disturbing features of these poor white families. Through this set of terms, new forms of etiquette for policing the boundaries of white racial identity in relation primarily to class concerns become manifest.

FROM CLASS OTHERS TO RACIAL SELVES

Northern whites were riveted in 1877 by unnerving images that emerged from the hinterlands of rural New York State. Richard Dugdale's (1877) *The "Jukes": A Study in Crime, Pauperism, Disease, and Heredity* presented a lurid account of backwoods degradation and depravity. The image of the "Jukes"—an incestuous, crime-ridden family—profoundly impacted white middle-class audiences, and Dugdale's initial study was soon replicated, confirming his basic finding that a distinctive "kind" or "type" of people could be associated with the range of social problems that were increasingly troubling whites in the nation's rapidly urbanizing regions. Initially, for social observers and commentators, the significance of these families lay in their transgression of middle-class norms of domesticity, as was the case for southern aristocrats' views of white trash, which also seemed to operate independently of explicit racial concerns. The interpretive framework brought to bear in explaining poor whites drew largely from newly developing discourses on sexuality and criminality (Walters 1974). Only gradually did a more disturbing dimension come to dominate attention to these families: their very palpable whiteness.

As eugenics discourse impacted middle-class white identity in the 1910s and 1920s, the most shocking and sensational images of these poor white families were displaced or at least adumbrated in popular writing by an anxious attention to the racial constitution of "good" families. The eugenical depiction of threats to the race posed by the breeding habits of poor whites brought into play a far more unnerving focus on the need for middle-class whites to engage in racial self-interrogation.[13] Connecting the early emergence and the later full development of this interest in poor whites is a new form of racial and class etiquette, a decorum that addresses anxieties over the shifting and mutable forms of racial identity, offering middle-class whites a new means for labeling *those people* and a novel basis for self-objectification.

"The Jukes" opens in a New York county jail, as social researcher and reformer Richard Dugdale discovers that six prisoners are blood relations. Collectively, their crimes ranged from vagrancy to burglary, attempted rape, and murder, but this was a modest series of offenses compared to the lin-

eage of criminality and bestiality of the whole extended family. In tracing out these relations, Dugdale "penetrated the social hades of the dangerous classes, and in their own abodes so photographed them as vagabonds, as offenders, as the out-door poor of a country, as felons and miscreants—that their unvarnished picture is recognized by all who ever saw these 'Jukes' *or any of their kind.*"[14] What he found in this "social hades" was a "kind" of people who looked remarkably similar to the white trash that troubled the previous generation of social commentators.

Dugdale (1877, 13) luridly described the "nests" in which the Jukes resided: "They lived in log or stone houses similar to slave hovels, all ages, sexes, relations and strangers 'bunking' indiscriminately. One form of this bunking has been described to me. During the winter the inmates lie on the floor strewn with straw or rushes like so many radii to the hearth, the embers of the fire forming a centre towards which their feet focus for warmth. This proximity, where not producing illicit relations, must often have evolved an atmosphere of suggestiveness fatal to habits of chastity." Though comparison with "slave hovels" offered an opportunity to flesh out possible associations with relations in the South, Dugdale instead stressed the "pure" Anglo-Saxon origins of this "strictly American family," as would the numerous researchers who followed his lead. "These six persons belonged to a long lineage, reaching back to the early colonists, and had intermarried so slightly with the emigrant population of the old world that they may be called a strictly American family. They had lived in the same locality for generations, and were so despised by the reputable community that their family name *had come to be used generically as a term of reproach*" (8; original emphasis). Such observations bolstered Dugdale's suspicion that he had discovered a kind of social collective; yet he was unsure whether or how this type could be abstracted out into a broader perception of a troubling social condition emerging among the Anglo-Saxon stocks in the United States. That would entail, first, confirmation of this kind through subsequent family studies and then theoretical elaboration through the explanatory efforts of eugenicists in the next century.

Yet, well before families like the Jukes were invoked to support the racial interests enshrined in eugenical ideals and legislation, middle-class whites found them fascinating for representing a world of class otherness. The features of the Jukes and subsequent families that researchers insisted matched their "horrible" profile fit a tightly predetermined representational frame that mirrored the pretensions and interests of this class of professionals.[15] In a fashion similar to southern aristocrats' view of white trash, social researchers and commentators in the North at first perceived only extreme differences of class when they regarded these disturbing white families in their midst: concerns of racial solidarity or identity were scarcely broached. Dugdale asserted that the Jukes represented a "class," one that was criminal in nature and defined by sexual depravities stemming from their lack of forms of decorum that middle-class whites relied on to distinguish themselves from the working and lower classes (Stallybras and White 1986; Frykman and Lofgren 1987). When Dugdale (1877, 12) concluded ominously from the above depiction of the Jukes that "domesticity is impossible," he articulated a frame of reference that tightly bounded the Jukes as a scene of terrifying otherness to the middle-class ideal of domesticity (see Matthews 1987; Bushman 1992; Frykman and Lofgren 1999; Stanley 1998).

"The Jukes" is often understood in relation to the eugenics movement, in which it played a central representational role. Even though Dugdale did not mobilize a "genetic" perspective (environment and heredity were equally powerful in his assessment, and he even leaned toward the former) and his work preceded eugenics writings by U.S. authors by several decades, his study is typically depicted as a precursor to the eugenics movement. There is a basis for this association, but it is just as critical to recognize, first, that it emerged in a distinct discourse of white, middle-class male anxiety in relation to sex (Barker-Benfield 1976; Bederman 1995; Tylor 1977). Sexuality is the molten core that generates his fixation on the Jukes. Dugdale emphasized that "sexual passion approaches to an instinct" among the Jukes, insisting that "it is more persistent in its entailment than is the sense of sight. In other words it is organic, and therefore transmitted by inheritance more certainly that the pigment of the negro's skin" (quoted in Rafter 1988, 40). This class and sexual condition, Dugdale asserts, reflects a deeper set of predispositions than even those associated with race. Through indiscriminate sexuality, they are "breeding complex social disorders growing out of these physiological degenerations." Sex is key, not heredity. Not only is their sexuality the key focus of interests, but it is also the behavior that defines them as a class: "In other words, *fornication*, either consanguineous or not, is the backbone of their habits, flanked on one side by *pauperism*, on the other by *crime*. The secondary features are *prostitution*, with its complement of *bastardy*, and its resultant neglected and miseducated childhood; *exhaustion* with its complement *intemperance* and resultant unbalanced minds; and *disease* with its complement extinction" (1877, 13).

The effect of this image on middle-class whites' imagination was profound and sustained. "The Jukes" went through three printings in several months and quickly became the central representational resource in a slew of discourses on crime, pauperism, and prostitution as problems in the northeastern states. The long life of the book and its central imagery of poor, degraded whites evolved in two distinct stages, which reflect a basic shift in interpreting this family, first as a form of class otherness and then as a disturbing mirror of racial sameness. The image of the Jukes was reinvigorated and sustained by a subsequent series of family studies modeled on Dugdale's work (discussed below), but the clearest glimpse of these distinct interpretive registers is provided by the two books that sought directly and explicitly to reinvigorate the figure of the Jukes: A. E. Winship's (1900) *Jukes-Edwards: A Study in Education and Heredity* and Arthur Estabrook's (1916) *The Jukes in 1915*. Estabrook's work recast Dugdale's research into a specifically eugenical frame by applying the methods of eugenics field studies to track down the family's descendants. But Winship's *Jukes-Edwards* strove to make emphatic the class representational dynamics by ratifying the otherness of the Jukes with the counterimage of the exemplary lineage of Jonathan Edwards's family.

Winship (1900, 15) embellished the figure of the Jukes by accentuating their relevance to concerns over class identity: "The story of the Jukes as published by Mr. Dugdale has been the text of a multitude of sermons, the theme of numberless addresses, the inspiration of no end of editorials and essays. For twenty years there was a call for a companion picture. Every preacher, orator, and editor who presented the story of the Jukes, with its abhorrent features, wanted the facts for a cheery, comforting, convincing contrast." Winship accomplishes this by recounting highlights of *"The Jukes"* and bringing them into seamless correspondence with a contrasting portrait of their class superiors. As a representation, the Jukes were recast in an overdetermined frame of class otherness: "Whatever the Jukes stand for, the Edwards family does not. Whatever weakness the Jukes represent finds its antidote in the Edwards family, which has cost the country nothing in pauperism, in crime, in hospitals or asylum service. On the contrary, it represents the highest usefulness in invention, manufacture, commerce, founding of asylums and hospitals, establishing and developing missions, projecting and energizing the best philanthropies" (15). The object lesson in Winship's account of the Jukes lay squarely on the need for the white middle class to increase its social investment in forms of decorum and self-control. This is a subtle but significant shift from the set of concerns and anxieties related to the image and logic of Otherness that Dugdale mobilized and honed in the 1870s.

The image of this poor white family clearly held a mesmerizing power and inspired other social observers to confirm the veracity of this image, and the extent of the threat so posed, by finding others of the Jukes kind across the Midwest and Northeast. Nicole Rafter (1988, 2) asserts that the major impact of these family studies was on eugenicists and those who promoted eugenical legislation, such as reform of marriage laws, the "segregation or sterilization" of the "feebleminded," and restrictions on immigration:[16] "The eugenics movement generated a large body of literature on topics ranging from alcoholism to zoology, but in terms of ideological impact, the family studies genre was its most influential product. The family studies gave the movement its central, confirmational image: that of the degenerate hillbilly family, dwelling in filthy shacks and spawning endless generations of paupers, criminals, and imbeciles. For the interpretation and control of social problems, the genre created a new, sociological paradigm, a master symbol that supported an ideology of power justified by biology." Rafter analyzes the way these studies worked as a genre of social observation by tracking their authors' core representational practices: "Combining genealogical techniques with those of a primitive social science, these studies identified tribes whose inferior heredity was considered the source of alcoholism, crime, feeblemindedness, harlotry, hyperactivity, laziness, loquacity, poverty and a host of other ills. The eugenic implications seemed obvious: if those afflicted with 'bad germ plasm' could be prevented from 'breeding,' society would be cleansed of social problems" (1).[17] Depicted "tribes" featured copious evidence of degeneracy: "Animal and insect imagery pervades the family studies. The cacogenic 'mate' and 'migrate,' 'nesting' with their 'broods' in caves and 'hotbeds where human maggots are spawned.'" The symbolic dimensions were plain: "The haunts of the cacogenic become outer manifestations of their inner decay. Many are located in forests, long associated in imaginative literature with mystery, danger, and the illicit" (27).

Such imaginative scenes mirror the descriptive accounts of white trash in the pre–Civil War era, and the family studies offered many opportunities to tap into the white trash migration narrative. Indeed, the first effort to replicate *"The Jukes,"* Reverend Oscar McCulloch's (1888) project, "The Tribe of Ishmael: A Study in Social Degradation," raised such an association. McCulloch described this "tribe" as a family of "murderers, a large number of illegitimacies and of prostitutes. They are generally diseased. Their children die young. They live by petty stealing, begging, ash-gathering. In the summer they 'gypsy,' or travel in wagons east or west. We hear of them in Illinois about Decatur, and in Ohio about Columbus. In the fall they return. They have been known to live in hollow trees on the river-bottoms or in empty houses" (quoted in Rafter 1988, 51). In explaining this urge to "gypsy," McCulloch implied associations with the southern poor white: "We find the wandering tendency so marked in the case of the 'Cracker' and the 'Pike' here. 'Moving' on." Such moments pass undeveloped, though, as McCulloch preferred to maintain symmetry with Dugdale's depiction, laying emphasis on sex and "the general unchastity that characterizes this class. The prostitution and illegitimacy are large, the tendency shows itself in incests, and relations lower than animals go" (51). As Rafter noted, McCulloch and others strove to appear scientific, and the discourse on sexuality, its control and its sources of peril, as part of the increased medicalization of sexuality probably bestowed that air of authority far more profoundly than could references to crackers or white trash (Martin 1987; Barker-Benfield 1976).

Each of the representational elements delineated by Rafter contributed to depictions of poor whites that fit a tight frame of class otherness. But as studies continued, and especially after they received institutional support from the Eugenics Records Office, the whiteness of these families complicated this representational framework. The second study attempting to replicate *"The Jukes"* began forefronting the racial subtext. Frank Blackmar, a professor in history and sociology at the University of Kansas, tracked "the Smokey Pilgrims," a similar "family or tribal group with loose habits of association." Stressing points of comparison with the Jukes and the Tribe of Ishmael, while also developing connections with Charles Booth's study of the London poor, Blackmar laid primary emphasis on how this tribe reflected the distinct dynamics of "the peopling of the great West" and the burden of those "poorly equipped for life." "There have marched, side by side, in the conquest of the West, the strongest, most energetic, and the best, along with the vicious, idle, and weak; in fact, with *the worst of the race*" (quoted in Rafter 1988, 60; emphasis added). The solutions he suggested ranged from optimistic calls, similar to Dugdale's, for "better home influences, which means a breaking up of the family group, steady enforced employment until the habits of life are changed and become fixed" (135) to the much more ominous demands for "social sanitation" to purge society of this degraded "residuum," anticipating the logic if not the social control efforts of the eugenics movement. By invoking such solutions and by distinctly highlighting racial concerns, Blackmar's work registers a critical shift in the family studies as concern over uncontrolled, licentious sexuality was reconstituted via eugenical attention to heredity and race. With this focus on race, the fact that all of these families were white received increasing attention.

Throughout the family studies genre, the whiteness of these families and their "pure" racial origins was noted, but the significance of their racial status moved to the fore only as the explanatory framework of eugenics came to dominate white middle-class thinking in the United States.[18] Notably, in an era when fears of miscegenation and immigration pervaded public discourse, the racial dimension of these families did not feature a sense of whiteness imperiled by racial Others, but rather as threatened from within both the white race and the white middle-class self. This aspect of the threat was accentuated as the whiteness of these families received heightened attention through the 1910s and 1920s. Oscar McCulloch insisted that the origins of the Ishmaelites derived "from the old convict stock which England threw into this country in the seventeenth century" (quoted in Rafter 1988, 51). The "Hill Folk" (1912) in Massachusetts featured a similar, though less extensive, genealogy:

> Into one corner of this attractive town there came, about 1800, a shiftless basket maker. He was possibly of French origin, but migrated more directly from the western hill region. About the same time an Englishman, also from the western hills, bought a small farm in the least fertile part of the town. The progeny of these two men, old Neil Rasp, and the Englishman, Nuke, have shifted through the town and beyond it. Everywhere they have made desolate, alcoholic homes which have furnished State wards for over fifty years, and have required town aid for a longer time. (quoted in Rafter 1988, 86)

Among "the Pineys" (1913) of New Jersey, Elizabeth Kite found no clear line of ancestry, but the confounding sources were encompassed by "the Swedes, the original founders of New Jersey," as well as once prosperous Tory families and outcasts from Quaker society. Then, too, "there have been men of leisure, young men of good families, foot-loose men of no character, adventurers of every sort, who for shorter or longer periods have delighted in losing themselves in the pleasures of the Pines. . . . All these revelers came back, leaving a train of nameless offspring to complicate still further the mixed social problems of the Pines, so that today, in tracing the ancestry of any particular group, one runs up continually against the impossibility of proving exact ancestry" (quoted in Rafter 1988, 172). Despite the uncertain lines of origins, the racial contours are quite clear and obviously white.

Given that the eugenics movement is so often characterized as primarily animated by concerns over immigration and miscegenation, it is striking that the objects that formed the centerpiece of their field research efforts were so consistently delineated as American and white.

Kite goes to great length exactly to characterize the degenerate condition of poor whites in the Pines in explicit and unfavorable contrast to local immigrant families. "No study of the component forces of the Pines would be complete without mention being made of the thriving Jew colonies established at different points, and of Italian communities" (1913, 10). Despite acknowledged superficial resemblances, Kite underscores the following contrast between poor white and immigrant families: "On one hand, loose disjointed living, with attendant lack of intelligence, absence of ambition, dearth of ideals of every sort; on the other, solid, compact organized existence; the father head of his home, protecting his wife and daughters, teaching the same attitude to his sons; both parents training their offspring to thrift and industry" (10). Kite points to one local immigrant, "Italian Mike," as an upstanding citizen who supports his family, in contrast to a poor white family "on the same road, under the same natural environment," but where the children are institutionalized and the parents lack any indication or moral fortitude. Indeed, the risk here is that "the foreign population" will "lose its characterizing virtues and assume our vices more quickly than the reverse" (10).

The emphasis on Anglo-Saxon origins of these troubling white families is sharpest in relation to the family that was even more widely cited than the Jukes in the 1910s and 1920s. The Kallikak family, studied in the field by Elizabeth Kite and then made the subject of eugenical theorizing by Henry Goddard, who coined their name from the fusion of the Greek words *kallos* (beauty) and *kakos* (bad), replaced the Jukes in importance for the eugenics movement because they so seamlessly "proved" assumptions about heredity promoted by the movement. The Kallikak story illustrates how a "good" family can be responsible for the generation and inheritance of "bad blood." Goddard (1913, 50) depicts a similar uniquely white genealogy as the Jukes bore: "We have here a family of good English blood of the middle class, settling upon the original land purchased from the proprietors of the state in colonial times, and throughout four generations maintaining a reputation for honor and respectability of which they are justly proud. Then a scion of this family, in an unguarded moment, steps aside from the paths of rectitude and with the help of a feeble-minded girl, starts a line of mental defectives that is truly appalling. After this mistake, he returns to his family, marries a

"What's wrong with this picture?" A family tree depicting the two branches of the "Kallikak" family, named and studied by Henry Goddard. From Amram Scheinfeld's *You and Heredity* (New York: J. B. Lippincott Co., 1939); illustration by the Amran Scheinfeld.

woman of his own quality, and through her carries on a line of respectability equal to that of his ancestors." As the story goes, this progenitor, on returning from duty in the Revolutionary War, paused long enough at a tavern on his journey home to have a frolic with "the Nameless Feeble-minded Girl," who was to give birth to Martin Jr., or "Old Horror," as the locals and Americans at large came to know him. The repercussions of this "unguarded moment," as we shall see, are tremendous.

The Kallikaks dominated discussions of eugenics for a variety of reasons—this institutionally supported study was widely promoted and designed specifically to prove eugenical arguments about the relation of heredity to "social problems"—but prime among these is that this family so clearly illustrated the two key sources of threat facing middle-class whites. One lay all about them, in the fear that lower-class whites were out-reproducing them; the other lay *within* each of them as individuals: the possibility that they, too, could succumb to such an "unguarded moment" or that, dreadfully, one of their ancestors already had succumbed. Goddard (1913, 71) intoned: "There are Kallikak families all about us. They are multiplying at twice the rate of the general population, and not until we recognize this fact, and work on this basis, will we begin to solve these social problems." His somber conclusion is "that all this degeneracy has come as the result of the defective mentality and bad blood having been brought into *the normal family of good blood*, first from the nameless feeble-minded girl and later by additional contaminations from other sources" (69; emphasis added). This point, one that provoked a distinctive sense of self-anxiety among many readers, was stressed as accounts of these poor white families were widely broadcast in the early 1900s. Increasingly, *the normal family of good blood* is foregrounded as a source of concern in popular writings on eugenics developed a new focus on the tenuous dimensions of racial and class self-constitution rather than on lurid forms of otherness.

Taken as a whole, the family field studies etched a stark, pulsating figure of poor whites as "the worst of the race." But how did that figure circulate and powerfully affect white middle-class audiences? The images were clearly riveting, but they did not speak for themselves, nor did they immediately impact whites broadly. If, as Rafter suggests, the family studies provided the core "conformational image" for the eugenics movement, then it was the popularizers—writers, educators, and editorialists—who broadcast this image as they strove to promote eugenic reforms, fashioning an interpretive framework by which the relevance of these families to white racial and class consciousness was made perceptible and compelling. Promoters of eugenics, to whose efforts we now turn, used notions of "race poisons," "racial betterment," and heredity, to transform the Jukes and Ishmaelites from representing specific families to projecting a far larger, more disturbing social collective. In the work of Dugdale and McCulloch, the family names are amplified from their local operations as a "generic term for reproach," but the eugenical framework deployed by popularizers effected a far greater transformation, rendering these families as illustrations of powerfully naturalizing, medicalized terms like "feebleminded" and "cacogenic." Indeed, this fusion of imagery and interpretation in popular writings on eugenics fashioned and instilled a new mode of etiquette offering middle-class whites innovative ways to label *those people* and to reorganize their self-constitution in relation to racial and class identity.[19]

"THAT HE MAY BE BORN OF OUR FLESH"

Etiquette provides a means to make sense of why, though the figure of debased, licentious, and threatening poor whites endured as a focal point of middle-class white anxiety, the epithet "white trash" was not consistently associated with this image in eugenical writings. The answer lies in the centrality of concerns over self-constitution and self-control, which is at the basis of both the cultural work of etiquette and the concerns addressed by the eugenics movement in this era. Daniel Kevels (1985, 72) locates the rise of the eugenics movement in the growing anxiety among middle-class whites in the United States and England over increasing social turmoil in the early 1900s, noting that "neither the literature of eugenics nor the preexisting climate of social Darwinism in which it came to flourish were enough to create a eugenics movement." The explanations proffered by eugenicists framed these problems in naturalistic terms, as irremediable matters of blood and heredity. Scenes of class conflict and unruly mass movements took on new significance for anxious middle-class whites as eugenicists spun horrific depictions of the threats posed by crime, disease, and spreading slums. Eugenicists condensed the various social insecurities to which these whites were prone and rendered them into frighteningly credible explanations, linking these disorders to irremediable difference in "blood" and "heredity." At the same time, compelling new forms of social observation heightened middle-class perceptions of the world as imperiled by the surging ranks of social misfits. As Kevel describes, "Statistics revealed, with seemingly mathematical exactitude, that afflictions such as 'mental defectiveness' and criminality were worsening every year" (72). And the statistic that most unnerved middle-class whites in the United States and England was the differential birthrate by which "the weak and unsound stocks" were out-reproducing their "social betters" in the middle and upper classes. "Race suicide" and "racial poisons" were central tropes in the eugenical discourses that seized white middle-class imaginations in this period.

But just as powerful as the explanatory framework were the accompanying terms: the charged labels "feebleminded," "imbecile," "idiot," and "moron." Eugenicists offered white Americans an apparently scientific set of terms for objectifying *those people* as "not our kind." "Imbecility," Charles Davenport explained in 1911, "is the outcome of bad breeding; the trouble will disappear if marriage matings are made more wisely" (16). Likewise, it cannot be cured because "the imbecile is an imbecile for the same reason that a blue-eyed person is blue-eyed." What made labels like "imbecile" more powerful rhetorically than "white trash" is that they appeared scientific and assumed an objective basis. Striving to make designations of imbeciles objective, Henry Goddard fabricated quantitative criteria: any adult whose "mental age" ranged between three and seven years as determined by intelligence tests (see Zenderland 1998; J. Smith 1985; Ryan 1997). Goddard also claimed to quantify "idiots" as possessing a mental age of one to two years, and "morons," a term he transposed from a Greek word for "dull" or "stupid," fell between eight and twelve years of mental age, all according to scores on completely dubious intelligence tests. The writings of Davenport, Goddard, and numerous others who mobilized these terms, consistently using either the family studies or vignettes from various institutions for the "feeble-minded" as means of illustration, profoundly transformed the way white Americans talk about "us" and "them." This enduring form of etiquette—one that remains active today in this repertoire of disparaging epithets (imbecile, idiot, and moron) that continues to embellish the charged class distinctions between "smart" and "stupid" (Kadi 1996)—derived largely from the eugenics movement that powerfully shaped middle-class whites' rapidly changing experience of race and class.[20]

Etiquette as a cultural dynamic has two critical, thoroughly intertwined dimensions: it delineates a series of labels for morally charged categorical identities, and it materially inscribes semiotic codes by which these identities are recognizable.[21] Labels perform a basic cultural operation by depicting these subject positions as natural, and codes establish modes of conduct by which these positions become tangible in daily life. Images of the families were deployed by eugenicists to illustrate this freshly minted set of abstract labels, ones that powerfully coalesced long-standing but perhaps somewhat vague assumptions about blood in relation to class and race that required such vivid, "horrible" images to make their relevance to everyday life palpable. The eugenics movement fused a set of technical terms with the images of these poor white families; as well, popularizers articulated a range of means by which this eugenical perspective could be applied in daily life to decisions that fundamentally turned on matters of belonging and difference.[22] In this regard, etiquette delineates a threatening locus or image of otherness and circumscribes the boundaries of a self requiring diligent examination, which can be a source of great anxieties. The images of poor white families circulating in popular publications in the 1910s and 1920s reveal these dual dimensions of etiquette, as much concerned with self-constitution as with depictions of otherness.[23]

The significance of these families in relation to white racial and class identities developed through a host of editorials and articles in a wide range of popular magazines, books, and college and high school textbooks, and displays and health promotions in county and state fairs held throughout the Midwest. During the 1910s, the family field studies were featured in articles on eugenics and its ties to a range of social concerns in *Ladies' Home Journal, Scientific American, Atlantic Monthly, McClure's Magazine, Harper's*

Weekly, The World's Work, The Survey, Everybody's Magazine, and *Popular Science Monthly.* These were part of a slew of publications on eugenics that also appeared in *Good Housekeeping, Saturday Evening Post, The Outlook, Literary Digest, Century Magazine, The Living Age,* and *The Independent.* Additionally, a range of books for popular audiences and textbooks for college and high school students also deployed images of the family studies to illustrate an array of claims ranging from marriage advice and hygienic guidance to calls to support sterilization and institutional segregation for these poor whites. On the whole, these secondary, popular publications eschewed the lurid details that were a feature of the actual family studies; they did not feature graphic depictions of these debased white others. Instead, they made reference to these families to shore up advice that today would easily be construed as "self-help." In magazine articles and editorials as well as textbook chapters and political tracts, the consistent emphasis was on promoting self-examination and developing a mode of racial consciousness tuned primarily to the task of self-constitution rather than to the direct maintenance of a clearly bounded color line.[24]

Poor white families made an easy and productive fit with the discourse of race betterment as it developed in the United States in the 1910s, and they were critical to the discursive efforts to convince middle-class whites of the need for white racial consciousness. These families were regarded as a threatening source of pollution confronting the white race, for, as Philadelphia physician J. E. Mears (1910, 19) claimed in one of the earliest books on this subject in the United States, *The Problem of Race Betterment,* they are "able to perpetuate the infected strain and promote degrading influences of the continually flowing stream of transmitted pollution" through the population at large. But it was the scientific conception of heredity that most profoundly recast the sense of threat posed by these poor white families. "Hereditary degeneration is as pronounced as hereditary genius—the one we cultivate and promote in order to maintain and transmit the elevated standard of the human race; the other we must prohibit as destructive to all of those conditions which give character, not only to the individual but to the community" (19). By way of illustration, Mears turned to the Jukes and the Ishmaelites: "You are familiar no doubt with the history of the Jukes family, a family of criminals, stretching through seven generations, and including, in the aggregate, some twelve hundred descendents, who had been burdens on the communities in which they had lived as paupers, imbeciles, or criminals." Of the Tribe of Ishmael he reminded readers: "Murderers, prostitutes, and illegitimates hang upon their genealogical trees. One member of one of these families raised fourteen illegitimate children." The solution, as would be advocated relentlessly over the next two decades, was sterilization or segregation, which was regarded as "efficient in securing control of degenerate subjects" (21).

Noted sexologist and progressive Havelock Ellis also prominently featured the Jukes in *Race-Regeneration* (1911), a work that impacted middle-class audiences in both England and the United States, but with an emphasis that further fleshed out the overriding concerns of eugenicists in this era: instilling and developing racial consciousness and warning of the threat of feeblemindedness. Of the Jukes, he wrote, "These are the kinds of people— tramps, prostitutes, paupers, criminals, inebriates, all tending to be born a little defective—who largely make up the great degenerate families whose histories are from time to time recorded" (30). One word, feeblemindedness, summarized the source of these manifold problems and grounded them in racial concerns. "Feeble-mindedness is an absolute dead weight on the race; it is an evil that is unmitigated. The heavy and complicated social burdens and injuries it inflicts on the present generation are without compensation, while the unquestionable fact that in all degrees it is highly inheritable renders it a deteriorating poison to the race; it depreciates the whole quality of a people" (41). Ellis lamented the "energy and money spent in improving the social environment during the past fifty years," when what mattered most in solving these problems was the development of racial consciousness (43). He noted hopefully, "We have realised, practically and literally, that we are our brothers' keepers. We are beginning to realise that we are the keepers of our children, of the race that is to come after us. Our sense of social responsibility is becoming a sense of racial responsibility. It is that enlarged sense of responsibility which renders possible what we call the regeneration of the race" (46). Eugenicists sermonized that whites had to learn to think in terms of "the race" in a distinctly self-conscious, more guarded manner. Ellis, and many other writers at the time, preached the need for a new mode of race consciousness, with a dual nature, directed simultaneously to what *those people* are doing while also making the middle-class self an anxious locus of intense scrutiny.

Popularizers of eugenics convinced middle-class whites that race encompassed far more of their social dealings than they previously imagined, provoking them to engage in quite elaborate forms of self-examination. The visages of the Jukes, Kallikaks, Ishmaelites, and the various other poor white "tribes" were mobilized by these writers in a variety of efforts to promote eugenicial legislation and thinking. Most scholarly research on eugenics has emphasized the former, but in much of the popular writing that sought to explain eugenics by way of these poor white tribes the overriding concern was with inducing white Americans to "think eugenically" in their daily lives. Indeed, these "cacogenic" families often appeared as a morally charged tangent to give readers a shudder of unease that drove home the central argument of these editorials and essays: that whites must change their orientation on the world and emphatically "think in terms of the race."[25] What did this change entail? Presumably, racial consciousness had been methodically instilled in middle-class whites since birth. But here was a new perspective that required a transformation of whites' disposition toward a host of what previously would have been considered class concerns: parenting most keenly, but also dating and marriage, as well as maintaining clear class boundaries in a range of challenging social situations, reinterpreted now in terms of race. What makes these writings and this imagery distinctive is that it unfolded primarily in an intraracial discourse, without relying on an active invocation of racial Otherness. That is, in this new mode of racial thinking, whites learned to regard a gamut of class relations in specifically racial terms, where previously their racial significance was unrecognized or muted at best.

Notably, given the whiteness of the objects of concern and the whiteness of the subjects addressed by this movement, each of these basic dimensions of etiquette was explicitly and emphatically cast in terms of race. Though the objects and subjects might be distinguishable in terms of class, white audiences were inveighed to "think eugenically," to think "in terms of the race" in their daily lives. The practices promoted in popular magazines and in books and textbooks were not oriented toward direct action in maintenance of the color line. Rather, they framed a range of sources of self-anxiety and provoked examinations of middle-class whites' self-constitution in relation to race. The labels were not just technical, abstract terms, but were instead racially charged and deployed to make the significance of race far more tangible and the source of critical concern. The decisions about belonging did not just impact decisions about membership in the white race, but provoked in middle-class whites a great deal of anxiety over the racial content of their self-constitution.[26]

This heightened consciousness of race was applied to matters of mate selection and breeding, themes that were staples of the popular magazine articles featuring both the poor white families and eugenics.[27] The central concern, as Seth Humphreys wrote in the *Forum* (1913), was that mundane but profound "starting-point of all race improvement and race-deterioration—parenthood" (157). Eugenicists were concerned with the "wholesale promotion of a better parenthood among the fit," but "the more immediate and desperate necessity is to rid the race of its paralyzing inheritance of unfitness by denying parenthood to the hereditary unfit" (158). As writers cast about for a way to convey the "practical" aspects of eugenics, they found it in the processes of selecting a mate and breeding. Charles Davenport (1911, 19) urged potential couples to "mix intelligence with their wooing" by instilling a eugenical perspective. The advice literature made this racial dimension central, as illustrated by a feature article in the *Ladies' Home Journal* in 1912, "When a Girl Is Asked to Marry": "Within certain limits women are the selectors, and in so far as this relation holds they determine the heredity of the race. Women therefore hold in their hands the opportunity *to interpret selective mating and parenthood in terms of race culture and progress*" (Nearing and Scott 1912, 70; emphasis added). Interestingly, as women's selections were cast in explicitly racial terms, there was no discernible attention to maintenance of the color line or expressed fears of miscegenation. Rather, matters of class belonging and difference were at stake. This article used Winship's comparison of the Jukes and Edwardses to depict starkly the terrain on which these choices were to be made: "One family produced twelve hundred social burdens or social scourges, while the other gave to the race nearly fourteen hundred social servants." The subject of scrutiny in this ponderous choice was the Self of the middle-class reader rather than the degraded other of poor white families. One essay's title put the matter quite bluntly: "Are You Fit to Marry?" (Millard 1913). Self-interrogation was a key feature of these writings.

Good Housekeeping featured a series of articles on eugenics in 1911 and 1912 that sought to explain its practical relevance to daily life by addressing issues of birth and marriage. The editorial claim was blunt: "The welfare of the race depends upon a general spread of knowledge of eugenics and the encouragement in every way of the application of eugenic principles" (Polk 1912, 131). These featured a practical demonstration of how such racial decisions could be made through the application of basic criteria: "The father who endeavors to prevent his son from marriage to a tuberculos [*sic*] young woman is practicing eugenics; the mother who urges her daughter against marrying a youth who drinks or who has made a criminal record is doing the same thing; the laws which are endeavoring to prevent the propagation of the habitual pauper classes, the mentally deficient, epileptics, habitual criminals—all these are practical applications of the science." None of the

exclusions posited in this scenario directly foregrounds issues of miscegenation or maintenance of the color line; rather, the elements in this series all
feature transgression of class mores, as underscored by the reference to "the
habitual pauper classes."[28] Here, a form of scrutiny is promoted by which
other whites were subjected to a racial perspective that did not parse or
distinguish between races as much as between carriers of "good" or "bad"
traits. "Let the young girl remember, when she studies the young man she
fancies, that his defects as well as his excellences are a part of him and will be
part of all the children he may father. Let the young man remember, when he
seeks a mate, that a wife's transmission of her qualities, physical, mental, and
spiritual is inevitable. Traits, as they may be termed, spring from the beginning; no matter how minute the cells may be in which they have their origin,
their perpetuation is as certain as the perpetuation of the color of hair, eyes,
and skin" (133). The physical markers of race are clearly mobilized here, in
color references related to "hair, eyes, and skin," but they are melded with
the categories of "mental and spiritual" features, which, taken as a whole,
constitute the broader frame for reading race by "stature" and "comportment" that are key to understanding how class distinctions were so effi-
ciently encompassed by racial discourse (see chapter 1).[29]

The effort to solidify the social grounds for middle-class identity through
this fusion of racial and class markers of difference turned on the need to
assure this class's reproduction through proper and respectable marriages.
Extreme forms of class difference, such as the Jukes and Kallikaks, evoked
such senses of disgust and horror that they presented little direct threat to
young middle-class whites in search of marriageable partners. But what of
less obvious cases? The popular writings on eugenics strove to answer this
question by supplying selective criteria for decision making, delineating
characteristic signs for detecting these racially suspect whites. But the sense
of anxiety and dread revolving around this topic stemmed from the fact, as
Gertrude Davenport (1914, 170) explained in an essay in *The Independent*,
that appearances are deceiving: "If the feebleminded always married in their
own class the result would be the building up of a separate and defective
class. The presence of such a class would, of course, be an annoyance or even
a menace to normal society, for the imbecile is usually also either the pauper,
the prostitute or the criminal. *But the greatest menace of imbecility is not that
the imbecile may break into our house and steal our silver or that he may set fire
to our barn, but that he may be born of our flesh*" (emphasis added). This
depiction of the "greatest menace of imbecility" locates the source of threat

not just within the race but importantly within "good families" and individuals, promoting a mode of self-anxiety and self-examination that was a defining feature of this racial discourse.[30]

These concerns over marriage and race betterment, revolving around matters of selecting those of or not of "our kind," led to a far more developed concern over self-analysis in relation to the race. The image of poor whites that made eugenics a matter of pressing concern for middle-class whites arguably had its greatest effect by inducing an intense form of increased self-scrutiny that middle-class whites undertook in relation to matters of racial belonging. The image of poor whites galvanized this interest and made tangible the sense of threat that might be lurking within the individual constitutions of middle-class whites; but the location of the anxiety was clearly an inward self-reflexive matter, perhaps outweighing or certainly stiffly competing with concerns over sterilization and segregation of "unfit" whites in society at large. This impact is apparent in that, surprisingly, amid all the publicity on the poor white family studies were widely circulated, many middle-class whites responded by wanting to participate in them, desiring to produce similar investigations of their own families.[31]

In 1912, Charles Davenport published *The Family History Book*, citing the more than ten thousand requests received by the Eugenics Records Office for "blank schedules" that people could use to examine their own lineages. These charts were staples of the demonstrations of the racial threat posed by the Jukes and the Kallikaks, and yet thousands of whites wanted to apply them to their own families. Two years later, as these requests to the Records Office doubled, Davenport offered a revised set of schedules and published *How to Make a Eugenical Family Study* as a do-it-yourself kit, including an individual analysis card, a pedigree chart (a "family tree"), and the distribution of personal traits (C. Davenport and Laughlin 1915). By 1939, when the Eugenics Records Office finally closed, its files included hundreds of thousands of entries from such cards, making it "perhaps the most extensive genealogical collection ever compiled in the United States save for that of the Mormon Church" (Riley 1991, 58).[32]

Participating in producing a family history involved emphatic assumptions about race, and participants could not mistake the racial aspects of such an endeavor. As Davenport explained in the introduction to *How to Make a Eugenical Family Study*, "Eugenics has to do with the racial, inheritable qualities of a population. The peculiar importance of such qualities, as compared with purely individual qualities, is that they inevitably pass through the generations; that they are essentially immortal and that, in consequence, if good they bless, if bad they curse, the race or strain which carries them, and in time they tend to disseminate throughout the population" (C. Davenport and Laughlin 1915, 3). This image of racial qualities disseminating "throughout the population" suggests an unbounded sense of race, where "good families" could not be assumed to be a safe bulwark against decay nor relied on to shore up the color line. Davenport summarized the purposes and benefits of producing and participating in eugenical studies as "the interpretation of one's own *constitution*, the securing of data for the future uses of society, assistance in the choice of vocation, assistance in education and marriage selection" (5–6; emphasis added). This mode of objectification was not primarily directed toward displaying the threat of racial others, but rather to render tangible the terrain of the self in relation to racial identity.

The most important element of the charts to be completed in this kit was the individual analysis card, which required the most thorough rendering "of the physical, mental, and tempermental constitution of as many as possible of the individuals charted" (C. Davenport and Laughlin 1915, 9). Completing this card opened a constitutional perspective onto an individual's racial being. Following an initial section for providing detailed bibliographic information, the card offered multiple groupings of traits that could either be underscored (if the "predilection or the possession" is above average or high) or crossed out (if the trait is notably absent or below average). Through this process, one's racial identity, composed of physical, mental, and temperamental traits, was quite literally inscribed.

The data required and secured by the individual analysis card involved a fairly elaborate cluster of bodily and behavioral elements, requiring "a record which should comprise not only the usual statements about birth and marriage and also the biological and social data so commonly found, but in addition, and above all, physical and mental data including build, proportions, pigmentation, quality of sense organs and other important physical traits, also mental equipment, tastes for particular occupations, tempermant and social reactions" (C. Davenport and Laughlin 1915, 32). These diverse features are all rendered here in a clear racial frame.[33] Tied in with pigmentation and proportion are the all important matters of comportment and decorum, from "quality of sense organs" to "tastes" and "social reactions." The element of comportment, once objectified in racial terms, could become selected for or weeded out. The section on physical traits ranged from complexion to "conditions of speech," histories of eating, "habitual exercise," and "falling hair" or "tooth decay," and finally "natural walking gait" and "use of hands." Speech was broken down into a series of activities, graded by quality and strength. Eating was analyzed according to details of amount, "balance of rations," and "mastication." The matter of complexion involved a notable difference from the charts fieldworkers used to record the distribution of traits in cacogenic families. Under skin color, fieldworkers could code any of the following: "bl. (blond), i. (intermediate), br. (brunette), d.br. (dark brown), n. (Negro), y. (yellow)." But the individual analysis card offered only three options for complexion and skin color: "blonde, intermediate, brunette." Clearly, the subject of this self-analysis was assumed to be white, and yet this individual's racial constitution was the subject of intense scrutiny—not to discern and ferret out instances of miscegenation, but to locate and eliminate internal signs of racial deterioration and pollution. With the eugenical family studies, both in the field and through individual analysis, race is conceptualized as more than simply an epidermal fate or a matter given at birth, and increasingly becomes a matter of internalized, disciplined bodily orders, actively maintained through attention to class distinctions.

The elements of race consciousness promoted by eugenicists are evident in this do-it-yourself family study kit; skin color was only a modest portion of the big picture, and competed with forms of comportment and posture to determine racial belonging or difference. But what purpose would this knowledge of individual constitutions serve? For Davenport and other eugenicists, the most profound effect to be achieved by this new racial consciousness lay in the transformation of middle-class whites' view of themselves in relation to the world. And the one practical decision on which all this could be realized was in the selection of a mate. Davenport warned:

> There are those who adhere to the obviously false doctrine that men are born equal and therefore it really doesn't matter who marries whom. It is, however, easy to show that it does matter tremendously. Also I think it quite within the range of possibilities that it will become incorporated into *the mores* that persons who are thinking of marrying should learn something about the genealogical history of the proposed parents of their children. And, again, it is highly probable that, after we have learned the method of inheritance of racial traits and can state the consequences (certain or probable) of particular matings, that such precise knowledge *will influence human conduct* even as a knowledge of the causes of yellow fever has influenced human conduct and has led to a vast reduction in the morbidity from that disease. When our knowledge of the inheritance of

racial characteristics becomes fairly complete and widely diffused it can-not be doubted that such knowledge will influence many selections of mates. (C. Davenport and Laughlin 1915, 29)

Influencing "human conduct" was an objective of the eugenics movement as much as, if not more than, their legislative agenda to segregate or sterilize the feebleminded, to limit access to marriage, and to restrict immigration. This emphasis on comportment profoundly impacted how whites thought about race.

"HERE ARE THE FOES THAT NEED WATCHING"

But if the eugenics movement and its host of scientized terms—*moron, imbecile, feebleminded*—eclipsed the incipient spread of white trash outside of its region of origin in the South, how was it that this epithet returned to prominence as it circulated in broad usage throughout the nation in the 1930s and 1940s? Certainly, the same figure of poor whites animated the labeling practices of the Civil War period and later of the eugenics move-ment; the same cultural image of licentious, lazy, dangerous, ill-bred whites is active in each of these eras. The representational practices and the anxious fusion of racial and class concerns that figured the first nationally circu-lated uses of "white trash" clearly also inform the images of the Jukes, the Kallikaks, and the legions of the feebleminded that eugenicists perceived as heralding the demise of the race. Part of the answer lies in the demise of the eugenics movement as much of its scientific basis was subject to withering criticism in the 1930s. A host of educated, influential critics systematically assailed the methods, theories, and truth claims that initially invested "mo-ron" and "imbecile" with an aura of objectivity; these labels lost the very connotations of technical neutrality that made them so appealing when they were first mobilized by eugenicists. In their wake, usage of "white trash" to describe the disturbing sense of threat posed by poor whites was reinvigo-rated, as will be shown in the next chapter. But why did "white trash" win out over the host of synonyms—"mean white," "poor white," "sandhiller," "bob tail," or "cracker"—against which it was juxtaposed in the 1850s and 1860s? The answer lies in the cultural logic manifest in "trash." This term, more than all these other labels, articulates exactly what is at stake in intra-racial efforts to maintain white racial identity—it encapsulates the self-conscious anxiety among whites over threats of pollution that threaten the basis for belonging within whiteness. "White trash" succinctly examples the cultural work ideas of pollution generically perform in delineating the center of power and the sources of contamination within a cultural order (see chapter 3).

The link between the epithet and the figure of white trash is that both rely on a conception of pollution and a discourse of contamination that are common features of cultural identity. From the early articulations of race betterment discourse, when Mears warned of "the continually flowing stream of transmitted pollution" coursing through the lineages of the feeble-minded, to the heyday of eugenic discourse and rhetoric, as evidenced in Lothrop Stoddard's writings, the cultural concept of pollution was critical to depictions of the threat posed by these poor whites, an emphasis that clearly echoes Weston's concern in 1857 over the contaminating effects of white trash as they migrated north from the slave states. For Stoddard, one of the principal ideological proponents and popularizers of eugenics, the concept of pollution was critical to explaining how and why poor whites presented such a threat to the race. Stoddard (1920, 250) did not write and proselytize simply to garner support for eugenics legislation, but also to promote "the development in the general populace of a true racial consciousness—what may be termed a 'eugenic conscience.'" In this effort, he strove to convince middle-class whites of the need to transform their thinking and personal conduct in relation to the future of the race. Race consciousness was his all-consuming concern, and he asserted that white Americans should recognize it as the basis of international relations. Trying to convince whites of the need for "white racial solidarity," Stoddard depicted global populations in the "yellow," "red," "brown," and "black" lands as already animated by this central principle. His most notorious book, *The Rising Tide of Color* (1920), depicts the operation of white racial anxiety and the totalizing worldview that whites developed. But of similar import is his subsequent effort, *Revolt against Civilization* (1922), which lucidly demonstrates the logic behind the cultural figuring of "white trash." Stoddard's exposition reveals critical dimensions of racial thinking in relation to white trash and shows how race turns on fundamental cultural dynamics—categorical identities that sort out belonging and difference.

Like Charles Davenport, Stoddard grounded the contest over racial purity and consciousness within the individual self. Influenced by Freudian theory, Stoddard described an internal struggle that all whites must engage in against "the rising tide of color." Against this threat he proposed a defensive response composed of an elaborate array of "outer dikes"—blocking encroachments by the "yellow," "red," "brown," and "black" races—and "inner dikes," which all whites must develop as a means of internal fortification to maintain "white racial solidarity."[34] But even as his and other eugenicists' efforts achieved legislative victories, Stoddard grew increasingly concerned that a far greater threat lay within the white race, potentially more devastating because its features were subtle and perhaps not easily recognized. This threat was the subject of *Revolt against Civilization*, which relied on images of the Jukes and Kallikaks to depict "the foes that need watching."

As suggested by his notion of inner and outer dikes, Stoddard propounded that the developing white racial consciousness needed to be turned toward the task of boundary construction and maintenance. The problem, he noted, was one similarly raised by Gertrude Davenport: "The defective classes are not sundered from the rest of society; they are merely the acutest sufferers from defects which, in lesser degree, spread broadcast through the general population. These defects, continually spreading and infecting sound stocks, set up strains, discords, and limitations of character and personality of every kind and description" (Stoddard 1922, 253). Thus, Stoddard insisted that distinctions had to be drawn more sharply than allowed by the intraracial terrain of white skin color. Hence his insistence—a central creed of eugenicists—that the race is both improved and threatened from within, and his obsession with pollution and the linked concern with constructing boundaries and instilling a consciousness that regards them quite seriously and sees them everywhere.

More than any other eugenic theorist, Stoddard succinctly delineates the contrasts between the nature of these inner and outer threats presented by the "savage" state of the colored world. The concept of pollution is key to this contrast. He explained:

> As civilization advances it leaves behind multitudes of human beings who have not the capacity to keep pace. The laggards, of course, vary greatly among themselves. Some are congenital savages or barbarian; men who could not fit into any civilization, and who consequently fall behind from the start. These are not "degenerates"; they are "primitives," carried over into a social environment in which they do not belong. They must be clearly distinguished from the true degenerates: the imbeciles, the feebleminded, the neurotic, the insane—all those *melancholy waste products* which every living species excretes but which are promptly extirpated in the state of nature, whereas in human society they are too often preserved. (1922, 22; emphasis added)

In contrast to the clearly delineated savage Other, "degenerate" whites are not properly "extirpated" from the race; the problem they present stems from the veneer of sameness that offers no easy tangible basis for boundary maintenance or their expulsion from whiteness. These "melancholy waste products," whose image he illustrated by turning to the family studies, constitute "the vast army of the unadaptable and the incapable," for which he coined a term, the "Under-man," "the man who measures under the standards of capacity and adaptability imposed by the social order in which he lives" (22–23).

As with current uses of the term "underclass," the Under-man was identified by antisocial behavior, characterized by actions "*against the social order itself*" and as "incorrigibly hostile to civilization" (Stoddard 1922, 24; see chapter 5 on poor whites and the underclass). Stoddard, like Charles Davenport, stressed the critical inward dimension of self-peril. The social landscape of threat was mirrored internally:

> Not only is society in the grip of its barbarians, but *every individual falls under the sway of his own lower instinct*. For, in this respect, the individual is like society. Each of us has within him an "Under-man," that primitive animality which is the heritage of our human, and even our pre-human, past. This Under-man may be buried deep in the recesses of our being; but he is there, and psychoanalysis informs us of his latent powers. This primitive animality, potentially present even in the noblest of natures, continuously dominates the lower social strata, especially the pauper, criminal and degenerate elements—civilization's "inner barbarians." (27; emphasis added)

In this characterization, Stoddard depicts a landscape of struggle and conflict that is intraracial and individually internalized.

The shape of this internal threat facing every individual is coded in class terms, with the threat of "racial impoverishment" vying against the maintenance of "racial values." As Stoddard explains, "The truth is that, as civilization progresses, *social status tends to coincide with racial value*" (emphasis added). He depicts a racial terrain where the terms of belonging and difference depend on class status rather than simply skin color (1922, 77). In place of the threat posed by the colored races, Stoddard is chiefly concerned with "the Nemesis of the Inferior," and warns, "These are not pretty facts. But we had better face them, lest they face us, and catch us unawares. Let us, then, understand once and for all that we have among us a rebel army—the vast host of the unadaptable, the incapable, the envious, the discontented, filled with instinctive hatred of civilization and progress, and ready on the instant to rise in revolt. Here are foes that need watching. Let us watch them" (87). The faces of these foes, not surprisingly, are drawn from the ranks of the Kallikaks and the Jukes, whose "melancholy genealogies" Stoddard recounts at length (93–99).

The combined weight of their example conveys a threat grotesquely spreading from the "centers of pollution" where these clans are located: "The rapidity with which feeble-minded stocks spread, and the damage they do, are vividly illustrated by numerous scientific studies which have been compiled. Both in Europe and America these studies tell the same story: feeble-minded individuals segregating in 'clans,' spreading like cancerous growths, disturbing the social life and infecting the blood of whole communities, and thriving on misguided efforts to 'better their condition,' by charity and other forms of 'social service' " (Stoddard 1922, 94). Before all the grand plans for race betterment can be undertaken, Stoddard ominously demands "race cleansing" first be accomplished, "to cleanse the race of its worst impurities" (249). The means for achieving this end were promoted with emphatic consensus by eugenicists: segregation or sterilization of the "unfit." The basis for their belief in the efficacy of these invasive solutions lay in the logic that these poor whites represented a long-accumulating racial trash heap that had to be purged. "The degeneracy with which we have to deal is an old degeneracy due to taints which have been carried along in the germ-plasm for generations. If, then, this mass of degeneracy, the accumulation of centuries, could be got rid of, it would never again recur" (248).

In all these operations targeted on poor whites, Stoddard (1922, 244) patiently explained, "A racial view-point is needed." In concluding *Revolt against Civilization*, he turned again to the ever reliable Jukes: "A single degenerate family like the Jukes may cost the state millions of dollars. And to these direct costs there must be added indirect costs which probably run to far larger figures. Think of the loss to the national wealth, measured in mere dollars and cents, of *a sound, energetic stock ruined by an infusion of Jukes blood*. Think of the immeasurably greater loss represented by a 'tainted genius,' his talents perverted from a potential social blessing into an actual social curse by the destructive actions of a degenerate strain in his heredity" (247; emphasis added). This is not fear of miscegenation nor of dilution of the Anglo-Saxon stock by migrants from southern and eastern Europe. Rather, it is a fear of "bad breeding" within the white race and its effects on the class order. The point that bears stress here, especially because it runs counter to many current conceptualizations of race, is that "racial" clearly encompasses such class concerns. As Stoddard himself stressed, "Social status tends to coincide with racial value" (77).

Stoddard's writings strive to generate and promote white racial consciousness, believing that whites are imperiled exactly because they lack a racial viewpoint on matters ranging from marriage to geopolitics. Hopefully, he wrote, "When public opinion acquires the racial view-point, the present silly and vicious attitudes toward birth control will be abandoned, and undesirable children will not be conceived" (1922, 251). Beyond all legislative objectives, Stoddard strove to channel white public opinion into an explicit racial consciousness: "The point to be emphasized is that this can be effected almost wholly by a broader and more intelligent application of processes already operating and already widely sanctioned by public opinion. Segregation of defectives, appreciation of racial principles, wise marriage selection, birth control: these are the main items in the programme of racial purification" (252). It is notable how critical a role class distinctions and hierarchies play in both promoting and instilling this white racial consciousness. The notions of racial purity and boundaries, even in this moment when racial identity was so actively contested and maintained in terms of "white" and "colored," importantly turn on intraracial dynamics of class belonging and difference. White racial solidarity is predicated on distinctions of class and the conception that the race is at risk of being polluted from within.

The eugenics movement was eclipsed by political events in the 1930s and 1940s, particularly as Nazi practices—predicated, in part, on legislative efforts in the United States and Europe—demonstrated the horrible implications of eugenical thinking. The regimens of intelligence testing in the United States, too, were effectively assailed by critics, who also challenged and disproved the biased assumptions that animated eugenics research efforts such as the family studies. Though the scientific basis of "moron," "idiot," and "feebleminded" was eroded by these critiques, the menacing figure of poor whites never dissipated. Indeed, in the 1940s, as middle-class whites looked around for another means to designate *those people*, they found "white trash" still easily at hand. Unlike any other term, "white trash" makes explicit and emphatic the perception of pollution that plays such a critical role in white racial consciousness.

The term was ready at hand because "white trash" never entirely vanished during the rise of the eugenics movement; in fact, the epithet expanded its range during this period. When Lothrop Stoddard wrote on "Worthwhile Americans" (1925) for the *Saturday Evening Post*, he took pains to distance one of his subjects, Abraham Lincoln, from such nomenclature when his rural upbringing in Illinois potentially cast him as of this "submerged class": "Lincoln was supposed to have come from poor white trash of a very mediocre order. But careful investigation proves that this was emphatically not the case." The allure of white trash as a means to characterize a threatening and degrading white social collective was powerful even in this era.[35] Indeed, one of the later family studies, by Maud Merrill (1918)—an account from Minnesota of white "families which show a strain of defect and degeneracy appalling in its scope and social cost"—drew on local usage that associated white trash with the source of the problem: "Minnesota, too, has fallen heir to a share of the refuse from England's house-cleaning," which, in the popular narrative, refers to "the old convict stock which England threw into America" and that developed into white trash. In explaining these families, Merrill traces their origins from this original stock, along a "trail of pauperism and crime from Virginia across Carolina, Kentucky, Indiana, Missouri, even to California and Oregon"; the means of their dissemination, though, was now explained as follows: "The builders of the railroad in one country financed the[ir] scheme by importing poor white trash from the south" (562). "These mountaineers and their descendants" left behind after the railroads were finished, Merrill estimates, "have cost the taxpayers, in jail sentences and reform schools, state prisons and other state institutions, hundreds of thousands of dollars."

With the eugenics movement, the image of poor whites as a distinct threat to white racial identity was reconstituted as a subject of middle-class concern via a series of purportedly scientific studies and an array of "technical" terms that naturalized this ominous class figure. But it is also important to recognize that eugenics discourse and the movement's extensive research and explanatory apparatuses largely worked to confirm what middle class whites already suspected about the dubious status of poor whites—the key lies in the shift from identifying "white trash" with particular families or individuals to seeing it now as a sprawling, dangerous social collective. And yet, for all the ways "white trash" fleshed out concerns and anxieties of the eugenics movement, there was also a view from which the elaborate apparatus of eugenical explanation was quite excessive in relation to the broad-based, contemptuous regard for such whites. As psychologist H. A. Miller (1914, 394) retorted in a critique of eugenicists' notion of heredity in *Popular Science*, "We need no germ plasm to explain the difference between 'the first families of Virginia' and the poor white trash. That is exactly the sort of thing that mores explain." In pressing his critique, he turned to that staple of the eugenical discourse, the Jukes: "Now let us consider the classic example of bad heredity, the Jukes family. Almost everything that is said about the Negro can also be said about them. They lived in New York in the nineteenth century, but they were not a part of it. They were socially ostracized, and built up mores among themselves that had no part in the current civilization. It is barely possible that they averaged mentally inferior to their more socialized neighbors, but the sociologist does not need the inheritance of base characteristics to explain their criminality, prostitution and poverty" (396).

No, the explanations of white trash, as with "the Negro," relied, in the end, on naturalized notions of belonging and difference, or superiority and inferiority, that were deeply imbibed by middle-class whites. Though the vogue of eugenics held sway for a while and profoundly transformed the way whites experienced racial and class identities, the cultural work of boundary maintenance enacted by "white trash" preceded and continued long after this important era.

BY WAY OF CONCLUDING

This chapter sketched aspects of the historical emergence of white trash from a regional epithet to a nationally recognized and circulated label for poor whites who both excited and disturbed northern middle-class whites' racial sensibilities. As well, this chapter traced the development of a social perception of *those people* as a class and racial threat to whiteness. My central objective was to show a particular cultural dynamic at work in the formulation of a perception of white trash as a kind or type of people, and of the meanings associated with this cultural figure. In this regard, it is important to keep in mind that white trash is neither just a name nor a distinct social group. Rather, it is a form of objectification developed by a range of social commentators who tapped the cultural perception of pollution to make their fellow citizens recognize a fearful, debased white threat to domestic order in the United States. This process of objectification had profound effects, primarily in the practices of sterilization and institutional segregation as conducted on poor whites to curtail their ability to circulate "racial poisons." This aspect of the eugenics movement has been well documented (see Reilly 1991). Less well understood are the intense effects that images of poor whites had on white middle-class audiences. The racial, sexual, and class threat posed by white trash was met not simply with social control efforts enacted on the bodies of poor whites, but also with the emergence of a regimen of self-examination by which middle-class whites learned to think anxiously about racial identity in far broader terms than simply black and white.

Racial analysis currently is often focused on dynamics of othering, on projections of difference, or on discerning racist ideology at work behind ostensibly nonracial discourses or practices. I hope this chapter demonstrates that these do not account for all that we need to know about how racial identification operates and why race matters. I have tentatively sketched another series of dynamics at work, those of self-constitution and of intraracial assessments of the limits and nature of belonging, that are, at root, cultural, and I have argued that these cultural aspects of racial identification are critical to our understanding of race. The value of this cultural perspective is that it lets us grasp the broad and overlapping range of registers (class and gender as well as race) by which judgments and perceptions of belonging and difference are forged in relation to shifting social concerns and interests. Granted, the historical account offered here is skewed by emphasizing the anxieties and interests in self-constitution among middle-class whites. A fuller account would have included a rendition of the prevailing techniques of racial othering operating among whites in this same era, which surely influence or inflect the contests over belonging examined here. But because the cultural dynamics I have emphasized are so little understood and recognized, I feel they warrant the singular attention paid to them in this chapter.

In addition to this theoretical point concerning racial analysis, I also hope that this chapter contributes to the burgeoning literature on whiteness. I opened with an invocation of Matthew Jacobson's important work on "the alchemy of race" in the United States between the 1840s and the 1920s. I built on his attention to the "fracturing of whiteness" in this period, but he also concludes that at the end of this era, "a pattern of Caucasian unity" was achieved (1998, 93). Similarly, historian Matthew Guterl (2001) sees the close of this era as heralding a new era of racial discourse in which "absolute whiteness" developed, when a uniform and homogeneous racial order replaced the previous fractured social terrain. The account I have related here of the historical emergence of white trash supports their view of fractious forms of racial identification prior to 1930, but it also provides a basis for questioning this notion of "absolute whiteness." The forms of intraracial distinctions I have detailed here, and the anxieties over racial self-constitution provoked by white trash, did not cease in the 1920s. Rather, as the subsequent chapters show, the cultural work performed by "white trash" continued throughout the 1900s and remains quite active today as a means of internally policing participation in whiteness.

CHAPTER 3

UNPOPULAR CULTURE:

THE CASE OF WHITE

TRASH

What is white trash? This question is easily posed and perhaps too easily answered. In response to the question, I find that people readily reel off a list of attributes, with complete confidence and assurance that they are in no way associated with *those people*. In a political moment when derogatory labels and innuendoes for ethnic groups are rigorously policed in social and institutional exchanges, white trash still incurs little self-conscious hesitancy on the part of the user. The confidence with which people are labeled white trash derives from a long tradition of social contempt and a complex process of racial and class stereotyping.[1] White trash continues to be sustained socially by an almost unconscious naturalness, which the influential culture critic Greil Marcus (Arnold 1992, 62) has noted in his own upbringing: "I grew up in a very liberal household, where no degrading word said about black people would be tolerated, a household very sensitive to bigotry. But there was one group that I somehow got the message that it was okay to be bigoted about, and those were the backward, white Southerners—white trash. I'm not saying that I got the message from my parents, but I did get it somehow."

Marcus's comments fleetingly reveal an intense process of socialization by which middle-class whites learn the proper and improper means of drawing class and racial distinctions. This process of socialization has deep roots in American culture, stemming back to mid-nineteenth-century debates over the significance of slavery and the bounds of white racial solidarity examined in the previous chapter. But for all its historical depth, this dynamic of sorting out belonging and difference in relation to whiteness has received far too little attention from scholars, partly because the social contempt embedded in perceptions of white trash is so deeply naturalized.

This situation is changing, and a critical assessment of the cultural work white trash performs may be impelled and facilitated by both the recent proliferation of uses of this racial epithet in public discourse in the United States and by the way poor whites are responding to this label. The term's usage in popular culture began changing in the 1990s, partly in response to Americans' self-consciousness about "politically correct" speech, but also because the representational dynamics of this epithet shifted.[2] Quite rapidly, white trash is passing from an unambiguously derogatory label to a transgressive sign under which certain whites claim a public speaking position. Until very recently, white trash was used solely in disparaging fashion, inscribing an insistence on complete social distance from problematic white bodies—from the actions, smells, and sounds of whites who disrupt the social decorums that support the hegemonic, unmarked status of whiteness as a normative identity in this country. But in current popular cultural productions, white trash increasingly serves as a means of self-identification. Such usages were rare prior to 1980.[3] Assertions of white trash as a form of self-designation, though, have not dispelled the term's negative connotations; rather, they coexist in a confusing series that ambiguously plays out in cultural exchanges between whites of distinct class backgrounds. This makes white trash a particularly tricky subject for cultural analysis.

This chapter provides a provisional sketch of the historical roots of white trash in novels and films and of the recent proliferation of such references and images in popular culture during the 1980s and 1990s, in order to analyze the complicated status of white trash as a cultural object and identity. The surge in references to white trash can be mapped in relation to a range of dramatic, unfolding social and economic processes in the United States. Some of these pertain to reformulations of the significance of whiteness, heralded as "the transformation of white identity" (Alba 1990; Lieberson 1985) and also as "the crisis of white identity" (Winant 1994). In response to multifaceted critiques of and challenges to the hegemonic status of whiteness, whites have developed a range of rhetorical responses that amount to "ethnicizing" in the face of political demands articulated in ethnic and racial terms. Another significant factor is the increase in downward mobility for whites in the middle and working classes. And then, too, there have been subtle changes in the production of popular culture whereby certain poor whites are gaining a limited degree of control over their own public representations. Each of these developments is examined below, but first I will sketch the basis for my interests in this "contaminated" identity (Stewart 1991).

I became interested in the phenomenon of white trash while pursuing ethnographic fieldwork in West Virginia in 1985. In the southern coalfields of West Virginia, the term "white trash" named those families deemed most backward (socially and economically) by the residents of the coal camps. In each holler, it seemed, there was always one family that was used to mark the edge of sociality, through either their unruly behavior and lifestyle or their isolation from the rest of the community. While the name designated a singular, shameful condition established in relation to the local community, it also entailed a set of consistent features or characteristics that were commonly recognized throughout the Appalachian region and the South in general. In this regard, white trash named a strange collective order, one that manifested only locally in detached isolation. There were no white trash neighborhoods or groups, just particular, solitary families and individuals.

White trash also bore another striking feature in this area. As we searched out and studied the culture of the coal camps, the "natives" consistently directed us to some of these spectacularly grotesque families. In one holler, people continually asked me if I had visited the Wick family, a brood of about eleven parentless teenage and preadolescent children, most reputed to be "retarded," living in a sprawling shack surrounded by half-cannibalized car bodies with their indigestible innards chaotically strewn about. The family bore every feature of the white trash stereotype. Rather than cover up this profusion of "backwardness," the locals directed us to them, assuming that it was this stereotypical instance of Appalachian culture that we were really after. These natives were familiar enough with the variously reproduced images of "mountaineers" and "hillbillies" that they easily reified our interests as researchers.

By the end of the 1980s, I noticed a surge in usage of "white trash" in popular cultural productions. These instances of the term (detailed below) are quite removed from the way the term typically operates in West Virginia, Tennessee, and Kentucky. In Appalachia the name bears an immediately infuriating and shameful charge, but its uses in popular cultural productions carry an invigorating, assertive edge. Indeed, the insulting features of the term, with its transgressive charge, actually provide a basis for representations that can challenge, rather than reproduce, naturalized forms of racial boundaries. In popular culture, white trash at times functions as a fulcrum for confronting or at least framing whites' hypocrisies concerning race (e.g., the movie *Poor White Trash*, 2000, directed by Michael Addis). Such transgressive uses may seem meager or modest given the huge challenge of effectively engaging the breadth and diversity of white racism, and they make an uncomfortable fit with the blatantly disparaging and contemptuous uses of the term to debase poor whites. But this range of connotations and usage provides an excellent vantage point on the dense issue of how white Americans make sense of race.

Before addressing the transgressive uses of white trash, a few cautionary considerations are warranted. First, its negative connotations are an irreducible remainder, active and proximate even when the name is used as a means of positive self-identification. Merely formulating questions about white trash participates to some extent in reifying "it" as a real object, thus naturalizing the forms of class loathing that animate the term. But without a critical attention to uses of white trash there are few means to objectify those reservoirs of contempt that play such a fundamental role in the reproduction of class identities in this country. Some researchers have instead attempted a redemptive approach to the people and lifestyles labeled white trash, striving to refute or eschew the contemptuous aspects of the term. Several historians have tried to redress the stigmatization and ostracism of white trash by portraying a valorized social history of poor whites. Key works in this effort include Charles Bolton's (1994) *Poor Whites of the Antebellum South*, Bill Cecil-Fronsman's (1992) *Common Whites*, I. A. Newby's (1989) *Plain Folk in the New South*, J. Wayne Flynt's (1989) *Poor but Proud*, and Grady McWhiney's (1988) *Cracker Culture*. These social historians, conducting something of a salvage operation in the wake of a broad master narrative in American history, largely constitute their objects of study in contradistinction to white trash.[4] In their efforts to construct a sympathetic account of the "poor" or "plain white" tradition, they explicitly discount the application of white trash to their subjects. Newby makes the case most forcefully in his introduction, "Plain Folk, 'Poor Whites,' and 'White Trash' " (1–19). He asserts that his object of study is

> roughly the poorer half of the white population . . . who had never evoked much sympathy and whose history has been more often over-looked or caricatured than studied systematically and evenhandedly. Alternately disparaged, patronized, and ignored, these people have never received what every group is entitled to—a sympathetic look into their history that seeks to understand them on their own terms. Historians, like other

people, have stigmatized all or many of them as "poor whites," "white trash," "crackers," "rednecks," or "lintheads," and smeared them with the demeaning qualities those terms convey—benumbing poverty, social wretchedness, assorted bigotries, moral and physical degeneracy. Few labels of wide currency have embodied, and still embody, more elitism and sanctimony than those, and only the kinds of racial and ethnic slurs no longer admissible in public discourse have served so widely as substitutes for informed and open-minded inquiry . . . *Terms that embody such prejudices are not useful for historians and should be discarded. They are epithets at best, moral judgments at worst.* Even the most neutral of them—"poor whites"—focuses attention exclusively on the economic aspect of identity and, in turn, on victimization and degradation. (3–4; emphasis added)

Newby makes a strong case for discarding such loaded, derogatory nominations as white trash in favor of compiling a sympathetic account of a disparaged and exploited people. But such a tack is counterproductive, in that it leaves unexamined and unassailed the operation of social contempt mobilized by white trash. Critical engagement with this cultural figure's history and significance requires objectifying, rather than disregarding, this wellspring of loathing. If images of poor whites in popular cultural forms were reduced to a generic, neutral form of reference, the rhetorical identity of white trash as a function of a discourse of difference would be rendered unintelligible, though hardly inoperable. We should not hold out for a better approximation (a more valorized account) of the social bottom of whiteness. Rather, by tracking the charged racial work performed by white trash, we can directly see the means of boundary maintenance through which white identity operates, containing or expelling certain whites from the social and political body of whiteness.[5]

The problematic status of white trash as a cultural identity can be effectively framed with the benefit of two theoretical assertions about the name's significance: first, white trash is a rhetorical identity; second, the term functions as a category of pollution through which white middle- and working-class Americans evaluate the behaviors and opinions of other whites of similar or lower class status. The rhetorical dimensions of white trash and its important role in organizing perceptions of pollution (particularly regarding contaminations of racial boundaries) are tightly intertwined. Uses of white trash in popular culture assert and maintain racial and class boundaries, while the rhetorical association of trash with certain whites who breach the social decorums that allow whiteness to remain unmarked and normative. This latter point speaks directly to the earlier suggestion that references to white trash should be discarded in favor of some neutral referent for *those people*. I argue that it is exactly this confidence in some neutral space where disparaging social judgments can be rendered more politely that gives white trash part of its enduring momentum. We cannot begin to understand white trash by trying to transcend its contaminating markings; rather, these must be at the forefront of any such inquiry.[6]

In its long career, white trash has functioned as a means of what Werner Sollors (1986, 27–28) refers to as "rhetorical boundary construction," an operation whereby, from a certain perspective, "contrastive strategies— naming and name-calling among them—become the most important thing about ethnicity."[7] The examples that Sollors draws on to make this point are taken from minority racial groups in the United States: "A series of recent slurs, often hurled by some in-group speakers against other people who threaten the fixity of mental boundaries based on race, scolded blacks as Oreos, Asians as bananas, Indians as apples, and Chicanos as coconuts—all with the structurally identical criticism 'they're white inside!' The warning had no specific cultural content but served as an interchangeable exhortation to maintain boundaries."

White trash derives from a similar intraracial, contrastive strategy by which whites have long demarcated a certain form of racial detritus, composed of other whites who, through their poverty and ungainliness, fit insecurely within the hegemonic order of white political power and social privilege. In one regard, no one is white trash unless so labeled by somebody else. This rhetorical boundary construction is historically developed and quite supple. Rather than referring to a static list of character traits and bodily features, white trash continues to be applied in innovative ways.[8] As a rhetorical identity, instances of the name offer a certain perspective on the formation of white identity and demonstrate a means by which whiteness is maintained via an intraracial contest in which the active marks of Otherness are read on ill-fitting white bodies.

The cultural work of white trash is further revealed by turning to the work of the anthropologist Mary Douglas (1966), who detailed the constitutive role of pollution in establishing and maintaining cultural orders. Dirt, garbage, and trash are all materials that must be excluded from a cultural system in order that its modes of identity operate as naturalized conditions. Out of place, these materials rupture the smooth decorum of conventionalized existence. Douglas argued that instances of dirt and trash provide a means of discerning "the underlying system of norms and categories" at work in a culture, revealing "the structures of signification which govern the assignment of meaning to objects and events" (9). From this perspective, it is easy to understand how a certain normative cultural identity is maintained through a series of exclusions that are achieved by inscriptions of pollutions as stigmatized, threatening excesses. Jonathan Culler (1985, 2) summarizes Douglas's reading of cultural forms as an insistence that "dirt is vital evidence for the total structure of thought in a culture because it is an omnibus category for everything that is out of place. To investigate what counts as dirt helps to identify the categories of the system."

In each of these regards, instances of the name white trash register racial pollutions: moments when the decorum of the white racial order has been breached and compromised or, perhaps more important, where the imagined boundary between whiteness and blackness is undermined. White trash is used to name those bodies that exceed the class and racial etiquettes required of whites if they are to preserve the powers and privileges that accrue to them as members of the dominant racial order in this country.[9] White trash is also applied to whites whose lifestyles, speech, and behaviors too closely match the "marked" cultural forms associated with blackness or other symbolically informed forms of racial identity and difference.

Tracking white trash as a category of cultural pollution and the mobilization of a rhetorical identity in a discourse of intraracial differences provides a perspective on a particular naming strategy that is a basis for maintaining the unmarked status of whiteness. It also opens a means for understanding how such an unpopular cultural form provides a representational dumping ground in which excessive forms of whiteness that blur racial boundaries can be exorcized. As an unpopular culture, the images and instances of white trash in mainstream media productions work as examples of what whites cannot afford to be if the propriety of their implicit racial privileges are to be maintained. Rather than simply providing a glimpse of a certain social group, instances of white trash open a perspective on the broad social order from which they have been exorcized, and which they transgress.

I use the notion of an unpopular culture to objectify the tensions inherent in assessing the status of white trash in popular cultural productions.[10] White trash is difficult to place in the polarized realms of high and low cultural forms, primarily because it plays an important role in reifying these two poles as absolute orders. And it is a mistake to consider white trash as simply a "popular" expression of an aesthetic value of "the people," because the term is often also used by lower-class whites to stigmatize whites who fall even lower than themselves down the social ladder. Rather than constituting a unique cultural object or identity, white trash is a function of complex and charged cultural poetics (see chapter 4). The meanings, effects, tendencies, and images that the name assembles do not simply reside in individual bodies or a group of bodies but, rather, are generated in complex code struggles between classes and races and over what will count as sexuality or gender.[11] In this sense, white trash exists as much in middle-class fears and fantasies as it does in the "trashy" bodies of poor whites and their shared stories and talk.[12]

With this theoretical orientation, I turn now to survey uses of white trash in various popular cultural media. This perspective requires, first, a historical orientation on the term's central connotations. The roots of this cultural figure extend deeply in American history, as examined in the previous chapter. But perhaps of greater relevance to the meaning of white trash today are two enormously successful novels that became extremely popular films: *Gone With the Wind* by Margaret Mitchell (1936) and Harper Lee's (1960) *To Kill a Mockingbird*. Although other novelists, travel writers, and journalists conveyed explicit instances of white trash to an interested American public, these two works have a prominence based on the continued fascination with their figures and plots, particularly in the case of *Gone With the Wind*.[13] These works play a crucial role in assembling the connotations of white trash that inform its usage today. They presented views of the South to the nation at large, depicting an etiquette-laden world in which social orders were naturalized and enduring. But as representations of white decorum, honor, and pride, these dramas also relied on objectifications of white trash as an image threatening that cultural order.

Perhaps the most notable aspect of the role of white trash is the way it links what might be regarded as two antithetical perspectives on the "old South." *Gone With the Wind* is drenched in nostalgia for the antebellum era, soft-pedaling its evils, while *To Kill a Mockingbird* presents an indictment of the continuing travesties entailed by white domination. Yet, in both works, white trash play critical and quite similar roles. In *Gone With the Wind*, arguably the most sinisterly depicted figures are the Slatterys, a white trash family that galls and disgusts Scarlett; their haunting, lurking images recur throughout the novel. They "kill" Scarlett's mother by infecting her with typhoid, and they stake an unrightful claim to Tara, attempting to acquire the plantation for the cost of back taxes. The unrelenting dread of sinking as low as these whites drives Scarlett insatiably to reestablish her previously privileged social status, at whatever cost. White Americans' attractions to this story are surely disparate, but I suspect one of its most alluring aspects is the images of a social world in which racial power and privilege were absolute, a world where blacks "knew their place," and poor whites as well were maintained at a conventionalized, contemptuous remove from polite society. References to white trash play a critical role in naturalizing this view of society.

To Kill a Mockingbird dramatically criticizes this same society, depicting the perverse maintenance of a racially segregated social order where whites brutally preserve their dominion. Lee's tale, though, also depends on white trash to make its point. Respectable whites, who are willing to believe the false accusations of a white trash girl, are depicted as hypocritical and morally corrupt for condemning an innocent black man, but the most sinister figures in this novel are the poor whites. And while Lee's drama made a compelling case for contesting and overturning the operations of everyday life in the South, which were so brutally effective in grinding down blacks, what remains unquestioned in his exposé is that a certain class of whites is always to be held beneath contempt. Defense attorney Atticus Finch sums up Mayella, the pathetic white trash accuser: "She committed no crime, she has merely broken a rigid and time-honored code of our society, a code so severe that whoever breaks it is hounded from our midst as unfit to live with. She is the victim of cruel poverty and ignorance, but I cannot pity her: she is white. She knew full well the enormity of her offense, but because her desires were stronger than the code she was breaking, she persisted in breaking it" (1960, 206).

Both before and since To Kill a Mockingbird, the blight of white racism has been conveyed to well-meaning (or at least mildly interested) whites via images of the fury and rage, manipulativeness and desperation, of poor whites. The question here is not whether such depictions are more or less accurate in their portrayals. Rather, the white trash figure allows an insidious belief to stand: that it is only *those people* who are racist, only *those women* who are so licentious that they would engage in miscegenation, only *those men* are so cruel and desperately violent in maintaining the color line. The dramatic backgrounds projected by both To Kill a Mockingbird and Gone With the Wind are decorum-drenched worlds, where instinctive, naturalized differences between whites are indelible. Even in a work such as Lee's, which promotes a hope and insistence that whites, broadly speaking, change their views and understandings of the position of black people in this country, the Ewells (the white trash family) are held up as that which cannot ever change. They remain in the end as the "kind of men you have to shoot before you say hidy to them. Even then, they ain't worth the bullet it takes to shoot 'em" (1960, 272). This assessment is based on transgressions quite apart from their connection to racism and the oppression of blacks.

These nationally broadcast images of white trash dramatize what historian Joel Williamson (1984) describes as the "grits thesis," a certain interpretation of politics and race relations in the South championed by conservative white elites who located the blame for racial violence solely among "the great unwashed" population of poor whites. Promoted strongly around the turn of the century, when populist stirrings threatened to expand the franchise first extended under Jacksonian democracy, this grits thesis obfuscated the fact that "upper- and lower-class whites have actually worked in tandem on the racial front. They have functioned, not against each other, but both against the Negro, the intermittent, sporadic, open violence of one complementing the steady, pervasive, quiet violence of the other" (294–295).

What Williamson found disturbing in the grits thesis is its endurance and the effective means it provides for masking the pervasiveness of white racism.[14] He notes:

> The Ku Klux Klan of the Reconstruction era was at first organized and headed by upper-class whites, and studied terror and violence were its chosen instruments. Turn-of-the-century mobs included "respectable" persons sometimes as participants and ordinarily as spectators. When the physical subjection of the black man was achieved, when he was down and out and seemingly promised to stay there, the necessity for violence decreased, and upper-class Southerners could very well afford to see themselves as the even-minded children of light and peace. The whole idea of a specially vicious attitude towards blacks prevalent among lower-class whites is an upper-class myth. It was primarily a technique that the elite used to divorce itself from unflattering deeds no longer productive, and thus to arm itself to take the lead in peacefully putting things back together in a lasting order with itself at the top. (1984, 295)

As Mary Douglas (1966, 13) explains, categories of pollution function "as analogies for expressing a general view of the social order." One of the pollutions that trash is used to name and achieve some distance from are those volatile social dangers of racism and sexism. Part of what the epithet white trash expresses is the general view held by whites that there are only a few extreme, dangerous whites who are really racist or violently misogynist, as opposed to recognizing that racism is an institutional problem pervading the nation and implicating all whites in its operation. In this naming operation, "bad" whites perform as examples by which the charges of racism can be contained. Sociologist David Wellman (1993), in *Portraits of White Racism*, details some of the discursive strategies by which middle-class professionals depict their efforts at preserving racial privilege as distinct from the prejudiced sentiments of poor whites. Wellman also points to the persistence of sociological placements of prejudice in the "poorly educated; the aged; those living in rural areas; poor minorities; dogmatic religious groups; those of low socioeconomic status; social isolates; people raised in authoritarian families. If Archie Bunker is fiction, sociological theories about prejudice have helped create him" (9). In this regard, instances of white trash in popular culture function as an economy of examples that delimit the contaminating effects of association with racism and that negotiate confusions, anxieties, and uncertainties over racial, gender, and class identities. Trash is the label applied when a white social decorum is ruptured. In tracking white trash we discern the structure and texture of this decorum, a class and racial etiquette, that is too often invisible, conventionalized as a normative condition on which others are marked by their racialness.

Given the mythic role of white trash and its reproduction through popular culture from the mid-1900s onward, it is interesting to ask how the operation of the racial and class etiquette grounded in usage of white trash is transforming in concert with the dramatic changes of the post–civil rights era and the rise of postindustrialization in the United States. We can begin answering this question by tracing the surge in references to white trash in a range of public culture forums, as noticed by a variety of commentators. The reporter Margo Jefferson in *Vogue* pointed to this trend in 1988: "While books, magazines, and TV have been wallowing in the lifestyles of the rich, richer, and famous, a counter-trend has evolved—downmarket chic. Part nostalgia, part condescension, it's a campy attitude toward trailer parks and diner food, redneck rock and inarticulate heroes, bowling-for-fun and the Mafia school of interior decorating." Jefferson offered an explanation:

> The rich are clearly more different from you and me than we might hope, and the poor are clearly less different than we would like. And so there seems to be a change of focus. Our insatiable curiosity, our desire to spy on, gape at, fantasize about, and revel in the doings of the wealthy elite has shifted; now we want to SPY on, gape at, fantasize about, and revel in the doings of the downscale and the declasse. You see the impulse in the graffiti and the trailer-park photography that fills art galleries, and in the

self-proclaimed "white trash" cookbooks and guide books. You see it in the rise and spread of hitherto "ethnic regional" and "underclass" music like Cajun and rap, and in the popularity of decorative accessories like plastic flowers and thick layers of chunky costume jewelry. What was once considered the province of people who didn't know any better has been claimed, upgraded, estheticized, and turned into chic Americana. (344–345)

Another journalist, Amy Spindler (1993), called attention to the popularization of white trash in an essay, "Trash Fash," in the *New York Times* (1993): "The trendy genre film of the 90's seems to be trash run amuck. And whether it is Ms. Arquette in *True Romance*, Drew Barrymore in *Guncrazy*, Ione Skye in *Gas, Food, Lodging*, or Juliette Lewis in *Kalifornia*, Hollywood has mobile-home-park fashion pegged to the last tattoo and peekaboo bra strap." This interest in white trash, Spindler noted, has spread from the realm of movie fantasy to the fashion industry, evidenced in Arquette's posing for Armani and the "lawn chairs, carnival rides and, of course, the omnipresent house trailer" featured in Wayne Maser's photo spreads for Guess? jeans and album covers for John Cougar Mellencamp. Such explanations for this surge of fascination with white trash are keyed largely on the realm of aesthetics: "Part of it seems to be pop culture's romance with the disenfranchised. The fascination with trailer-park esthetics neatly parallels a trend that has left whites by the side of the road: hip-hop and gangster rap, with their emphasis on impoverished roots and violence. This is poverty and violence in a white setting" (10).

The observations of these cultural critics are useful because they adroitly draw into view the aesthetic dimensions of such representations. This attention to aesthetics as the basis for explaining how white trash operates in popular culture has advantages and drawbacks. Like the subject itself—diffuse, sprawling, and unattainable—trash is grasped clearly and succinctly in images from movies and advertising. But in this mode of attention it is easy to trivialize the demographic and social shifts underway in America's class and racial formations. Even when these broad social transformations are associated with the aesthetic dynamics, the power of these insights are easily blunted. In a wide-ranging survey of popular culture and politics, Tad Friend (1994, 24), in the magazine *New York*, links the emergent "age of white trash" to the expanding "white underclass." Unfortunately, as is common with any invocation of the underclass, Friend immediately reifies behavior as the defining feature of this group rather than suggesting that class identities are relational, changing as economic transformations develop and unfold: "What's alarming is not so much the burgeoning number of people with low-rent circumstances as the exponential spread in stereotypically white-trash *behavior*, whether exhibited by those in the underclass or by figures like Roseanne Arnold or Bill Clinton" (24). The end result of a singular attention to behavior is an inevitable implicit or explicit assertion of simple "childishness" at root. Friend concludes: "True trash takes what it needs and claims it's what it deserved. True trash is one long boiling tantrum, primed to explode. True trash is the terrible twos forever. The culture is in a panic to find its collective inner child. Well, here he is" (30).

An alternative mode of tracking the significance of white trash shifts attention from the consumers to the subjects of this excessive, anxiety-filled commentary. Interests of the middle class provide a key momentum to the proliferation of white trash in the realms of popular culture, but it is also the case that poor whites are grudgingly gaining certain degrees of control over their own representations. Performers and writers, more than ever before, are now actively willing to claim this debased identity. Mojo Nixon, who gained renown on MTV for such works as "Debbie Gibson Is Pregnant (with my two-headed love child)" and "Don Henley Must Die!," explains how this works: "When I sing about Cheez Whiz and barbecue and Beenie Weenies, it's all part of this weird white trash sensibility. I call them the front porch food groups. You see, we were supposed to pretend to be middle class, but I come from a group of people who grew up in small towns in North Carolina during the depression. Their whole modus operandi was to try to deny that—to try to be the 'Donna Reed Show.' But I'm the next generation and I can embrace all that stuff that made them so uncomfortable" (Plotnikoff 1990, 1E).

In Mojo's reading, there has been a distinct, class-specific generational shift in how whites negotiate the assumptions and impositions of class decorums; a few whites who have grown up hopelessly removed from, and incapable of assimilating to, the normative markers that more privileged whites have maintained find themselves able to fashion their remove and distance from the body of whiteness as an expressive and articulate subject position. Does this suggest a contrary, lower-class aesthetic sensibility, counterposed to a middle-class disposition toward consuming images of white trash?

From the television show *Roseanne* to *Trash*, a collection of short stories by Dorothy Allison, it is possible to read images of white trash as a carnivalesque aesthetic, a transgressive celebration of the *grotesque* body (with its illicit sexuality and propensity for cathartic emotions) that will not be constrained by (white) middle-class social decorums (Bakhtin 1984). But this view risks being either too celebratory or simplistically valorizing of counterhegemonic aspects to the name and the image, losing sight of how socially uninhabitable the space is that white trash designates. The key to such a reading is to resist the urge to identify the term with an undifferentiated sense of the working class or of the people and instead remain attentive to the active distancing and stigmatizing work of this term among those most closely associated with this cultural figure.

Turning to those who use the term as a means of self-designation, the contours of social contempt and tenuous economic standing become increasingly apparent. In these contours, the struggles to resist the contaminating connections of trash are amplified. No matter how transgressive the potential that resides in this label, what is irreducible in white trash is the inscription of social difference that is relentless even among members of the white working class. Considering white trash an unpopular culture maintains an attention to this distancing work, while resisting a tendency in discussion of popular culture to homogenize producers and consumers of everything that does not count as high culture.

There is a social bottom to "the people," as Marx first designated in *The Eighteenth Brumaire* with the term lumpenproletariat, and in the United States that boundary is policed and maintained with the label white trash. Evidence of this boundary work is apparent even in the current proliferation of references to white trash in popular culture. Attempts to regard "white trash" positively, to redeem it as a cultural identity, reveal an active remainder of social contempt and loathing that cannot be fully expelled. White trash carries an irreducible debasing connotation for those who rupture white social etiquette. This is most evident in attempts to take white trash seriously, such as Ernest Mickler's (1986) *White Trash Cooking*.[15] In this self-proclaimed "authentic" effort to depict a poor white cultural tradition in relation to food, Mickler, in the very first line of the introduction, claims an inability to "write down on paper a hard, fast definition of White Trash." What he comes up with, though, is this statement: "The first thing you've got to understand is that there's white trash and there's White Trash." The lower-case version is common and worthless; the upper-case has tradition and pride. Even when the name is being redemptively put forth as a proud identity, white trash is divided against itself and is still called on to perform the distancing duty of designating *those people* as low-down and beneath contempt.[16] Each effort to take it seriously seems to reproduce this rhetorical distancing gesture of marking a form of cultural contamination.

This play of upper- and lower-case namings of trash is also at work in the writings of Hunter S. Thompson, whose dexterity in assigning the term authoritatively both derives from and serves to efface his personal connection with the identity.[17] The following quotes appeared in his syndicated weekly column:

> No more wretched example of high-powered White Trash exists in America today than Lester Maddox. When the Great Scorer comes to write against Lester's name, he will get the same chance as Knute Rockne. There will be no question of whether he won or lost but how he played the game. And there will be a special dung heap in the low-rent section of hell for that brute. (14 July 1986)
>
> Oral Roberts is a greed-crazed white trash lunatic who should have been hung upside down from a telephone pole on the outskirts of Tulsa 44 years ago before he somehow transmogrified into the money-sucking animal that he became when he discovered television. (30 March 1987)

These two instances, the capitalized and the small-case namings, squirm between deeply powerful evil (Lester Maddox) and the merely disgusting (Oral Roberts), labeling those who do not know their place or disrupt too many assumptions about how power and money work in this country.[18] This set of authoritative comments illustrates another problem in making sense of white trash as a cultural object: such an effort has to constantly forestall confident inscriptions between a valorized and a debased, or a loathsome versus ridiculous, representation of such poor whites. A critical analysis of white trash has to work against these confident claims to define exactly what white trash is. If we accept that there is something that simply and objectively is white trash, these would most likely be the representative connotations. But white trash, like any symbolic material, is eminently "good to think with." So instead of trying to generate an authoritative sketch of a distinct cultural type as white trash, we need instead to analyze the work the term performs in marking and negotiating the social distinctions that inform racial and class boundaries in the United States.

This work is notably on display in country music.[19] The most striking aspect of white trash in this genre is that it stands in stark contrast to other derogatory labels for poor whites that have been redemptively claimed as forms of self-identification, such as redneck and hillbilly. The different subject positions each of these loaded terms entails are examined in detail in chapter 5. Here I only briefly touch on the contrast between hillbilly and white trash in country music to underscore how the distancing dynamic of white trash operates even in a domain of popular culture with which many poor whites identify, where the badge of social scorn is often worn proudly.[20]

In contrast to white trash, hillbilly became an accepted, seemingly neutral term for a long musical tradition. As folklorist Charles Seeger characterized it in 1946, "Hill-billy music seems to be a super-hybrid form of some genuine folk elements which have intruded into the mechanism of popular culture" (512). Folklorist Archie Green (1965, 205) claimed that "the term hillbilly music was born out of the marriage of commercial industry— phonograph records and some units of show business—with traditional Appalachian folksong." To this day, though, hillbilly carries a remnant of its once solely contemptuous marking; it remains critically useful for designating a certain cultural style that remains removed from a broader identification with the "mainstream" of the white middle class. Green summarized the ambiguous nature of the term's historical connotations: "Not only does High Culture frequently downgrade the artifacts that document hillbilly music—record, folio, radio transcription, barn dance show, rural drama—as trash, but for two centuries it has labeled the very people who produced the music as poor white trash" (206). The term *hillbilly* developed an ability to refer to a valorized past before the commercial success of this music. White trash has not experienced a similar transformation.[21]

Part of the transformation of hillbilly and redneck derives from the broad rise in social mobility experienced by many white country music fans and performers. Richard Peterson (1992, 58) notes that the numerous songs that have "redefined the word 'redneck' are important not simply because this term of derision was turned into a positive, but because it was made into a kind of badge voluntarily worn. To call oneself a redneck is not so much to be a redneck by birth or occupational fate but rather to identify with an anti-bourgeois attitude and lifestyle." Peterson quotes one of country music's most influential disc jockeys, Hugh Cherry, who notes, "While being a 'hillbilly' was something you were born to and fated to remain in the 1930s, anyone who is a 'hillbilly' today is a 'hillbilly' by choice. By the latter 1980s, all of these terms of prideful identification [redneck, hillbilly, country boy] had become virtually interchangeable with each other in connoting a working-class lifestyle and consciousness. Thus, using any of these terms was tantamount to evoking working-class consciousness" (58). White trash, however, retains the indelible imprint of the stigma of poverty and unending social contempt that sets it apart from these other means of self-identification.

In country music, white trash never received much prominence.[22] With rare exceptions, it is still used largely as a means of differentiating between whites at the bottom of the social and economic ladder. The megagroup Sawyer Brown had a hit in 1992 with "Some Girls Do." The chorus: "Well I ain't first-class, but I ain't white trash / I'm wild and a little crazy too / Some girls don't like boys like me, but some girls do." Clearly, trash has yet to stray far from its contemptible connotations or its usage as distancing technique. Another reference to white trash is Reba McEntire's 1990 remake of the late 1960s country classic "Fancy" by Bobbie Gentry. This song recounts a dying, impoverished mother's last-ditch attempt to move her daughter "uptown" by making her into a socially viable, sexually marketable attraction. The song features the daughter's defiant assertion, "I may have been born just plain white trash but Fancy is my name." But the clearest instance of the distancing role of the term occurs in the Bellamy Brothers' parodic follow-up to their hit "Redneck Girl." The chorus runs: "She's trash, white trash / Shooting that bull and slinging that hash / long on nerve and short on cash / she ain't nothing but white trash." This song, as well as providing a sense of comic distancing from the vulnerability implicit in valorizing the ideal "Redneck Girl," highlights the sexual charge carried in degraded objects. This usage is amplified in Confederate Railroad's hit, "Trashy Women": "I like my women a little on the trashy side / When they wear their clothes too tight and their hair is dyed / Too much lipstick and too much rouge / gets me excited leaves me feeling confused / I like my women just a little on the trashy side."

Men have rarely self-identified as white trash in country music, but that changed somewhat with the rise of "Alt Country" in the 1980s. White trash surfaced briefly as a way to name the social discrimination and scorn for lower-class whites. Steve Earle deployed such usage in the title cut on his *Copperhead Road* (1988) album, in a song that relates the story of three generations of men in a backwoods, white trash family. In this case, white trash names those whites who, along with blacks and Hispanics, bore a disproportionate burden in Vietnam.[23] "I volunteered for the army on my birthday / They draft the white trash first round here anyway / Done two tours of duty in Vietnam / I came home with a brand new plan / Take seeds from Colombia and Mexico / just plant 'em down the holler on Copperhead Road." Dwight Yoakum adds a "country" twist to his cover of The Blaster's song "Long White Cadillac," with a self-debasing usage of the term, "I'm gonna take this white trash on out of here."

Whereas country music performers and producers remain squeamish about the label, musicians in other genres actively took up the term in the 1980s and 1990s, when "white trash music" was linked to the producers of grunge or heavy metal sounds. Bands claiming the name range from White Trash to Cracker, the White Trash Debutantes, and Dirty White Boy.[24] Rather than drawing on any regional origins, "family traditions," or social standing, these bands make productive use of the transgressive, shocking position the label entails. Grunge bands, though, hardly have a monopoly on the term. The "tradition" of invoking this position/identity can be loosely sketched from Edgar Winter's *White Trash* live album (Epic, 1972) to Alice Cooper's *Trash* (Epic, 1989) and includes Bad Religion's song "White Trash" on their *How Could Hell Be Any Worse?* album (Epitaph, 1988). It continued in Exene Cervenca's "White Trash Wife" on *Old Wives' Tales* (Rhino, 1990) and The New Duncan Imperials' "White Trash Boogie" (*The Hymns of Bucksnort*, Pravda, 1993) and also included uses ranging from high art to folk, from Orchestral Manoeuvres in the Dark's "White Trash" on *Junk Culture* (A&M Records, 1995) to the collection of East Coast up-and-coming folk artists, *White Trash: N.Y. Folk, Volume One* (109 Record, 1989).[25] As with hillbilly, in grunge and alternative music the early 1990s popularity of white trash perhaps indicates a loosening of the visceral inscription of class identities and the cultural capital earned in effectively transgressing certain white versions of mainstream culture.

The role of white trash in other expressive cultural forms, such as literature, is also complicated. The lineage of figures and images of trashy whites in popular writings in the United States is quite lengthy and cannot be effectively surveyed here (McIlwaine 1939; Cook 1976). Instead, I turn succinctly to consider the "expressive" role of white trash and the problematic question of an "authentic voice" of trash, by juxtaposing the work of two successful authors, Carolyn Chute (*The Beans of Egypt, Maine*, 1985; *Letourneau's Used Auto Parts*, 1986) and Dorothy Allison (*Trash*, 1988; *Bastard Out of Carolina*, 1992).[26] Both Chute's and Allison's work revolve around stories of poor whites that are drawn from their personal experiences of poverty. Critics applied the label white trash to their characters, but the authors responded quite differently to these assignations. Chute rejects the label "white trash" as just another instance of the class contempt that maintains the painful stigmas of poverty. She objected to its use as a means of identifying her or her characters and reacted furiously to the numerous reviewers who, like Bertha Harris in the *New York Times Book Review*, have used the phrase to describe "her people." Allison, however, promotes usage of the label. Her approach to writing is openly autobiographical. Her novel *Bastard Out of Carolina* is, in part, a careful chronicling of the author's developing understanding of the social position in which the inscription white trash placed her and her family. The central character, Bone, laments early in the novel: "Just for a change, I wished we could have things like other people, wished we could complain for no reason but the pleasure of bitching and act like the trash we were supposed to be, instead of watching how we behaved all the time" (1992, 66).

The contrasting reactions of these two authors to the label white trash relates, in part, to their distinct positions in literary markets. Chute's works were marketed to a mainstream audience (published by Warner Books and Harper and Row), and reviewers questioned both the suitability of her subject matter and whether or not her writings counted as literature. Allison (published first by Firebrand Books and later by Dutton), on the other hand, offers very personal accounts of her developing lesbian sexuality and was initially marketed to an "alternative" audience that is attracted to transgressive actions and identities.[27] Asserting a shared white trash voice or identity in these writers, based on similarity of class circumstances in their works, covers over the important differences in reception and presentation of these authors and their characters.[28] Chute's discomfort with the term being applied to her work by well-educated cultural critics highlights the problem of blithely assigning the term to any object or product that matches a mental checklist of what white trash supposedly is. When wielded by a member of the middle or upper classes, the term cannot be neutralized of its stigmatized charge simply by the good intentions of the user.[29]

Despite Chute's discomfort with the label, there are tempting reasons to use it in relation to her work, primarily because she so effectively conveys the intimate clashes between the social bodies differentiated by white trash. Apart from Chute's characters and general style, the dramas that she depicts offer a compelling version of what is at stake in white trash. More so than Allison's writings, Chute conveys the civic stage on which classed conflicts between upper- and lower-class whites continue to be waged in small towns all over the United States. In this regard, she objectifies the gaze that inscribes white trash and the position that cultivates the reservoir of social contempt that animates the term's usage. The narrative of *Letourneau's Used Auto Parts* features the efforts of the city council to pass and enforce building codes that will eradicate a precarious grouping of trailers at the edge of town. The novel follows the steady strides of the "Code Man" and the sheriff's deputies as they make their rounds, depicting the people who are driven from their trailers, resulting in suicides or random acts of violence. White trash helps develop and expand the significance of the charged class dynamics dramatized in this narrative. Scenes throughout the book position trash in a way that makes the political and economic stakes quite clear in instances that only seem to involve a contest over aesthetics. In a scene where bad neighborness might be the simple middle-class effort at thematizing an incident, Chute's account articulates another perspective. In the following description, Maxine has just been told by her new, upwardly striving neighbor to stop her guests from turning around in his driveway and not to park in front of his property:

> Maxine's thick neck quivers. "What do you care where people park. . . . This aint Connecticut. This is the woods!" She is starting to tell him about how she has no control over what her company does, about how one of them might whip right into his dooryard to turn around before she could stop them . . . but he is walking away from her.
>
> After his trailer door closes, the quietest door-closing Maxine has ever heard, she heads for her door. She has to step high because of no porch. Inside, she crosses the kitchen to the sink, stands there looking into the drain.
>
> "What happened, Mama?" Ryan asks. He comes up behind her and gives her pretty blue cowboy shirt a little pull.
>
> "The usual," says Maxine, mashing her Tiparillo in the sink. "The usual half-brained idiotic mother-fucking crap represented by eighty-nine percent of the human being population. . . . Damn them all to hell. I've HAD it."
>
> "What are you going to do?" he asks, looking around at the bright open door to the yard.
>
> "I don't know," she snarls. "We're outnumbered, for crissake." (1986, 81)

Does applying white trash here help to bring into view a minority discourse?[30] Does white trash refer uniquely to that minor population of poor whites whose lives and dreams are ground down in the interests of white middle-class desires and projects? Does this label help name the class conflicts that are too easily parsed as neutral or worthwhile efforts at civic code enforcement? These questions should be answered in the affirmative, but with a tentative ear to the repercussions from such assertions. As a front in the continued internal wars of capitalism, the exclusionary strategies and the disciplinary tactics that disperse the recognition of class conflict into multi-faceted bodily concerns (over hygiene, over decorum, over consumerism) make of white trash a vulnerable, threatened social position. The attacks come from within a body labeled trash in the forms of self-doubt and self-contempt, as much as from the neighbors. This makes "positions" difficult to articulate. But the heavily naturalized investments in middle-class order (materialized through lawn care and quiet streets) and the support they receive in legislation and policing need to be identified as aspects of class conflict. And the violent forms of anxiety and contempt they generate must be named in relation to the base of power from which they derive. My use of white trash attempts to implicate the very interests in status that police public discourse against such unpleasantries. "White trash" insists on the ties that bind the detached, well-composed observer in a particularly nasty way to this disturbing subject.

Another domain of popular culture that offers a broad collection of instances of white trash is the movies.[31] In this realm of cultural productions, there are few question of "authenticity" or "voice"; with scant exceptions, white trash do not produce their own stories in Hollywood.[32] The compelling question about films that feature white trash is whether these images are largely objectifications of a contemptuous Other to white middle-class moviegoers, or do they present Americans with a figure that, in symbolic terms, is quite good to think with regarding the dynamics of racial and class identities? Two films identified by Spindler as accurately pegging white trash, *Kalifornia* and *True Romance*, present radically different depictions of this subject. *Kalifornia* offers up an extreme caricature of white class positions and, through their polarized interplay, presents a keen rendition of how class operates intraracially in the United States today. *True Romance* is more of an idealized fantasy made compelling and dramatic because of the desperate financial straits of its central characters. Running from mob hit men is not the same as driving in a car cross-country, sitting side by side with a contemptible and dangerous class Other.[33] Both films are obviously fantastic, and yet within this mythic realm one makes more of a direct gesture at tapping into and dramatizing the class anxieties that animate usages of white trash. Does that make *Kalifornia* a more accurate depiction of white trash than *True Romance*?

Rather than authoritatively judge and list which films "really" are or are not about white trash, I prefer to point to a few ways such characters have been used to figure and refigure shifting subject positions and identities in the 1990s. The decade opened with three prime instances in 1991 of films relying on white trash characters to think through or to ground shifting cultural orders and social realities: *New Jack City, Silence of the Lambs,* and the remake of *Cape Fear. New Jack City* dramatized myths and realities of the inner city while critiquing the visual economy of spectatorship that thrives off such representations. The vast majority of the characters are black, and there is a well-developed tension over the white gaze and the participation of whites within the drama. As well, *New Jack City* highlights the precarious basis of black male bonding between "brothers" on the street and the confused connection between blackness and "the streets." To valorize a white male position in the film, and to establish the depth of his sincere interest in the drama's outcome, the white cop, Nick Paretti (Judd Nelson), is designated as white trash. There are few objective indicators of his status as trash, but in the crucial bonding scene between him and his partner Scotty Appelton (Ice-T), Paretti names himself as "white trash." When his presence is most tenuous, after their undercover connection, Pookey (Chris Rock), has been murdered by the gangsters, Paretti asserts, on a rooftop drinking scene with Ice-T, "I used to be Pookey."

An incredulous Ice-T replies, "Hows that?"

Paretti answers, "I was a poor white trash Pookey."

After a dramatic silence, this claim allows Paretti to speak the moral of the film: "This whole drug thing. . . . It's not a black thing; it's not a white thing. It's a death thing. Death doesn't give a shit about color."

The white trash figure in this film assails racial barriers and reveals that underclass entrapment, despair, and devastation transcend racial lines.

Silence of the Lambs, a brooding, tension-filled film on the perversity of transformations, deploys a completely different usage of white trash. Agent Starling (Jodie Foster), a young woman desperately out of place in the fiercely male institution of the FBI, transforms herself through a series of humiliations and moments of intuitive brilliance into a professional agent. The gendered aspect of her struggle is heightened by the class divide she must overcome. In her first meeting with the imprisoned Hannibal Lecter (Anthony Hopkins), he blunts her efforts to "dissect" him and turns the objectifying gaze back upon her. Lecter reads her: "You're so ambitious aren't you? You know what you look like to me, with your good bag and your cheap shoes? You look like a rube, a well-scrubbed hick. Good nutrition's given you some length of bone, but you're not more than one generation from poor white trash. Aren't you, Agent Starling? And that accent you try so desperately to shed—pure West Virginia."

The beat-up Ford Pinto to which she retreats, distraught, in the parking lot seems to confirm his reading. But her class background is both a blemish and the means that enable her to track the murderer, because the killer stalks women in the small towns of West Virginia and along the Ohio river. As she tracks the killer to his lair, she comes face-to-face with the women she might have become if she had not transformed her class identity and left behind these backwater towns. In the end, Agent Starling's triumph effaces any trace of her connections to the past, a past that had haunted her and that she was required to eradicate.

Cape Fear offers a more stereotyped use of white trash, but one that, like the film itself, was updated for the 1990s. As with the succeeding generations of The Terminator and Freddie, the second version of Max Cady is white trash with a vengeance, more terrifying than most previous male trash figures. The momentum of his rage derives from a desire for class vengeance. His lawyer, disgusted by and contemptuous of Cady and realizing he is illiterate, deprives him of effective counsel, ensuring that he will be found guilty. The new *Cape Fear* depicts a nightmare of the illiterate ranks of white trash rising up and lashing out: in jail Cady learns to read and discovers the true nature of the crime against him. The original film featured a suave, if ominous, Robert Mitchum as Cady, and the extent of his social failings are conveyed in the now mild designations of being "rock bottom" and "the lowest." With Robert DeNiro's tattoo-covered body and the repeated refer-ences to white trash, there is no ambiguity about the class divides between these whites. Cady describes being raped by white and black men in prison, invoking the kind of perversity that has long been an accent on white trash figures. The 1990s *Cape Fear* still explores the durability of the social system to protect "decent, law-abiding citizens," but the depths of the class divide between privileged and underprivileged whites has spawned new terrors that would have seemed unimaginable in the 1950s and early 1960s.

These films present a composite of the threatening visage of white trash that terrifyingly figures aspects of the expanding social bottom for the white middle class. In the early 1990s the image of white poverty resurfaced in U.S. public discourse in a novel manner, more threatening and ominous than before (see chapter 6). Images like those in *Kalifornia*, of rural white trash on a lethal cross-country road trip, and in *Cape Fear* depict this threat, cer-tainly, but they are also oddly juxtaposed and conjoined with images of the threatening black, inner-city underclass, as in *New Jack City*. This latter film evidences one of the enduring features of representations of white trash: that it corresponds in some manner to the color line between whiteness and blackness in the United States.

But how do we weigh these images against the voices and narratives drawn from the novels of Chute and Allison, or from the positions articulated in the references to white trash in country music? Are the demonized filmic depictions more revealing of the true significance of white trash, or are they just one medium by which this cultural identity operates? These questions return us to the opening of this chapter and lead on to the subsequent chapters. To say that white trash is a projection of white middle- and working-class fears of the lower social orders entails a set of assumptions about its realness or its stereotypicality; to say that white trash is a debasing name for a real stratum of the white population leads in another direction, toward efforts to redemptively develop a more valorous counterimage of poor whites. Neither of these options is an adequate means of framing the dense cultural work of white trash, but they do each develop important perspectives on this challenging subject, which are respectively developed in detail in the following two chapters.

What is irreducible in all of the usages of white trash reviewed here is the rhetorical quality of the name and the contaminated charge of trash. From any position, these two aspects of the name are active; there is no stable referent to the term: uses continue to be fashioned anew, different bodies and speakers emerge that are inscribed with old labels, positions are established and contested in acrimonious exchanges of "white trash." This chapter has briefly surveyed uses of white trash from the 1930s to the early 1990s. Instances of the name, related here, are in complicated and often confusing agreement. In thinking through the future career of white trash, in tracing its further dissemination, it is important not to become obsessed with assuring that its uses remain authentic or true to a certain presumed origin. The term will continue to be unevenly used. The reactions that I have evoked when I tell people of my interests in white trash vary greatly by region. In Tennessee and West Virginia, people consistently respond with the suspicious, loaded question: "Who are you calling 'white trash'?" In California, people have been enthusiastic about a means of naming whites that transgresses or rejects the etiquette that maintains whiteness as hegemonic. In this state, with so many rootless whites, white trash is an oddly comfortable assertion of a self-identity. These disparate reactions belong to the same moment but point to the always critical matter of position and location that fundamentally determine the meanings and effects of white trash.

The means I've settled on here for considering all of these varied usages is to think of white trash as an unpopular culture. It is not the product or the sign of an undifferentiated "people" from a mass audience in the United States. Though aspects of its connotations aptly fit the carnivalesque aesthetic that Mikhail Bakhtin (1984) described as the relational, competitive Other to the elite, "classical" forms of high culture, the negative markings of the term make it equally active as a means of differentiating among partisans of "low culture." Whether it is taken as a self-identity or applied as an inscription of social difference, the relentless core of white trash remains its remove from the mainstream of proper class and racial identities among whites. While other derogatory terms for lower-class whites have been transformed, it seems that white trash, at least for the time being, will remain an improper name.

CHAPTER 4

READING TRASH:

DELIVERANCE AND THE

CULTURAL POETICS OF

WHITE TRASH

Wherever there is Man there is Trash. This chapter examines the cultural poetics by which the two are distinguished from each other in the United States. The distinction is a cultural matter in two regards. Cultures mobilize notions of pollution or trash to articulate their form and content via the material they consider "out of place" and dangerous, thereby subject to exclusion (Douglas 1966; Douglas and Wildavsky 1982).[1] As well, trash is a means for categorically organizing and evaluating an internal hierarchy of cultural productions. Differentiating designations of "classics" and "trash" are crucial operatives in the inscription of the division of a culture into high and low realms.[2] The figure "white trash" is a function of cultural notions of pollution in the United States and, as such, falls problematically and productively along the disciplinary divide between anthropology and cultural studies. Rather than providing a unique, locatable, ethnographic object (an authentic culture for anthropologists) or an expressive culture (a category cultural studies uses to distinguish creative dimensions of ethnic or racial experiences), white trash exists as a rhetorical identity. That is, white trash is a naming practice by which racial and class identities in the United States are maintained.

The name white trash is used to make an example out of the contaminating extremes that undermine the ability of white bodies to stand as unmarked identities, synonymous with social norms in this country. In racial terms, white trash is a stereotype asserting that there are only some "bad" whites who are racist, while institutional racism remains faceless. With class relations, white trash is an image of abject poverty, where the obviousness of a body's decay or lack of decorum and comportment "explains" the economic condition, overwhelming any suggestion that systematic market forces are responsible for producing such conditions. White trash is the label given to those white men and women who are considered sexually dangerous. As much fantasy as reality, trash is a floating image of loose, cheap, rough sex that forms the border ratifying middle-class sexual mores. The epithet is a label for those bodies that, in their speech, comportment, and actions, exceed white social decorum and rupture the forms of politeness that allow racist, sexist, and classist ideals to operate effectively in everyday life.

Typically, the purpose of a cultural analysis of such a stereotype is to demystify and disprove its existence. The disciplinary options here divide between ethnographic accounts that demonstrate, in place of stereotypes, the humanness of the subjects, and a cultural studies analysis that either contests the representational economy behind such depictions or examines how its expressive forms are commodified and reproduced by and for dominant groups.[3] Each approach reflects certainty about their subjects that is distorting or deceptive with a cultural figure like white trash. The very use of the label risks reproducing the charged perceptions of class contempt and stigma that animate this figure. But eschewing the term in favor of some neutral designation allows that reservoir of contempt to escape critical attention. Making sense of white trash depends neither on disabusing people of received images nor on finding a more valorized basis for the origins of such images, but rather on attention to the poetics at work in the constitution of racial and class subjects via this figure.[4] White trash poetics involves the effort to demarcate Self and Other within a frame of reference drenched in ambiguity by its appearance as a surface of sameness: whiteness, for instance. The terror and tension in this poetics involve uncertainty over whether the Other is really, threateningly there or if it is a projection of a repressed Self that class, sexual, and racial decorums produce. In this regard, the figure of white trash exists as much in middle-class fears and fantasies as it does in the rural southern hill country or in the northern urban communities of migrant Appalachians. The figure gives dynamic shape to transgressions of the intangible boundaries and decorums that constitute whiteness as a cultural identity.[5]

The operation of this poetics is active in the movie *Deliverance* (1972), a film that endures in American popular culture through nervous references and knowing invocations that revolve around its shocking depiction of white middle-class masculinity being ravaged in the woods by violent hillbillies.[6] Just the first few notes of its theme music, the "dueling banjos" melody, are enough to summon the film's depiction of classed sexual fears dramatized in a nightmarish scene. In 2001, Chevrolet ran full-page ads in *Time* and *Newsweek* for their Tahoe SUV, emphasizing its OnStar navigational system. Over an image of a desolate swamp ran the banner "One word before you venture off into the wilderness without OnStar: *Deliverance.*" The lasting presence of this film derives as well from the role it played in transforming popular cultural representations of poor rural whites. Based on a novel written by a southerner, James Dickey, the movie breaks from the buffoonish, comical representations of the Otherness of poor southern whites that predominated on television shows (*Beverly Hillbillies, Green Acres,* and *Hee Haw*) in the late 1960s.[7] *Deliverance* marks an important shift in the narrative forms that make use of poor whites.[8] Earlier films, such as *Gone With the Wind* and *To Kill a Mockingbird*, depicted lower-class rural whites as clearly Other. They were either comic or pathetic, but always unmistakably clearly debased in relation to middle-class whites. *Deliverance* signals the first time the cultural certainty supporting this difference is called into question; the terror in this film is generated as much by its interrogation of white middle-class self-construction as it is in projections of threatening forms of class Otherness. In this regard, *Deliverance* is a key precursor to the current wave of cultural productions by those who personally claim a white trash identity.

Deliverance unfolds a tense narrative landscape in the zone between Nature and Culture. Nature, in this case, "the last wild, untamed, unpolluted, unfucked up river in the South," is being destroyed by a large dam project to bring more power to Atlanta. This Nature is inhabited by strange "natives," poor whites who live in a contaminated zone of junked yards. Referred to as hillbillies and mountain men, they represent an inability to become fully "civilized" humans; their "backward" location in the woods perversely confuses the boundary between Culture and Nature, problematized in this narrative by the conjunction of trash and natives. *Deliverance* dramatizes the way white trash operates as an internalized figure of the Primitive, a figure of wildness and lack of constraint that forms civilized Man's symbolic Other.[9] The desires that operate in and on this figure are complex, even if considered only from the viewpoint of a Western subject. When the space in which this figure is encountered is elsewhere, a Pacific island perhaps, or some other "natural" setting somewhere on the periphery of "civilization," the bodies it animates are dark, exotic, and sensual. This Primitive occupies an external site of difference. But when the body is white and dwelling within the identifying boundaries of civilization, as with white hillbillies, then the desire for the primitive becomes confused, lacking clear markers of distinction for managing Otherness. Its "difference" loses external characteristics such as race and even gender, and expands uncomfortably and uncontainably through internal zones; its sexual charge is marked as incestuous and perverse.

The difference that does emerge here is generated by class distinctions. Bodily differences are polarized by the markers of economic refinement: straight teeth, clear skin, good posture. In this situation, the Primitive is animated by the corruption of implicit codes by white lower-class bodies that fail to maintain decorum, shaming themselves with a crude remark or a disgusting display. The poetics of this internal Primitive fashion a figure of sprawling trash heaps, junk-strewn yards, distorted, ruined faces; the distinction of "civilized" and "wild" easily molds the bodily differences between middle and lower classes. The dramatized images of white trash as backward, degenerate, incestuous, living in filth piles of relations or kin are complexly motivated representations that effectively exteriorize behaviors and attitudes that undermine white middle-class propriety.[10] What is fascinating and disturbing about *Deliverance* is the way a drama about Nature and Culture so easily maps a conflict about proper and improper sexuality between distinctly classed white male bodies.

As the opening credits roll, the camera tracks four city men driving from Atlanta through scenes of storm clouds and rain falling on steep, densely wooded hills. Over these images a voice asks, "Are there any hillbillies up here?" Lewis (played by Burt Reynolds) promises the men, who are nervous about their adventure, that he will have them "back in your smug little suburban homes" in time for Sunday football. Though not a homogeneous unit, the four men, Lewis, Ed (John Voight), Drew (Ronny Cox), and Bobby (Ned Beatty), form a conflicted, composite image of middle-class masculinity. The driving interest of the movie's narrative is whether a coherent portrait of a proper Self can emerge from these four men. The contest for that Self unfolds in a series of shifting forms of ambiguity that the movie works strenuously to maintain. The central ambiguity is whether the Otherness that threatens this middle-class Self impinges dangerously from without or emerges disturbingly from within. A stark class opposition, between white trash and suburban men, initially poses the external threat as predominant, but by the end of the film this threat seems more a repressed Self projected on the screen of the class Other.

The thematic shift from Nature as challenge to Trash as threat is immediate. The men pull off the road in a collection of run-down houses somewhere in the woods, clustered around an old gas station that appears abandoned, surrounded by junked cars. "The river is inaccessible in all but a few places," Lewis says. They have to find some way to penetrate the woods to reach the river, and in this effort the hillbillies become a tense obstacle. In the first encounter with these peculiar natives, and the first time that we actually see the city men, only the filth and squalor of the setting stands out. The city men silently look about the scene, calling for anybody. Bobby wanders open-mouthed: "Will you look at the junk?" He strolls amid the decrepit structures: "I think this is where everything finishes up. Gentlemen, we just may be at the end of the line." Drew hisses, "Keep it down, Bobby, we don't want to offend these people." "*People*?" Bobby guffaws loudly. "What people?"

As no natives yet appear, Bobby prowls around the place until he comes upon some junked cars in the front yard. "This is my car," he jokes. "That is my '51 Dodge." The others giggle and laugh. "All of my youth and passion was spent in that backseat. It's all gone, you see. Rust in dust.'" As a scene of internalized Otherness (a setting where whites inhabit a liminal zone), a landscape of de-eroticization and devalued objects unfolds where "everything" is worn out and collapsing in a tired heap. In stark contrast, Nature is the virile, erotic force for transcendence in this film. "Wait until you feel the water," Lewis keeps saying. "It's the second best sensation in the world." In contrast, when some hillbillies finally emerge, they are old and move slowly, looking decrepit and filthy. The tension between the two groups is alleviated, momentarily, by the appearance of a boy with his banjo. The boy, who looks extremely retarded, sits on the front porch and answers the tentative notes that Drew strikes up on his guitar—the dueling banjos theme. Studying the boy and the other men who come to hear the music, Bobby remarks, "Talk about genetic deficiencies. It's pitiful." After the song, Drew excitedly offers his hand in friendship, but the boy abruptly turns away. He refuses to or can't speak, and the ideal of speechless communication is perverted by becoming a literal condition: "genetic deficiencies." Lewis looks for somebody who will drive their vehicles back down river. The men he finds are "rough looking," and Bobby whispers to Lewis, "Let's just go back home and play golf." But Lewis haggles a deal with the men while Bobby whines that they will never see their vehicles again.

The shift from conflict on a natural terrain to such a classed landscape reconfigures the sexual adventure that is unfolding. As many activities of the 1990s "men's movement" would confirm, male bonding that occurs in the wild is socially sanctioned. But when class lines blur the mythic clarity of the natural setting, the specter of perversity emerges. The sexual imagery of the movie operates in two distinct registers. The middle-class men's jokes about "getting your rocks off" in the wild river seem good-natured, and the shots of Lewis's bulging biceps, accentuated by his black rubber suit vest, seem only virile—rather than explicitly homoerotic—against the natural back-drop of the water. In contrast, the hillbillies are left on shore and become blurred and diffuse, lurking figures, obscured by trees, watching as the men start down the river. In this moment of merging with the freedom of the "last wild river," the trash men are indelibly marked as suspicious natives, perversely watching, immobile in a society of upward mobility, unable to enact the adventure rituals for attaining full manhood.

Being on the river is a lyric encounter with Nature that suspends all other aspects of the city men's lives, heightening their primal sexuality and male identity. The "first explorers saw it just like us, by canoe," a comment that further inscribes the native-versus-adventurer theme. "I know how they felt," remarks Drew. Male bonding (often a problematic between ideal and bodily experiences) in this sense is achieved across nature and the past by sharing a common experience of the river with the first adventurous white men. But sexuality among the men starts slipping; the river unleashes the restraints of propriety. The proper Self of the middle-class male depicted here is stretched between Bobby, an insurance salesman, and Lewis, the wild man survivalist. The strain shows most on Ed, who is deeply attracted to Lewis but uncertain of his own virility. In the sensual experience of the wild river—the transcendent experience of a heightened maleness—their roles become detached and ambiguous; they experience a suspension of all mean-ingful ties with the social world. They discuss whether they are happy or not with their wives and families, and the meaning of "the system." None of these ties is part of the natural man that the river allows to emerge. Their talk runs into apocalyptic images of the collapse of society.

In a camp scene, as the men make ready to sleep, sexual images become pervasive and unruly. Sprawling about, bodies close together, a conversation begins about "something in the woods and the water we've lost in the city." "Not lost," Lewis insists, "sold." Bobby refuses to take up the ensuing argu-ment over the corrupt system and society. "The system's done all right by me. After all it produced the air mattress, better known in the industry as the 'instant broad.'" The sexuality of the immoderate and half-naked male bodies is temporarily shifted by Bobby into another register by invoking a commodified rubber woman. "Now, if you'll excuse me," he adds, "I'm gonna go be mean to my mattress." The sensual tension in this scene dwindles with the firelight as Ed drunkenly mumbles, "I know that no matter what problems might be happening, no one can find us up here." But this tension—over male sexuality, the relation of bodies to identities and roles, the experience of nature—is only deferred until next day, exploding in a confrontation with white trash men in which the implicit meanings in these relations are violently made emphatic.

The hillbillies represent a rude irruption of the perverse dangers of male sexuality in this setting. The threat to the proper Self is dramatically figured in class terms when Bobby and Ed encounter two white trash men in the woods who take them at gunpoint. In the movie's most notorious scene, the threatening uncertainty posed by the uncivilized, natural male sexuality is externalized into a terrain of class conflict. Ed, in lofty tones, nervously smoking and fondling the tobacco pipe he has smoked throughout the film, makes distinct the class differences between them and their attackers. "Gentlemen, we can talk this over. What do you require of us?" "We *re*-quire that you get your ass up in them woods," one replies. The trashy features of the hillbillies—squinty eyes, bad teeth, filthy clothes, and rough language—are graphically accentuated in this confrontation.

Ed is lashed to a tree by his own belt, and watches, fairly fascinated, while Bobby is made to slowly strip. Bobby then breaks down in desperate pleading, trying to hug and hold his attacker while the hillbilly forces him against a log and sodomizes him. As their attention turns to Ed, the other hillbilly observes, "He's sure got a real pretty mouth." Lewis arrives in the background and fires an arrow into the back of the hillbilly holding the rifle, while the other white trash man escapes into the woods. Lewis has restored sexual order, asserting a disembodied, quasi-mythic phallus over the literal and perverse real penis of the rapist. The cracker's body is ruptured and spews blood. His gaze is empty and staring as he slowly collapses; his face glazes over in a gross caricature of the primitive's silent gaze. Lewis admires the phallus and its destructive power, fingering the blood- and gore-coated tip of the arrow protruding from the dead cracker's chest.

From this point on the body (literally of the trash man and figuratively of Man) is forefronted as the key problematic. Should it be turned over to the Law or buried and forgotten? Drew, playing the conscience of the group, insists that they take the body downriver and turn it over to the highway patrol and involve the Law. Lewis shudders at bringing the social world into the game of natural drama that is unfolding. He points out that "this is a mountain man, a cracker. That gives us something to consider." Invoking an enduring stereotype, he then argues that "all these people are related," and any jury chosen would probably be stuffed full of his kin. Unlike the families of the city men, which are detachable portions of their identity, kin is a tangle of relations, not clearly delineated or hierarchized. Such perverse relations negate the humanity of the dead cracker and justify his immediate disposal.

The body bears the contaminating result of disrupting the mythic order of the adventure and of sexually transgressing class boundaries. It has become grotesque.[11] The encounter with perverseness and the degradation that Bobby has endured are too much to bear, and so Lewis suggests, "Let's just forget the whole thing"—just bury the body. The city men assert an ability to efface the body and its marks, to return to the mythic state of adventure and not be hindered by this ruptured body. Shame is a relation of power; bodies bear its mark to the extent that they cannot achieve distance from its ruptures of decorum. The middle-class men assert their ability to dominate such relations by burying the marked body. Only by doing so can the Nature/Culture divide be resolidified.

Though the body seems contained, the proper Self of the middle-class men, contaminated by sexual contact with white trash and by the killing, begins to disintegrate. The men fight bitterly over how to proceed. Through the process of burying the body they are hurried on by the fear that the other cracker is watching them. He could be anywhere, or gone and got his kin. The feeling of being watched is a distinct sense developed by the camera movement that follows the men from behind trees that, at times, fill the whole frame. He is somewhere, anywhere, or maybe nowhere. Two terrors emerge here. One is of a pervasive, threatening landscape, animated in hostility by absorbing the lurking forms of the native. A fear of perversity disembodied, having erupted from the body, infuses the entire landscape. The other terror follows from the earlier image of genetic deficiencies due to perverse inbreedings, a consistent image of white trash. It is as if all distinctions have been washed out or become unintelligible. The intention of the trash men in the movie is consistently impossible to read; now their difference becomes bodiless and haunting. Decay also marks the remains of passion, of excess. Like the junked cars, the hillbillies are a site where desire has been used up and the passion of killing has worn off. This other threat of the wild, the erosion of distinctions, now affects the difference in the classed bodies.

The tangles of kin, of the woods, and of the grotesque body are what the city men must extract themselves from when they try to get going again. As they proceed downriver, the canoes enter a steep gorge. Drew, after looking ill and disturbed, topples from the canoe and is lost. In a moment, both canoes are overturned and the men tumble wildly down a steep waterfall. Lewis screams that Drew's been shot by the other cracker. They are trapped in the gorge, fearful of being shot if they try to venture further downriver. The clear frame that the narrative provides for the crude irruption of male sexuality has dissolved into a host of unrelenting uncertainties about where the threat is coming from. Was Drew really shot? Is the cracker up there waiting to kill them? The truth of the stereotype that the rape confirmed now seems unsteady, and the men are about to lose poise and control. They fear the descent into sheer desperation as much as they fear the nameless, invisible cracker. The repressed Self has been loosed in the first killing and now runs unrestrained.

Ed decides to scale the steep cliffs in the night to kill the hillbilly, who *must* be there. As dawn breaks, a man does appear on the cliffs. Ed takes him by surprise and quickly kills him with the bow and arrow. He exalts at his success, then suddenly freezes in horror as he gets a closer look at the man's face. "No! No!" he cries. The corpse looks different from the man he encountered in the woods. He, too, has a ruined, fouled mouth, but has false teeth. Ed fondles the man's face, almost affectionately, feeling for an identifying deformity, but collapses at last, uncertain whether this was the other cracker. Either way, there is another body to dispose of now.

In the following scene, an elaborate act of distancing from this ruptured, grotesque body is performed. Ed has to lower the body of the dead man down the cliff by rope so that it can be properly disposed of in the river. The perversity of the cracker or the desperation of the killing must be carefully removed. But as Ed is lowering himself by the same rope it breaks, and they both tumble into the water. He becomes tangled not only in the rope but in the dead man's arms under the water. Again he must extract himself from fatal perversity and ambiguity while wrapped in another man's arms. Bobby asks if he is sure this is the cracker, and Ed replies, "I think so." "It's not some hunter who was just up there?" Bobby whines uncertainly. "You tell me," Ed snaps back, but Bobby cannot tell.

The quality of this scene, as with so much of the movie, lies in the way the literal frame is drenched in figurative meanings. Ed's struggle with the dead man unfolds an archetypal struggle of Self with conscience, in this case, the other dead man, Drew. Ed's horror here is of the transformation that has

"Is this the right cracker?" A hillbilly character in the film *Deliverance* (1972, directed by John Boorman).

turned him from a domesticated man into a killer. He tried to kill the threatening Other but was perhaps mistaken. The innocent Self was washed down in the water with Drew's body, and the remaining Self slowly assumes the most terrifying aspects that once so neatly fit the projected Other.

When they find Drew's body further downstream, his arm horribly twisted out of its socket and wrapped around his head, they cannot tell if any of the skin's ruptures were caused by a rifle bullet from the cracker. They cannot read the ambiguous marks but decide to bury him in the river as well; he has been marked and contaminated by either the cracker or the river. As a casualty of ambiguity he must be disposed of. Bobby laments, "There is no end to it." Unlike the journey, which has a clear beginning and end, the encounters with the poor whites are an endless diffusion of meaning, irruptions that threaten to go on ceaselessly: a narrative out of control.

The drama of the movie now turns to a contest over narrative. After the last set of rapids, their surviving canoe drifts slowly by a half-submerged junked car in the river, the first signs of their departure from the realm of Nature. Ed reminds them that the sheriff will investigate, and he insists that they say everything happened at the last set of rapids so the police won't search upstream and find the other bodies. They construct an account that will explain away or efface their involvement with the trash. But uncertainties that undermine this narrative surface as the men come ashore near a town. Ed stumbles through the crushed landscape left in the wake of the dam's construction and, on reaching the road, finds their waiting vehicles. To his shock, the hillbillies kept their word and delivered the vehicles. The previous ambiguity over the second man's death gradually rises. A new nightmare begins as they are questioned by the sheriff. The clear bodily distinctions of class that they have previously encountered are no longer apparent: all of the locals have clean faces and straight teeth. A local hunter is mysteriously missing, and wreckage from their canoe is found upstream from the spot where they had agreed that "everything" happened. Their ability to control the narrative is uncertain.

Indeed, the structure of middle-class male identity and sexuality on the whole becomes uncertain. The repressions that restrain male homoeroticism seem to have produced projections as terrifying and dangerous as any reality encountered by the men when they stumbled into the woods. The movie relies on the stereotypes of white trash perversity to represent men being raped, demonstrating how the anxieties that animate those stereotypes are projected fears of the Otherness of poor white bodies. In the end, whether the projections or the stereotypes are more real doesn't matter as much as the demonstrated power over the world of the repressed wild Self of the middle-class male.[12]

But there is still the question of narrative that the movie marvelously dramatizes. Figured in this drama is much of what is at issue in understanding narrative as a theoretical or critical term. In one regard, the film illustrates Julia Kristeva's (1984) statement that narrative is always a gendered form of domination. The natives cannot account for the disappearance of the trash men and are left speechless, like little children. But Kristeva's formulation is too abstract and lacks a cultural sensibility. Narrative is not an absolute form; its structuring principles vary by class (Theweliet 1987). *Deliverance* exactly figures the culturally classed differences involved in a contest between two distinct narrative forms.

Like the clear-cut line of progress, in this narrative the middle-class men must detach themselves from the wreckage that lies in their wake. The poor whites disrupt this narrative intention with a host of details that protrude from this seamless account. The determination and challenge of wills that this involves is portrayed in a scene formed between Ed's cold stare and the sheriff's elusive and mumbling questioning, valorizing Ed's refusal to participate in the construction of meaning that storytelling necessitates (Stewart 1996). They refuse to help reconstruct events, leaving the community disrupted. The proper Self is back on stride with its narrative line that it must maintain against disruptions at all costs. But the bodies and the fantasies that Ed has tried to bury in his narrative refuse to stay put. As he is preparing to leave, he encounters an eerie scene. The bodies in the local graveyards are being dug up and moved to escape the rising waters of the dammed river. The movie closes with a nightmare: looking over the still, murky waters of the lake, a hand slowly breaks the surface and jarringly fills the frame. Ed jolts awake in his bed. There is no escape from the body that the narrative allegedly sealed over. And the Self, loose against its dangerous Others, now spreads out over the boundaries of fantasy and the real. In these drifting, haunted scenes is an unarticulated play of meaning that stands poised in the refuse of a civilized narrative, waiting to rupture that line.

We can sense this other dangerous aspect of narrative in the wreckage that the men's journey leaves behind. Trash involves a construction of meaning based in diffusion, of repeated tangles, and being stuck. The Self is disrupted and cannot remove itself, constructing meaning of events that leave open an unaccountable edge to the world. The ruptures are not sealed over, and the account becomes a diffusion of meaning through a compilation of details and images that are fed or heaped up in the story.

Too often, efforts to conceptualize culture rely on unconsciously classed perceptions of bodily conduct and narrative coherence.[13] As well, a certain sense of propriety deflects interest in such taboo objects of our culture as insults and degrading names. Ethnographies that include white trash seem at a loss as to what to do with the name (Foley 1990; Gitlin and Hollander 1970; Howell 1973). It appears as a bit of data, but the content and form of its designation seem analytically inaccessible.[14] The notion of white trash poetics, derived from the example of *Deliverance* and other mass-produced cultural objects, offers a means of understanding both the charged, degrading content of the stereotype and the formal class relationhips that structure its use and appearances (Fox 2004). This poetics is a means of grasping the aesthetic dimensions of class relations—in narrative and other expressive cultural forms—that too often are either dismissed as irrelevant to social analysis or disregarded by the use of value-laden artistic criteria that implicitly devalue products of "low" culture. Making these aesthetic aspects of class conflict the centerpiece of cultural analysis is the subject of the following chapter.

CHAPTER 5

TALKING TRASH:

WHITE POVERTY AND

MARKED FORMS OF

WHITENESS

Disadvantage is a key basis for assessing the significance of race in this country. Discrepant life chances associated with race are primary evidence that racial discrimination remains active and powerful. Cumulative forms of racial disadvantage—financial, social, and in terms of health—provide the grounds for generalized assertions about whiteness as a form of privilege and blackness as a condition of subordination. But a closer look at poverty and race in the United States should make us more cautious about such generalizations and the ambiguous complexities of racial matters. For instance, there are two glaring and enduring facts about poverty in this country: a disproportionate number of Latinos and African Americans are poor, but whites compose the majority of poor people in the United States. The first fact leads many commentators to stress the correlation between poverty and race, yet this emphasis dismisses or ignores the far larger numbers of poor whites. But does taking into account the condition of poor whites necessarily undermine an attention to the relationship between race and poverty? It should not. Analyzing the situation of poor whites actually provides a critical basis for grasping why and how race matters, but it does entail moving beyond generalized statements about whiteness and blackness.

Arguably the greatest insight generated by whiteness studies is the assertion that whites are racially interested and motivated social actors rather than unmarked, normative paragons of the mainstream. Yet this fundamental recognition is limited by the insistence that whiteness is strictly equivalent with forms of domination and privilege. If we are to understand the fast-changing significance of race—the way racial identities and formations are being remade and reinvented today—then we also have to examine whites who are not in positions of privilege. And we have to do this with specific attention to race, understanding it as more than an absolute bipolar relation of advantage and disadvantage or domination and subordination. Such an approach certainly risks muddying the view of the association between disadvantage and racial discrimination, but it brings an ability to understand race in a far more nuanced manner, which is necessary as racial matters become more complicated and mutable.

This chapter takes up this task by examining a series of labels for poor whites: hillbilly, redneck, and white trash. These marked forms of white identity each derive from and respond to the dissonance raised in the American cultural imaginary by linking whiteness and poverty. But they also reflect distinct forms of social positioning and cultural representations that lead us further in understanding how white racial identity operates. Usage of these terms in popular culture evidences the tangled interplay of cultural poetics and social conditions as poor whites articulate a discursive identity in the dense conflation of race, gender, and class. In contrast to an innocuous self-referent like "white guy," which makes a passing, often dismissive, self-effacing gesture toward acknowledging racial identity,[1] redneck, hillbilly, and white trash bear traces of the history of drawing boundaries between whites and people of color and of traditions of intraracial distinctions in this country. These terms emphatically inscribe a charged form of difference marked off from the privileges and powers of whiteness, each demarcating an inside and an outside to "mainstream" white society. Though it is easy to assume that these racial labels are synonymous, the differences from which they are historically derived and that they continue to inscribe reflect fundamental social dimensions to whites' lives and interests that are obscured by the concept of whiteness and are critical to the task of rendering this racial identity in specific terms rather than abstractions or generalizations. The manifold uses of these derogatory terms in U.S. popular culture offer an excellent means to grasp both the enduring intraracial dynamics that have long maintained the unmarked status of whiteness and the intriguing, complex current forms of name-calling that whites engage in as they attempt to navigate increasingly fraught social terrains in the United States from economically tenuous subject positions.

These terms reflect distinct processes of racialization and thus frame a challenge facing whiteness studies. Whites need to be examined not just as shaped by ideological operations of whiteness as a hegemonic construct, but as racial subjects. This entails recognizing whites as subjects whose identity is nested within a variety of overlapping discourses on belonging and differ-ence, generated in particular social relations, and indexing a host of cultural positions or statuses—and not simply as reproducers of latent or blatant forms of racism. Just as the broad cultural and political dimensions of blackness cannot be reduced to a response to racism, the significance of white racial identity, developed through class- and gender-based intraracial contests over belonging and difference, cannot be wholly equated with racist perceptions, beliefs, or actions. Tracking the uses of these epithets through popular culture in the United States today, where the racialness of whites is close to the surface, should make this point apparent.

Current uses of redneck, hillbilly, and white trash reveal critical dimen-sions of the stratified social terrain of white social identity, as well as the rhetorical means of boundary maintenance work that whites pursue in stabilizing and reproducing the homogenizing practices that both occult these differences and project an ostensibly nonracialized (i.e., unmarked) social position of authority and dominance. These instances of name-calling evidence the forms of decorum or etiquette that whiteness depends on for its hegemonic position and that are consistently threatened by the words, ac-tions, bodies, and lifestyles of various strata of whites who reveal the tenuous and artificial nature of these social conventions by their inability to conform to the decorums of whiteness. Tracking these terms in popular culture is a means to view gaps within the body of whiteness in order to understand how they may be further exploited.[2]

STOMPING ON BABY CHICKENS

There are few better places to begin such a survey than statements by John Rocker, a baseball pitcher initially with the Atlanta Braves, who incited a flurry of antiracist protest and commentary across the nation when he voiced his dislike for New York City in an interview in *Sports Illustrated* magazine. Rocker explained that his loathing for the city derived from "tak-ing the 7 train, looking like you're going through Beirut with some kid with purple hair and some queer with AIDS right next to you." He also complained about all the foreigners: "You can walk an entire block in Times Square without hearing a word of English" (quoted in Pearlman 1999, 60). These comments, among others from the interview, instigated a wave of public protests and accusations of racism against Rocker that led the commissioner of baseball to levy a stiff, twenty-eight-game suspension and $20,000 fine on Rocker. The beleaguered Rocker tried an interesting tack to counter his depiction as a clear public example of the enduring operation of white racism. In a subsequent ESPN interview, he insisted that he was not a "racist," just a "redneck." Rocker was soon traded to Cleveland, where he struggled to fit in with teammates and to get along with fans, due, in part, to his public notoriety. One source of conflict in the clubhouse came to light when Rocker derisively labeled a teammate white trash. However, this epithet received scant media attention and provoked no public outcry at all.

The example of Rocker helps to highlight distinctions in the usage of these three terms. Quite simply, redneck is something Rocker doesn't mind being; it is an identity that can be invested with valor, in contrast to the loathsome image of the white racist (though, for some, redneck and racist remain synonymous). In contrast, white trash is something even John Rocker holds in low esteem. It operates here intraracially, inscribing a sense of contempt and distinction that even a self-identified redneck and publicly pilloried racist feels is critical to maintain. The lack of public outrage over his use of white trash also evidences a key component of this term's operation. White, middle-class liberals learn very young not to use epithets with racial connotations, but they receive quite different messages from their parents concerning labels for poor whites, the most naturalized of which is white trash.

Rocker's is only one of many instances of the use of redneck in popular culture, but this form is the most common, featuring the term as a means of self-identification. There are certainly instances where redneck is applied in public contexts in a disparaging and dismissive manner, but most usage involves individuals claiming this marked social identity.[3] These forms of self-identification are distinctive in that they continually allude to the charged terms of difference between whites; they underscore rather than efface the distinctions that inform the severely sloped terrain of power and privilege of whiteness by animating and inhabiting the most extreme caricatures of white rural poverty and ignorance. Within this position of marked whiteness there are two distinct strategies employed by those who self-identify as redneck: one approach seeks to actively counter the stereotyped connotations of this label, whereas an opposite tack asserts a stance squarely within these disparaged features.

Two great examples of these different strategies of self-identification are the Redneck Games, held annually in Dublin, Georgia, and the American

Redneck Society. Membership in the latter comes with a year's subscription to the society's newsletter, the *Mullet Wrapper*, plus a certificate of membership, an inscription of the redneck creed—"Just because we talk slow doesn't mean we think slow"—plus two bumper stickers. The American Redneck Society uses the *Mullet Wrapper*, with a subscription base of ten thousand, to counter stereotypes of poor whites, such as those voiced by one reporter covering the society, who noted: "Apparently, not all rednecks look like extras from *The Dukes of Hazard* and decorate their lawns with old appliances. In fact, they come from all walks of life and from every corner of America" (Marchand 1997, 12). Against this grudging acceptance and fairly benign acknowledgment that rednecks might be everywhere—a point best evidenced by the enormous popularity of Jeff Foxworthy's comic routine, "You might be a redneck . . ."—other whites so labeled sound a very loud, contrary claim, asserting the disreputable, southern connotations of the term, as brazenly promoted by the Annual Redneck Games.

This event, which has drawn a combined crowd of fifty thousand people between 1996 and 2003, puts on display a range of buffoonish activities that purport to represent this distinctive white tribe. Contests feature bobbing for pigs' feet, hubcap hurls, seed spitting, the armpit serenade, and dumpster diving; festivities commence with a ceremony displaying a propane torch. As the torch suggests, the games originated as a spoof of the Olympics and other established athletic venues. Confederate flags are displayed enthusiastically, either worn emblazoned on shirts, hats, bikinis, or pants or hung on boats and campers or carried about on poles. The mud pit produces a bit of "color" on participants, viscerally marking their redneck status as one pale white body after another plunges into a mud pool to emerge dripping red. Such public performances might start out critiquing the stereotypes but end up actively reproducing them—perhaps because, in the end, participants tangibly feel the weight of the social distinctions that animate the stereotype and recognize that these cannot be easily dispelled. In that regard, why not at least retain an identity, one that does provide performative room for maneuver? As one of the Redneck Games organizers put it, observers "seem to think we are portraying Southern people as unintelligent, beer-swilling hicks." Rather, "we just like to have fun" (Pappas 1999, 45).

Such public displays by rednecks are not merely reflexive responses to widely circulated, disparaging depictions of lower-class whites. Each element of these performances bears some link to actual social practices and a certain cultural condition. The most systematic attempt to survey the cultural content of redneck is quite likely Bethany Bultman's (1996) *Redneck*

Heaven: Portrait of a Vanishing Culture. Bultman compiles beliefs and practices, stories and traditions, even recipes and advice that define and inform "redneck culture," which she argues evidence Celtic origins.[4] Bultman travels the nation interviewing people who both claim this charged label and follow a set of "codes" or "values" that she discerns as central to "redneck ideology." These largely hinge on Attitude, "a genetic inability to kiss butt," derived from both the necessity and the willingness to flout social conventions. Jim Goad's (1997, 84) *Redneck Manifesto* asserts a similar definition: "A redneck, as I define it, is someone both conscious of and comfortable with his designated role of cultural jerk. While hillbillies and white trash may act like idiots because they can't help it, a redneck does it to spite you. A redneck is someone who knows you hate him and rubs that in your face." This antagonistic, disparaged stance can be seen as informing a core of cultural practices from music to athletics to work. Bultman's compilation of aphorisms, culinary practices, forms of ingenuity, sexual habits, styles of labor and recreation, and devotional dispositions amounts to a range of cultural practices framed by, but not reducible to, responses to economic constraints or social stigmatization. This cultural view, though, is predicated on a charged contrast to hillbillies and white trash, who, as Goad notes, "can't help" the way they act, reflecting brute economic determinism rather than cultural identity.

The core feature Bultman discerned in redneck, a socially boisterous Attitude, also often undercuts claims to a serious and coherent cultural identity. In its place, the transgressive dimensions of redneck countervail against efforts at asserting a "respectable" identity in the stratified terrains of whiteness. An example of this tension is framed by two Web sites that, at first impression, seem to have a good deal in common. Dixie-Net and RedNeck.org each assert a form of separate southern white identity, rupturing a public decorum of whiteness that eschews direct invocations of racial self-identity; but each does so in ways that reflect "respectable" and "disreputable" class divisions. Dixie-Net features petitions for southern reparations as well as various states' rights efforts and in opposition to "Southern ethnic cleansing." The site also features the League of the South's Declaration of Southern Cultural Independence, which opens: "We, as citizens of the sovereign States of the South, proclaim before Almighty God and before all nations of the earth, that we are a separate and distinct people, with an honorable heritage and culture worthy of protection and preservation. Standing in the very place where our President Jefferson Davis stood in 1861, we declare that Southerners are entitled, like all peoples, to self-determination." The site is packed with notices of conferences and associations, links to journals and newsletters, and copious lists of events that promote white southern distinctiveness. Interestingly, my keyword search of the site for "redneck" revealed "no matches on this site."

RedNeck.org, on the other hand, wallows in many debasing images of poor, rural whites. The page opens with a warning that immediately asserts a sense of difference from the mainstream of white society: "Caution. You are entering RedNeck.org. Sissy Yankee Boys and eny uh y'all born north of the Red River, may need to git a note from yore mamma's or flash a lil red skin round tha neck ta git in. Don't step in anything, stomping around in here." The self-deprecating use of vernacular English and misspellings reflects the transgressive emphasis of the site, a point that is further underscored by the site's claim to be "more fun than stomping on baby chickens in yore bare-feet." Links, images, and text on the site conform to an aesthetic of the grotesque, featuring deranged deer hunters, sex with farm animals, public urination, and a slew of redneck jokes. Each caricatured depiction asserts a stance that, quite in contrast to the efforts of a site like Dixie-Net, inhabits, ratifies, and indulges stereotypes of poor rural whites, finding them enjoyable rather than abhorrent.

Tara McPherson (2000), in "I'll Take My Stand in Dixie-Net: White Guys, the South, and Cyberspace," assesses how such sites operate in the post–civil rights public discourse of the United States. McPherson deftly uses Dixie-Net as an example of how "cyberwhitening" occurs in online discussions and virtual communities. She finds that "the default setting is all too white" at this site, because discussions of racism are directly squelched and invocations of the South as an imagined community consistently promote an implicitly white racial subject. But McPherson asserts that it takes more than an attention to racism to analyze these sites because participants "do not believe themselves to be racist," and "labeling them and their cyberspaces as 'racist' does little to help us understand how they understand either whiteness or blackness" (124). After detailing how the play of images and texts interpellates the viewer into a white subject position, she then demonstrates how, by coining new languages and investing old signs with new meanings, these sites surprisingly fashion a "subaltern counterpublic." This leads Mc-Pherson to a challenging question: "What does it mean that white, mostly middle-class men—the group that we usually see as important players in the public sphere—feel the need for alternative publics?" She adds, "These men clearly see themselves as marginalized because of their southernness, and they actively construct spaces in which this origin can be discussed, celebrated, and protected from attacks, real or imagined" (126).

Whiteness, as McPherson (2000, 126) observes, is reproduced through these sites, particularly as discussions of white southernness couched in terms of ethnicity deflect attention to "the privileges whiteness confers and often functions as yet another form of covert racism." Yet McPherson also regards this experience of perceived marginality—exaggerated or not and certainly varied in its intensity along a continuum of class positions—as a means "to make whiteness strange" by amplifying the forms of difference its homogenizing practices obscure. In terms of the experience of social marginalization, we can discern in these two Web sites different strategies: one striving for the "respectability" of social practices like conferences, petitions, and redemptive, scholarly research to valorize this condition; the other, conversely, flouting social conventions and underscoring the debasing differences. This latter, redneck approach acknowledges the indelibleness of class markings and the interminable importance of class distinction in determining matters of belonging and difference.

The work of redneck in popular culture in the United States opens up a space within whiteness, one that clearly features the diacritics of class and regional difference that importantly score the social landscape of white identity. Caricatured behaviors and beliefs may be claimed as forms of self-identification under the label, but they still resonate with usages of the term to inscribe a contemptuous form of difference among whites. These connotations are notably on display in the computer game "Redneck Rampage." The designers claim that it is "far and away the most profane computer game in the history of mankind," which, along with the excessive amounts of blood and gore, are clearly a strong selling point. The distinguishing feature of "Redneck Rampage" is that it enthusiastically animates the most debasing tropes from the poor rural white stereotype. The representational dynamic is underscored by the fact that rednecks are the ones being slaughtered in the game. The storyline features "Leonard and Bubba's" efforts to "get back their prize-winning pig who's abducted by aliens . . . in the fictional town of Hickston, Arkansas." Players blast their way through country bars and trailer parks, slaughtering rednecks left and right. The game's promo reads: "If you thought navigating a melted-down Los Angeles or sneaking around ogres' castles was tough, then just try your hand a-whoppin and a-stompin the good ole boys at Stanky's Bar & Grill." Clearly, part of the allure here is bloodletting in a scene of socially disparaged poor whites.

Hillbilly applies to a social collective similar to that covered by redneck, but rather than defined by Attitude, its usage entails greater regional specificity and perhaps more historical depth and coherence. Public uses of hillbilly also provoke a sharper response from whites so labeled. Hillbilly burns sharply and poignantly in the memory of many poor whites and engenders strong antipathy. One source of this sentiment is that hillbilly has a longer record of use in the public domain than redneck; it entered the popular lexicon quite early and served active duty as an acceptable, derisive term. What makes the label insidious is that its connotations often seem comic and buffoonish rather than offensive, which renders its effects harder to confront. This comic dimension is underscored in the effort by CBS to revive *The Beverly Hillbillies* as part of their reality programming, featuring a new family of "real" hillbillies cast in today's Beverly Hills and offering Americans yet another way to see poor whites debased in public.

However, the most common current usage of hillbilly is in relation to music, reflecting the term's historical status in popular culture. In the 1920s, hillbilly was used by record companies to characterize and market the music being produced by whites in both rural and urban areas throughout the South. This marketing practice paralleled the "race records" approach of the major labels, segregating early jazz and blues recordings. In this regard, hillbilly was racialized as white but also clearly marked as distinct from the mainstream audiences and musical practices of white society broadly. Tony Scherman (1994, 42) relates how music producers and marketers tried to fix a label to this emerging regional style of music: "Record companies restlessly tried out 'Old Time Songs,' 'Old Familiar Tunes,' 'Mountain Ballads.' Gradually a single name emerged; mingling amusement and derision, it neatly encapsulated America's feeling about the new genre: hillbilly." Through fits of fashion and in conjunction with the dramatic midcentury demographic shifts in the United States as rural people migrated to industrialized urban areas, the popularity of hillbilly rose and fell over the next eight decades. Rural whites derided as hillbillies in the North at first took solace in the image and the music; as they assimilated to middle-class urban lifestyles, they gradually rejected the genre and the label. Beginning in the 1980s, hillbilly commenced one of several returns to modest popularity, reflecting discontent with white suburbia or the disillusionment of downward mobility and deindustrialization.

Hillbilly is currently enjoying a resurgence, as noted by *Billboard* magazine: "Now, a crop of current entertainers, including Toby Keith and Mont-gomery Gentry, are bursting out of the proverbial closet and proudly waving the hillbilly banner" (Jessen 2000, 60). These performers appeal to whites who find themselves distanced from middle-class society or on the fringe of economic survival. Montgomery Gentry's hit "Hillbilly Shoes" earned an early release from Columbia "because radio jumped on it early." Audiences were enthused over the song's depiction of righteous rejections of conde-scending social judgments. "You want to judge me by the whiskey on my breath / You think you know me but you ain't seen nothing yet / Till you walk a while, a country mile / In my hillbilly shoes." Studio executives characterize the group as "raw" and "gritty," claiming, "There's nothing slicked up here," invoking the rustic realism that is a consistent feature of efforts to aestheticize cultural expressions of poor whites. Strikingly, though music industry representatives in Nashville continually try to distance them-selves from the "hillbilly stereotype," they repeatedly are drawn back into reproducing and marketing just this imagery, largely because it is lucrative, with a strong appeal to those who feel distanced from white social forms of respectability and belonging (Appel 2000).

Hillbilly may command a significant market share in current popular culture, but it is not hard to find many accounts of those who are closest to the stereotype and resent the term, refusing its relevance and rejecting it as a form of self-identification (Goster and Hummel 1997). Nationally, attention to the disparaging features of this stereotype intensified during the period when Bill Clinton campaigned for and won the presidency. Hillbilly was a label alternately applied to Clinton, his running mate, Al Gore, and a key portion of his constituency—mostly rural southern whites. Particularly af-fected were white residents of Arkansas. As noted in the *Los Angeles Times*, "Eight years after Bill Clinton first ran for president, reporters there still seethe at the hillbilly image produced by outside reporters" (Kolker 2000, A15). One sustained response to this image is the documentary *The Ozarks*, which "attempts to counter the stereotype of the lazy, moonshining 'hill-billy' image of Ozarkers with a view of a strong, proud, hardworking and independent people."[5] But more typical are the kinds of first-person ac-counts featured in an essay in *Newsweek* titled "Who's a Hillbilly?," relating stories of rural whites who are unable to escape from the "hillbilly stigma." Author Rebecca Kirkendall (1995, 22), drawing on her personal experiences of being derided and disparaged in jokes and comments about her rural upbringing, reflects both on the reproduction of hillbilly stereotypes in popular culture and the curious way some whites participate in these forms of commercialization: "Despite their disdain for farm life—with its manure-caked boots, long hours and inherent financial difficulties—urbanites rush to imitate a sanitized version of this lifestyle. And the individuals who sell this rendition understand that the customer wants to experience hillbilly-ness without the embarrassment of being mistaken for one." The best examples of this are the booming novelty shops of Pigeon Forge, Tennessee, just outside the Great Smokey Mountain National Park, that purvey all forms of hillbilly caricature and stereotyping, largely for white southern tourists.

Social commentators, political observers, editorialists, and comedians throughout the 1990s deployed hillbilly stereotypes without much restraint, reflecting little of the self-consciousness that is increasingly afforded to depictions of ethnic and racial groups. Most notoriously, perhaps, the *Wall Street Journal* did not hesitate to ask in a headline "Who Is This Sex-Crazed Hillbilly?," referring to Bill Clinton (Ferguson 1996, A9). But the most intriguing dimension of uses of hillbilly in the past three presidential campaigns is the way it materialized across party lines. The same imagery that was invoked to characterize Clinton's supporters was also mobilized in relation to George W. Bush's 2000 campaign. In both cases, what mattered most was the sense of difference posed by lower-class, rural, southern whites. One story in *Time* featured a first-person account of a campaign reporter, Steve Lopez (2000), who leaves Bush's bus to head out on his own through the rural areas of South Carolina in order to understand Bush's popularity. Along Highway 178 Lopez stumbles into The Roadkill Grill and meets the people of the "hillbilly nation." "The hillbillies, it turns out, liked Bush, as did plenty of God-fearing family folk, party loyalists and the professionals who fit more comfortably into the new South Carolina." But in pursuing reasons for this support, Lopez found only confirmations of the most stereotyped features of hillbillies: "More often than not, when I asked people, 'Why Bush?' it was as if they had a zinc deficiency. The smile would freeze, the eyes would cloud and all signs of intelligence would fade" (36). This image reproduces the most enduring representations of rural poor whites: faded or absent intelligence, stemming from some sort of indelible physical deficiency. Obviously, despite challenges to such stereotypes in the popular media, this image is entertaining enough and gives voice to anxieties sufficiently deep to warrant its continued circulation.

Though hillbilly imagery is caustically active from California to Washington, D.C., it has burrowed most deeply in Appalachia, where concentrations of poverty and illiteracy have long nourished its most disparaging connotations. Residents feel the impact of stereotypes that construe them as backward, lazy, and dangerous. This region has been exploited for over a hundred years by various corporate interests and government agencies, producing a degrading dynamic of dependence that continues to this day, accentuated by rampant environmental destruction caused by ongoing mining operations. Many whites in this region are far from powerful or privileged. School programs in Kentucky work to counter hillbilly stereotypes by imbuing a sense of positive cultural content through exposure to bluegrass music and other aspects of "mountain culture." Dan Hays, executive director of the International Bluegrass Music Association, relates, "Many kids who live in these mountain areas still suffer under the hillbilly stereotypes. If you can take something that's an important part of their culture and history and turn it into something they can be proud of, then they don't have to be ashamed of where they came from" (quoted in Simon 2001, 36). What's tricky about such a strategy is that it does nothing to drain the reservoirs of contempt that feed such stereotypes in the first place. Indeed, these efforts risk reanimating the very cultural distinctions that are the bases for disparaging uses of hillbilly.

"AND THERE IS NOT-US, THE WHITE TRASH"

Countering poverty-related shame is certainly a challenge in Appalachia, but more difficult problems arise for the poor whites with Appalachian roots scattered in pockets of inner-city neighborhoods in the Midwest. The prejudice and discrimination confronting urban Appalachians is well documented (Mead 1995; Obermiller and Philiber 1987; Pasternak 1994). Their rates of unemployment and dropping out of high school are double that of African Americans in some neighborhoods of Cincinnati, the city with probably the largest concentration of urban Appalachians. As has been the case since they first migrated to the midwestern cities, urban Appalachians face discrimination in hiring and housing because their accents, lifestyles, and relations are indelibly marked as hillbilly. Their situation underscores a basic point in relation to each of these forms of name-calling: these rhetorical identities make it clear that whites are not uniformly privileged or powerful because of their skin color. But the more fundamental point to be drawn from hillbilly, as well as redneck and white trash, is that these stereotypes derive their enduring currency from the way they ratify a host of anxieties that white Americans hold concerning the white underclass. This nexus of anxiety and contempt is clearest in uses and depictions of white trash.

If "hillbilly" burns, "white trash" brands. What distinguishes this term from the others is not the cultural content that it grounds, but the highly emotional response of loathing and disgust the image congeals among the middle class. Even among white lower classes, white trash is primarily a distancing technique before it is an identity. As with John Rocker's quote, claims to a redneck identity are frequently accompanied by disavowal of and distancing from white trash. A central dictum of the "redneck value system," according to Bultman, is to "never accept a handout, 'cause if you do you're white trash." Goad favorably contrasts rednecks to white trash, and as the Redneck Web site emphatically asserts, the first in the list of "What a Redneck Ain't" is white trash. We see in white trash the dynamics of distancing and boundary maintenance that informs redneck and hillbilly distilled into a concentrated and virulent form. Further evidence of this distillation is the effect on social perception of this rhetorical identity. Hillbilly and redneck easily conjure collective images of poor whites as a social order, but white trash, perhaps because it so keenly draws attention to breaches of racial decorum, singularly renders poor whites in isolation, as evictees from the social compact. Rednecks' anxiety over being perceived as white trash brings another dimension of this term's usage into view. The ease of this "misperception" reflects the fact that, in terms of cultural content (body type, lifestyle, and beliefs), these two terms can be regarded as synonymous. Thus, it is not the *content* to which white trash refers that distinguishes this term's usage. Rather, its rhetorical dimension demarcates an order of whites definable strictly by transgressions of the social expectations that maintain the unmarked status of whiteness and facilitate its claims to power and privilege.

White trash also demarcates the end of the class spectrum where extremes are heightened, thus allowing for bizarre transpositions to occur. White trash becomes chic in a way neither redneck nor hillbilly could ever attain. White Trash Charms is a line of jewelry from a designer in Los Angeles who bedecks Hollywood stars with bracelets, earrings, and necklaces festooned with diamonds, rubies, and sapphires bearing "trashy" logos such as "Lady Luck" and "Punk Rock." Across the country, in Manhattan, the East Village store White Trash sells "kitschy items" that cost hundreds of dollars. Or consider how the fall 2002 fashion season featured the theme of "dust-bowl glamour," heralded by a photo spread in the *New Yorker*'s "Style Special" issue that restaged Dorothea Lange imagery of poor white migrants bedraggled and besmeared in undershirts by Dolce & Gabbana, dresses by Chanel, and cardigans by Louis Vuitton. Yet another dimension of the way white trash chic operates is its invocation as an aesthetic, a representational approach that purports to merge high and low culture. The most recent example is the movie *Scotland, PA* (2001), an adaptation of *Macbeth* set amid the fast-food pits of rural Pennsylvania. Billy Morrissette, the film's director and writer, asserted, "I tried to keep it just pure white trash, with a touch of Shakespeare" ("Film Capsules," *Dallas Observer*, March 16–22, 2000). Similarly, Peter Steinfeld, the screenwriter for *Drowning Mona* (2000), characterized that movie's motif as "the white-trash *Murder on the Orient Express.*" In addition to these, films like *Poor White Trash* (1999) and *Joe Dirt* (2001) all claim free license to use poor whites as a stage for fashionably depicting themes that breach an array of social decorums, even for speaking out against whiteness and racism.

The forms of defensiveness that accompany redneck and hillbilly, discussed earlier, are not similarly generated by these uses of white trash, perhaps because the term's boundary maintenance work allows little room for valorized self-identification. As well, maybe with white trash we reach a terrain where the depravities facing poor whites are so stark or severe that representational struggles are simply not a priority. Among the various strata of poor whites, white trash most readily applies to those who cannot afford membership in the American Redneck Society or who have neither the time nor the social capital required to write angry letters to the editor over depictions of hillbillies in the *Wall Street Journal*, the *New Yorker*, or the *New York Times*.[6] Instead of angry outcries over such debasing uses of white trash, though, there is a notable resignification of the term under way in U.S. popular culture, whereby whites who have been subjected to the label claim it now as a form of self-identity. But grasping the cultural significance of the rise of rap star Eminem or the popularity of comedian Roseanne first requires a deeper attention to the way the label has long policed the spheres of public discourse in the United States.

The emergence of these and other self-professed white trash performers flies in the face of the traditional usage of this term to restrict a segment of whites, their interests and concerns, from being regarded seriously in public forums. Social critics use the term not just to specify a particular group but to degrade a certain condition or behavior. This is evident from Charles Murray (1993) berating "white trash culture" in the *Wall Street Journal* to Oklahoma governor Frank Keating characterizing methamphetamines as "a white trash drug" ("Oklahoma Governor Criticized" 1999, A32). Governor Keating made his usage of this label explicit, explaining that such drug use is practiced "by the lower socioeconomic element of white people, and I just think we need to shame it." The distinctive characteristic of this very public form of debasement or name-calling is to depict certain behaviors or thoughts, words or actions as outside the realm of social acceptance. And it applies wherever the traces of poor white social conditioning can be detected, as is evident in the surge of white trash references to Bill Clinton following his departure from office. As the *Boston Herald* proudly declared on the day following George W. Bush's inauguration, "The white trash is out of the White House. Our long national nightmare is over" (Carr 2001, A14).

But, as Clinton's resilience in the face of social contempt perhaps indicates, a notable transformation is under way in U.S. public discourse, a possibility best glimpsed in the rise of Eminem. "White trash" is derisively applied to the singer by cultural critics, but he also enthusiastically performs the poetics informing this abject cultural figure. Critics initially dismissed Eminem and, as with Kid Rock before him, by deploying "white trash" to levy their judgment. P. J. O'Rourke, writing in *Rolling Stone*, characterized Eminem as "a beyond-Faulknerean specimen of double-Y chromosome white trash who mimics all that's loathsome and stupid in ghetto thug culture—resulting in a toilet mouth recording." This characterization reproduces a hackneyed image of "bad breeding" in the extreme, but one that has yet to lose its social luster for "respectable" whites staring out at the likes of white trash. Eminem, as with Roseanne before him, responded to critics by embodying and performing the object of their condescension, claiming the degrading epithet as a form of self-identification.[7] In considering this claim, it is important to do more than assess the accuracy of this label or the authenticity of his usage: Did he really grow up as poor as he claims (Echlin 2002; Eddy 2000)? Rather, the important question is whether or how his usage draws from and reworks the connotations and representational elements of white trash in U.S. public discourse.

In a variety of interviews, Eminem described his impoverished childhood in Detroit as a white trash existence. He makes the claim lyrically as well, when he describes his upbringing in "If I Had" (Aftermath Records, 1999): "Tired of being white trash, broke and always poor / Tired of taking bottles back to the party store / Tired of not having a phone, tired of not having a home to have one in if I did have it on." But more than just claims about his personal past, Eminem performs white trash. Two aspects of his rapping style stand out in this regard. As several commentators have noted, though Eminem is drawing on the black aesthetic form of hip-hop, his nasal vocal style and the content of his lyrics clearly inscribe him as white; in crossing over or appropriating rap, he is not attempting to masquerade as black (Hancock 2003). Eminem is not just white but trashy, and he performs a distinctive fusion of signifiers of whiteness and impoverishment that have long composed images of white trash. Unlike any self-respecting black rapper, he performs an identity of stupidity and debasement. In "Role Model," he ironically asks, "Don't you want to be just like me?" then flushes out lurid details that figure both abjection and the grotesque: "I've been with two women that got HIV / I've got genital warts and it burns when I pee / I tie a rope around my penis and jump from a tree." He relies on tropes of being diseased, "clinically brain-dead," and having "mental problems" that extend back to the eugenics family field studies. And he even draws on images of incest, as in "Kill You" (on the *Marshall Mathers* LP, Interscope Records, 2000): "Just bend over and take it like a slut, okay Ma. Oh, now he's raping his own mother." Such lyrics both preemptively respond to critics' disparagement and fill out a stereotype that has a long history in American culture. And in "White America," he ominously invokes a "fuckin' army marching" of similarly debased whites rising up against the conventions and decorums of the white mainstream: "I've shoveled shit all my life / and now I'm dumping it on white America."[8]

Why, then, is he so popular? There are many answers to this question, as his performances encompass a broader range of elements than those addressed here. In his own assessment, Eminem stresses the fact that many poor white kids identify with his gestures and posturing: "What people don't realize is that there are so many poor white kids in America. They just go unnoticed, know what I'm sayin', just because of like, statistics. There's white trash in America, and as soon as they see a white-trash kid like me that lived a [expletive] life that they can relate to, then they go buy it because they understand it" (Wartofsky 1999). This claim links his familiarity with minimum-wage existence and all of its forms of debasement (in "If I Had," he describes being "tired of jobs starting off at $5.50 an hour" and "tired of being fired every time I fart or cough / tired of having to work as a gas station clerk, for this jerk breathing down my neck, driving me berserk / I'm tired of using plastic silverware") with his transcendence of those conditions, as in "Who Knew," which relates how, in the past, "I used to get beat up, peed on, be on free lunch, and change school every three months."

Does the success of Eminem herald a transformation of white trash?[9] If so, the most intriguing dimension of the alteration of meanings associated with this epithet will be its racial boundary-crossing popularity (L. Holloway 2002). But whether or not Eminem's megastar status will transform his representativeness as white trash, the term's enduring usage will also continue to be to inscribe contempt and loathing between whites. This work typically is removed from public scrutiny and all the more effective for its ability to not draw undue attention—except for those rare occasions when the boundary maintenance work of the term is dragged into the open, as it was when Lizzie Grubman, a New York publicist, rammed her wealthy father's Mercedes-Benz suv into a crowd outside a Hamptons nightclub, injuring sixteen people before fleeing the scene. This appalling act was instigated when a bouncer asked her to move the vehicle from a fire lane. She spat the epithet "white trash" at him, then turned the suv into a weapon, injuring the bouncer and others in the crowd in the process. This incident is instructive not simply because Grubman used the term but also because this was one of those rare instances when its usage was publicly critiqued and evaluated for its implications and assumptions. A host of social critics commented, and their reflections offer an excellent synopsis of the boundary work accomplished via this label.

For upper-class whites who noticed, Grubman's usage was primarily a mortifying breach of etiquette, in that it led to a public spectacle. An essayist for the *Washington Post* used this incident as an opportunity to opine that "it has not been a well-mannered summer" and to discuss her informal investigation of whether the "social graces have disappeared," an endeavor that involved keeping close "track of every service interaction I've had" over the summer, assessing the distinction between informality and indifference with plain rudeness and disrespect (Janis 2001). Another essayist, in the *Hartford Courant*, also used this incident to nominate Grubman as "the poster girl for bad behavior" for her indiscretions. However, she was cited as just one among a host of "famous faces [who] seem to be working overtime these days at cursing, bending the truth, evading responsibility and airing their dirty laundry" (Morago 2001, D1). Such commentators fixated on the rupture of decorum of being caught publicly using such a vulgarism enacted by social climbers like Grubman.

Another line of commentary fixated on the uneven social terrain illuminated by Grubman's usage. Roberto Santiago (2001), in an editorial in the *New York Daily News*, pointed out that in her use of white trash, Grubman "made a social statement: 'white trash' remains the only slur that is not labeled as hate speech—and the only slur used unabashedly by all races." Santiago notes that, with a term like white trash, there is no reciprocal, equally visceral, debasing, or morally charged name for upper-class whites. "In a fair world, 'white trash' would refer to those who sneer at maids, doormen, messengers and minorities. But because the slur is all about white class distinctions, the worst one can call a Lizzie Grubman is a pampered, spoiled brat." Perhaps reflecting on the rise of white trash chic, Santiago commented further, "Sad to say, the final arbiters of what is 'white trash' and what is 'cool' are the world's Grubmans. Body piercings, tattoos and Harleys used to be 'white trash' but now are embraced by the socially hip." A view from England, the land where class culture has long been a central obsession, was conveyed in the *Daily Telegraph* by Zoe Heller (2001), who observed, "For the most part, the media have pitched the Grubman story as class war—a story about rich, 'arrogant' blonde girls using enormous cars given to them by their daddies to mow down the little people. This doesn't preclude a certain kind of aspirational voyeurism of Miss Grubman's 'lifestyle'—gleeful accounts of where Lizzie gets her hair blown out, articles of advice from fashion experts on how she should 'tone down her pampered look' for her court appearances, and so on." Heller's attention to the upper-class fascination with this spectacle extends further, as she comments on the multivalent nature of this epithet and the way its derisive social charge can cut in many directions at once: "For all their private outrage on behalf of the humble working stiff, the reporters covering this debacle have betrayed a distinct snobbery of their own—a disdain for uppity Jewish princesses with too much privilege and no real 'class.' As far as the hacks are concerned, it's Miss Grubman who's white trash and this, no doubt, is why they have felt so free to stick the boot in." Quite in excess of whatever cultural content or social position may be considered proper as this term's range of reference, Heller identifies the premier purpose of white trash as a form of social distancing: inscribing an inaccessible upper sphere as well as a debased lower realm.

Finally, an editorial in the *Washington Post*, in what I assume to be a sarcastic vein, declared "pity Miss Grubman. She is a victim of our culture if ever there was one. How was she to know that it was impermissible to run over white trash? Miss Grubman knows what we all know. There is us—us in the VIP rooms, us in the VIP schools, us in the VIP jobs. And there is not-us, the white trash, and there are very different rules for what each can do to each other" (Kelly 2001). Uses of white trash inscribe and make emphatic a realm of "us" and "not-us" for whites. On one side are all the social practices, conventions, and resources, access to which assure whites a privileged and powerful status in this society. On the other side are all those reminders of both the artificial nature of these conventions and the tenuousness of claims to these resources. Antiracist critiques have long targeted "naturalizing" discourse in relation to assertions of social superiority, but the manifold ways these discourses operate in relation to class identities is largely unacknowledged in the public sphere. White trash insists on the naturalness of class identities, but in every instance of its usage one can detect as well the anxious uncertainty as to how long or how well those identities will be maintained in the face of changing economic or social circumstances.

The distinctions among these key terms—rednecks, hillbillies, and white trash—are tangible and active, reflecting historical developments and varied current circumstances for lower-class whites. But these distinctions do not countervail against the fundamental similarity that links each term: they demonstrate that the social landscape of whiteness is far more complicated than we can comprehend via assertions that it is generically an unmarked, hegemonic identity. These terms reveal contests over belonging and difference in relation to whiteness that are fundamentally shaped by class. Historically, these terms have been deployed and projected to maintain the unmarked status of whiteness. But the range of current usage of these labels suggests that this tradition is changing and that poor whites are carving out identities that reference a condition of relative disadvantage within the privilege of whiteness. This identity is tangible but multivalent, shifting in intensity of its effects—at times no more real for some whites, in social terms, than any other "symbolic ethnicity," while for other whites it is a daily inscription of social contempt and distance.

These terms specify class and regional distinctions in a manner that demonstrates that assertions about whiteness as an unmarked normative identity are only a starting point for thinking about how race matters in relation to white social identity. Their usage in popular culture also offers only an initial glimpse of the forms of significance that animate white racialness. To comprehend more fully how white racial identity is constructed and experienced it is necessary to move from the realm of representations to that of the field, to the social settings where white people perceive and project race in dense daily circumstances. The following chapter pursues this level of inquiry, but it also portrays the difficulties inherent in empirically framing social circumstances. No perspective from the field is ever transparent; rather, such views are always predetermined by theoretical orientations, political interests and debates, and the biases inherent in human observations.

Eminem makes much of his experiences in Detroit, but does he represent the white underclass in that city? Chapters 6 and 8 represent my effort to examine poor whites in Detroit: first, in relation to debates about social science knowledge production concerning poverty; then, in terms of critical deployments of the whiteness concept. To do so, I engaged in debates about the urban underclass and the role race played in producing the conditions of concentrated poverty in American inner cities. As suggested by my comments in opening this chapter, I found that theoretical and political debates and discourse on urban poverty revolved around and reproduced delimited meanings of race. As well, I realized that much of the social knowledge being produced about the urban underclass is generated at a great remove from the actual circumstance of these people's daily lives. What I encountered in Detroit was surprising, in terms of both social science definitions of race and popular impressions of the urban underclass. Chapter 6 strives to convey the novelty of circumstances in the inner city, but it also represents my effort to depict the conditions of poor whites in that city within the overdetermined political and theoretical discourses on race in the United States. The term "urban underclass" is only obliquely useful for representing people, particularly poor whites, living in the inner city, but it is a term that can be usefully wielded to think critically about academic discourses on race and class.

CHAPTER 6

GREEN GHETTOS AND

THE WHITE UNDERCLASS

This brings us to the emergence of a white underclass. In raw numbers, European-American whites are the ethnic group with the most people in poverty, most illegitimate children, most women on welfare, most unemployed men, and most arrests for serious crimes. And yet, whites have not had an "underclass" as such, because whites who might qualify have been scattered among the working class. Instead, whites have had "white trash" concentrated in a few streets along the outskirts of town, sometimes a Skid Row of unattached white men in large cities. But these scatterings have seldom been enough to make up a neighborhood. An underclass needs a critical mass, and white America has not had one.

—Charles Murray, *Wall Street Journal*, October 29, 1993

The "urban underclass" is a notorious social science objectification that generates large amounts of research and intense criticism of the representational dynamics related to this concept.[1] As with white trash, urban underclass is a degrading label, keyed to "socially deviant" behaviors that transgress middle-class decorums rather than to economic and social dynamics, to the point of obscuring these important dimensions. Similarly, images of both play crucial roles in processes of middle-class identity construction (see chapters 1 and 2). Depictions of the urban underclass, whether in sensational journalistic accounts or in reserved academic reports, shore up the conviction of middle-class whites that *those people* are different—debased and abhorrent. The important distinction between these terms, though, is that the urban underclass became an object of social knowledge production, whereas white trash still largely operates in the realms delineated in the previous chapter. This chapter considers the question of whether the debasing label, urban underclass, can be effectively deployed despite its stigmatizing connotations and in direct challenge to the tradition of stereotyping the urban poor from which it derives. The answer hinges, in part, on the extent to which the predicament of poor urban whites can be in some way figured through this charged objectification. The urban underclass progressed from a phrase used by journalists to serve as a key term for organizing and explaining social research on the drastic transformation of inner cities in the United States during the 1970s and 1980s. At its worst, the term served as a seemingly objective, scientific means of designating contemptuous, dangerous urban subjects. But it bore the potential, only half realized in the important work of William Julius Wilson, to articulate a new way of speaking about the significance of race. Wilson used the term in two novel ways: first, to move away from blanket generalizations about race, specifying racial dynamics in terms of class relations and spatial transformations, and second, to examine factors other than racism that were shaping the plight of inner-city residents. That these efforts to think differently about racial matters were only partially realized by Wilson should not preclude us from considering further, with circumspection, what the urban underclass can refer to and mean. This chapter pursues such a consideration by using the term in relation to concentrations of urban poor whites.

As with my attention to white trash, I am interested in "urban underclass" as much for what it can reveal about the assumptions we bring to the task of understanding the dense linkages between race and poverty as for its ability to objectify a certain social condition or subject position. In a manner similar to my use of white trash to get at the reservoir of contempt that animates the term, I deploy urban underclass not simply to render and analyze a social collective but also to understand the limits and presuppositions of social science discourses on class and race. This chapter critiques the preconceptions about race built into this concept that inhibit us from recognizing the forms of racial heterogeneity that are also an aspect of urban poverty. Grasping this heterogeneity, in turn, offers a basis both for critically rethinking homogenizing assumptions in racial analysis and for opening new perspectives on the conflation of race and class.

But I also turn to the urban underclass because it offers a means to move out of the realms of popular culture examined in the previous chapters. This social science concept is geared toward the task of examining social dynamics and can be deployed in objectifying the lived conditions of daily life. This terrain, though imbued with multiple forms of public culture, offers a different and crucial perspective on the key question of how race matters. Additionally, I wrestle with this concept because it offers a challenging angle onto the predicament of poor whites. To comprehend fully the multiple and rapidly changing ways race matters, we have to grapple with the situation of poor whites. This chapter shows the difficulties and potential in rendering the lives of urban poor whites via the concept of the urban underclass, with its clear and determined forms of racial coding. The term's debasing connotations remain active and require the sustained critical attention to representation that characterized earlier chapters. But, as with white trash, what matters most is that we objectify the relational dynamics in which these disparaging meanings operate and make them part of the overall account from the field that this concept permits.

As when Charles Booth strode into impoverished districts of London in the 1880s, we are in a moment when urban poverty, in the extremity of its transformation, compels close study and comprehension. But we may be no closer to understanding such conditions—even with all the sophistication of current statistical models and modes of ethnographic inquiry—because social science discourse still is informed by and actively reproduces the monstrous, demonized imagery of the poor that circulates broadly in popular culture. Perhaps we are even further incapacitated in this endeavor by the overspecialized academic approaches to race and class, which increasingly construe these fundamental social forms as distinct rather than coconstructed. The hope articulated here is that by transforming the processes of objectifying social subjects by encompassing the interests and imaginary of observers and audience alike, it will be possible to grasp something of a social setting that is so revealing of how race and class matter and, at the same time, reflectively comprehend the role social science plays in reproducing the very class dynamics it sets out to analyze.

Urban cores in the United States are transforming rapidly; they are home to novel social forms and complicated spatial transformations. From a distance, the inner city appears as a generic, nightmarish image in media representations, but up close and on the ground, in cities like Detroit, these collapsing central zones reveal disparate and highly nuanced cultural conditions. This chapter provides a glimpse of the inner city in Detroit, a zone that in many ways epitomizes the startling effects of deindustrialization in midwestern and northeastern cities. With its stretches of green fields where

The white underclass?
Photograph by John Hartigan Jr.

hundreds of houses once stood, the Briggs neighborhood, an area within a mile from the city's downtown, is hardly unique as an inner city.[2] However, the residents of this zone, where I did fieldwork from July 1992 through February 1994, make an uneasy match with characteristic depictions of the urban underclass (Hartigan 1999).

Before turning to Detroit, though, I want to confront two predicaments that shape social science representations of inner cities. One is that a preponderance of the knowledge produced about these sites is generated at a great physical and social remove. So much of what is known derives from statistical accounts that measure demographic change across census tracts. Obviously, such approaches produce critical insights that convey the drastic scale of changes affecting inner-city dwellers. We would be largely ignorant of the broad scope of transformations of urban life without quantitative depictions of economic shifts under way in the United States and across the globe. However, because many of the statistical registers rely on behavioral or lifestyle categories, it is precarious to depend so excessively on numerical renderings of conditions in these zones. Take, for instance, the assertions that the cultural uniqueness of the urban underclass is generated largely by inner-city zones themselves.[3] This may not be an invalid claim, but it remains a dubious assertion without concrete evidence that could confirm it, drawn from daily life among the disparate social groups within such neighborhoods (Hughes 1989). Ethnographers produce exactly this type of social knowledge (E. Anderson 1990; T. Williams 1989; Bourgois 1995; Sharff 1998); yet, the findings and approaches from ethnographic studies concentrated on issues of the urban underclass have made only meager inroads into the composite picture of what is known about the urban underclass.[4]

The second predicament involves uncertainty and ambivalence over how conditions in these sites are linked to race. What are the racial factors that have contributed to the emergence of inner cities where populations are vastly African American and Latino? Provisional answers to this question, derived, again, largely from statistical measures, paint these ghettoes in uniquely colored terms. Such answers, though, delimit our attention to the disconcerting complexity and nuance of how race continues to matter, not only in this country's ghettos, but in the political debates and the research agendas of those charged with objectifying these troubling sites. Whether or not this matter is adequately resolved or answered depends in part on our willingness to address core uncertainties about race broadly. As producers of social science knowledge we need to enter into a discussion, first, about the degree to which racial stereotypes active in the culture at large implicitly inform or affect the research done on these zones, and second, the extent to which we have been content to allow "racial" to refer solely to the behaviors, lifestyles, and speech of people of color.

In this predicament, ethnographers are no more above reproach than are demographers; their firsthand accounts have done little to challenge racialized perceptions of the inner city.[5] The problem is that poverty and blackness are largely synonymous in the minds of most white Americans. Combine this presentiment with the overwhelmingly disproportionate presence of African Americans in the urban underclass population, and you have a cultural representation that is difficult to deconstruct. My point here is not to provide either more "positive" views of inner-city residents or penetrating indictments of the racist nature of American culture. Rather, I want to suggest that the novelty of urban conditions provokes a rare opportunity to fashion an equally innovative attention to the subject of race and its continuing cultural significance in the United States. Taking advantage of this opportunity, though, depends on our ability to move closer to these sites, attending to their unique and their stereotyped elements; it, too, hinges on whether, as social scientists, we are willing to examine and challenge what is presumed when we argue and talk *about* race.

Conditions in Detroit, a city used to epitomize the apocalyptic meanings that social commentators have read into the emergence of inner cities, allow the implications of these two predicaments to be both displayed and revised

(Chafets 1990; Herron 1993). For all of the routinized scenes that are drawn from this city to illustrate the extreme effects of deindustrialization, Detroit also provides a glimpse of the emergent social forms still grasped only clumsily in the rhetoric of social scientists. The physical nature of slums here is being reconfigured. The key problem is no longer overcrowding, with its correlates of ill health and rampantly spread diseases. Rather, those who remain living in the deteriorating housing stock in the blighted zones of this city are threatened primarily by a collapsing infrastructure that can no longer support its extension over residential areas that have lost more than a million people in the past forty years. When I began fieldwork in the Briggs neighborhood, the most striking aspect of this area was the vast expanse of green fields that dominated the landscape. On some blocks, only one or two houses remain standing, and there are no blocks that retain all of their structures. In this neighborhood of 0.6 square miles there are more than 450 vacant, grass-covered lots (U.S. Bureau of the Census 1990). On summer days, the loudest sounds are from crickets, and pheasants hide in the tall grass.

Briggs is one of many Detroit neighborhoods where fields now outnumber houses. The city's population peaked in 1952 at just under 2 million people. This apex was hardly evident at that moment, as city planners were still imagining and designing an infrastructure for a projected population of around 3 million. Who could have predicted the severe hemorrhaging of people that was soon to follow? Between 1950 and 1990, Detroit's white population declined by 1.3 million; today approximately 1 million people still reside in this city, which continues to lose residents to the suburbs.[6] As a result, the city is pockmarked with huge empty spaces that officials are dubious about ever refilling with residents. This unusual situation has forced a search for equally unique solutions.

Borrowing a metaphor from the corporate maneuvering that has transformed the world of work in the United States, city ombudsman Marie Farrell-Donaldson in March 1993 suggested that the city begin "downsizing" its operations.[7] Because it has become too expensive for the city to provide basic services to neighborhoods that many residents have long since left, the downsizing plan called for relocating remaining residents in sparsely populated areas, preferably moving them into the seven thousand to twelve thousand vacant city-owned houses, razing whatever structures are still standing, then fencing off these zones and letting them go "back to nature." The plan was dubiously received by city politicians, but many Detroiters (60 percent in a *Detroit Free Press* poll)[8] favored the idea as a beneficial

solution to the problems arising from their increasing isolation in neighborhoods where vegetation is reclaiming sidewalks and illegal dumping is destroying streets.

Residents in these neighborhoods are ambivalent about the fields that
now surround their homes, fields that symbolize the city's inability to provide basic services that any urban dweller might expect. In Briggs, people
joked about bringing in cows to graze or running horses in the "meadows."
Such an arrangement, they laughed, would crimp drug dealing in the area:
"You can't sell crack to cows," one old white man told me. More practically,
though, they found numerous uses for these overgrown lots. Large gardens
of corn, tomatoes, greens, and other vegetables spread over lots that once
held houses. Another popular use is to turn empty corners into car repair
sites. Pickup trucks converted into homemade wreckers tow cars to and
from these corners, as junkers are turned back into operating vehicles or are
cannibalized for parts until they are sold for scrap. These uses are an active
means of countering one of the hazards that result from all this open space:
illegal dumping. As in the city at large, the primary product dumped here
is used tires. By conservative estimates, over 2 million tires are illegally
dumped in such fields all across Detroit.[9] These piles house rats and occasionally catch fire, burning and smoldering for days at a time.

At first glance, Briggs epitomizes conditions in Detroit generally. But this
neighborhood highlights the uneven effects of seemingly uniform processes
such as white flight and deindustrialization that summarize what happened
to large urban areas in the United States. The population in Briggs began
declining after 1930, at a time when this area was home to approximately
twenty-four thousand people dwelling in six thousand housing units.[10] Today, fewer than three thousand people live in this inner-city zone, and only
about twelve hundred housing units remain.[11] The inner city in Detroit was
taking shape even while the city was experiencing unprecedented economic
growth and increases in population due to the boom in wartime production
during the 1940s (Darden et al., 1987; Sugrue 1996). As well, the economic
and social problems in this zone largely predate the massive shift in racial demographics. White residents began leaving this neighborhood before
blacks began moving in large numbers to the area. And while whites have
poured from the city, until those that remain account for just 22 percent
of the population, Briggs continues to be a white-majority neighborhood;
52 percent of the population is of European descent. Although white flight
has been a convenient and largely objective means for labeling a crucial
factor in Detroit's deterioration, it has also somewhat distorted the racial

contours of this particular green ghetto. The whites that remain in Briggs today demonstrate that whiteness did not entirely take flight from this city.

The preponderance of whites in Briggs undermines the neighborhood's representative quality in relation to Detroit at large; its ability to epitomize conditions in the city is also undercut because economic conditions are much worse here than in Detroit as a whole. As Table 1 indicates, the proportion of residents in Briggs living below the poverty line is larger than for the city as a whole.

Given the extent of blight and social disadvantage in Briggs, is it clear that this is an underclass neighborhood? Researchers and social commentators generally agree that underclass refers to novel transformations in the structure of class relations across the United States, yet there is still much debate over how this "new" stratum is to be defined, typified, and analyzed. One strategy focuses on the geographic concentration of the poor in urban areas; another tracks behavioral indicators regarding the rates of joblessness, female-headed households, high school dropouts, persistent low income, and reliance on public assistance.[12] These measures demonstrate that inner-city neighborhoods are radically different places from any that ever existed in the United States before; they also make clear that African Americans and Latinos disproportionately occupy these neighborhoods.[13]

Briggs fits part of this description. It is an extreme poverty zone where 47 percent of the households are female-headed with children, where only 34 percent of people over 25 have a high school diploma or a GED, where the unemployment rate has stood for the past twenty years at more than 20 percent, where 51 percent of the total population and of the children age 17 and younger live in poverty. This neighborhood is also predominantly white. The case of an inner-city neighborhood that is so white runs counter to scholarly and popular images of underclass areas. Although Briggs may not be representative of Detroit in most regards, in terms of the city's poor white population, this neighborhood is quite typical.[14] In Detroit, these whites complicate the assumption that the underclass is a uniquely racialized phenomenon.

From its earliest uses in social science and political discourses in the United States, "underclass" has borne a clear racial component.[15] The concept gained broad resonance and notoriety with journalist Ken Auletta's (1982) work *The Underclass* and was further elaborated by William Julius Wilson (1987) in *The Truly Disadvantaged: The Inner City, the Underclass, and Public Policy.* Wilson used this term specifically "to depict a reality not captured in the more standard designation *lower class.* In my conception, the

Table 1. Statistics for Underclass Status, in percentages

	1980		1990	
	Briggs	Detroit	Briggs	Detroit
White	54.5	33.4	52	21.6
Female-headed households	46	40	63	46
Households with children				
High school graduates, or GED	32	54	48	61
People in poverty:				
Total population	48	22	51	32
Children age 17 and younger	61	32	51	32
Persons age 65 and older	41	32	80	42
Unemployment Rate	22	18	28	18
Households on public assistance	38	21	38	26

Sources: U.S. Census of Population and Housing, 1980, 1990 (Summary Tape Files 1A, 3A); Planning Department, City of Detroit, Report no. 34, January 1986; Gerald Leudtke and Associates, Detroit, "Briggs Community Survey," 1991.

term *underclass* suggests that changes have taken place in ghetto neighborhoods, and the groups that have been left behind are collectively different from those that lived in these neighborhoods in earlier years" (8). The "collective difference" that Wilson particularly highlighted was racial: the dramatic outmigration from central cities has left behind populations that are predominantly nonwhite and poor. Yet, conditions in Briggs, as in other sites of concentrated poverty where large numbers of whites reside (Alex-Assensoh, 1995), suggest that assumptions about racial formations and identity need to be reexamined as part of the ongoing debate over how to analyze the underclass.[16]

In *The Truly Disadvantaged*, Wilson emphasized the fact that very few whites live in the areas of most concentrated poverty. Although that may be the case nationally, the situation in Detroit, a city that, for Wilson and others, epitomized the new reality of the underclass, presents a more diverse racial picture. In Detroit in 1990, 52,148 whites lived in census tracts where the poverty rate exceeded 40 percent.[17] Whites occupy neighborhoods that are distressed (tracts with high levels of poverty and joblessness, female-headed households, teenage school dropouts, and people drawing public assistance income) and severely distressed (which includes the above indicators plus "exceptionally high" rates of school dropouts) in greater numbers than in any of the other ten largest cities in the United States. In Detroit, 87,149 whites live in distressed and 47,977 in severely distressed neighborhoods.[18] In New York, 77,036 whites live in distressed areas, and only 12,921 whites dwell in severely distressed areas. The distressed portions of Chicago are home to 19,525 whites, and only 5,902 whites in Los Angeles live in such neighborhoods; the severely distressed areas in Chicago hold 5,781 whites, and in Los Angeles only 3,373 whites live in such zones. These figures suggest that the white underclass may be an unusual class formation in that it manifests unevenly across urban areas and the scale or scope of its identity is greatly contoured by local conditions.[19] Surprisingly, Detroit is the one city in this country that best exemplifies the presence of a white underclass.

The emergence of a white underclass has been heralded with catastrophic imagery and language by social scientists, politicians, and policy advocates and experts (Page 1993; Will 1993). The white underclass shifts the polemical aspect of how to characterize *those people* (i.e., poor, white, inner-city dwellers) into a scientized realm of allegedly neutral detachment. The white underclass was initially publicized by Charles Murray in the *National Review* in 1986; he used the term explicitly to counter a growing unease among social researchers over the not so subtly racialist aspects of their obsession with the underclass generally. Acknowledging that the relentless equation of antisocial behavior among the poor with African Americans living in poverty had a racist air, Murray announced, "At this moment in the dialogue about the underclass, there is no more salutary activity for whites than to inquire into the nature of white illegitimacy, illegitimacy being perhaps the best symbol for the social and family problems of the poor who stay poor" (30). He further elaborated on the notion of a white underclass in the *Wall Street Journal* (1993) by contrasting this "new" population with the group he refers to as white trash. The difference, he asserts, lies in the increased concentration of poor white families in inner-city zones, whereas white trash historically referred to a few isolated individuals or families.

The working definition of the white underclass proffered by Murray involves an interesting, though often overlooked dynamic of racial discourse in this country by which intraracial distinctions are drawn. But before considering this point further, I must make clear the stakes in coloring the face of the underclass. Wilson, whose research has primarily set the terms of debate on the underclass, crafted a complex evaluation of how race and poverty interrelate. Initially, in *The Declining Significance of Race: Blacks and Changing American Institutions*, he made the case that class divides among African Americans have steadily developed since the 1960s, to the point that "the life chances of blacks have more to do with their economic class position than with their day-to-day encounters with whites" (1978, 1). He characterized the contemporary United States as becoming increasingly dominated by class inequalities over racial inequalities. In his subsequent study, *The Truly Disadvantaged*, Wilson took pains to note that the population that resides in the zones with the highest concentrations of poverty and social disadvantage— his central defining characteristics of the underclass—is disproportionately black: "Whereas the total white population in the extreme-poverty areas in the five largest cities increased by 45 percent and the white poor population by only 24 percent, the total black population in these areas increased by 148 percent and the poor black population by 164 percent" (1987, 46–47). Wilson highlights this discrepancy to make the effects of racist institutions clearly recognizable as a factor in the plight of inner-city blacks, and he dismisses the notion of a white underclass by calling attention to the disproportionate extent of white and black experiences of extreme poverty.[20]

The crux of this matter is a question of scale. At stake is the possibility of quantifying a calculus of social disadvantage by which an equation can be drawn demonstrating that the magnitude of black suffering clearly indicates a racial or racist determinant. This "new" population is predominantly black, but it is not so absolutely. Dismissing the 45 percent increase of whites in extreme poverty areas may make a racial analysis more compelling or convincing, but it also distorts the racial heterogeneity of the populations that dwell in such zones.[21] The assignment of "racial" to a particular problem or condition has largely been an all-or-nothing matter: the underclass registers as a racial problem when this distinctly colored group reaches an order of magnitude that borders on absolute. But, in making the case that whites, too, are part of the underclass, does this necessarily mean that race is no longer a factor in its development?

"Racial problems" typically refers to intergroup conflicts and discrepancies, as if race was solely manifest in corporally distinguishable populations whose uneven social positions derive from lengthy histories of exploitation and domination. In this line of approach, the underclass is one more instance of the racialist domination that whites continue to maintain in this country. But there is no reason the analysis of racial matters need be as simplistic as the binary logic relentlessly alternating between black *or* white dictates. As the social orders in the United States (especially within its cities) become more complex and heterogeneous, social scientists must develop analytical approaches that are adequate to the novelty of these forms and identities. Acknowledging the presence of whites in the underclass does not negate or counter the role that racism plays in confining large portions of the black population to the new green ghettos in our cities. Rather, calling attention to the white underclass suggests that, inevitably, "racial" also involves complex intragroup dynamics of social differentiation.

This becomes apparent when we return to Murray's assessment of the white underclass. Ostensibly, he drew attention to a certain strand of poor whites to alleviate the impression of racist motivations on the part of social scientists who obsessively and voyeuristically document the social "failings" of poor blacks. Yet, the way he makes a case for the existence of this distinct class reveals a more convoluted set of interests. Murray defines the white underclass by deploying what he titles his "white trash hypothesis," which stresses the way rates of illegitimacy among a certain group of whites now rivals the rates that held for blacks in the 1960s, rates that prompted Daniel Patrick Moynihan's public panic and prophesies of impending social collapse. In contrast to the "misguided" "Farah Fawcett hypothesis" (Murray's coinage), which suggests that illegitimacy among whites is a phenomenon that crosses class lines (movie stars being the most prominent "class"), Murray offers the

> "White Trash Hypothesis," which has been around for as long as parents have lectured children, and which says that illegitimacy is essentially a lower-class phenomenon. The children of good families don't get pregnant, and if they do get pregnant they get married, or, these days, they get an abortion. We cannot measure from census data whether or not someone is from a "good family" or "white trash." We can, however, measure poverty and levels of education in a community and thereby ask whether or not a link exists between illegitimacy and socioeconomic class. (1986, 31)

Like white trash before it, in Murray's use of the term white underclass operates a key policing mechanism by which whites are intraracially distinguished. Whiteness, in this sense, is hardly a given property of white bodies (Weismantel 2001). The realm of social privilege and power that is broadly equated with whiteness in this country is also keenly a matter of class position and status within that racial order. The conclusion that Murray points to "is that there does seem to be a white underclass, and the illegitimacy problem among whites is concentrated there, not in white society as a whole" (35). In this usage, the unmarked propriety of white decorum is maintained by delimiting a social problem among the dominant racial order in the United States to a "stupid" subset.[22]

In this judgment, Murray neatly effaces the connections between whites in some innocuous "mainstream" where "middle-class values" still reign and those who are mired in the same conditions that are equated with the condition of blacks and blackness in this country. This scholastic act of boundary maintenance is reproduced, playing an even more critical role, in Murray's most audacious effort to demonstrate the natural order of social hierarchies, his collaborative work with Richard Herrnstein, *The Bell Curve: Intelligence and Class Structure in American Life* (1994). Essentially, Herrnstein and Murray assert that naturalized registers such as "cognitive classes," evident in a range of behavioral dispositions, are more relevant for explaining "social problems" than are socioeconomic registers of class identity. In this demonstration, Herrnstein and Murray quite purposefully state their case, first, by relying on an entirely white sample from the National Longitudinal Survey of Youth, their central data set. All of part 2—with its chapters "Poverty," "Schooling," "Unemployment, Idleness, and Injury," "Family Matters," "Welfare Dependency," "Parenting," "Crime," and "Civility and Citizenship"—is focused on a problematic white population, wherein "a lack of energy, thrift, farsightedness, determination—and brains" (131) outweighs the detrimental condition of being born in poverty. The motivation for such a focus probably involves a preemptive effort on the authors' part to diffuse the charges of racism that have been generated by the section "Ethnic Differences in Cognitive Ability." However, also evident is Murray's relentless lambasting of scholars for being too polite in their examinations of social problems, a gesture that echoes Wilson's effort to encourage scholars to be less restrained in objectifying classed forms of debasement. Hence Herrnstein and Murray's assertion: "The reluctance of scholars and policymakers alike to look at the role of low intelligence in malparenting may properly be called scandalous" (213). That their preference for morally outraged, demonized accounts of the "dumb" portion of society is primarily articulated by making an example of poor whites has largely gone uncommented on in the flurry of denunciation of this polemical work.[23]

This type of intraracial policing effort is clear, too, in the division of whites in Briggs. There are two groups of whites in this neighborhood: natives, who were born in Detroit between the 1920s and the 1940s, and "hillbillies," whites who migrated to this city from Appalachia, predominantly between the 1940s and the 1960s.[24] The designation hillbilly extends to those whites who were born in Detroit, as long as their parents (and, in some cases, their grandparents) came from West Virginia, Kentucky, or Tennessee. There is a long-simmering distrust and animosity between these groups. Native white Detroiters remain nostalgic for an idyllic time back before the boom years of World War II dramatically changed this city. When I asked these whites what happened to bring the neighborhood to such a devastated state, they uniformly cited the arrival of the "damn hillbillies." Although many factors were involved in the decline of this part of Detroit, the whites who lived through that transition and remain in the areas succinctly collapse these into one scapegoat: the hillbillies.

There are rather clear class divisions between these groups of whites. The remaining native white Detroiters are mostly homeowners, whereas hillbillies, even those born in Detroit, are typically renters. Native whites are largely retired and living on pensions, while hillbillies continually scramble to find odd jobs and part-time work. The stark regional distinctions between these groups of whites are accentuated by the class divide, leaving their differences largely undissolved. In part, the cultural distinctness of the hillbillies is maintained because many either make trips "back home" to the South or have family members from home towns come for visits. The cars belonging to hillbillies frequently bear license plates from the Appalachian states; their drivers may have bad records in Detroit, or they find it cheaper to keep the cars registered in their home states. As well, hillbillies refuse to participate in any way with the local community group, while native whites regularly hold board-level positions in this organization.

Given the stark contours of these two groups of whites' distinct lifestyles, I was surprised to find that there is only a meager sense of solidarity among the hillbillies. These whites, though they generally socialized with other hillbillies, also fought most regularly with other southern whites. The social ties that brought them close together were also the connections that imbricated them in elaborate conflicts that developed between families, enduring over lengthy time periods. And, too, not all southern whites were comfortable being referred to as hillbillies. The ones who successfully assimilated to northern mores, largely by becoming respectable homeowners, used the term disparagingly, singling out a certain stratum of "rowdy" and "dangerous" whites with whom they shared regional affiliations. Hillbilly remains a charged term that poor whites alternately use as a means of self-designation and as a provocation to other whites who fail to match their standards of decorum and comportment.

The cultural heterogeneity of whites in Briggs makes any generalization difficult, especially when it involves such a loaded term as the white underclass. Although this neighborhood fits the general description of an underclass area, the people who live there constitute a diversity of class positions.

Even among those whites closest to the figure that characterizes the under-class, none ever used this term. Indeed, when I asked residents, white and black, about the underclass, they offered me back the sound bites they had heard on the news about this problem group. People would tell me about "welfare cheaters" they had seen on TV.[25] Even if they themselves had been on welfare or disability for years, they were most interested in dissecting media images of "welfare queens" and violent "gangstas" as members of the underclass. As with most Americans, the term referred to somebody else, somebody in another neighborhood or perhaps even around the block.

Still, I think the term white underclass is useful in referring to a segment of the white population in Briggs. In part because the term has such loaded connotations that cannot be avoided, it gets to the core dynamic that ani-mates the intraracial class divide between whites in this inner-city neighbor-hood. Underclass both mimics and objectifies the perception that is the basis for more economically stable whites to refer to some of their white neigh-bors as hillbillies. This mimetic function, while raising the specter of com-plicity in the reproduction of social contempt, more importantly provides a basis for what Kathleen Stewart (1991) refers to as a "contaminated critique" of this class dynamic. The underclass clearly is the latest technical term used to objectify a long tradition of social contempt between professionals and the poor (Gans 1993). Indeed, Wilson directly addresses the queasiness that some researchers feel over this term, insisting that liberal scholars must use charged designations such as the underclass in spite of their connota-tions. Wilson acknowledges "that certain groups are stigmatized by the label *underclass*, just as some people who live in depressed central-city commu-nities are stigmatized by the term *ghetto* or *inner city*, but it would be far worse to obscure the profound changes in class structure and social behavior of ghetto neighborhoods by avoiding the use of the term *underclass*. Indeed, the real challenge is to describe and explain these developments accurately so that liberal policy makers can appropriately address them. And it is difficult for me to see how this can be accomplished by rejecting a term that aids in the description of ghetto social transformations" (1987, 8). Following this line of argument, it is clear that using the term *white underclass* is just as critical, because it brings greater specificity to complex shifts in racial for-mations within this country, which are shaped in concert with changes in the structure of class relations.

Furthermore, pointing to the white underclass in Briggs is a means to begin complicating the assumptions about the social isolation that Wilson has argued is a key factor in generating this new population. Inner-city dwellers may be isolated from the suburban middle classes, but they remain in intimate, though strained contact with the working class and professionals. The white underclass in Briggs lives side by side with somewhat more financially secure, working-class neighbors, and they engage in routinized exchanges with professionals who, as social workers, doctors, or police officers, are charged with regulating the urban poor. In this context, the underclass are part of a relational order; these whites are not simply a unique population formed in isolation. Rather, every day they encounter the solidity of class boundaries constituted in bodily and behavioral registers that manifest a naturalized register, distinct from obvious connections to the means of production. And whether the term is hillbillies or white underclass, the inscription of absolute class difference achieves similar effects. Although these encounters or instances of name-calling do not produce an unproblematic or articulate sense of class consciousness, the texture that these class relations give to social experience in this inner-city zone needs to be named.

Does the condition of poor whites in Detroit and Briggs clearly demonstrate the reality of this cultural identity, the white underclass? What can be said about the white underclass from a national perspective? Have we established that such a class truly exists, or merely laid bare the discursive exchanges in which this identity is mobilized and inscribed? The question of whether or not there is a white underclass requires a provisional response of yes and no. The necessity of affirming that this class exists is impelled by the fact that whites, too, suffer from these processes that have devastated and degraded the cores of America's cities. The negation of this assertion, however, must also be posed, because the term entails a nefarious implication. The danger of the term white underclass is that it imposes a conceptual form of segregation on these inner-city populations: over here are the whites in poverty, and over there are the blacks who share a similar predicament. In Detroit, at least in neighborhoods like Briggs, the two groups are not that easily kept distinct. In fact, their lives and situations relentlessly overlap and intermingle; key social spaces regularly feature racially mixed gatherings, from front porches to the corner bars and in the aisles of the party stores where people shop for their overpriced necessities. The dangerous implication in Murray's invocation of the term is that "we" (as whites) have "ours" to worry about, and "they" have "theirs." Such a rendition allows the intraracial policing of class identities to proceed as a natural matter, asserting that this is no longer about race but about the natural hierarchies of *civilized* and *savage* that have long legitimated class rankings.

Murray's trumpeting of the drastic increase in white rates of illegitimacy prompted many social commentators to follow his lead in effacing the primacy of race in relation to the intransigence of inner-city problems. One of these commentators, Bill Clinton, stated, "What you see now happening is that the economic hardship is also creating a white underclass, with the same sort of family-separating pressures at work, so that now the out-of-wedlock birth rate among whites is now above 1 in 5. So it is now credible for us to argue that this is not a racial issue."[26] But it is not the case that race suddenly ceases to be a factor when whites begin to match a behavioral trend that had long been associated solely with blacks in this country. Race clearly still matters; only the scale at which it registers as significant, and the specificity required of us to describe its effects, has shifted in scope. The presence of whites among this "new" class should not distort the disproportionate effects of current economic and social transformations on blacks and Latinos. Rather, the place of whites among the underclass demonstrates that the structure and content of racial formations are changing in concert with the massive restructuring of class identity in the United States.

Statistical discrepencies between the life chances of whites and nonwhites in the United States are plentiful, and they have been effectively deployed to make the case explicitly that race remains of immense significance and, more or less implicitly, that white racism provides the motivational core of this continuing significance. The certainty of this conviction has relied on a steady equation between the social or economic bottom and the condition of the most disadvanataged minorities. This equation, however, is challenged by the predicament of poor whites in Detroit and other cities. Yvette Alex-Assensoh's (1995, 15–16) study in Columbus, Ohio, "show[s] not only that poor whites in concentrated poverty neighborhoods are on par with poor African-Americans in terms of welfare dependancy, low educational attainment, the perception of criminal activity, unemployment, and a lack of neighborhood role models but also that whites are even more disconnected from the broader society and beleagured by the stigma of social and political isolation than are African-Americans." Her point is clearly echoed by Jay MacLeod's (1995) ethnography, *Ain't No Makin' It: Leveled Aspirations in a Low-Income Neighborhood.*

An awareness or recognition of the white underclass bears relevance for a broad range of approaches to issues of race and class, particularly for those that have posited the social bottom as essentially a racial predicament or whiteness as unproblematically equivalent to privilege. As Doug Henwood (1997, 184) demonstrates, a distinct class rift complicates that latter assumption: "White privilege these days means that your wages fall more slowly than those of non-whites, unless you're a high school dropout, in which case racial advantage is actually eroding." The point, though, is not to undermine the clarity regarding the social and political problem that white privilege continues to present to this and other countries around the globe. Rather, by articulating with specificity its ongoing transformations, the social construction of whiteness becomes increasingly tangible and susceptible to interrogation and, ideally, decomposition. What researchers into the problem of whiteness need now to grasp is that the types of intraracial class divisions and dynamics that have characterized African American inner-city communities, where the underclass was first recognized, are active and unfolding among whites as well. We must treat whiteness with the kind of class specificity that we have learned, through studies of the underclass, to apply in discussing and analyzing blackness. Just such a perspective is formulated in the second part of this book.

PART 2

CHAPTER 7

ESTABLISHING THE FACT

OF WHITENESS

When surveying the range of public discourses on race in the United States, it is hard to escape the conclusion that, as anthropologists and academics, we are struggling to keep pace with the innovations and obsessions this subject generates in popular culture. Granted, a certain mind-numbing redundancy characterizes most widely circulated representations of race: scenes of intergroup conflict predominate, to the exclusion of the array of social interactions between whites and people of color that are not conflictual;[1] an "extreme gulf" generically summarizes the contours of interracial coexistence; and analytical views offered by commentators, newscasters, reporters, and politicians are woefully simplistic in comparison with the nuance and complexity manifest in many "racial" situations. Still, what stands out is the number of public forums (ranging from books to talk shows, music, and political speeches) given over to discussing or arguing about what race means and how it matters.

There is, however, one racial subject where an upsurge of interest by academics may precede and effectively recast public formulations or means of attending to race: the subject of whiteness. Through the efforts of literary and film critics, historians, sociologists, and, gradually, anthropologists, whiteness as an analytical object is being established as a powerful means of critiquing the reproduction and maintenance of systems of racial inequality within the United States and across the globe.[2] Apart from the concept's usefulness to academics, discussions of how whiteness operates provide a means of altering the terms of racial debates in the United States. Listening to whites respond to the way racial inequality and the continued insidious effects of racism are highlighted in a range of public discussions—whether in relation to the O. J. Simpson trial, the spate of church burnings across the South, or more individual tragedies such as the death of Cynthia Wiggins in Buffalo—I consistently hear the laments that *now* racism is "everywhere" or that "race is an excuse for everything these days."[3] Rather than recognizing the pervasive effects of race, these white complaints dismiss the relevance of racism to current social conflicts in the United States, asserting that anything so apparently omnipresent must be mythic or imagined. Whiteness offers a different purchase on the attention of whites by framing effectively what Ruth Frankenberg characterizes as a structural position of social privilege and power. Studies of whiteness show that whites benefit from a host of apparently neutral social arrangements and institutional operations, all of which seem, to whites at least, to have no racial basis. But this powerful form of objectifying white racial interests also bears the potential to distort as much as it reveals about how race works. This chapter frames both problematic aspects of whiteness and suggestions ameliorating by considering how this concept works in empirical rather than critical contexts.

Whiteness emerged as much from a series of distinct disciplinary developments as in response to the ongoing need for more effective analyses of racial dominance. For anthropologists, the call to study whiteness is linked to long-simmering efforts to "decolonize anthropology" (Harrison 1991) as well as to critiques of how the logic of Otherness perniciously informs ethnographic accounts of non-Western subjects and the move to include within the scope of anthropology studies of "nonexotic" people, such as whites in the West (Varenne 1986; Nader 1969; DiLeonardo 1998). The convergence of these various disciplinary developments is evident in Helan Page's (1995, 21) depiction of the turn to examining whiteness: "One of the most important things to be done is to encourage our students to seriously study white people. Here is a population that has achieved dominance. How did this happen and what are the lessons? . . . We shouldn't stop studying the 'Other,' but we need to study those who are reproducing themselves as dominant groups. We shouldn't study white ethnics, but how whiteness is constructed." Increasingly, as Page directs, the ethnographic gaze is being deployed on those who wield power and (consciously or unconsciously) reproduce structures of dominance.

A problem arises, though, in the linkages between whiteness, dominance, and the racialness of white people. In whiteness studies, all three are typically treated as equivalent, which promotes a unified view of white people as a collective order sharing a common cultural identity. The power and problem of *whiteness* as a subject of cultural critique is exactly this treatment of white racial identity as a uniform cultural construct, a coherent, historically determined ideology of dominance. This view runs counter to the developing attention to the place-specific functions of racial meanings and to the stress anthropologists lay on the continual conflation of racial, regional, gendered, and class-specific terms of identity and difference (P. Jackson and Penrose 1993; Brackette Williams 1991). In these latter views, plasticity is a prevailing feature of race; in the former, race is primarily treated as an order of structured inequality, and whiteness can practically have only one meaning: dominance. Undeniably, it is important to pursue what Faye Harrison (1995, 63) characterizes as "a cultural critique of whiteness as the key site of racial domination." But the insights gained from this critique will be skewed if in the process whiteness is considered a homogeneous order or identity— as simply "white culture" (Frankenberg 1993)—and not, additionally, a conflicted and heterogeneous social position. The challenge lies in striking a balance between the critical power of whiteness and the often contradictory, muddled effects of race in everyday life as encountered in ethnographic contexts. This second half of *Odd Tribes* details how this kind of balance can be developed and sustained via an empirically based form of cultural analysis, an approach that arises out of anthropologists' effort to critically rethink homogenizing assumptions that inflect the culture concept. Such assumptions are also evident in whiteness studies and need to be reevaluated if this new analytical purchase on race is to realize its potential.

Whiteness was formulated as an interdisciplinary subject of study by an array of scholars struggling with the task of making visible the operations of racial privilege and advantage that structure the lives, attitudes, and actions of white people. Out of these studies, several characterizations of whiteness have been asserted, all to some degree related but also often involving subtle disjunctures or contradictions. Film and literary critics fashioned a view of whiteness as a relational identity, constructed by whites defining themselves as unlike certain ethnic or racial Others (Dyer 1988; Morrison 1992; Nelson 1992). In this view, blackness serves as the primary form of Otherness by which whiteness is constructed. Historians have followed a similar model in describing the centuries-long development of white identity; their emphasis, though, has been on both the relational construction of whiteness in opposition to blackness and on the ever changing content of this identity, highlighting that whiteness has excluded certain ostensibly white European groups only to incorporate them at a later date (T. Allen 1994, 1997; Roediger 1992; Saxton 1990). The complicated matter of the cultural content of whiteness has also been examined as a repressed synthesis of many African or African American styles and practices (J. Holloway 1990; Lott 1993; Piersen 1993).

In contemporary social settings, whiteness has been identified as a core set of racial interests often obscured by seemingly race-neutral words, actions, or policies (Jamieson 1992; E. Jackson 1993; Page and Thomas 1994; Lipsitz 1995). From the terms or subjects of debate that compose political campaigns to the placement and funding of freeway projects and waste dumps, in the limits determining access to home financing and the varied practices that constitute and reproduce medical professions in the United States, a set of institutional routines and "white cultural practices" establishes and maintains privileges generally associated with being white. Indeed, whites benefit from "white skin privilege" whether or not as individuals they hold supremacist notions, harbor racist sentiments, or are made anxious by the physical presence of people of color (McIntosh 1989). The phrase "white culture" is proffered to convey the material relations and social structures that reproduce white privilege and racism in this country, quite apart from what individual whites may feel, think, and perceive (see Frankenberg 1993, 196–205, 228–234; Hitchcock 2001). As an analytical register, then, whiteness stands as a sweepingly broad, effective means to characterize the racial content of white people's cultural identity.

From this perspective, the central use of whiteness as an analytical concept is that it identifies how the unmarked and normative position of whites is maintained by positing race as a category of difference.[4] "Racial" and "race" are typically used to characterize difference and deviance from social norms that have been seamlessly equated with what white people, generally speaking, do and think. Phrases such as "race relations" and "racial problems" have effectively focused on only one side of the equation, on the conditions of people of color and not on the position of dominance that whites maintain. Whether in Frankenberg's (1993) definition of whiteness as a structural position conferring privilege and power or in historian George Lipsitz's (1995) characterization of whiteness as an organizing principle in social relations, the common concern is in naming and objectifying the content of white people's character. Whiteness thereby stands as a concept that reveals and explains the racial interests of whites and links them collectively to a position of racial dominance. The problem, though, is that this formulation, while opening up newly insightful analyses of how racial inequality is structured, promulgates an assumption that whiteness simply exists and is real, thus undermining a potentially productive opportunity to reframe the long, contentious debate over what race is and how it matters. This problem, as well as the means to correct it, lies in the limited role that culture plays in these studies of whiteness.

In these definitions of whiteness, culture is used in a twofold manner. Primarily, it establishes a register apart from individual identity that affects and defines white people collectively while also suggesting the broad range of means by which racial matters influence and inform the lives of white people, asserting that they, too, are racial. Second, and most problematically, the notion of white culture, developed and consistent through the long centuries of white global domination, reifies whiteness as a definable entity.[5] This moves dangerously close to undermining the basis of social constructionist views of race. The conviction that there are no inherent affinities between people sharing a collective racial identity is destabilized by such a singular, unified definition of whiteness. In place of race as an artificial category, we increasingly have accounts of whiteness and blackness as distinct historical traditions and identities; such is the consistency with which they can each be traced through the past four hundred years of global history. But asserting the "fact" of whiteness—the durability of its dominance and the pernicious nature of its effects—may have the unintended effect of undermining the concept of race as "constructed." Without emphasizing that race is socially constructed, cultural critiques of race risk reproducing the pernicious notions that have long linked racial identities with immutable, inherent characteristics. The way to avoid this lies in developing a broader and more nuanced understanding of how culture works, which can be gleaned from a range of ethnographic perspectives on the constructed aspects of racial identity.

Daniel Segal (1993, 81) articulated this perspective in the course of describing the function of race and color in pre-independence Trinidad: "Such groupings are fundamentally contingent, though this is precisely what is obscured when they are called 'races,' for these denominations represent historically contingent groupings as facts given to us by objective reality." When the fact of whiteness is asserted with certainty, the contingent basis of the significance of white racialness and the arbitrariness of racial categories and distinctions become less easy to grasp. The distinction here is rendered more clearly by contrasting Frankenberg's approach to Lisa Douglass's ethnographic study of white, upper-class families in Jamaica. Frankenberg, in defining whiteness "as a set of normative cultural practices," asserts plainly, "White women are, by definition, practitioners of white culture" (Frankenberg 1992, 228). Although there are structural similarities in terms of dominance between the whites in northern California that Frankenberg interviewed and the whites that Douglass studied in Kingston, Jamaica, Douglass views racialness in a more strictly constructionist frame, as an arbitrary system: "I view gender, color, and class not as descriptions of particular groups or persons, but as categories that act as principles of distinction. . . . What these categories (or principles) mean, how they may combine in different ways, and how they affect a person at a given time vary; they are neither rigid, nor fixed, nor timeless. Above all, they are not 'real,' even though they often have concrete effects. Principles of distinction serve both as analytic and as commonsense categories that inform the way Jamaicans relate to one another and affect the way they explain and experience the world" (12).

In treating racial categories primarily as a means of organizing and interpreting everyday life, Douglass draws on the work of Jack Alexander (1977), whose study of "the culture of race" among the middle class of Kingston examined racial identities as interpretive categories rather than relying upon them as a means to strictly define his ethnographic subjects. Alexander draws the following contrast: "Where previous studies sought to define the meaning of racial terms by applying objective instruments, here the meaning of racial terms is determined by linking them to the larger problem of how informants use their ideas about race to make sense of society" (413). This characterization elaborates on the contrast between Douglass's and Frankenberg's approaches as a difference between treating race as a generic subject and analyzing the perpetuation of a historical, cultural tradition of white domination. The distinct emphases in these studies of white people is further fleshed out in Frankenberg's deployment of whiteness to present a view of white privilege and dominance as a unified operation, implicating and influencing, to varying degrees, all white people, linking the racialness of whites to an inherent, motivational core. This emphasis does not necessarily limit the extent to which whiteness is seen as contemporarily constructed in distinct settings, but it raises the question of whether racial interpretive structures are best understood as strictly historically determined ideological operations or as cultural modes that are as mutable as the changeable, place-specific contexts in which they operate.

Assertions about the fact of whiteness are based on its historical duration and its ideological coherence and effective power. In establishing the "social reality" of race, Audrey Smedley (1993) grounds the durability of this cultural construction in its historical determinants; applied to whiteness, this view orients analysis toward confirming the continuing effects of this historical order rather than toward assessing the permutations this construction may be undergoing:

> Accepting the fact that race is a cultural construct invented by human beings, it is easy to understand that it emerged out of a set of definable historical circumstances and is thus as amenable to analysis as are other elements of culture. No amount of comparative definitions and synchronic explorations of modern race relations will lead us to more refined definitions and understandings of race. On the contrary, *it is a complex of elements whose significance and meanings lie in historical settings in which attitudes and values were formed.* We should be able to analytically isolate the central components, investigate their probable genesis, and determine how they evolved over time. (16; emphasis added)

The durability of whiteness is confirmed by this view of race's social reality, but this stance makes it difficult to grasp or learn from the settings where the significance of white racialness is currently in flux. Singularly stressing the historical determination of racial significance delimits recognition of how the meaning of race is currently being reformulated in relation to fast changing social and political dynamics in the United States.

The asserted ideological coherence of whiteness leads to a similar problem, as evidenced in David Roediger's (1994) oft-cited work, *Towards the Abolition of Whiteness.* Finding that whiteness is "infinitely more false" than blackness, Roediger calls for "a sharp questioning of whiteness" that will lead to its eventual abolition (3, 12). "To make its fullest possible contribution to the growth of a new society, activism that draws on ideas regarding the social construction of race must focus its political energies on exposing, demystifying and demeaning the popular ideology of whiteness, rather than on calling into question the concept of race generally" (12).[6] Aside from the question of how to validate an activist interest in abolishing an ethnographic subject of study, however clearly in the interests of humanity, this focus on whiteness apart from the "the concept of race generally" is a mistake. Rendering whiteness as unique, a special ideological case apart from race, limits inquiries into the way changing racial terrains are discursively negotiated by whites in their daily lives, in workplaces and at home. Out of confusions over race in these sites, new versions of racial identity are being articulated; heteroglot rather than homogeneous, these new forms are oriented as much toward an unfolding present as they are bound to a determining past (Holt 2000). The conditions through which racial identities are articulated will only become more complicated, not less so. Unless whites are examined with this in mind, ethnographers, historians, and cultural critics will generate only accounts that confidently link whiteness back to some originary historical impulse rather than as something continually being restructured, revised, and disfigured in a host of discrete, local settings.

Neither Frankenberg nor Harrison asserts that the cultural coherence of whiteness derives from a simple, ontological condition. They both stress the relational construction of whiteness in opposition to blackness, and they both acknowledge that "race is always lived in class- and gender-specific ways" (Harrison 1995, 63). But, in the final analysis, their definition of whiteness emphasizes the unifying interest in and reproduction of dominance, diminishing the extent to which its meanings are contested or rearticulated through local "racial idioms" (Segal 1993), inflected by the contours of distinctly constructed regions and place-specific contests over forms of class and gender identity. I am not certain that their conceptualization of whiteness allows for a view of the plasticity of race in relation to white people. Race still eludes emphatic definition; though its association with forms of domination and subordination is consistent, there is certainly a diffuse range of racial phenomena that are not all easily subsumed under this definition. The question is whether or not white racialness bears treatment through the type of racial analytics that have been devised largely through studies of the cultural forms generated in conditions of racial subordination.

In Harrison's (1995, 47) survey, whiteness is one of a range of topics that emerged as "anthropologists have revitalized their interest in the complex and often covert structures and dynamics of racial inequality." The centrality of whiteness in this "revitalized interest" rests primarily on the recognition that "the ideology and materiality of white supremacy provided the historical precedent for subordinate racisms by providing the most systematic mode of classifying and capitalizing on race" (50). Importantly, whiteness is framed as a global order or identity: "Despite its uneven development and varying systematization, racism is characterized by an international hierarchy in which wealth, power, and advanced development are associated largely with whiteness or 'honorary whiteness' " (50). In this summation, the definition and description of whiteness is emphatic and unambiguous: though its contents may be mutable and shifting, the coherence of whiteness is consistently equated with domination: "Racial meanings and hierarchies are unstable, but this instability is constrained by poles of difference that have remained relatively constant: white supremacy and the black subordination that demarcates the social bottom. Although whiteness and blackness have not had fixed meanings and boundaries, the opposition between them has provided the stabilizing backbone for the United States' racialized social body. The most visible instability has occurred between the poles" (59).

Whiteness invites broadly devised analytics—both the sweeping scope of its reign of dominance and the insidious nature of its current effects make this clear—but the instability of what constitutes race and the overriding importance of emphasizing the localness of culture underscore the necessity of analyzing white people as more complicated, conflicted, and ambiguous racial subjects. Comparative studies of white supremacy in South Africa and the United States by George Fredrickson (1981) and John Cell (1982) offer a view of the complexities involved in treating whiteness as a unified subject of study. While the cultural similarities between whites in the two countries are striking, these historians differ in their assessment of white supremacy's historical origins and reach contrasting conclusions about whether or not white supremacy possesses an identifiable core. Fredrickson suggests that, rather than tracing whiteness as a consistent cultural order, constructions of white supremacy are best understood as resonant but distinctive structures:

> The vagaries and variations that I have found in the actual evolution of racial attitudes and policies in North America and South Africa drew my attention away from common cultural influences and towards differing environmental circumstance and political contingencies. I have not therefore found it possible to treat "white supremacy" as a kind of seed planted by the first settlers that was destined to grow at a steady rate into a particular kind of tree. On the contrary, I have found it more plausible to regard it as a fluid, variable, and open-ended process. Major shifts in both societies in the forms of white dominance and the modes of consciousness associated with them belie any notion of a fixed set of attitudes and relationships. (xxviii–xxix)

The notion of whiteness as "a fluid, variable, and open-ended process" does not necessarily counter Harrison's depiction of it as "the key site of racial domination," but Fredrickson's discounting "common cultural influences" in explaining the distinct versions of white supremacy in these two countries suggests a notion of white racialness as something more than a unified ideological order. Dominance is no doubt key to the processes that Fredrickson analyzes, but the interplay of "differing environmental circumstance and political contingencies" makes the matter of generalizing about race relations in the two countries somewhat tenuous because they constitute such distinct cultural, demographic, economic, and political domains. Shifting "topics and angles of vision [and] even units of analysis" between the two countries, Fredrickson relates that this comparative effort "has strengthened my sense that race relations can best be understood in the terms of interaction of specific groups in particular historical situations and that attempts to generalize broadly about entire societies over long periods of time usually distort more than they illuminate" (1981, xx).

John Cell, in his comparative study of white supremacy, is not as hesitant to find a common core of beliefs and attitudes among whites. Describing "two traditionally racist societies dedicated to maintaining white supremacy," each facing stressful social transitions in the developing forms of industrialization and urbanization, he sees segregation as a comparatively recent articulation of white racism, emerging only after 1890 in the United States and around 1910 in South Africa (1982, 230). In this key word, segregation, he discerns a common "growing consciousness, synthesis and ideological crystallization" among whites of both countries. Even so, in defining segregation he stresses attention to a matter that I think is easily overlooked in attempts to theorize whiteness, and that is ambiguity:[7] "The most impressive characteristic of segregation was a complex fabric of structural ambiguity" (18). As it changed rapidly from a "de facto tendency or practice" into "both a de jure system and a coherent, articulate ideology," segregation produced a "state of ambiguity and contradiction [that] was skillfully and very deliberately created" (3, 18–20). While a good deal of this "structural ambiguity" involved the "facade of constitutionality," a critical aspect of its operation was to obscure the conflicted and disjointed nature of the "white world": "The principal function of the segregationist ideology was to soften class and ethnic antagonisms among whites, subordinating internal conflicts to the unifying conception of race" (234). The conflicted aspects within whiteness are precisely where an attention to cultural dynamics can make a significant contribution to this area of inquiry.

Vincent Crapanzano (1986), in *Waiting: The Whites of South Africa*, makes the case for studying dominant whites based on the complexity of their cultural identity. Noting that, despite numerous studies of the effects of domination on the dominated, "anthropologists had never bothered to study the dominant" (22), Crapanzano examined how "the discourse of domination" was spoken and defended by South African whites: "Pathos, terror, guilt, the joy of power and acquisition, the weight of responsibility and the resentment of such responsibility, feelings of solitude, misunderstanding, and un-understanding, to name only a few of the dispositions and predispositions of the dominant, have to be understood if any understanding of domination is to be achieved" (23). Such dispositions are not easily rendered in a generic sense of whiteness, especially when they are articulated through intense, intraracial contests animated by the severe distinction between English South Africans and Afrikaners. Qualifying his findings as drawn from a specific field setting, Crapanzano suggests "that the Blacks, Coloureds, and Asians were not 'significant others' from whose standpoint the white could look reflectively at himself and discover, so to speak, his identity. They were too different—and too distant" (39). Instead: "What I found extraordinary about the identity play of the two white groups was the insignificance of non-whites. They simply did not enter the self-constituting discourse of the whites, although their potential threat to the whites' 'way of life' (not their personhood) was certainly acknowledged" (39). Crapanzano finds the "psycho-ontological dimensions of apartheid" demonstrated in this structured white obliviousness to South African blacks. But this cultural dynamic indicates that the complex matter of how race remains significant will not be determined by exclusively keying on contests between the poles of whiteness and blackness. These views of whites, comparatively and in the field, contrast with Harrison's depiction of whiteness by emphasizing heterogeneous aspects of white racial dominance.

The consistency of white hegemony speaks to a unified definition of whiteness, but the changing demographic and political circumstances unfolding in this country suggest that we also maintain a view to the changes under way in how racial identities are established and contested. In the course of my ethnographic fieldwork in Detroit, I found that racial matters in different neighborhoods were articulated through local idioms, discourses that whites and blacks spoke, with varying degrees of commonality, in positioning themselves, neighbors, and strangers in relation to marked and unmarked identities. Whiteness was not readily apparent as either a unifying ideology or a shared sense of identity between these neighborhoods (see chapter 8). Partly, this is due to the fact that whiteness is not a normative identity in this city. As whites, their racialness is rarely unmarked. But more important, in the most salient labels and categories, race was rarely established in pure form. Rather, it was conflated with class distinctions in a series of terms that negotiated the significance of being white without drawing in a uniform manner on a historical notion of whiteness or a clear opposition to blackness. The interpretive struggles these whites engaged in over the meaning of race in these communities were fiercely oriented toward the volatile present. In Detroit, white hegemony has been shattered, and in its wake whites assess, accentuate, or efface the significance of race through discourses that are complicated by class difference and relentlessly local in focus.[8] An attempt to read whiteness as uniformly at work in Detroit would obliterate the novelty of these settings and the heterogeneity of racial matters in these discourses.

My purpose here is not to insist blithely that acknowledgments of the "diversity" of whites need always qualify analyses of whiteness, nor am I attempting to simply complicate the cultural critique of whiteness by stressing the conflation of racial and class identities according to place-specific dynamics. What I am sketching here is a certain analytical dilemma that the cultural critique of whiteness presents. The question is whether to wield whiteness as a means of identifying the ideological core of white people's identity or to sketch the discursive predicaments in which whites are entangled as they operate—and are operated by—racial idioms of identity and difference. My concern is that generalizations about white culture undermine an attention to the disparate circumstances of whites in various settings around the globe. Certainly, an analysis of domination and subordination pertains to locales throughout North and South America and the Caribbean, but the diversity of racial dynamics suggest that understanding whiteness remains contingent on grasping how the heterogeneous functions of race alternate between stark definition, absolute positions, and swirling ambiguity (Hoetnik 1985).

This approach regards "white" as a cultural construct whose content and uses vary by locale and whose significance in relation to global forms of domination may be oblique or attenuated by place-specific dynamics. Ethnographers in a variety of settings around the world are honing a perspective on race that is informed by whiteness studies but that also takes into account distinct local dynamics by which racial objectifications are formulated, deployed, and interpreted. Research by Galen Joseph, Mary Weismantel, and Ira Bashkow reveal that representations of whites in the field operate like other cultural forms: they perform a host of local uses that ratify a sense of difference and belonging, sometimes directly but often obliquely in relation to understandings of global operations of power and privilege.[9] Breaking down the "phantom objectivity" of the concept of whiteness, their fieldwork projects bring into view a range of relationships between people, as well as proximate uses of power and positions, that are negotiated and interpreted via figures, images, and narratives of whites. Bashkow's work among the Orakaiva of New Guinea, in particular, demonstrates how the cultural figure of "whitemen" is deployed and manipulated to articulate and sort out complex concerns through their indigenous moral system. Rather than delineating problematic aspects of their position in relation to colonial and postcolonial orders, the Orakaiva's symbolic usage of whiteman is oriented toward explicating, sifting through, and altering local relations via a powerful moral discourse of values and beliefs. Mapping these local uses requires cognizance of the potential for these representations to respond to or reference global power relations, especially the forms of privilege and advantage that are the focus of whiteness studies. But it also hinges on recognizing and understanding both the place-specific, contingent social dynamics and the explicit rejection, particularly in the case of the Orakaiva, of a global subject of address.

An ethnographic vantage point on such racial constructs raises a range of questions concerning the analytical status and uses of representations of whites by natives, Others, and subordinated populations (Roediger 1998). Representations of "the white man" are bountiful as historical and contemporary social artifacts, and they certainly bear potential in contributing to critical whiteness studies (Nowicka 1984; O'Nell 1994; Basso 1979; Holden 1976; McClellan 1970). But they need to also be recognized as cultural objects, that is, as multivalent, nontransparent forms of signification. Accounts of whites and whitemen require a deft understanding that, despite similarities, these stories and figures are not all about the same thing and they do not uniformly critique a generic, homogeneous whiteness. Instead, as with any cultural object, they play any number of roles in local efforts to sort out matters of belonging and difference or as means of interpreting and negotiating proximate, personal relations of power and position. These place-specific, cultural dynamics, potentially lost from view in abstract formulations about domination and subordination on a grand scale, are an important dimension of how race works and key to understanding racial situations.

The importance of this cultural dimension and the insight it potentially bears in assessing how and why race matters can be glimpsed in the commonplace racial objectification, "acting white." As with uses of "whitemen," acting white can be construed as an insight into how whiteness as a form of cultural domination operates. But such assignations are also products of cultural struggles—thus partial, interested, and contingent and often shaped by or defining intraracial contests over belonging and difference (Fordham 1996; Uriciuoli 1996). Acting white, as with the whiteman or *pishtaco* (Weismantel 2001), is a means of policing group boundaries and of asserting forms of social homogeneity in relation to racial identities. These representations of whiteness perform intense cultural work, replicating racial groups rather than deconstructing them, ratifying and policing conformity to racial identities such as blackness as much as critiquing forms of domination. Understanding these dense, local uses of whites is important to comprehending how race works and matters, and it is just such a cultural perspective that offers ways to move beyond generic discussions about whiteness.

Perhaps this point is best underscored by the simple assertion that efforts to theorize whiteness need to be informed by the long struggle to establish that blackness is a heterogeneous rather than a homogeneous social order (V. Green 1970; Harrison 1988; Wade 1993). As Livio Sansone (1994, 173) argues, "The development of a world system of culture not only brings about cultural homogenization but also buttresses heterogenization." In his account of "the transformation of Creole culture into a black subculture centered on the aestheticization of blackness," Sansone demonstrates that "their black culture and ethnicity is highly complex and eclectic—cacophonic rather than symphonic" (193). It is so because of the considerable degree of participation in white society that "the management of this new black ethnicity" requires; because "the leisure industry, music industry, and mass media play a key role in the marking of what is commonly considered black and white"; and because the development of young people takes place amid a host of new "facilitating conditions" where ethnic and racial identities are not simply preserved, but actively refashion and "replace one ethnicity with another" (175, 192–193). Sansone insists that "a major barrier to constructing an anthropology of black people" has been the belief "that black culture is more 'genuine,' 'traditional,' and 'natural' than white culture, and that black ethnicity is given, static or scarcely manipulated" (175). These types of spurious distinctions are replicated when the racial complexity that constitutes blackness is not seen as also at work in constructing whiteness.

There are many ethnographic studies of whites that do not raise questions about race; such works largely confirm the basic critique of whiteness: that whites, especially those in racially homogeneous zones, are treated as normative rather than racial. But there are also an increasing number of studies that deal with racialness and whites simultaneously; these works are currently untapped by theorists of whiteness. Principle among these are linguistic studies that track how language usage shapes social worlds (Heath 1983; Hewitt 1986; Labov 1990). In her study of rural, working-class whites and blacks and their social distance from townspeople, black and white, in the Piedmont Carolinas, Shirley Brice Heath examines language as a medium both riven by racial and class distinctions, yet too fluid and mutable to be reified in simple terms of white and black patterns. Teresa Labov examines reports "by liberal whites of conflicts with blacks" in a food cooperative in a racially mixed neighborhood in Philadelphia. Rather than abstracting out black or white "styles in conflict" (Kochman 1981), she pursues the question of "when and how ideological themes, which do not appear relevant in one situation, can come to become defined as relevant" (Labov 1990, 155); this allows for a view of shifting definitions of "collections of people" that are only partially (and convolutedly) linked to matters of racial belonging and difference. Both ethnographers emphasize the medium of language as the means by which race is produced, reproduced, and continually reconfigured.

Interracial urban settings provide the most frequent depictions of whites negotiating racial matters (Merry 1981; Schneider and Smith 1973; E. Anderson 1990; Brett Williams 1988). In these situations, whites and blacks often come from different regions to the city and are differentiated in terms of class backgrounds. But at times, too, class and regional lines blur the stark racial divides, even to the point where the "social bottom" is no longer assuredly linked to blackness (Alex-Assensoh 1995; Macleod 1995). Racially mixed urban neighborhoods range from volatile to benign, but they are commonly defined as grounds where the changeable and uncertain nature of urban terrains often makes abstract notions of race tenuous. Surely, too, in these settings racial identities are typically the handiest, bluntest means for making blurred identities emphatic, but this tension shapes a cultural poetics patterned as much by the mutability of urban situations as it is by historically determined principles of racial distinctions. The forms of "street etiquette" that Elijah Anderson details are an interpretive set of rules that middle-class whites and blacks make use of in maneuvering through volatile public environments. While whiteness and blackness organize one level of perceptions, the unresponsiveness of these environments to "a formal set of rules rigidly applied to all problems" compels these middle-class city dwellers to additionally develop more sophisticated interpretive structures that draw on class distinctions as well (1990, 210).

Attempts to objectify whiteness and establish its facticity have deep roots. Arguably the first social scientific attempt to analyze—rather than champion—whiteness was W. E. B. Du Bois's account of the "white world" in *Dusk of Dawn* (1940/1980). Du Bois rendered the white world as a sociological object and insisted that "it is impossible for the clear-headed student of human action in the United States and in the world, to avoid facing the fact of a white world which is today dominating human culture and working for the continued subordination of the colored races" (145). This statement of the white world's facticity was asserted through a model of race in which whites constitute "the environing race" that "entombs" the "colored world" (138–139). He described the segregation that maintains these races as "some thick sheet of invisible but horribly tangible plate glass" (137). An initial glance at the United States confirms the continued relevance of Du Bois's model. Race still fundamentally determines the places, largely homogeneous by race and class, where people live, and segregation is clearly influential in creating "intractable" problems such as the underclass (Massey and Denton 1993). But, interestingly, a city like Detroit, the most segregated metropolitan area in the United States, raises a discordant qualifier to Du Bois's objectification of the white world (Farley et al. 1993). Du Bois (1940/1980, 138) dismissed the notion of whites ever "being possibly among the entombed or capable of sharing their inner thought and experience," but today, at least structurally, such an emphatic stance is problematic; whites, too, are entombed in concentrated poverty areas like Briggs. In this regard, Du Bois's sociological rendering depicts the central tension in this chapter: whiteness seems unchanging in its consistent position of dominance, but racial orders are rapidly being rearticulated and contested. We have to be able to discern these changes, keeping in mind the type of qualifications Du Bois himself offered when he characterized "the concept of race" as featuring "all sorts of illogical trends and irreconcilable tendencies. Perhaps it is wrong to speak of it at all as 'a concept' rather than as a group of contradictory forces, facts, and tendencies" (139).

Conceptually, whiteness is powerful and provocative, but it can also be an encumbrance. The power of whiteness lies in its ability to describe the coherence of privileges that white people, broadly, have developed; its encumbrance lies in this generic view, in rendering white people as a homogeneous cultural identity or order, which, as anthropologists explain, can be only a partial version. Homogenizing accounts stem from what has rightfully been established as a key function of whiteness: that it homogenizes whites from a range of ethnic and class positions in order to assert a normative social identity from which privileges can be secured and maintained. But it is important to maintain an awareness of the distinction between the process and the population to which it pertains, as Crapanzano (1986, 22) suggests, trying not "to confuse dominance within a system with the domination of the system." Indeed, Helan Page and R. Brooke Thomas (1994) describe "white public space" as a homogenizing process specific to professionals as a class and that includes, often through coercion and manipulation, black participants as well. But homogenizing accounts are overwhelmingly common in analyses of race, and it will be hard for studies of whiteness to do otherwise.

If whiteness stands definitionally as equivalent with homogenizing processes in the workplace, at home, in neighborhoods, and in public debates, then we should additionally have a means of designating the heterogeneous aspects of white racial identity that are not effortlessly processed into whiteness—that, through ruptures of class decorums or other forms of social etiquette, undermine the unmarked status of some whites. Lest whiteness and blackness become static versions of the Marxist superstructure/base paradigm—discrete, separate entities rather than constantly entangled registers—we must devise means to analyze how whites, as racial subjects, are embroiled in predicaments where the meanings of race are unclear and shifting, subjects of discourses or local idioms that are fashioned in fast-changing sites.

Where does whiteness end? Where do whites begin? At their core, these questions highlight the problematic issue of scale when regarding racial matters. This shift between singular and plural orders (whiteness and whites) materializes differently depending on the domain in which it is located. Whiteness may be fixed as a unified or unifying phenomenon when regarded ideologically at the national level, but on the ground that unity quickly becomes illusory. Instead of one firm ground, there is a shifting series of domains (local, regional, national, transnational) across which whiteness materializes according to distinct centers of significance, assimilating or effacing a varying array of internal differences and projecting or excluding a host of corporal others. Each level displays a certain intermittency of effects. Whiteness may be inhabited and active at every level, but the order of replication in each domain is not absolutely determined by those "above" or "below." The intervals and gaps between domains create an irregular and unpredictable basis for the cultural reproduction of this racial category, white.

The interminable difference and distance between whiteness and whites became apparent to me while conducting fieldwork in Detroit. Over a twenty-month period I worked in three distinct class communities: two inner-city neighborhoods, one gentrifying and the other underclass, and a working-class neighborhood on the city's far west side. Initially, I assumed that by studying the everyday lives of whites in this city, I would be able to abstract out some order of solidarity or cultural coherence that was identifiably whiteness that linked them all. What I found, though, was that articulations of the significance of white racialness varied widely among these class zones. The differences were amplified further when I shifted geographic focus from these neighborhoods to the city and region as political entities and when I attempted to link them to national forms of discourse on whiteness to provide an overarching context. Whiteness, which can be ideologically and discursively distinct when viewed from a national or global perspective, appeared on the ground in Detroit to be inundated with heterogeneous social materials that were not abstractable into one racial category. The differences among whites were magnified across the distinct geographic orders of the neighborhood, the city, the region (southeastern Michigan), and the nation.[1]

In grappling with the cultural complexity revealed by shifting scales of reference in relation to whiteness, I found Marilyn Strathern's (1991) reassessment of cross-cultural comparisons quite useful. Strathern suggests that interdisciplinary and comparative projects should model the scaling of cultural phenomena on the chaotic nature of the transmission of information and the "not quite replication of fractals, which generate patterned irregularities" (xxvi). This approach focuses on the gaps between levels and the new backgrounds of significance that emerge as one analytically shifts attention between distinct domains. Strathern contrasts this theoretical tack with a "segmentary model," which assumes that levels are "generated by the division of a pre-existing entity into discrete parts through distinction or opposition like a unit dividing or doubling itself" (xxvii). Considered through a segmentary model, whiteness appears to be a top-down version of ideology. Rather than assuming an intrinsic order of connections, Strathern asserts that the emphasis should be placed on drawing out "partial connections" that link the distinct domains across which the phenomenon in question, in this case, whiteness, replicates in increasingly irregular yet relentlessly connected patterns.

This chapter engages the complexity of whiteness by elaborating the partial connections that exist among distinct domains and situations of whites. The significance of whiteness is inconsistent across the variety of levels at which whites may be examined collectively: the terms of inclusion and exclusion by which racial decorums and conventions are maintained or contested among whites involve a specificity according to place and time.[2] Toward this end, I examine whiteness as something akin to a message or transmission in which varying occurrences of errors repeat their irregularities at each increasingly minute level of attention to the content of the message/error. The gap between whiteness and whites generates numerous locations, which, like points on an initial line scored by intermittency, may be interrupted infinitely, forming increasingly distinct positions while retaining a patterned similarity across escalating irregular extensions. "The result is that, however numerous, the points never exceed the quantity contained in the initial level. And however sparse, they never lose the complexity that the initial level was capable of conveying, for each point is capable of further interruptions. For every piece of information lost, information is gained" (Strathern 1991, xxvii).[3] In this regard, a thorough objectification of whiteness requires a recognition, first, of the provisional or relational character of racial matters, and, second, the deployment of an analytic mode of attention that facilitates shifts between distinct orders of phenomena. The question of scale is never resolved into a final ground of comprehension and understanding but is replicated at each level, where each answer produces more questions and each insight leads into more tangled quantifications and instances.

Applying Strathern's method for analyzing gaps and partial connections to the study of whiteness in the field helpfully recasts the orientation of established analyses of racial orders. In the course of my fieldwork, I was compelled to tinker with the notion of racial formation developed by Michael Omi and Howard Winant (1986). Although I certainly confirmed their finding that racial meanings are never static or absolute, the singular order of focus implied by racial formation delimited my ability to detail the linked but divergent articulations of whiteness in Detroit. Omi and Winant define racial formation in the following manner: "The meaning of race is defined and contested throughout society, in both collective action and personal practice. In the process, racial categories themselves are formed, transformed, destroyed, and reformed. We use the term racial formation to refer to the process by which social, economic and political forces determine the content and importance of racial categories, and by which they are in turn shaped by racial meanings. Crucial to this formulation is the treatment of race as a *central axis* of social relations which cannot be subsumed under or reduced to some broader category" (61–62). This broad frame of reference and the national scale of attention Omi and Winant deploy in rendering historical and political versions of racial categories and their meanings obscures the nuanced modes of differentiation that obtain in distinct geographic zones within the nation. Detroit, rather than simply providing an instantiation of national discourses on race, is a location in which the meanings of race and the significance of racial categories are interpreted and negotiated in situations quite distinct from those assumed to be the norm in the United States. To detail the local dynamics by which the significance of racial matters was interpreted, I began to consider Detroit as a particular racial formation. In this regard, I found it more relevant to think in terms of plural (racial formations) rather than singular orders.

Shifting attention from singular to plural forms extends the scope of the analytic perspective articulated by Omi and Winant in three key regards, each of which elaborates on rather than criticizes their project. The first elaboration entails a recognition of multiple racial formations in the United States instead of one unified formation; this draws attention to the level of regional specificity wherein distinct operations that maintain or transform racial categories can be seen as functioning simultaneously across the nation.[4] The social, economic, and political forces they refer to have differential effects across the United States; regions emerge from and, in turn, shape the uneven consequences and determinations of these forces. So, too, the contours and scope of the connection between whiteness and positions of privilege vary distinctly by region, continually being reconfigured and reasserted in relation to local pressures and challenges. The clearest instance of the regional variations of whiteness is glimpsed in the demographic revolution now under way in the United States. Already in most of this country's largest cities whites have lost their majority status. This same shift is occurring as well in the nation's most populous states, including California and Texas, with others like Florida sure to follow. In locations such as Detroit, Chicago, Miami, San Jose, and Atlanta, the contours of whiteness have rapidly mutated and reformulated; the background of significance against which whiteness is articulated, the gaps that have emerged between whites in these locales and those in the nation at large, have generated new racial meanings too heterogeneous to be summarized into one abstract racial order of significance.[5]

A second elaboration follows from this last point. Omi and Winant's (1986, 66–67) articulation of racial formation divides levels of analysis too rigorously between the abstract individual and the social collective: "At the micro-level, race is a matter of individuality. . . . At the macro-level, race is a matter of collectivity. . . . The racial order is organized and enforced by the continuity and reciprocity between these two levels of social relations." In between these levels is perhaps the most critical site for the generation and reproduction of racial formations: the cultural unit of the family.[6] The meaning of race depends to a large degree on whether particular families reproduce homogeneous or heterogeneous racial categories. Families process social relations (friendships, animosities, kin networks) in addition to reproducing cultural subjects.[7] As I explain below, the family is a distended and nebulous location, a scale of reference between individuals and the broader society that generates a great degree of variation in how racial categories gain and lose their significance.[8]

The third elaboration required by the notion of racial formation involves Omi and Winant's insistence that race is "a central axis of social relations." The problem with this formulation is that it requires that race be a unified phenomenon, not reducible to or subsumed by other orders. Such a requirement results in interminable debates over how to prioritize race with competing central axes, such as class, and undermines a recognition of the fundamental heterogeneity of objects produced simultaneously by class and racial systems of domination.[9] In this elaboration, as in the other two, the key shift in attention is from the implicit assumption that racial categories are homogeneous orders to the recognition that they are inevitably heterogeneous constructs (see chapters 1 and 2).[10] Even at the level of greatest abstraction, the nation or the globe, racial categories are rarely so rigorously delimited as to produce a consistently homogeneous content. With whiteness, gaps continually emerge between whites in different regions, in distinct families, and in various class positions. These gaps reveal distinct backgrounds of significance against which whites varyingly articulate and interpret the scope of their racialness.[11] The extent of this heterogeneity in racial categories becomes clearer with increasing attention to specific locations.

"WELCOME TO DETROIT . . ."

As a racial formation, Detroit is quite the opposite of the United States at large.[12] Whiteness may be hegemonic nationally, but that condition is bracketed in this city where blacks form 82 percent of the population.[13] Within the city's boundaries, blackness is hegemonic in terms of politics and culture.[14] This black hegemony has limits, of course. The surrounding suburbs are vastly white, and the inhabitants are quite interested in asserting regional mastery over certain operations of the city's infrastructure. At this level, the metropolitan Detroit area mirrors aspects of the seemingly absolute social divide between blacks and whites in the United States (see Massey and Denton 1993). Yet, within the city proper this mirror is shattered, leaving whites and blacks to negotiate the significance of their racial markings in contexts that are quite unfamiliar to most Americans.

As a racial formation, Detroit provides a context in which the meaning of race generally, and of whiteness and blackness in particular, diverges from national assumptions and understandings. The most important difference is that whiteness here is rarely an unmarked or normative condition. In fact, whiteness is often read as being out of place in this "black metropolis." A primary form of this reading of whiteness involves critiques of the racial interests of white suburban politicians who are striving to "regionalize" certain operations of the city's infrastructure. White suburbanites who make incursions into the city for entertainment and recreation also provide instances for reading whiteness as out of place in Detroit. Since the 1984 World Series victory celebration-turned-riot, Detroiters have been quick to note that white suburbanites are responsible for some of the most notorious instances of havoc that are regarded nationally as evidence of the lack of discipline among blacks in the city. The national media covering the chaos following the World Series in 1984 reported that once again Detroiters were destroying their own city. But a more thorough examination of the "rioters" by local reporters revealed that they were predominantly white suburbanites who had come into the city for the Series.

Such forays by whites into the city are often read popularly as moments of contamination. This connection between white incursions into the city and pollution is illuminated by Mary Douglas's (1966) continually relevant insight that cultural boundaries are ratified through an obsessive marking (as dirt or trash) of matter that is out of place. Illegal dumping is a huge problem in Detroit. By conservative estimates, discarded tires piled in vacant lots and in abandoned buildings outnumber city residents by more than two to one.[15] And most of this dumping seems to be carried out by city residents. The issue of pollution, though, garners little attention or symbolic charge unless the matter can be cast in racial terms. The city hosts an annual hydroplane race in the Detroit River off Belle Isle, a city park. In the summer of 1993, the crowd on the island was, as usual, vastly white, and they left behind mounds of trash, some of which was spectacularly burned in their wake. The next day's headline of the *Detroit Free Press* read: "Boat Race Fans Trash Belle Isle" (June 8, 1993). The article reported that "some Thunderfest revelers went too far this year, torching piles of trash and discarded couches which forced city parks crews to work overtime to clean up the mess." In an accompanying frame, the article highlighted a quote from the city parks director, Alonzo Bates: "Most of the folks who came in were whites. . . . They feel that this is a black city and we don't care. They think they can leave dirt and destruction behind and nobody will do anything about it. . . . They go wild and we look bad, but it's not Detroiters doing it."

The article also featured a debate over the accuracy of this racial assessment, and the matter was also fiercely discussed and featured in subsequent letters to the editor.[16] Suburbanites who took offense at being lumped together and read in reductively racialized terms charged Bates with making "racist comments." One resident of affluent Grosse Pointe Woods complained, "Why is he assuming all Thunderfest fans were non-Detroiters? Simply because the majority of them were white? How can you be so sure some of those fans weren't Detroiters?" A Detroit resident placed the blame for the problem on city officials and police who grant suburbanites "carte blanche" when they come into Detroit. Others insisted that race was irrelevant because the offending fans were simply "slobs." But what stands out in the collection of statements is the simultaneous ease and explosiveness with which whites are considered out of place in Detroit.

This connection between whiteness and pollution in Detroit is quite active at one level, but appears to scarcely impact the significance of racial categories in particular locations within the city, such as the Briggs neighborhood where I did the majority of my fieldwork, a blighted, extreme-poverty area adjacent to Tiger Stadium and within a mile of the city's downtown.[17] Residents here are ambivalent about the vastly white crowds that appear for the baseball games. Suburbanites do leave behind their garbage and frustrate some of the few remaining homeowners by urinating on lawns and in empty lots before and after the game, but most people in the area welcome the crowds because of the money they bring. Some residents make cash off these spectators by selling them parking spots, game tickets, and drugs. During the time I lived in this neighborhood, I never heard black residents racialize these incursions by white suburbanites.

The crowds at the Tigers' games illustrate one of the complexities involved with assessing the content of racial formations. Although the broader characterization of Detroit as black and the suburbs as white may be accurate, certain locations within these orders are subject to periodic fluctuations that disrupt the clarity and stability of such characterizations. Residentially, this census tract is 54 percent black, which establishes a certain order of racial dominance in the neighborhood. But the frequent appearance of these massively white crowds (96 to 98 percent of spectators at the stadium are white)[18] for the eighty-one home games each year undermines the facile equation of residential demographics with a certain racial balance. As well, the fluctuation in racial composition points to a crucial connection between local and national racial dynamics: the economic advantage of the visiting white suburbanites is a facet of the privileged mobility that distinguishes them from the impoverished residents of this zone, white and black. A racial reading of these periodic reversals might seem the most obvious, but for white residents the class component of the baseball crowds was a more compelling issue. I heard local whites expressing anxious discomfort about these visitors, emphasizing the fact that they were wealthy and hence arrogant and contemptuous. Local whites reported hearing snide comments from these suburbanites as they parked their cars in the vacant lots where houses once stood or purchased tickets from local scalpers. Such exchanges distinguished whites who seamlessly manipulated the privileges associated with their racial position from whites whose very racialness accentuated the degraded coding of their class standing.[19]

Over the course of my fieldwork, I often observed acquaintances among the white residents working in the lots parking cars before the games. Their difference from the suburban white visitors involved a complex of class distinctions: not just their occupational differences, but the fact of their particular location (poor whites in Detroit) mattered greatly.[20] Whites in this neighborhood did not participate in the same order of racial privilege and power with which whiteness is typically associated. For suburban whites, their racialness was an advantage; for the poor whites in this neighborhood, their racialness was a matter of shifting, everyday contexts; their whiteness might mark them as vulnerable to a host of black reactions or leave them open to contemptuous sneers from suburban whites, sparked by their lack of shared position of status that a common order of whiteness should have ensured.

The position of poor whites in Detroit points to an aspect of racial meanings that may or may not vary from formation to formation: that the significance of race fluctuates in relation to other modes of interest.[21] Racial meanings are often quickly rendered and asserted in Detroit, but there are also many situations in which they are suspended, held in abeyance, or simply do not come to mind. Any analysis of racial categories and meanings must be able to take into account the play between active and passive articulations of racial identity. The distinction between active and passive *does not* imply alternate modes of presence or absence such that, at times, a person's racialness might simply not be present. Rather, the value of this distinction is that it points to an interpretive continuum according to which the racial aspect of an event or situation registers either as significant or not to the participants. This type of analytic awareness involves an ability to understand how racial readings are prioritized among a host of other interpretive interests and concerns that assemble the cultural complexity of social subjects. In other words, analyzing whiteness is not simply a matter of specifying certain sites and determining how they shape and contour racial categories; it also entails locating whiteness among a host of concerns and values that occupy the realm of a person's consciousness in everyday or ritualistic registers. The meaning of race varies from location to location, but it also depends on the set of concerns against which it is prioritized and the other forms of consciousness or modes of reading with which it is ranked and arranged.

This variable aspect of whiteness is illustrated by the complex situation presented by another periodic event that temporarily shifts the racial content of this zone: the annual Saint Patrick's Day parade. The southern portion of the area is known as Corktown, after the county in Ireland that offered up many of the first Irish immigrants to settle in Detroit. Though the ethnic content of the area has shifted with the changing generations, becoming inhabited subsequently by Mexicans and Maltese, the neighborhood's Irish identity remains quite visible, supported largely by the "Irish" bars along Michigan Avenue. As well, the parish of Most Holy Trinity remains home to the Irish Americans who grew up here and to their children raised in the suburbs. They return annually during the high holy days surrounding Saint Patrick's Day, which is capped off by the parade.

As a slice of the racial formation of Detroit, the parade presents a stunning picture. Its content is only partially ethnic; in between the line of floats featuring scenes of Irish history and demonstrations of Irish culture march all-black bands from the city's high schools and junior highs.[22] On one frigid day in March, I stood with the other huddled spectators, white and black, watching the "ethnic" parade as it rolled down Michigan Avenue with its dozen or so bands from the city schools. For the white spectators I spoke with, the presence of black high school bands presented no disruption of the ethnic nature of the event, even if only one of the bands performed a traditional tune, such as "Danny Boy." These whites seemed to be intrigued by the seamlessness with which blacks moved in this performance of ethnicity, as if it confirmed the fundamentally ironic nature of ethnic identity in the United States (see Chock 1987). Nor were the black spectators that I talked with perturbed by the presence of white suburbanites packing the streets of downtown Detroit. People of both races were fascinated by the ability of this parade to unfold yearly with its heterogeneous racial content.

Inside the Gaelic League, a huge Irish American club located along the parade route, a more traditional performance of ethnic heritage and identity ensued. Bands there played an onslaught of standard jigs, reels, and waltzes; ballads and patriotic songs were thrown in to give the grandparents whirling their excited grandchildren across the floor a few moments' rest. On one stage the microphone was opened to those who wanted to come up and sing their favorite songs from Ireland, and the kitchen ran full bore late into the night. Here, all the participants were white, and yet in the most public performance of Irish ethnicity, the parade down one of Detroit's main avenues, the order of participants was racially heterogeneous. The racialness of all present at the parade was never absolved, but simply remained in a passive modality, paused on the cusp of some unarticulated threshold, waiting for something to be made of it.

The significance of racial materiality in this particular zone depends largely on alternating active and passive modalities. There are thresholds across which race matters absolutely, but they compete with a diverse array of other thresholds that individuals rely on to determine when other abstractions matter more, such as crime or violence or poverty. On the streets and in social spaces, on front porches and in corner bars, whites and blacks move alongside each other continually, mutually inhabiting the same blighted zone where the poverty rate runs at 51 percent. Few people actually own their own homes; most are on welfare or currently unemployed. Yet, with all this in common, everyone here is an obviously racial being. They all notice and are marked by race; they think and talk about race; they recognize it as a substance that inexorably links and divides them. Although race never materializes as exclusive residential zones within Briggs, neither is it simply a matter of individual attitudes; it depends on the context and on the significance people are interested in making out of racial difference.

FAMILY, RACE, CLASS

Jerry

The family I lived next door to in the neighborhood was a group of "hillbillies" centered on the relations of three brothers: Jerry, Sam, and David. (Three other brothers and two sisters lived in the city's suburbs.) They were one family among many who came to Detroit from West Virginia, Kentucky, and Tennessee. Such Appalachian migrant families form an "invisible minority" of inner-city whites in cities throughout the Midwest.[23] In the case of Jerry and his brothers, their parents were both born in the South and met and married in the North. The brothers used "hillbilly" as a term of self-identification, but with a great deal of ambivalence. The designation marked their difference from the older generation of white native Detroiters who remained in the neighborhood in the wake of the mass exodus of whites from the city that began in the early 1950s.[24] Hillbilly was also used to distinguish them from other southern whites who had achieved more financial security and assimilated into the suburbs.[25] Whenever hillbilly was used, it carried a volatile charge of social contempt, a contempt these brothers alternately reveled in or rejected, inscribing a particular class difference that divided the whites in the neighborhood. Objectifications of a collective order among these whites were quite rare, and hillbilly operated as the most salient common identity recognized by them.

One afternoon, I joined the brothers around David's Ford LTD, watching and sometimes helping Jerry tinker with the failing water pump. David was trying to decide which problem was more critical: the transmission, the brakes, or the water pump; he could afford to repair only one. I had been moved in for a couple of days, and the brothers were still sizing me up. Sam wanted to know why I had not gone "to school" yesterday. I went over again how I was doing a study of the neighborhood rather than taking classes or literally going to school. Jerry asked, "What is it you're studying again?"

"Race relations," I replied.

They exploded, laughing. David said, "Oh you come to the right place for that. Just keep going to the bars with us, you'll learn all you need to know about race relations."

Sam offered, "I'll take you over to them bars on Third, and you'll sure learn something."

David: "Naw, man, you want to learn about race relations, you just walk from here through them projects over to the freeway on the other side. That's an education! 'Cause I'll tell you what, you won't come out the other side. You walk in there and you're gonna learn more than you can handle what race relations is. You won't come out the other side."

Sam: "Yeah, go in there at night, you won't get a hundred yards." They giggled over this, then their talk turned back to more concrete matters involving the LTD. The bars on Third Avenue, I later found out, had been their stomping ground as slightly younger, rowdier men, when Third Avenue was the spine of the concentration of hillbillies in Detroit. They now visited them only occasionally, in part because increasing age had made the brothers less adept at negotiating the dangerous contexts of such places. They preferred O'Leary's, around the corner, which was frequented by slightly more whites than blacks and featured a mix of honky-tonk and rhythm-and-blues tunes on the jukebox. The "projects" were directly across the broad, three-way intersection from our house. When a graduate student from nearby Wayne State University was shot to death by a thirteen-year-old boy on the street in front of the projects, the brothers were all quick to point out that this proved their assessment: "See, I told you. That's what happens to researchers."[26]

It was not until many months later, when I began to wrap up my field-work, that this exchange came back to me as quite striking. The brothers immediately connected the abstraction "race relations" with the absolute racial zone of the projects, not simply for the degree of blackness of that demographic site, but because if they entered or passed by it they would be out of place and read reductively as strictly racial objects: whites. The basis for their sense of direction stemmed from an awareness of place and location. In this neighborhood, they were one family among many, white and black, who held elaborate and lengthy knowledge of each other reaching back over the tumultuous past three decades. But across the intersection, they were simply whites, partly for their skin color, but also in terms of location and being out of place.[27]

What I found fascinating in their response was the way it ignored their immediate setting, which they obviously did not regard as racial. Jerry maintained the three remaining houses on this corner for their Maltese landlord. Jerry, his wife, Jessi Rae, and his brother Sam, his wife, and their two children lived in the first house. There were three black men living in the other rental rooms in that house; this number varied, as one black tenant took in fluctuating numbers of friends from off the street. The middle house was a two-family flat; I lived in the bottom flat, and David lived upstairs with his wife and their son. Two black couples, one white couple, and a single white man lived in the third house. One of the black couples in this house, Marvin and Charlotte, had a long friendship with Jerry and Jessi Rae. They celebrated birthdays together at O'Leary's and collaborated on some mean barbecues in the yard. Marvin and Jerry had worked together for at least the past two years, using Marvin's truck for various hauling and towing jobs. Jerry enjoyed waxing on about the past bad winters and how, if it had not been for Marvin and he working together, they all would have gone hungry.

Yet this relationship and the general living situation did not spring to mind when I asked them about race relations. They shared their houses with blacks and faced similar economic dilemmas with their black neighbors, but they did not feel that met the criteria of the academic abstraction I had posed regarding race relations. The problem of whiteness arose for them when they ventured out of their place in the "hood," but it did not starkly signify in the immediate context of their homes.[28] This is not to say that they did not recognize themselves, or understand the ways their black neighbors regarded them, as whites. But whiteness preeminently gained active significance as a feature of their identity when they were challenged in biracial contexts.[29]

As social aggregates, whites and blacks in this neighborhood are diverse and distended associations, but they do not materialize into reified, spatial orders. Instead, race is a matter of scattered instances and inexorable histories. Whites and blacks resisted narrating the conflicts that arose between neighbors as being of racial origin. The most consistent generalizing phrase I heard from people of both races was "There's good and bad in everybody." Or as Bill, a black man in his sixties, explained to me, "Peoples is like dogs: there're some you get along with, and there're some you're born to fight. Can't change that." Such distinctions often fall within racial categories rather than characterizing the difference between two collectives, which leaves the significance of race open to varying interpretations. Such benign renderings would evaporate on occasion in conflicts that were racialized by one or both parties, but racial polarization was not sustainable for long because the social worlds and economic circumstances of whites and blacks in this area were too enmeshed.

The members of this hillbilly family showed no consistent attitude concerning blacks. Just distinguishing between and explaining the range of understandings and experiences of each of the three brothers regarding blacks would require more space than this chapter allows. David was aloof from the rest of the family. He was going to school to get a cosmetology degree, and he made a point of emphasizing his disgust and distrust of his brothers whenever possible. He was also usually quite emphatic in his contempt for blacks. Sam, at times quite suspicious of blacks generally and prone to bitter racial sentiments, was the one brother who most emphasized the importance of moments of racial transcendence when they occurred. He cared, too, about specifying that he developed a sense of racial animosity on his own, rather than have me think that he was just raised that way.

Late one night, Sam and I were sitting out in the yard. In the few weeks that I had known him, he had dissected for me the roots of his suspicion toward blacks. It began in elementary school with being shaken down daily for his lunch money by black kids who controlled the bridge over the freeway that led to their school. Other childhood recollections centered on trying to get back home from Tiger Stadium and being chased by black kids through these very streets. "Every year we'd go up there on Bat Day, and not once did we make it back to Canfield with those bats. When they caught us, they'd beat us up and take them bats." He had a number of tales of being jumped by black youths, which resonated with those told by his brothers and other whites who grew up in that neighborhood. But that night what came to mind for him was a warning to me, a prediction drenched in memories, a past that continued to return. He began explaining to me the formula that produced racial violence, describing how he had been caught up in its inexorably arbitrary logic. The times he had been jumped were mainly on those hot summer nights when people are irritable and reckless. "It's quiet now," he noted, looking down Martin Luther King Jr. Avenue. "But one of these nights, it's gonna be too hot to sleep. A bunch of them are gonna come down that street looking to kick your ass. They don't know you, but they're looking for you. It's happened to me, it'll happen to you, too, if you stay here long enough. One of these hot nights, they're gonna come right down that street." Sam's wariness developed from his particular past rather than drawing on an essentialized sense of otherized difference. For Sam, racial antagonism was a contextual order; individual relations did little to obviate the relentlessly volatile nature of arbitrary racial violence; all one could do was "watch out."[30]

As vulnerable as they were to sporadic racial violence, I was surprised to find that this induced no general sense of solidarity among whites in the area. In fact, these hillbillies were more animatedly detached from other whites than they were from many black families. One afternoon a couple of weeks later, while we were sitting out on the porch, I asked Jerry about a white family that lived around the corner. He disgustedly snarled, "They're a bunch of assholes. Well, Tommy's all right, and so is Billy if he ain't drunk. They all hang out at O'Leary's some, but they just go down there looking to fight. They get stupid and make trouble. They're a bunch of assholes. The grandfather, old man Johnson, he's all right; he'd talk to you. But watch out for the rest of them." I almost laughed when I heard Jerry's response. Since I had moved in, other whites had similarly warned me about Jerry's family, and in particular, told me, "Don't trust Jerry." Whereas unknown blacks might present a degree of uncertainty for Jerry and his brother, the depth of distrust or contempt reserved for fellow whites was typically profound and intense.

During the course of my fieldwork I realized that conflicts in this zone tended to follow family divides: the largest embroilments were produced when family members were drawn into conflicts in defense or support of their relatives. The repercussions of such conflicts produced elaborate fractures and rifts among residents in the neighborhood, such as that between Jerry and his brothers and the white family that lived around the corner.

What this dynamic reveals is that the strength of family solidarity here problematizes any stable, collective notion of racial allegiance. Jerry's family is ostensibly a homogeneous racial site, and yet it erodes any certain, larger sense of racial commonality because it demands a sense of allegiance that is much more compelling than any notion of a shared whiteness. The many differences generated by past conflicts prevented whites from enacting a solidarity that might have provided the basis for a collective identity. Along with the fact that they resided with and among blacks, their preference for responding to conflicts as family members was yet another reason whiteness was rarely objectified as a shared racial order in this zone.

This is not to say that there were no similarities among the white residents. The sense of a displaced regional identity was strong among the whites with connections to the South. Some traveled back home to register their cars and to visit families with regularity; they also received visiting family members who came north for a weekend or longer. But another common condition for these white families was the extent to which they were divided from their own family members by the city's boundaries. I expected the city limits to uniquely signify a racial divide separating black from white, but for these inner-city whites, the borders of Detroit predominantly indicated a stark class division. Detroit's population peaked around 1952; its hemorrhaging of people has been largely steady since then.[31] Over time, as the city limits became increasingly racialized, those who left grew more estranged from both their old neighborhoods and their own family members who still reside here. Broadly speaking, class mobility marks the difference between whites who stayed in this zone and those who left, but an interesting racial significance developed as well regarding this relocation of whites.

Late one evening, after it became too dark for Jerry to keep working on the ruptured fuel line on his Gremlin, we slipped into a long conversation about family. At the moment, he was furious with his brother Sam, who was living in the house rent-free. The landlord had finally realized that Jerry allowed Sam and his family to live there on the sly. Though Jerry bought him several free months by fooling the landlord, now, when the game was up, Sam was still refusing to make any gesture toward paying rent. This conflict played out over the next month and a half, but that night it got Jerry and Jessi Rae, who joined us in the yard, talking about raising kids and strained family relations. On the matter of discipline, Jerry was proud of the restraint he had shown with their kids.

Jerry: Those kids got only five whippings between 'em their whole lives. That's it. Just five. That was enough. After that I could just raise my voice and they listened.

Jessi Rae: Well, kids know, if you don't raise your voice you don't really mean it.

Jerry: Just five whippings. I never beat them up or slapped them around 'cause that ain't right. And they minded, too. And my brothers and sisters were all the time giving me shit, saying they were gonna grow up all fucked up 'cause we lived in Detroit. Barry was the worst of them. He was saying, "Your boy's gonna be in the pen, and your daughter's gonna be a nigger lover."

Jerry's face drew into a sneer as he repeated his brother's predictions.

Jessi Rae: That's right, he said she'd grow up to be a nigger lovin' whore.

Jerry: That's what he said. And every one of them have given us shit about staying here. They all live in the suburbs and they shit on us because we never left. We never left the inner city of Detroit. We never tried to, either. We've never lived any more than a few blocks from where we grew up. Those kids grew up between here and Third and Alexandrine. We never left this city. And those kids all went to the Detroit schools, and they all turned out fine.

For Jerry's brothers who left Detroit, his position challenged notions of racial allegiance that might have been based on family ties. The term "nigger lover" makes their offended sense of racialness clear. The only other time I heard this term used in Detroit was in the context of arguments between local whites and those from beyond the city's boundaries. To whites like Jerry, the term was no more offensive, it seemed, than a host of other insults that could be applied; if he was ready to fight anyway, then any mode of name-calling offered sufficient cause. But "nigger lover" points to a reservoir of anger and confusion felt strongly by whites who left the city toward those who stayed behind. While their other brothers' fears of (and disgust for) blacks were so great that they left the city, Jerry stayed because he loved the area, David stayed because it was cheap, and Sam came and went ambivalently. These three brothers remained for reasons that are not racial, but their other brothers left for reasons that predominantly involve race and the felt need to reestablish a sense of whiteness in a more homogeneous zone.[32]

Whites' motivation for leaving the city significantly involves race; it also complexly and inextricably involves a sense of class division. Although the range of sentiment among Jerry and his brothers regarding race is interesting, Jerry was far more concerned with the great degree of class variation that had developed within his family. When Jerry recounted Barry's predictions, it was the classed tones of contempt his brother articulated that bothered him deeply. Jerry survives on various hustles, government checks, and his work as a bouncer at the corner grocery store; Sam was regularly out of work, but his wife was a cook at a fast-food restaurant in Taylor, a thirteen-mile drive each way. Several of the other brothers had made good. Barry had taken a job training program while he was on welfare, started in a maintenance job for a large hotel firm, and worked his way up to being in charge of maintenance for the company in this region. Another brother supposedly held a management-level position at a large brewing company. Barry stopped by Jerry's when he needed his cars worked on; the only other times I saw the suburban brothers were when their mother, who still lived in Detroit, was either sick or celebrating a birthday. What kept the other brothers away was not simply a contempt for the racial order in the city, but also Jerry's generally degraded class position, which recalled their own meager origins.

I heard from many other whites in the neighborhood that, for them, the city limits form a class divide that sunders their ties with family members who have "moved up in the world." Betty, a white woman in her late fifties, lives with her brother in one of the old workers' cottages that were thrown up all over this area in the 1880s to meet the city's burgeoning demands for cheap housing in the nineteenth century. Aside from her brother, the rest of her family lives in the suburbs, "way out there. They never come to visit us. They've got their noses up in the air, y'know what I mean. They won't come down here anymore." One afternoon I was helping Betty put up signs on the abandoned houses, warning "This house is being watched," in approach of Devil's Night.[33] She reeled off stories about the past occupants of each of the houses that now stood vacant and ruined. Between the mostly burned abandoned houses and the hundreds of lots now turned to prairie grass, the old neighborhood has changed drastically since the rest of her family left. "They never want to come down here, anymore. They just can't stand it. 'It's gross,' " she mimicked. " 'It's gross.' They're terrible." She cannot understand her sisters' attitudes because they were all raised in this neighborhood. "They even went to school here, too." But they refuse to come back, apparently not wanting to be reminded of their humble beginnings.

Now she sees the family only on rare occasions, "like weddings." The most recent time had been at the funeral for one of her sisters. "See, we don't have a car, so we can't get out there. And they won't come and visit us." Betty said that at the funeral, "we wanted to leave, 'cause we couldn't take anymore. So we asked if somebody could give us a ride. Well, my brother-in-law tells someone to tell us that he'll give us the money to take a cab. Can you believe that? I just told them to tell him 'We don't need your money,' then we just left." They never returned any of Betty's calls. "I believe my sister always made him call before, but now he just doesn't want to talk to us."

These instances demonstrate that family and kin groups are more than little social factories where ideological orders are homogeneously reproduced. The content and function of this site vary depending on its location and position.[34] Perhaps in more homogeneous racial zones, this site generates social units with little variation and the children inherit their parents' belief structure fairly intact. But even in such zones, the family is also the site in which social relations are magnified and changing experiences are examined, manipulated, and contested collectively. The family is never a static entity; members are typically added and lost over time, through birth and death, but also through various social relationships such as adoption, friendship, and marriage. What makes this site mutable is the variety of shifting social relationships that it grounds.

An interesting aspect of the role of families in constituting racial formations is that they fuse temporal and spatial orders. The racial materiality that composes a family is distended across a given past that cannot be perfectly replicated, a present in which members synthesize copious social relations and experiences as a group, and a future into which their given social materiality is refracted and extended through births, adoptions, and marriages. In other words, family is as much a process as it is an abstract social site. With this in mind, I turn now to a brief discussion of the role that adoption plays for families in this zone. Partly because of the general economic instability, families here dissolve, leaving younger members either to fend for themselves or to be (legally or informally) adopted into extant families. This process is a generative source for the racial heterogeneity of this zone.

Esther

One of the first people Jerry introduced me to at O'Leary's was Esther, a white woman in her late forties. Jerry affectionately referred to her as "Mom." She was a well-regarded regular at the bar, with an elaborate network of social relationships that she had developed over a lifetime spent in this neighborhood. I later interviewed her on a hot and miserable day while she was on vacation from her job of cooking and washing dishes at a westside club. Esther embodies many of the dynamics involving adoption in Briggs. She told me her father "sold" her to a family moving to Florida when she was a child. In Florida, she got pregnant at age thirteen. When her adopted mother took her baby and gave it up for adoption, Esther left in a fury and came back to her family in Detroit. She has never seen that child or her adopted family since. Though several of her siblings live a few blocks away and even frequent the same bar, she tries to avoid them. "They only live right there on Butternut, but I only see them twice a year. Because, I mean, it's just gossip all the time: who did this and who did that, and 'They ain't no good,' when they [her family] ain't no damn better." Although Esther remains disgusted with "living in the ghetto," she considers that her family "is used to living like that. My family wouldn't give a shit if there was a roof over their heads or not."

Esther gave birth to eight children, three were stillborn, and she adopted one of her brother's daughters after he and his wife gave up on raising the child. She was raising her "black" grandson, Jason, because her adopted daughter became "too wild" to care for him. Esther stays generally detached from her children. Only one son "got away" from the life that she hates so much. The others terrify or disgust her to varying degrees; she said they were too involved with drugs and crime.

"When it gets to the point that you start fearing your own kids, you don't need 'em around. And I wouldn't put nothing past them. My adopted daughter has been in prison three times for murder and got out of it; she got acquitted each time. They didn't believe that she could've done it—she's so small. But I knew she did it. I knew."

I asked her how she thought race mattered in this area.

"Down here? Well, there's a lot of mixed families—a lot. A lot of young girls, I think, to me, it has to be attention, it's got to do with attention. Because, a lot of times, because I've got it in my family, all my grandkids, most of them are all mixed. And it seems like it's their way of being noticed, if they're walking down the street with a black man. Because, it's just like my grandson, he's black. When we go somewhere and people hear him call me 'Ma,' they look. Y'know, 'cause he don't call me his grandmother, he calls me his ma. Y'know, people just look."

For Esther, in this case, race matters as a function of almost involuntary attention. Racial differences are accentuated in these couples whom she sees as being drawn together because of race, not in spite of it. Race also mattered for Esther regarding her daughters' relationships with black men, because the product of these unions had distinctly racialized her. The racial aspect of her reading is evident, but it is subsumed within a more fundamental class logic of treating all social relations as manipulative.[35] Esther described how her daughters' relationships had increasingly racialized her, largely against her will, it seemed. This surprised me, because I had noticed that her elaborate friendship network included many neighborhood blacks, mostly women.

Esther: It just kinda makes you, y'know, some of my best friends are black, but we don't get into all of that, y'know. It just irritates the shit out of me sometimes. It just makes me prejudiced in a way.

JH: How so?

Esther: It makes you kind of prejudiced against the black guy using the white girl. A lot of times the blacks use the whites.

JH: In what way?

Esther: A lot of black men use white women. Y'know, they just go, "I got me a white bitch," that's what the whole thing is about. They're useless to them, unless you're gonna go out and make him some money. That's about the way it goes.

JH: Do you see that a lot?

Esther: Oh yeah, with a lot of the young girls that hang out at the bar. I've got nothing against the races, it's just, don't use people. And that's the way it goes. Like my one daughter, she won't go with nothing but a black man. It just irritates the shit out of me [laughs].

JH: Because you feel she's being used?

Esther: No. She likes attention. My daughter thinks she's God's gift to man, y'know. She's got three kids and they all got three different black men for daddies.

JH: That's Jason's mom?

Esther: No, but she's got three kids, too, all by different fathers. I've got eight grandchildren and none of them are by the same father. I'm talking about the girls, they're the ones having the babies, and each one has a different father. And then they give 'em all different last names; that's what irritates me, too. If you're not married to him, why not at least give them the name you carry? These kids have got to go to school, and this one over here has got a different last name than this one, so how can we be brothers and sisters? And that irritates me.

For Esther, the "races" coming together did nothing to eliminate racial differences; the differences were only accentuated. But it is worth noting that when she considered the offspring of these relations, the confusion over family that bothered her was not that the grandchildren were different colors, but that they all had different names.[36] Her daughters' patronymic choices had left her disturbingly and legally estranged from the grandchildren she was increasingly called on to care for. In addition to the confusion of connections between the children, she also complained of bureaucratic problems when she had to sign their report cards or authorize any kind of medical care for them because she shared no family name with any of them. It was not the range of racial content that made their connection problematic, but that the familial basis that could process that range of difference had, from a bureaucratic perspective, been undermined.

Her irritation, though, did involve race, just not so much in terms of personal opinion. Esther was comfortable with her relations with blacks in the neighborhood, but caring for her daughters' "black" children had put her into situations that not only racialized her, but racialized her perceptions involuntarily to the point that it became harder for her to have race not matter: "It makes you kind of prejudiced." She could will good relations with blacks her own age and her own gender, but other relations were outside her control.[37] Even though she was estranged from her parents and siblings, she encountered the racially productive site of family in another generation. The generational shift had taken her out of her place in the neighborhood and moved her into problematic institutional settings.

Esther described how she had to deal with the verbal taunts of black students whenever she went to one of the schools to deal with one of her grandkids. The Detroit public schools are even more racially homogeneous sites than is the city in general.[38] "No white person wants to go up to that school for their kid," she told me. "I've had problems up there before. Well, the kids, they call you names and all: 'You're all this. You're snowflake,' and me, I get pissed, and I say, 'Okay chocolate drop'" (she laughed). "So, and then it starts confusion, so I try to stay away from it."

Relating to her grandchildren racialized Esther by bringing her into zones where her racialness would be read reductively as out of place; attending to her "black" grandchildren made her whiter even though she promoted no notion of racial superiority. It is notable that in such heterogeneous family sites, race retained an indelible content, no more diluted than if these members were in homogeneous family groups. This point is clear from the suspicion that Esther bore for both members of biracial couples. The issue of attention played both ways for her. She felt both sides were using the other race, though in unequal fashion based on gender differences. The fact of racial unions was not annoying, but the forms of manipulation she thought they embodied did "irritate" her.

JH: The attention you mentioned before, where is that coming from mostly, other whites, other blacks?

Esther: Well, no, it's them theirselves. What it is, is they like to get noticed. So if you take a real fair-skinned white girl with bleached blonde hair and you stick her with a man that's black as tar, people are going to look! And they like this, they like this. The white girls like this! I mean, it's your choice, do whatever you're gonna do. Just don't do it for the wrong reasons.

For Esther, the complexity of their racialness (hers, her daughters', their children's) had expanded exponentially. Where as an individual she could efface the significance of race with her friends ("we don't get into that stuff"), as a family member she had become racialized in a manner outside her control or will, both by her nurturing role and by the positions in which it placed her. She was put into positions where she was out of place and subjected to the judgment "You're all this." This was in stark contrast to social scenes in the bar, where black and white differences were more malleable matters and subject to discussion.

AND IN GENERAL?

In our efforts to analyze, dissect, and repudiate whiteness, it is critical that we keep in mind the problem of scale in relating to this racial construct. Jerry and Esther deal with and experience whiteness on a scale that is completely alien to most white Americans. This alienness is structured by their poverty, their social origins, and their position within the vastly black city of Detroit. Their modes of engagement with whiteness, in turn, differ in ways too numerous to adequately recount. However, their phrases resonate with common tropes and discursive tacks of whites across the United States. Esther's phrase "Some of my best friends are black" is the clearest example. But unlike most whites who speak this phrase, in addition to such friends Esther also has black grandchildren to tend to, and in the case of Jason, singly raise. For Esther, the fact of having black friends did not, as most often is the case when whites make this claim, assert that race is unimportant. Rather, it marked racialness as a mode of cultural significance that whites and blacks ineptly or deftly struggle with daily. Notably, it is not a phrase that Jerry was compelled to speak in our discussion of race relations. He did not reify his black friends and neighbors as a counterweight to his racial view of this zone. But this should not suggest that there is a qualitative distinction between his opinions on race and Esther's. It is not just the content and discursive character of her statement that matters, but the position and context in which it was articulated.

Esther noted of her black friends that "we don't get into all of that" about race. This phrase, like Bill's naturalizing comment comparing people's animosities to those of dogs, seems to be a form of avoiding race altogether, a discursive move that Ruth Frankenberg has shown is characteristic of white people's public assessments of race. But what do we make of the resonances between the comments of Bill, a black man, and Esther, a white woman? They are similar soundings of a domain in which race is every day in everybody's face. Race is something to be effaced in this inner-city zone where street violence is commonplace, where residents strive to find means of undermining motivating impulses that can polarize ambiguous or even accidental social exchanges. Where people find ample incitement to violence, race is just one excuse that black and white residents generally prefer to defuse, lest a conflict between individuals bleeds into collective matters. Rather than a form of avoiding race, such comments are a means of restraining the significance of racialness from becoming too abstract and totalizing.

It is tempting to conclude with a sweeping point such as, In a cultural regard, race is a materiality only partially under the control of individuals; its significance manifests in social relations and settings that an individual can attempt to manipulate, but are as often objects of others' manipulations. This would be an overly broad generalization. More to the point is that racial matters, like other social materials, are manipulable to varying degrees depending on a host of contexts and one's class position. What matters with race is as much a person's class position as his or her individual opinions and choices of whom to relate with. Locating class, geographically and in terms of structures of significance, is a simultaneous and overlapping function of locating racialness in general and whiteness in particular. The point of this chapter is to offer a perspective on the ambiguous contexts and exchanges that are easily overwhelmed by modes of analysis that abstract the significance of racial matters too broadly. This fieldwork convinced me that however whiteness may be regarded at the level of greatest expanse (ideology, for instance), no continuous motivating or informing impulse can be traced down through the various levels of increasing specificity with absolute consistency. Nor, in the obverse, can we compile a more or less thorough aggregate of whites, abstract out from them a common condition or an intrinsic set of connections, and have neatly defined by these efforts a succinct, abiding identity: whiteness. In each domain or level (nation, region, city, neighborhood, block, house, and yard), the material conditions of whites exhibit degrees of incomparability with those of other levels: the difference between whiteness and whites, in its continual repetition, ensures an irregular terrain in which some whites always sit insecurely in the larger body of whiteness. At each level, the gap between whiteness and whites opens distinct horizons of social and political contexts. An attempt to map all of these would be stymied by the daunting task of proposing a unified means of locating whites and whiteness into a range of domains in some standard, proportional relation to each other and under consistent forms of magnification.

Instead of generating such a map, I conclude this chapter by way of reinflecting a popular mythic image: the melting pot, the long-active model of Americanization that envisioned a continuous stream of conventionalized, homogeneous products/citizens. In a sense, Detroit put the idea of the melting pot on the map of this nation's cultural imagination. The image, after all, is an industrial one. It was never simply an insidious ideology promoted by progressive business leaders and capitalists who required an efficient means for assimilating the great stream of foreign immigrants and black and white migrants from the rural South who poured into U.S. cities looking for work. The melting pot was a material, pervasive reality for those workers and the very basis of the industrial order that drew them to the great northern cities. In the steel mills, coke plants, and smelting operations, they worked where the raw materials were melted, blended, pressed, forged, and molded into the infrastructure of the swelling consumer economy. For these workers, the image made sense at a more mundane level than could ever have been fully recognized or manipulated by publicists for the industrial order. Rather than an elusive object of desire, the melting pot was a livelihood and responsibility, and a relentless, dangerous occupation.

The melting pot was largely a paradigm of ethnic rather than racial melding; its operations primarily envisioned smelting the array of cultures brought from across the Atlantic into one seamless body of efficient, unmarked labor. As the vicious conflicts that unfolded in plants and on shop floors in Detroit attest, blacks did not fit easily into this scheme of things.[39] The process of molding and fusing foreign workers' bodies into expendable components of the production process involved a mode of racial reproduction that required blackness to remain an indigestible embodiment of Otherness. Through decades of struggle and conflict, though, the melting pot in cities like Detroit was grudgingly made to include and produce black workers as well.

Whatever is finally decided about the relative worth of that operation, whether the mode of assimilation that the melting pot provided was of positive or negative value to the Irish, Poles, Hungarians, Appalachians, and others who fell under its sway, the image is now defunct.[40] Detroit, once the symbol of America's industrial order, is now the setting for social commentators who want to demonstrate the tragic effects of deindustrialization (Vergara 1992; Herron 1993). In this desolate condition, Detroit remains charged mythic ground, symbolizing for whites in the nation at large both the unsalvageable refuse of the underclass left in the wake of the speeding new high-tech, postindustrial economy, and the shambles wrought by black civic self-rule. The future represented by Detroit differs distinctly from that of Los Angeles, a city similar in history and contemporary conflicts.[41] Where Los Angeles becomes the site for techno-conflicts by cyborgs in defense of humanity, as in *Terminator II*, the population of Detroit is subjected to the unrestrained lethal onslaught of the corporate cleansing agent, *RoboCop*. Aside from its mythic status as a playground for antipopulation technologies, deindustrialized Detroit can also be read figuratively, in the key of racial allegorizing, for a different emerging present and future. Detroit—in its deindustrialized condition, with the forges and furnaces shuttered and abandoned—also represents a current condition of racial material; it is no longer smelted or processed into homogeneous, purified metals, but remains heterogeneous, distended, and extractable from its location only at great cost.[42]

CHAPTER 9

OBJECT LESSONS IN

WHITENESS: ANTIRACISM

AND THE STUDY

OF WHITE FOLKS

For academics concerned with the problems of racial inequality and search-ing for a means to directly effect a change in the way racism is socially reproduced, these are exciting times. Antiracism is emerging as a coordi-nated and sustained means of both pursuing critical pedagogy and politi-cally engaging the institutions that racially structure society. This chapter examines efforts by social researchers to turn their scholarly training to-ward the broad goal of eliminating racism. Antiracism as a political prac-tice increasingly also encompasses efforts to generate critical knowledge about whiteness and its operations, while also challenging, destabilizing, and short-circuiting the social routines by which white dominance is repro-duced.[1] This work depends partly on the ability of antiracists to make use of historical or ethnographic research and, in some cases, to deploy techniques derived from the participant-observation practices of ethnographers. The focus of this chapter is on this interesting moment as scholarship and activ-ism merge in antiracist efforts to compile a systematic body of knowledge concerning the object of its interventions: whiteness.[2]

But this moment is not without problems and perils. As antiracism solid-ifies as a means of engaging racial inequality, it risks reifying both an object of investigation and a way of thinking about race that is inattentive to the dramatic ways racial identity is rapidly transforming. The growing con-fidence about what whiteness is has produced dogmatic political formulations, such as the call to "abolish" whiteness,[3] that have only limited purchase on the attention of whites who need to be engaged on the subject of race. Thus, in surveying the current crossings between academic work on race and antiracist writings and teachings, this chapter also offers some critical reflections on how this conjunction might be enhanced and sharpened. Tapping ethnographic perspectives on antiracism and whiteness, I argue that our ears need to be tuned to the ambiguous aspects of white racial thinking and that the uncertainties permeating whites' racial experiences are key resources for affecting the way whites identify racially. If antiracists can draw more widely from ethnographic findings and techniques, and if they adopt an orientation toward the interpretive work of their subjects, antiracism's critical engagements with the reproduction of white identity can perhaps be more powerful.

ANTIRACISM AND THE ETHNOGRAPHIC GAZE

Antiracism is the term for a movement that covers a broad range (historically and contemporarily) of efforts to directly counter the reproduction of racism in its manifest institutional and personal forms. In Britain, an antiracist mass movement emerged in the 1970s, organized by Rock Against Racism and the Anti-Nazi League. Paul Gilroy (1987) notes that these groups were committed to engaging the cultural dimensions of struggle, moving beyond the confines of formal politics into the realm of popular discourses. Characterizing antiracist sentiments, Gilroy asserts that these types of organizations "have been concerned not directly with the enhancement of the power of the oppressed or disadvantaged groups but with the development of racially harmonious social and political relations" (117). Rock Against Racism sought to bridge racial divides partly by stressing common class concerns between black and white youths, but it also asserted the need for whites to disavow their whiteness through the potent crossing points of popular and punk music. Antiracist goals were redefined by the Anti-Nazi League, which more sharply sought to engage fascist, nationalist political movements in Britain. These popular forms of antiracism influenced the establishment of what Gilroy terms "municipal anti-racism," a series of policy statements, publicity campaigns, and workplace training routines directed toward "the elimination of racism" in bureaucratic operations. Gilroy's critiques of these versions of antiracism are multifaceted, but he fundamentally stresses that "the unevenness of racism, its different forms in different institutional contexts and the correspondingly different forms of organization, tactics and modes of actions required to attack it are simply not acknowledged to be significant" (145).[4]

In the United States, antiracist politics have a long and diffuse history, but in the 1970s there emerged a range of awareness training methods and consciousness-raising strategies to provoke in whites a realization of their participation in the reproduction of racism.[5] These initial efforts emerged as Racism Awareness Training, an established series of techniques deployed in institutional settings, which most closely represents the form of antiracist practice I am concerned with here.[6] In this form, antiracism is achieving an established position in various institutional contexts, such as academia and corporate multicultural training sessions. George Sefa Dei (1996, 4) defines this version of antiracism as "an action-oriented strategy for institutional systemic change that addresses racism and other interlocking systems of social oppression. It is a critical discourse of race and racism in society that challenges the continuance of racializing social groups for differential treatment. Antiracism explicitly names the issues of race and social difference as issues of power and equity, rather than as matters of cultural and ethnic variety."

Ethnography—a view of the lived experiences, social relations, and symbolic dimensions of everyday life—shares certain features with antiracist interventions. Practitioners of both pursuits assume the importance of mundane matters (the realm of "everyday life") in the operations of society or culture. Congruent with a developed ethnographic tradition, antiracism examines and challenges the marginalization of certain voices in society. Similar to the work of ethnographers, antiracists detail the delegitimation or devaluation of the knowledge and experience of subordinate/minority groups. As Sefa Dei (1996, 6) explains, "It challenges definitions of what can be named 'valid knowledge,' and how such knowledge should be produced and distributed, both locally and globally." These points of resonance between ethnography and antiracism partly reflect the fact, as Dei further notes, that antiracism developed as "a consequence of ongoing transformations in social science epistemologies that offer alternative readings of how, as social beings, we live our lives in multiethnic, multiracial communities" (4). As a series of disparate projects, antiracism is partly informed by the efforts of anthropologists to understand such processes as transnational identity formation and globalization.

Indeed, some antiracist scholars are moving toward a more direct participation in anthropological knowledge production. This is perhaps best demonstrated by the collected volume *Racism and Anti-Racism in World*

Perspective (Bowser 1995). A significant portion of this work is organized as "area studies of racism and anti-racism," in which researchers examine "how racism is expressed in [their] national culture" and "comment on the nature and extent of dominant group anti-racism." Not surprisingly, they find the latter task very difficult, "largely because of the lack of attention to anti-racism from scholars, newspapers, and activists alike" (155). Still, they provide sufficient commentary for a concluding summary that highlights a range of goals, tactics, and objects of engagement for antiracists in distinct "national cultures" and specific "world communities" (303–305). Whereas challenges to the false consciousness of workers' attachment to "artificial and inaccurate" representation of national identity are a fundamental starting point in the United States and Western Europe, different tactics are called for in the Caribbean, "where the issues of racism and anti-racism are waged between peoples of color in a microsetting within the larger world economy" (156). And though the use of racism "as a way to maintain group control of the state and the material privileges that are derived from state control" is certainly as evident in Brazil as in South Africa, the contrasting histories and forms of diversity within these national populations makes problematic any formulaic agenda for critical antiracist interventions (Guimares 1995; Heringer 1995; Premdas 1995; Kushnick 1995).

Interestingly, as antiracists employ anthropological approaches in an effort to generate a broad, critical knowledge base to serve their goals of challenging multiple forms of racism, antiracism as a social movement has recently been subjected to ethnographic scrutiny, with intriguing results. Practitioners and interested observers have usefully applied the ethnographic gaze to interrogate both the implicit and not so hidden racial dynamics in the social interactions that compose antiracist interventions. Many critical observations are made of the power dynamics and rhetoric that serve to reproduce racial difference in antiracist workshops (Gurnah 1984; Ellsworth 1989; Mohanty 1989–90; Srivastava 1994 and 1996; Marty 1999). Work by Sarita Srivastava is particularly interesting, as it combines political criticism with the goal of producing ethnographic knowledge about antiracism as a social movement. Srivastava regards antiracist workshops, which she has observed as a participant, a facilitator, and an ethnographer, as "a privileged site for the performance and inscription of racialized identities." By objectifying workshop practices, she raises "questions about how knowledge of racialized identities, racism and antiracism is produced and circumscribed" (1996, 2). Her task of rendering "the specificity and diversity of these power relations" is directed toward the goal of transforming these relations.

Srivastava first delineates the range of variation that characterizes this social site, listing the assortment of identifying labels that are applied to this basic form of engagement around issues of interracial conflict: antiracist, diversity, cross-cultural, equity, conflict resolution, postequity, among others. "They have a variety of formats, but share a number of common features: they are events held outside routine schooling, and their participants are usually adults or adolescents. Their goal may be to cause awareness, reduce conflict, or initiate change, often within an institutional context, including schools. They are discrete but often regular events, in contrast to antiracist education, which is part of an ongoing, general educational programme. . . . Finally, they almost always use methods and ideas of popular education, in varying ways and degrees" (1996, 3). Additionally, this stylized form of social interaction features a common set of practices: "A variety of techniques—drawing, role playing, body sculpting—are used to discuss and collectively analyse participants' experiences, emphasizing diverse and enjoyable ways of learning. The participant's experience is seen as a valuable source of knowledge, and attention to technique, group dynamics, organizational contexts and physical space promotes a participatory and egalitarian environment to share and analyse experience" (6). Storytelling is usually central to the event; participants are frequently asked to "share personal experiences of racism." Srivastava asserts that this production of stories reproduces, rather than facilitates the deconstruction of, essentialized racial identities. Later in this chapter I expand on this insight on the role of stories in antiracist practice by examining the contrasting hermeneutical orientations of antiracists and ethnographers that shape knowledge production in relation to whites.

Srivastava details the implicit requirements of the solicited stories in these settings: people of color are circumscribed strictly "as victims of racism or as resources on racism." She relates instances of nonwhite students refusing to relate their experiences as "raw material" for group and social analysis and suggests that they are rejecting the way the requirement of

> having to present our experiences as knowers of racism, or as people of colour, produces and reproduces those categories. . . . Within this relationship, white participants may speak about their commitment, hope, solidarity, complicity, guilt, lack of complicity, failure to understand and disbelief, and about the hurt caused by accusations. This alternation between confession and performance of experience produces new racialized representations and corresponding labels. Constructions such as

"angry women of colour" and "weeping white women" surfaced frequently in my initial interviews about antiracist organizational change. (1994, 8)

Rather than effectively challenging the operation of racist practices in educational or occupational settings, these workshops often reproduce the power dynamics or stereotypes they explicitly intend to counter. "Because of these discouraging, draining and painful encounters, many people of colour are dropping out of, rejecting, and refusing to participate in mixed antiracist workshops" (9). Srivastava, though, suggests how to deal with this predicament: "I am also arguing that we should conceive of antiracism and antiracist education not only as objectives to be prescribed, evaluated and restructured, but also as a place to understand the relations we are seeking to change" (13). Regarding antiracist interventions in this light reveals implicit and invidious power dynamics, while also rearticulating the fundamental insights and interventions concerning whiteness that antiracists are committed to developing.

Srivastava's observation that the role of people of color in antiracist workshops is sharply circumscribed may open onto a broader criticism of antiracism generally. I think it certainly may be provocatively extended by considering how or whether whites, too, have a clearly circumscribed role in such workshops. Although I did not directly observe such workshops in Detroit, I did hear accounts from a number of whites who participated in a two-day antiracism session that was developed in relation to a controversy over the Malcolm X Academy in the neighborhood of Warrendale, a predominantly white, working- and middle-class neighborhood on the city's western boundary. Whites in this neighborhood are perched between racially polarized zones: the all-white suburbs, where, as they pointed out to me, blacks are effectively excluded through a host of both subtle and blatant policing techniques, and the rest of Detroit, which they generally regarded as all black. Many whites living in Warrendale remained behind as white flight gutted Detroit. A few whites, however, had moved into Warrendale quite recently from the suburbs where they were born and raised because they were unable to afford starter homes in these communities. Though the area had been largely unaffected by white flight, Warrendale residents were now facing some dire economic trends. Housing prices fell sharply between 1980 and 1990 as blight spread inexorably from Detroit's inner city, and poverty rates doubled or tripled in portions of the neighborhood during the same period.

The summer I began my fieldwork in Detroit (1992), the Board of Education reopened a local elementary school they had recently closed, citing insufficient funds to keep the building operating, as the Malcolm X Academy, featuring an Afrocentric curriculum (Hartigan, 1999). Whites in Warrendale protested the school board's decision for a variety of reasons, but their concerns appeared to reporters and city officials to be strictly based in racist sentiment. The concerned and sometimes angry voices of white residents resonated strongly with the history of working-class resistance to the racial integration of public schools. Framed by the background of their small, aluminum-sided tract homes, the image of violent white racism was hard to dispel. The controversy over the Academy was protracted but not violent, and there were many nuances to the positions local whites assumed, either in support of or in opposition to the school and its curriculum. I cannot present a detailed view of this ethnographic setting here, but I will briefly summarize the way whites described and critiqued the antiracism workshop, which was sponsored by two local Catholic churches.

The area churches, along with the Warrendale Community Organization, actively tried to calm white residents' anxieties about the Academy and its curriculum; members of these organizations were typically more concerned about the accumulating signs of deterioration in the neighborhood, which they associated with the influx of renters. They did not want to further undermine the character of Warrendale through its depiction as a racist white enclave. The workshop was conducted and facilitated by two white women, each with lengthy local histories of activism relating to racial conflicts. One ran her own business as a diversity consultant and the other was a dedicated social worker for a Catholic human services agency. I found white residents' accounts of the frustrations they experienced with this workshop to be indicative of the classed confusions over how race mattered in this conflict, where black professionals squared off against white working-class homeowners in a contest over control of civic resources represented in this neighborhood elementary school.

In my interviews with whites in Warrendale, the antiracist workshop typically arose as an instance of how they had been confronted with the assertion that blacks could not be racists due to their generally disadvantaged and disempowered status nationally. These whites would easily spout this position for me: racism is equated with power; without power—institutional, political, or social—blacks simply could not be racists. They questioned this assertion by pointing, first, to the local political dominance blacks have achieved in the city, and, second, to the characterizations of whites by school officials and promoters of Afrocentrism associated in some manner with the Detroit Public Schools. Whites referred to statements made by blacks in the course of this dispute, which ran the gamut from what might be cast as racial to racist (Goldberg 1993). They pointed to comments by callers on radio talk shows charging, "We have to keep the [City] Council black," or shouts at a school board meeting: "We're the majority now. We'll do what we want." Each of these statements was regarded by whites as a blunt assertion of black dominance, creating the impression that blacks were insisting that power operate along racial lines rather than in a "color-blind" manner. But primarily, they pointed to statements by advocates and promoters of the Afrocentric curriculum, such as characterizations of whites as "killing machines," "devils," and "ice people," or claims that melanin was actually a basis of black cultural and intellectual superiority. Such characterizations struck these whites as racist. Hence, they stressed that their opposition to the Malcolm X Academy was not because it was a "black school" (99 percent of the enrolled students were black), but because of the ideological threat they perceived in the curriculum that the school promoted.

The workshop leaders were guarded and suspicious of whites' claims that they were not opposing the school based on a visceral contempt for or fear of blacks, and they dismissed many of these whites' concerns over the Afrocentric curriculum as smoke screens obscuring fundamentally racist sentiment. In my interviews with the two women who directed the workshop, they described being confronted by "lots of rhetoric that was really hard to mush through" to get at what they believed to be the racist core of the whites' response to the Academy. This search for the tangled, submerged emotions and anxieties that animate whites generally in regard to race proved ineffective for the Warrendale whites I spoke with, because it made the workshop facilitators seem oblivious to the way class and power mattered in this particular situation. Their frustrations with the workshop are well summarized by Alastair Bonnett's (1997, 179–180) criticism of antiracists' conceptualization of white racism; he argues that it depends on "a myth of Whiteness. . . . This myth views 'being White' as an immutable condition with clear and distinct moral attributes. These attributes often include: being racist; not experiencing racism; being an oppressor; not experiencing oppression; silencing; not being silenced." It was exactly the projection of these attributes that most frustrated opponents of the Academy, because it ignored or dismissed their volatile, confusing experiences as whites in the public schools, of being objectified as whites by blacks, and of their precarious class position in the tumultuous setting of Detroit.

The antiracist workshop in Warrendale further strengthened the convictions of opponents of the school, in part because the dogmatic stance on racism seemed absurd to them, but also because it revealed the broad gulf between antiracist whites and those who were engaged in an emotional struggle over events in their own neighborhood. Their descriptions of exchanges in the workshop about the readings disseminated by the facilitators reflected the contrast between people mired in a losing conflict and the detachment of those who are trying to enlighten them with a broader view of their predicament. This rift was most evident in the different ways the Afrocentric curriculum was regarded in the workshop. White residents complained that facilitators would not talk about the aspects of the controversy that mattered keenly to them (the Afrocentric curriculum), refusing to examine its implications and ramifications, preferring instead to treat it as an innocuous expression of multiculturalism. The facilitators, instead, regarded the sentiments and anxieties as being expressed *in terms of* the curriculum, stemming from a deeper ideological conditioning about race.

Long after the Academy's opening, the school's Afrocentric curriculum remained an elusive, haunting concern for these whites—elusive, because school officials were reluctant to address the issue; haunting, because engaging this subject led them into a disorienting, powerful assemblage of racial imagery and narratives. Afrocentrism, a molten, formative array of assertions, claims, facts, and theories, confronted white residents as a bewildering perspective, challenging, threatening, and certainly racializing whites, whether or not they contested the Academy directly.[7] The dissonance generated in the workshop between the antiracist perspective and the view of whites from Warrendale centered on whether they regarded Afrocentric discourse as the issue. One participant, Jeff, who ran a lawn mowing service in the neighborhood, described to me how he tried to raise questions with one of the facilitators about the implications of teaching what he and others regarded as religious or spiritual material in the public schools:

> She didn't really want to hear anything about it. I asked her, "What do you know about this curriculum that you're teaching us about, and the way we're reacting? Do you know what they're preaching?" [He mimics her voice] "Yeah, they've got Kwanzaa." "Do you know what Kwanzaa is?" "Yeah, it's a holiday. I've been to . . ." "*Do* you know what it is? It's being taught in the schools. Do you know the religious implications, and the political implication behind it? Do you know anything about Maulana Karenga, the man who invented Kwanzaa?" I mean, I went right down the

line with her. Okay. "Are you familiar with the libation ceremony in Kwanzaa that's similar to partaking of communion in the Roman Catholic Church, and they're doing this in our schools, except that the children are drinking out of what they call a Timbiko cup, with their dead ancestors. *In school!*" Now that is a religious ceremony.

White opponents of the Academy, as shown in this account, were actually avid consumers of Afrocentric writings and pronouncements. Because they could not get their questions about the curriculum answered by school officials, they cast a broad net that drew in a range of claims, assertions, and charges that probably far exceeded the scope of the curricular program being developed by the Detroit Public Schools. But the disparate range of sources and versions also reflected their multifaceted readings of this neighborhood's political and social position in Detroit. The curriculum was not a euphemism for a racial threat; rather, it was a measure of the range of changes that were transforming the city and making the status of working-class whites increasingly uncertain. From one perspective, certainly, the version of Afrocentrism they compiled was self-interested, choosing extreme over reasoned statements, and perhaps naïve. But more important, the whites' perspective showed their vulnerability to seeing themselves in the white devil subject position in this discourse. Whereas antiracist whites can regard Afrocentric tenets as a benign, balancing addition to multiculturalism, these whites found that the discourse conveyed a deeper reality, reflecting their predicaments as whites in this Detroit neighborhood. Their political incapacitation in this controversy pushed them to emphasize the most racially apocalyptic versions of the future preached by Afrocentrists.

As racist became the definitive characterization of white opposition to the Malcolm X Academy, whites in Warrendale were subject to black objectifications of their interests and anxieties. Additionally, they were objectified by antiracist discourse that reduced their multifaceted concerns to simple expressions of racism. Bonnett (1997, 177) charges that the "essentialising dynamic" at the heart of the antiracist project "lead[s] towards the positioning (or self-positioning) of White people as fundamentally outside, and untouched by, the contemporary controversies of 'racial' identity politics."[8] In Warrendale, and in Detroit generally, antiracism as a political stance seems to disregard the dramatic shift in political and cultural power and does not recognize these whites as mired in fundamentally racial predicaments: trying to regain control of their identifying features, disoriented by the disjuncture between a projected social identity (as whites) and personal experience, feeling the inadequate fit of stereotyped depictions. Antiracism is also fundamentally guided by the conviction that white domination and black subordination define racial dynamics. However well this formula may address race relations in a national register, it badly distorts the experience of working-class whites contesting black city officials over scarce civic resources in a city that has been devastated by the emergence of the post-industrial economy. It is easy to assume that the correspondence between emotional, angry images of working-class whites and public representations of racism in the United States derives from an essentially racist class disposition. But this view ignores the difficult fact that the neighborhoods and jobs being used to rebalance the racial order in this country are predominantly those of working-class whites who have benefited little from the nation's recent economic boom (Kefalas 2003).

MODELING WHITENESS

The model of whiteness most widely promoted by antiracists posits a generic white subject both privileged and unconscious of the extent or operation of the privilege. This model perhaps pertains to the majority of white Americans. But its explanatory power diminishes for whites who are engaged in disputes such as the controversy over the Malcolm X Academy, and its sweeping assertions are seriously challenged by the process of racialization that whites are subject to in Detroit. Bonnett (1997, 174), drawing on the work of Ali Rattansi and Tariq Modood, asserts that "orthodox anti-racism appears ill-equipped to engage creatively with the fluid and complex forces of the racialisation process" because it is unprepared to acknowledge the contradictions, inconsistencies, and ambivalences in white and nonwhite identities. Such ambiguities and discrepancies are manifold for white Detroiters, who make up only 13 percent of the population. Their efforts to make sense of racial incidents—many of them have endured the harsh confusion of racial animosity and antagonism—are certainly somewhat unique for whites. Still, I think they are indicative of a range of ambiguous experiences that whites generally will face more frequently in the twenty-first century. To understand how these experiences arise in novel racial settings, it is critical that antiracists attempt to ground their insights about whiteness in an ethnographic orientation toward their subjects—that is, with an understanding of the powerful role of place, both as a specific location and as a concrete experience of larger structuring forces. The orientation I refer to here does not require actually pursuing extensive fieldwork; it can be accomplished by adopting a different interpretive stance toward the ways that whites objectify their perceptions and experiences of racial matters through stories.[9] But fundamentally, this entails an acknowledgment that the field is not solely a site of intervention, but a location for *learning* about the variable operations of racial identity—operations that their analytic perspective may not fully comprehend. To develop this point, I turn now to two of the most sophisticated examples of antiracist knowledge production, Ruth Frankenberg's (1993) *White Women, Race Matters* and Alice McIntyre's (1997) *Making Meaning of Whiteness*.

The findings developed by McIntyre and Frankenberg exemplify problematic aspects of projects that seek to produce knowledge about, or discern points of critical intervention with, whiteness. I focus on these two works for several reasons. Primarily, they each offer intriguing crossing points between antiracism and cultural anthropology; both authors characterize their projects as modes of knowledge production about whiteness and whites, as well as articulating political challenges to the social reproduction of racism. Aspects of these research projects, particularly Frankenberg's use of intensive interviewing and McIntyre's version of participant-observation and attention to social conversation, are certainly familiar to anthropologists. Their methods and findings have been taken up by other social researchers and antiracist activists. Second, Frankenberg and McIntyre do an excellent job of highlighting material in extended excerpted transcripts, providing rich and complex glimpses of whites thinking about race. In addition, the exchanges and comments that they analyze have a great degree of resonance; I found many comments similarly voiced in the course of my own fieldwork on whites in Detroit. But it was also through my own field research that I have come to critically regard some of their fundamental insights. The criticism I develop concerning their approaches is oriented first toward the general project of producing knowledge about whiteness and white people qua whites, and second, as a series of suggestions regarding how an ethnographic perspective might critically improve antiracist projects.

McIntyre both develops and applies the concept of "white talk" in a "participatory action research project" with a small group of white student teachers. In sessions with thirteen female education students of somewhat ambiguous class backgrounds, "a challenging journey of self- and collective reflections about the intersection of whiteness, racial identity, racism and teaching," McIntyre identified the continual emergence of "white talk": "talk that serves to insulate white people from examining their/our individual and collective role(s) in the perpetuation of racism" (1997, 45). She further explains: "During the group sessions, the participants used a number of speech-tactics to distance themselves from the difficult and almost paralyzing task of engaging in a critique of their own whiteness, some of which served to push the participants to be more self-reflective about being white and some that resulted in the perpetuation of white talk." These tactics, which she calls characteristic of white talk, consist of "derailing the conversation, evading questions, dismissing counterarguments, withdrawing from the discussion, remaining silent, interrupting speakers and topics, and colluding with each other in creating a 'culture of niceness' that made it difficult to 'read the white world'" (46). Based on my own experiences of teaching white students about race, I think McIntyre has identified a critical dynamic in the reproduction of white racial identity. I also think that this concept of white talk can be effectively deployed in ethnographic contexts to make sense of how whites respond to racial subjects. But in reading McIntyre's study I was unnerved by the way her analysis, which zeroed in on the task of discerning how these students were socialized into whiteness, disregarded a great deal of the ambivalent and highly contradictory aspects of their experiences. Any form of analysis that takes race as its basis runs the risk of treating reductively the complexity of people's social perceptions and behaviors. This type of reductionism certainly can be fruitful and critical, particularly in overcoming the obstinate refusal on the part of many whites to recognize that racial inequalities still exist. But, as is evident in McIntyre's study, there is a point of diminishing returns where we begin to lose insights into the more muddled and ambiguous aspects of racial situations as they develop in everyday life.

McIntyre has a keen ear for her subjects' use of stories. She explains, "The participants told numbers of stories during our project that illustrated the difficulty they had understanding the nature of racism as a system that privileges and maintains the social practices, belief systems, and cultural norms of the dominant group, and beliefs in the superiority of that group over the inherent inferiority of others" (1997, 48). She takes their stories as examples of racism, as material that reveals racial perceptions and judgments. McIntyre highlights a series of exchanges that she characterized as "waitress stories," where the students related and compared observations from their work as waitresses or restaurant hostesses. In particular, the women evaluated their perceptions that "Black people tip horrible." The discussion begins with one woman, Elizabeth, describing her thought process as she began to notice this "trend" among her black customers and how it was "confirmed" (in an unsolicited comment) by another waitress who made the same observation. Elizabeth explained:

> It was every time I got a Black party whether it was a single person or a family of six, whatever. Bad tips. So I just kind of kept to myself, well you know said "Well whatever" you know? But just thinking that I was like, "Well, am I just being racist or" you know? And I'm like "but isn't that kind of odd" (laughs) you know? And I just didn't know what to think. And so one day, I was um, I don't know how it came out but another co-worker said this to me. They said, "Oh, I had a bad day of tips. Well, I had a lot of Black parties." And I said, "Well, why do you say that?" you know? And they said, "Well, every time I get a Black party" and so then now every time you know, you get a Black party, you think or just everyone there is like, "Alright, how good is this tip going to be?" You just kind of expect a lower tip and every time I get a Black party I'm like, "What am I thinking? Did I think this" and I just, its horrible 'cause I say to myself, "I am being racist in expecting a lower tip" or maybe trying to go out of my way to be extra nice and hope for a good tip or whatever. But it kills me 'cause I know that just thinking it is being racist and I also know that I try my hardest not to be. (49)

McIntyre concludes emphatically:

> This story exemplifies how deeply ingrained racism is in "the souls of white folks." Elizabeth seems to "pick up racism" by osmosis. She notices that Blacks don't tip as well as whites "without anyone ever telling me." She describes it as a "trend" and that "you can just expect a lower tip" from Blacks. In addition, "it just about kills" her to be racist—to accept the stereotypes that have been created about Blacks by the white people in her restaurant. The "guilt inside of me" motivates Elizabeth to question her assumptions about Blacks. Her desire to "know if it's racist" to per- petuate the idea that "Blacks are horrible tippers," appears to stem from her need to be free of guilt. (50)

I hear this story differently, as an example of the problems inherent in reducing such stories to object lessons on white racism. It seems to me that Elizabeth's "desire to know" is related to an effort to make sense of an uncertain matter. She may be really striving to think through an ambiguous perception, resisting an unpalatable interpretation, rather than just relieving her sense of guilt. After all, her narrative frames her uncertainty rather than steadfastly insisting that this perception and the workshop folklore it is linked with are true. I do not think that "racism" adequately diagnoses or objectifies the interpretive process in which Elizabeth is engaged. Relying solely on racism to explain her thinking disregards the sources of ambiguity and ambivalence that enter into her interpretations. Instead, I think this story works just as well in demonstrating how our critical language and analytical skills have yet to match the complexity of racial matters: there is no term other than "racist" (or "antiracist") to be used to make sense of the perceptions shared by the white waitresses.

McIntyre is right to key on the socialization process that racializes this setting and on the exchange of racial observations; this is a great advance over locating racism as an individual failing or a somewhat abstract aspect of institutions. But her analysis is stymied when the women then proceed to develop this genre of stories—of their experiences as waitresses and hostesses serving blacks—rather than pursuing her questions about racism. Faith follows Elizabeth's stories with her own experiences from three years of working in a restaurant, relating similar perceptions of blacks and adding the elaboration of seeing patrons "pull away in their Mercedes" after leaving a meager tip. "It stinks because it's the money that you're taking home, you know what I mean? And it's hard. It's really such a struggle in your head but you know, I don't know. When you've been waiting tables for three years and it's like statistics. You can look at statistics. You can look at the numbers and know and lay it out and that stinks" (1997, 51).

McIntyre (1997, 51) relates being "disturbed at the direction of this conversation." She waited

for one of the participants to intervene in the discussion and highlight the myriad racist comments being made. . . . Instead, the participants revert to a "white-as-victim" stand and rigidify the boundaries that get established when white people talk to white people without self- and collective criticism. Elizabeth states: "It doesn't matter how hard you work." No one disagrees with Elizabeth's comment or, if they did, failed to make it known. Faith expresses her own frustration over not being rewarded by a Black patron for her "exemplary service" and by suggesting there are statistics to prove her point that Blacks are bad tippers. Her indignation that "they" would "pull away in their Mercedes" leaving her "thirty cents on a fifty dollar bill" seemed justified. It appeared to me that the other participants accepted her reporting of such incidents as a common occurrence, thereby, facilitating the growth of white talk. (52)

So much depends on tone and gesture that even detailed transcripts can be tricky to use reliably, but in contradistinction to McIntyre, I hear primarily the frustrated ambivalence of "you know, I don't know," that "it stinks" and that "It's really such a struggle in your head." Rather than hearing an insistence that there are statistics to back up her claim, I hear Faith saying specifically that "it's *like* statistics" in that "you can look at" them. She can recall "the numbers" of blacks "and lay it out and that stinks." She can make a serial observation and not come up with a better alternative conclusion or interpretation than to confirm and reproduce the stereotype of blacks as bad tippers. Rather than railing at their inability to self-reflexively grasp their participation in the generation of "racist speech" and "failing to attend to how whites perpetuate racist behavior," it seems to me that a more effective tactic might be to confront the social influences that make such conclusions seem obvious and inevitable, call attention to their ambivalence as instances of resistance or unwillingness to succumb to racist judgments, and articulate the specific points of disjuncture that might rupture the generic characterizations of blacks. I think what would be useful in this context is a keener attention to the interpretive processes whites are engaged in rather than focusing solely on discerning the ideological core or belief structure that might be revealed by their comments. As well, it would be helpful to have some means of assessing the social dynamics at work in this setting that generate the impression of "such incidents as a common occurrence."

But more than just offering an alternative reading of these stories, my point here is to distinguish two distinct but not irreconcilable approaches to the task of understanding white racialness. Antiracism, as evidenced by McIntyre, features what Hans-Georg Gadamer (1984, 54) characterizes as a "hermeneutics of suspicion." In contrast to what might be broadly cast as the "traditional" hermeneutic stance, deployed to grasp the structures of intentionality and the meaningfulness of a speaker's world, the hermeneutics of suspicion "challenges the claims to validity of ideas and ideologies." The interpretive work of antiracists (their stance as listeners) is geared toward "revealing the meaningfulness of statements in a completely unexpected sense and *against* the meaning of the author" (58; emphasis added), that is, revealing a true racist motivational core where whites strenuously claim to not be racists. In contrast to this stance, I suggest that the hermeneutic stance ensconced in ethnographic approaches might be more effective, not just in producing more reliable knowledge claims about whiteness, but in actually engaging the subjects' understanding of their racialization.

At the risk of broadly generalizing—and, as with my earlier sketch of antiracism, drawing a characterization geared toward framing key contrasts most productively—I regard the hermeneutic stance ethnographers assume to be oriented toward understanding (1) how specific situations countervail or complicate abstract generalizations; (2) that ambiguities are not to be rationalized away: they indicate both the unfinished process of cultural constructions and moments when researchers' assumptions grind against the categorical orientation of their subject; and (3) that the interpretive work of subjects—what criteria or means of prioritizing interests are evident, and what counts as a "good" interpretation—is important to understand, not to simply "correct" or "deconstruct." The criteria people employ in making sense of ambiguous situations provide a glimpse of the forces that economically and politically shape the places they inhabit, and these criteria reflect people's perceptions of the meanings of these forces. The hermeneutic disposition of ethnographers is geared toward grasping how place both shapes and reflects the interpretive work people pursue in everyday situations. And it is this kind of interpretive work that must be understood about the "waitress stories," whether regarded as points of intervention in the reproduction of racism or as sources of knowledge production about whiteness. Instead of singularly regarding these stories as reflective of a monolithic ideological condition, we should grant them consideration as active efforts to make sense of situations that may or may not reproduce categorical racial judgment. McIntyre's approach, though, pursues an opposite course regarding the stories that Elizabeth, Faith, and the others are narrating, relying on a reductive view of white racism formed from two critical assumptions: that racism is an absolute or totalizing phenomenon, and that only clear thinking can short-circuit its power.

The root of antiracism is the belief that racism is *the* problem and that white subterfuges must be penetrated, their confusions and contradictions about race clarified, in order to reach a point where whites stop reproducing and participating in a social order organized on racial privileges and inequalities.[10] McIntyre illustrates this stance well as she challenges the students' efforts to distinguish between active and passive modes of racism. She is upset that, for the participants, "intentionality is equated with 'blatant racism,' thereby, exonerating the participants from racist thoughts and actions *if* those cognitions and behaviors are not premeditated and intentional" (1997, 54). At one point, partly in response to McIntyre's stance that "we, as whites, have all internalized dimensions of racism," Faith remarks in confusion, "So everything, every encounter that you have with someone of an opposite, someone of a minority is racist? Every interaction? Whether it's blatant or intentional or whether it's blatant or not? I'm confused" (54). The students want to distinguish between the active production of racism, carried out through intentional acts, and the possibility that there is some state other than racism to characterize their thoughts and behaviors. They also seem to be striving to articulate a view from the position of everyday life where the relevance of race is changeable, shifting from being obviously active to being part of a dense, signifying background. But McIntyre insists on the absolute, all-inclusive power of white racism: they either actively resist its transmission, or they unconsciously reproduce its insidious effects.

Along with an insistence on the pervasiveness of racism and the uniformity of whites' participation in its reproductions, antiracists also promote clear thinking about race, relying on sharp definitions to bring this problem into view. Indeed, for McIntyre, ambiguities and confusions expressed by the students were strictly active forms of reproducing racism. When McIntyre finds the white women's comments becoming "convoluted" and "contradictory," she takes this as an indication that they are "resist[ing] a critical analysis of the consequences of racism for both people of color and for whites . . . resulting in these young white females accepting an ideology in fear and distortion." In particular, McIntyre reads the convolutions in their stories and expressions as signifying either their inability or resistance to embrace an antiracist activist mind-set, as well as their susceptibility to myth and fantasy. Indeed, "lack of clarity in defining racism and zero-sum thinking contributed to the group's construction of white talk for they are both strategies for insulating speakers from tackling the underpinnings of whiteness" (1997, 59–60).

While it is worth considering "lack of clarity" as a strategy for resisting antiracist analyses of whiteness, it is certainly also worth pondering whether such confusions are hopeful indicators of points where the certainty of racial logic is breaking down. Ambiguous moments are indicators that an ideological conditioning has been ruptured or has exceeded its confident reach. In Detroit, I found whites' lack of clarity about race to be a function of the changing political and social settings in the city; the instability in whites' opinions and views on racial matters reflected the fact that the ways race operated in the city were often unpredictable. The racial features of exchanges and conflicts were typically nuanced and ambiguous; they consistently involved interpretive efforts by individuals who had to decide whether to prioritize race in relation to competing frameworks for understanding interaction, such as class, family, and place. Their responses to race were shaped by contingencies in daily life that are not easily acknowledged by antiracist analyses. This has to be recognized and incorporated into antiracist approaches if they are to be successful in gaining some foothold in the realm of whites' everyday experience, offering them relevant insights that make sense of their daily routines. This is particularly true in the case of whites whose economic position does not reflect a status of power and privilege. In the case of these waitresses and the working-class whites of Warrendale, a similar anxiety over money and resources is too easily reduced simply to racism. This reductive approach undermines antiracists' interventions.

Ambiguity is very hard for antiracists to contend with, politically and conceptually, as is evidenced in an intriguing story narrated in Ruth Frankenberg's *White Women, Race Matters*, one of the early efforts to sociologically examine whiteness and notable for the sophisticated analytical apparatus she applies to this tricky subject. Frankenberg (1993, 21) developed "an analysis of how white people's positions in the racial order are produced through the interplay of discourses on race with the material relations of racism." Her approach to whiteness is similarly grounded in antiracist theory and pedagogy, but her theoretical approach to her interviews with white women is more ethnographic. Frankenberg uses these interviews to track "white women's inscription into discourses of race difference" (138). Essentialist racism is one of three discourses she hears resonating in these women's stories of their childhood and their contemporary relations to racial matters. Frankenberg suggests that "at a certain point in U.S. history a color- and power-evasive public language of race displaced essentialist racism as the dominant discourse on race . . . [and] remains dominant today; it has not been displaced in its turn by race cognizance." This third type of discourse, race cognizance, is characterized by rearticulations of the significance of racial difference by people of color. "Where difference within the terms of essentialist racism alleges the inferiority of people of color, in the third [discourse] difference signals autonomy of culture, values, aesthetics, and so on." Frankenberg asserts that, "although continually challenged by the third mode of thinking through race, the color- and power-evasive paradigm has incorporated elements of race-cognizance into itself, rather than being in any significant way displaced by it" (21). The illustration she offers is of the "watered-down" versions of multiculturalism circulating in institutions and popular culture.

Frankenberg's analytical approach helped antiracism draw into view the way whites' perceptions and statements are linked to an essentialist racism, even when designations of racial inferiority or assertions of racial superiority are not expressly articulated. Her fundamental effort lies in "showing the continuities across discursive repertoires from (ostensibly) 'left' or 'progressive' to apparently more conservative; the traces of essentialist racism, colonial discourse, and evasion of color and power in the discursive repertoires of women whose intentions are, in fact, quite different; the sharp cutting edges that reinforce racism, embedded in the discursive repertoires of color- and power-evasive women who might well, at the level of intention, be attempting to challenge essentialist racism" (1993, 20). This powerful interpretive stance has the capacity to continually discern racist kernels in whites' actions and comments, but I think that it will increasingly obscure more than it reveals about the novel range of situations in which whites today are confronting racial matters. This is apparent in Frankenberg's analysis of a story told by one of the actively antiracist white women in her study. Frankenberg is able to draw out the links to racism in Beth's predicament, yet I think there is much more to learn from this story about the ambiguities animating whites' racial interactions; it sharply reveals the gap between the antiracists' goal of revealing whites' links with essentialist racism and an equally pressing objective of beginning to understand the range of ambiguities operating in black and white social interactions.

Beth Ellision grew up in Virginia and Alabama and later moved to the San Francisco Bay Area. She related to Frankenberg how her experiences in California made her "aware of what a racist environment I'd grown up in, and how I had grown up with a kind of an unexamined racist attitude myself." Frankenberg uses Beth's narrative as an example of how white feminists had achieved "a sharpened awareness of how racism had structured their own lives and . . . continued to be informed by racism" (1993, 162). In Beth's story, she highlights the limits to the recognition these women articulate in how racism structures their lives:

> The other night . . . I was in a coffeehouse, and I had left my table for just a minute. Without thinking, I'd left a pack of cigarettes there, and when I came back to the table with a friend, there was a Black guy that was sitting there. I guess he thought nobody was sitting there. So we let him know that it was our table, and he got up and left. And then I realized that my pack of cigarettes were gone. So I approached him and asked him if he'd seen a pack of cigarettes there, if he picked them up. He became very insulted and drew himself up and said that, contrary to the stereotype that white people have, not every Black person is a thief.
>
> And if I hadn't felt so much like, "Uh-oh, am I thinking this guy stole

these because he's Black?" or "How can I redress his wound now?" If I had felt like this was just a guy that had a problem—I thought a few minutes later that I could have said is that contrary to the stereotypes, not all *white* people think all Black people are thieves. I think I would have said that if I hadn't been so drawn aback. . . . I still have some sensitivity that would make me stop immediately and say, "Oh, gosh, I'm being racist, I'd better quit this," even though I knew full well that I wasn't: I was only saying that to him because he was sitting there. (164)

Frankenberg's analysis of this story primarily emphasizes what she considers to be the revelation of the ongoing influence of childhood experiences. This is characteristic of how antiracists tend to weight evidence drawn from white speech: always toward a past where racism is inscribed or hardwired rather than toward a present or a future growing increasingly uncertain.[11] "As this story makes clear, Beth had a very elaborate sense of herself as mutually constructed into a dynamic of racial tension with Black people carried over from childhood. It is striking, in fact, that Beth's primary focus remained on her relationships with Black Americans rather than with other people of color, even though the San Francisco area is more multiracial than biracial. What is going on here, I suggest, is Beth's struggle to reexamine the particulars of the biracial dynamic in which she had been involved since childhood" (1993, 164). My impression of this story is the opposite of Frankenberg's: instead of highlighting a continued problematic from childhood lessons on race and blackness, I hear Beth trying to make sense of the current moment as she registers confusions generated from her incorporation of antiracist discourse or not adequately addressed—in fact, adversely affected—by her heightened attention to white racism.

Whether or not antiracism is implicated in developing a form of "sensitivity" that contributes to Beth's "treating the other person less as a human being and more as a representative of a certain group" (164), I think this story conveys that the vast repertoire of Americans' folk knowledge concerning race has hardly dissipated, despite the great strides made by social scientists and activists to dispel such beliefs and assumptions. Indeed, what seems most crucial in making sense of this story is that it provides a means of addressing situations when stereotyped assumptions and projections run riot, where suspicions might never be fully expressed, examined, or disengaged through antiracism's activist solutions. In my reading, the black man Beth confronts also employs racial stereotypes: he locates her in the subject position of white racist. The significance of her white racialness preceded her individual experience, perceptions, and convictions. She was located in a position in a black discourse about whites; she stepped into and reproduced the stereotype of whites as racists, suspicious of blacks, and predisposed to accusing them of social transgressions. Should she have reflexively grasped this potential and decided against saying anything at all, or preemptively brought up the stereotype herself, disarmed it somehow, and only then inquired about her cigarettes? Rather than debate which of these options, or others that might be suggested, should be emphatically endorsed, I think it is important to recognize that the significance of race in certain situations exceeds individuals' efforts, whether avowedly political or not, to engage its unruly range of potential meanings and implications.

This story can be used to consider how the significance of race is at its most riotous in such passing, chance encounters, settings perhaps concentrated in exchanges related to the service sector (at the cash register, in the checkout lane, in the movie theater line).[12] The dynamics shaping the significance of race in these settings are distinct from those operating in the maintenance of segregated housing and occupational forms of discrimination: the control of and access to limited resources is not directly at stake. Though the contours of privilege and disadvantage can be roughly discerned in the situation Beth describes, the reliable contrasts between whiteness (dominance) and blackness (subordination) are not so clear. Perhaps disjunctive forms of meaning are at work in these settings, suggesting that race is best treated not through a uniform analysis that distills the problem into racism and uniformly casts whites on one side (dominant, privileged) and blacks or people of color on the other (subordinated, exploited).

To establish and consider this possibility, though, we need to find ways to produce both knowledge about and the means to intervene in the everyday contexts where whites engage the significance of race. Rather than further refine an analysis of whiteness, we need to work on a means of understanding race whereby the contrasts of whiteness and blackness are not sharply drawn by differentiating two clearly opposed subject/social positions. This is where ethnography becomes a crucial tool in extending the insights of antiracist scholars and activists. An ethnographic disposition can frame the specificities of whites' talk and stories, and it can productively examine the sources of whites' ambivalence and ambiguity rather than reduce these in favor of certainty concerning racism's presence or absence. To illustrate this point through a closing example, I turn to Steven Gregory's (1998) ethnographic study, *Black Corona: Race and the Politics of Place in an Urban Community*. In this multifaceted study of interweaving historical forces, bureaucratic structures, and class discourses, Gregory examines how the construction of racial identity is linked to the organization and reconstitution of urban space. In one particular situation, Gregory relates the way white residents of an apartment complex in Queens mobilized in response to a massive influx of black tenants (rising from 25 percent to 80 percent of the population in a four-year period). He analyzes the way whites became politically active in response to this shift, developing a strategy to promote neighborhood "stabilization"—against the specter of instability associated with black youth and crime—by securing housing for low-income, elderly whites in these apartments. He tracks the way "black, crime, and 'welfare' were conflated in the public discourse of white community activists" who mobilized in response to this demographic shift, seeking a strategy to restore the "racial balance" of the complex. Gregory provides an excerpt from an interview with a white member of the local community board, noting that "his account provides a good example of the complex and shifting entanglements of race and class in white activist ideology."

> An official of the rental company "came to the Community Board and and he wanted us to fill his vacant apartments. So we got Section 8 [federal rent subsidies] approved [for low-income, elderly whites]. And he claimed—well in Section 8, that he would put 90 percent senior citizens in. You know, in order to . . . uh . . . stabilize the area. And also he claimed that the . . . the Section 8 would be used mostly for elderly white people. You know, because they were the ones being displaced and whatever. So we went along and he got the approval. And then of course it turned out that—you know, he gave all the Section 8 to the big minority families and not to the senior citizens he promised to. And even the senior citizens he promised—the security was so bad that they . . . they were . . . that they would run for their lives, 'cause they couldn't survive with the kind of people he was letting in. But again, it was nothing to do with the color of the black people. We had Indians, we had Chinese, we had all kinds of people here. But they was—it was a different class of people." (114–115)

Gregory focuses on the tricky class terrain that informs white community activists' perceptions and articulations, and it is this attention to class, manifesting as a series of distinctions and a contrasting array of advantages and disadvantages in a particular setting, that would well serve antiracist objectives. Gregory analyzes this story without relying on racism as a reductive assessment of white interests; rather, he shows how the counterposed images of "big minority families" and "senior [white] citizens" fused race, class, and age differences in a symbolic shorthand that encoded complex and at times conflicting ideologies and social forces. White oppositions to black welfare families converged symbolically and in practice with local resistance to the exercise of power by big government and big business. On the one hand, white residents felt that their neighborhood was being victimized by city officials because of its political weakness as a middle-class community: Low-income housing and other undesirable projects were "dumped" on Corona because, as one resident put it, "we were such a soft touch." On the other hand, many residents attributed the decline of Lefrak City to the greed and opportunism of the Lefrak organization which some held was resolving its lawsuit at their expense while failing to provide proper maintenance services. (1998, 115)

It is possible to hear other resonances than strictly white racial fear in complaints and laments about the "decline" and deterioration of life in these apartments. Gregory underscores the multiple "targets" of this discourse, noting that "opposition to black 'undesirables' in Lefrak City was entangled in white activist ideology with a resistance to the power of big government and corporate greed" (115).

The complicating role of class in the interplay of place and racial identity is made more apparent as Gregory analyzes the way black middle-class residents of Queens speak a "homeowners' discourse." Gregory details how black, middle-class residents also came to recognize, speak about, and fear urban "blight."[13] A nonprofit corporation's efforts to open a foster care diagnostic center in an area of Queens that is over 85 percent black elicited similar angry charges of "dumping" from black homeowners. Gregory quotes a statement by one black homeowner that could certainly pass as a racist assertion when spoken by a white person: "These are problem children. We as a block of people don't want this type of building on our block. This is a private neighborhood; there are no public buildings. What happens when your kids meet our kids?" (149). Just as when white homeowners make this type of statement, the racial implications are implicit and dense, and Gregory emphasizes the play of intraracial class distinctions at work in this predominantly black community.[14] Strictly racial implications can be forced to the surface and called racism, but I think the explicit statements themselves are important to consider for the way they reveal points of interracial commonalities along the lines of class interests. As well, such statements need to be analyzed for the ambivalences active in comments that strive not to be racially explicit or emphatic. In each of these cases, the attention to class I am promoting here is not simply a matter of adding nuance and complexity to racial analytics; rather, I see emphasis on class as recognizing discursive forms that cross racial lines. In the burgeoning novelty of racial situations in disparate settings throughout the United States, it is exactly these points of correspondence that need to be acknowledged and examined in any racial analysis.

CONCLUSION

Antiracists have staked out a clear means for both generating knowledge about the constitution of white racial identity and actively disrupting and undermining its ongoing maintenance by whites. Although antiracism holds much promise, social researchers have to be cognizant of the limitations that accompany its techniques and findings. My hope is that antiracism will continue to profoundly influence social research, but we need to be astute about the assumptions that inform this mode of generating knowledge and be aware of how the dynamics of its contexts—workshops, classrooms, and interviews—distinctly influence the type of insights antiracists produce. These settings effectively reduce the attention to place that is fundamental to understanding how whites perceive particular situations and identities to be racial. In the utopic (placeless) dynamics of antiracist workshops, racism emerges as a singular, profound, active force, but in the concrete lives of whites, racialness is hardly a uniform and consistent material. Because, in the end, it is the daily experiences of whites that antiracists hope to change, they must be able to engage the more distended and ambiguous meanings race can have in those settings.

Ambiguity can be frustrating from a political or scholastic perspective. Whether your objective is to generate change or knowledge, ambiguous matters typically stand as that which must be resolved logically into clear, distinct orders. I have not tried to frame ambiguity here as a means to discredit the confluence of social research and antiracist activism or to suggest an unassailable limit to this perspective's reach and scope. Rather, I pursued this subject because I think if this movement is to gain momentum and be effective, it has to deal with the ambiguities whites confront in relation to racial matters. Ambiguous situations reflect gaps that have opened in an ideological conditioning that has previously held answers for most experiences. That is why I consider the ambiguities evident in the "waitress stories" to be hopeful: they indicate instances where whiteness as a possessive invest-ment reaches its limits. The ambiguities in Beth Ellision's story are of a somewhat different, though related order, reflecting the increasing uncer-tainties faced by whites who are informed by antiracist perspectives in a social milieu that is rapidly changing—demographically, politically, eco-nomically, and culturally. Unless antiracists can treat these experiences in a nonreductive manner, they will lose their most critical audience, as was the case in Warrendale. Ambiguity also opens a view to the unfolding interpre-tive work of subjects. This is critical both because we need to understand how racial significance materializes in distinct settings and because it is whites' interpretations of race that those who want to short-circuit the reproduction of whiteness need to engage.

Scholars and activists who engage the subject of whiteness need to de-velop a means to negotiate the gulf between analytical/political insights and the murky realms of daily life where people are compelled to make sense out of their lives. The movement away from workshops and into particular places entails a shift from certainty about analytical dynamics to a con-frontation with the ambiguities of people's daily lives in specific settings, where they distinguish some and not other matters as racial. No matter how alluring the political goals of antiracism, we still need to generate a form of social knowledge that attends to less than perfect forms of social interaction based on changing modes of identification and differentiation. We also need to sharpen the analytical categories and methodological tactics that cultural anthropologists (and social scientists generally) deploy in making sense of racial matters.

A central theme developed over the course of this book is that racism is an insufficient explanation for the continuing significance of race. Without discounting the prevalence of racism in society, I have argued that the imbrications of racial discourses, perceptions, identities, and boundaries in American culture far exceeds the capacity of either white supremacy or racist ideology to account entirely for the confounding ways race matters today or will matter in the future. There are cultural dynamics at work shaping racial notions of belonging and difference that exceed the construction and projections of Otherness or the operations of an ideology that delineates strictly between whiteness and nonwhiteness. The purpose of this chapter is to describe in detail how cultural analysis more adequately engages these charged and convoluted dimensions of life in the United States in the early twenty-first century. The value of this approach is that it may offer a way to lead whites who have turned a deaf ear to discussion of racism to recognize the immense, enduring significance of race.

The power of cultural analysis lies in the ability to objectify a broad, pervasive phenomenon that informs people's daily lives and the multiple dimensions in which identities are posited, revised, and reproduced. Whether as patterns of behavior and belief or as discourses or worldviews, cultural analysis develops an attention to the forces that shape individual experiences and perceptions of sameness, as well as expressions and articulations of difference. This form of analysis provokes people to recognize dimensions of their lives that both exceed and inform their individuality: the idioms we speak, the ideas we express, the encounters that shape our biographies, all are socially contoured. This type of perception is crucial to the task of making sense of the enduring yet evolving significance of race, because of its capacity to link seemingly disparate domains, revealing similar dynamics constituting boundaries of belonging and difference that multiple aspects of social identity simultaneously (e.g., nationality, class, gender, region, as well as race). Certainly, as some analysts assert, racism can be found everywhere in American culture, and such assertions are easily substantiated with evidence gleaned from an array of social settings (see Bonilla-Silva 2001). But such claims tell us little about how members of distinct classes relationally construct, negotiate, or police social boundaries; nor do they convey all we need to know about how gendered distinctions are learned and reproduced.[1] Cultural analysis demonstrates how the coconstruction of race, class, and gender distinctions operates according to place-specific dynamics that ground and facilitate the concurrent production and reproduction of multiple overlapping and mutually reinforcing identities.

This claim for the power of cultural analysis confronts an immediate challenge from an array of critics who assign to the culture concept a good deal of blame for implicitly reproducing racial thinking and perception. This view of culture as part of the problem must be addressed first before considering cultural analysis as a means to comprehend the reproduction of racial identities and discourses. Specifically, I respond here to the charge that the concept of culture serves as a key means of refashioning racialized notions of difference into more palatable, seemingly innocent public forms (Trouillot 2002). Projections of distinct "cultures" come perilously close to simply transposing racial characterizations into a more innocuous but still insidious affirmation of social hierarchies. Responding to this critique, I review a series of recent ethnographic works that engage in discussions of whiteness and generate keen insights into how racial identities operate, exactly because they deploy an attention to cultural dynamics. These ethnographies suggest that the case against culture may be overstated, given their capacity to analyze both the reproduction of racial identities and the way such processes of identification are subverted or compromised in certain places and times. I then review criticisms of whiteness studies, drawing juxtapositions with similar critiques of the culture concept. This chapter concludes with a summary of what cultural analysis is and how it functions, along with some suggestions concerning how this approach offers greater vantage points than racism.

The potential for culture to reinscribe racial discourses was highlighted by the critiques of Orientalism and ethnographic authority (Said 1978; Clifford 1988; Clifford and Marcus 1986). Lila Abu-Lughod asserted in 1991 that "the concept of culture operates much like its predecessor—race—even though in its twentieth-century form it has some important political advantages" (143–144). Abu-Lughod argued that "culture" is conceptually flawed, "shadowed by coherence, timelessness, and discreteness," characteristics that distort more than they reveal about peoples objectified in cultural terms.[2] "Culture is the essential tool for making other," and in this role "the culture concept retains some of the tendencies to freeze difference possessed by concepts like race." The solution she proffers is to "write against culture" by eschewing generalizations and the power-laden entailments of objectivity in favor of "ethnographies of the particular" that focus "closely on particular individuals and their changing relationships" (154, 158) rather than on broad depictions of social dynamics and processes (see also Abu-Lughod 1999).

This case against culture was further elaborated by Virginia Dominguez (1992), who called attention to the political impact such invocations have in various spheres. Dominguez observed, "This 'thing' that anthropologists have for decades taken to be what we study, describe, decipher, and theorize about can be, and often has been, an ideological mechanism for subordination and social control" (22). In comparing the value of such objectifications against the power dynamics reproduced in cultural accounts, Dominguez framed the critical problem as "culturalism," a form of legitimation pursued by national governments that strives for a "minimization of divisiveness" by invoking culturally defined ethnicity:[3] "The switch from talk of races and immigrant groups to talk of ethnic groups and ethnic identity carries with it what I call the culturalization of difference. A public discourse that promotes intergroup tolerance employs the notion of cultural pluralism, not biological diversity, multilingualism, or class harmony" (32). These strategic forms of public discourse, Dominguez argues, point to the need for analysts to shift their conceptual focus, to refrain from deploying culture because of its racial impacts, and to be circumspect about its use in political discourses: "We need to move away from asking *about* culture—what belongs, what doesn't belong, what its characteristics are, whose characteristics are being imposed and whose are being excluded—and toward asking *what is being accomplished socially*, politically, discursively, when the concept of culture is invoked to describe, analyze, argue, justify and theorize" (21).

For Dominguez, part of the problem with invocations of culture is conceptual: "It is the concept of culture itself that carries in its continued discursive usage a huge social, economic, and political value" (1992, 35). But her critique extends as well to the basic elements of cultural analysis, which involve observing and describing cultural processes:

> I worry that in conceptualizing cultural politics too substantively, empirically, or regionally or locally, intellectuals, community activists, and politicians are, even in acts of resistance against European hegemony, perpetuating the very terms—of hierarchies of differential values—that constitute the hegemony. And in the process we may well be missing the more significant phenomenon—that these struggles are taking place now not because of existing or expanding or narrowing "cultural" differences among groups of people, but because at this point in time much of the world has internalized culture as the marker of difference. (38)

Thus, Dominguez recommends both a critical detachment from and attention to uses of culture.[4]

RACE IN ITS PLACE?

Following these suggestions for curtailing uses of culture because of its tendency to reproduce racial thinking, some anthropologists began to articulate a strong position that race instead needs to become the central concern of the discipline. There are two sharp statements of this view, one by Kamala Visweswaran, who draws on recent work in cultural studies and critical race theory to show both the paucity of anthropological accounts of "lived experiences" of race and to stress the centrality of race to contemporary power relations. In a somewhat different tack, Faye Harrison asserts that it is more specifically racism that needs to be a central focus of anthropological research and analysis. Taken together, these two perspectives make clear the crucial concerns at stake in this century-long interplay between these two powerful concepts, race and culture.

Visweswaran (1998, 76) builds on the line of critique delineated above, observing, "The failure to supply an account of our own role in propagating a notion of culture that lent itself to essentializing and fundamentalist tendencies signals not only an analytical weakness but a poverty of vision as well." But the problem Visweswaran diagnoses runs deeper than the tendency of culture to reproduce racial thinking; she additionally finds it inadequate to the task of making sense of contemporary race dynamics. Visweswaran asserts that "the modern anthropological concept of culture has lost any descriptive ability with regard to the construction of racial identities" (77). As a result, the relevance of anthropology to current circumstances has faded, and other analytical approaches have rushed to fill the void: "Multiculturalism and cultural studies have emerged as counterdisciplinary formations that radically foreground race and racial identity precisely because the modern anthropological notion of culture cannot do so." This is why, Visweswaran explains, "we do not usually turn to anthropology for accounts about what it is to function as racialized subjects" (77).

In place of the circumspection counseled by Abu-Lughod and Dominguez, Visweswaran affirms the importance of rallying around race as an analytic perspective, asserting the need to "see race itself as a productive and generative social category"; here, she champions approaches such as critical race theory "that radically foreground race and racial identity as modes of sociality and resistance" (1998, 77). Her attention to the "productive and generative" work of race stresses, first, "that the experience (and indeed, the category) of race is produced by racism and that different forms of racism produce differing effects of race" (78). This perspective emphasizes the enduring legacy of the racial constitution of collectives:

> The middle passage, slavery, and the experience of racial terror produce a race of African Americans out of subjects drawn from different cultures. Genocide, forced removal to reservations, and the experience of racial terror make Native Americans subjects drawn from different linguistic and tribal affiliations: a race. War relocation camps, legal exclusion, and the experience of discrimination make Asian American subjects drawn from different cultural and linguistic backgrounds: a race. The process of forming the southwestern states of the United States through conquest and subjugation and the continued subordination of Puerto Rico constitute Chicanos and Puerto Ricans as races. (78)

These racial identities define the type of subjects that Visweswaran advocates bringing into view via "a conception of race which is socially dynamic but historically meaningful" (78) and yet also responds to or counters the rise of sociobiological notions of race.

Such an approach, while bringing race to the fore of critical analysis, also bears the risks of reproducing racial thinking in much the way culture has been accused of perpetuating race. Herbert Lewis (1998) highlights the perils in Visweswaran's efforts to cultivate this broader sensibility concerning race.[5] Where Visweswaran strives to reanimate the "richly connotative 19th century sense of 'race,' " with its invocations of "blood" as a form of collectivity that encompasses "numerous elements that we would today call cultural," Lewis warns against a "return to the pre-Boasian conception that combines race, culture, language, and nationality in one neat package" (980). And though the equation of racial identity with the forms of persecution and exploitation highlighted by Visweswaran is insightful, Lewis observes that, pursued further, this logic reactivates a concept that "indissolubly connects groups of people and their appearance with beliefs about their capacity and behavior" (980). Given the criteria she lists, Lewis argues, "it follows presumably that we should recognize as 'races' all those who have suffered one or another form of ill-treatment. Certainly Jews would now return to the status of a 'racial' group (as the Nazis contended), as do Armenians, Gypsies (Rom), 'Untouchables' (Dalits) in India, East Timorese, Muslim and Croats in Bosnia and Serbs in Croatia, educated Cambodians in Pol Pot's Cambodia, both Hutu and Tutsi in Rwanda and Burundi" (980). Every similarly subjected group would thus be reinscribed with the charged terms used initially to distinguish them for exploitation and persecution. Dominguez's concerns about culture's propensity for "perpetuating the very terms—of hierarchies of differential values—that constitute the hegemony" seem equally relevant to this redeployment of race. As well, there follows the interminable question of subdividing and distinguishing races. Visweswaran's description of the processes that produce "Chicanos and Puerto Ricans as races" leads Lewis to question, "Are these two different 'races' or one? Can rich, powerful, and self-assured Puerto Ricans belong to this 'race'? Do Dominicans, Ecuadorians, and Cubans each get to be their own race, or can they all be in one race with Chicanos and Puerto Ricans because they all speak (or once spoke) Spanish? Can Spanish-speakers from Spain belong, too?" (981).The problem with formulating research in terms of race is that it becomes very difficult to proceed without reproducing various racialized logics that promote the notion that groups are essentially differentiated—experientially and in terms of innate capacities and dispositions—by race.

After raising similar concerns about how a reinvestment of race with critical authority would construe Asians ("Are South Indians and South Koreans in the same race?"), Lewis then turns to the important question of how this approach would incorporate various social collectives associated with whiteness: "If all these people belong to 'races,' how shall we categorize Yankees, the English, and the French, peoples who never suffered from racism—unless they lived in Quebec perhaps? If the Quebecois can be a 'race' because of their sense of persecution, doesn't symmetry demand that the English of Canada be another 'race'? If so, at the end of the twentieth century we have landed back in the nineteenth century, and we can all dust off our copies of W. Z. Ripley's *The Races of Europe* (1899) and assign it in our classes" (1998, 980–981). In addition to his point about the spiraling uncontrollability of any system for delineating races, Lewis raises the issue of symmetry. Without some form of equivalence in deploying racial analytics, the favorable aspects of Visweswaran's attention to race over culture entails inscribing essentialized distinctions between those who are racialized and those who deploy and cultivate racialized perceptions. This, of course, is a dynamic that culture, whatever its shortcomings, was used to short-circuit. In the Boasian view, everyone belongs to a culture; all identities are culturally constituted. This type of leveling gaze remains important to the task of analyzing race. As with the point about symmetry, it asserts the importance of some commensurate form of analysis to discern similar and linked dynamics within, say, both whiteness and blackness, a point I return to below. But first we need to consider a related take on race, one that instead lays a primary emphasis on highlighting the role of racism.

Faye Harrison similarly engages critically with the history of anthropology to arrive at a new analytical sensibility for the discipline. Harrison (1992, 1995, 1998) has diligently critiqued anthropology's tendency to avoid or ignore race; as well, she has worked to both document and cultivate efforts by anthropologists, historically and contemporarily, to counter this tendency. So it is notable that she is more optimistic than Visweswaran about the potential role anthropology can play in analyzing contemporary racial dynamics. In a special edition of *American Anthropologist* devoted to the subject of race across the subdisciplines, Harrison (1998, 623) asserts, "After an extended hiatus, anthropology has again reached a moment in its history when it cannot evade the pervasive power of racism." Avoiding some of the pitfalls in Visweswaran's approach, Harrison specifies that the focus must be on racism and points to "anthropology's unique role in interrogating, theorizing, and potentially disrupting the dynamics of racism." The crux of this distinction between race and racism lies in the way racist discourses have been reformulated to maintain invidious distinctions between social collectives without explicitly invoking race or white supremacist notions (see Balibar 1991; Fredrickson 2002). Harrison explains, "As racism assumes more subtle and elusive forms in the contemporary world, it is being reconfigured without 'race' as a classificatory device for demarcating difference" (1998, 610). This assertion, however, raises a perplexing question: What is racism without race? Certainly, there are many ways racialized perceptions and actions operate furtively, studiously avoiding direct attention to their racial basis or outcomes. The enduring impact of racist ideas and beliefs, despite many countervailing legal and political structures, indicates that their effectiveness derives from an ability to operate without ostensibly invoking race. But the functioning of "a classificatory device for demarcating difference" without explicit references to race opens onto a larger question of how such classificatory devices operate generally. Is it the case that, in the past, race has represented only one of several or many such devices? If so, in now functioning without race, has this historical mode of classification undergone such drastic changes that it will no longer be recognizable (a possibility that concerns Harrison), or do these changes rather reveal social dynamics at work in racial discourses that have long been obscured by the unique poignancy and insidious ease of seeing race? I raise this question not as an abstract philosophical concern, but because it brings heightened attention to the way Harrison's approach implicitly recoups some basic form of cultural analysis. Indeed, though she, too, argues against culture, her basis for seeing some redeeming perspective in anthropology implies some use for the culture concept in making sense of race.

Harrison makes the case for prioritizing racism by underscoring its cultural dimensions. She argues that racism "in all its subtlety and intricate multidimensionality actually works as *a complex social force*" (1998, 611; emphasis added). She also refers to racism as an "underlying cultural logic"; as well, she observes that "racists' *beliefs* about blackness are embedded in *a system of material relations* that produces and reproduces *taken-for-granted* power and privileges, such as those associated with whiteness" (612; emphasis added). These characteristics of racism reflect cultural dynamics, which become more evident when Harrison concludes her assessment: "As we devise anthropologically informed strategies for intervening more effectively in the 'culture of racism,' we should be reminded of the need to penetrate beneath the surface of ignorance and knowledge to educate and *enculturate against the very cultural logic of the manner in which ordinary people feel, think, speak, and live their everyday lives in this increasingly multiracial and multicultural society and world*" (613; emphasis added). Here, culture surfaces as both part of the solution and the crucial terrain of engagement against racism. Both Harrison's solution ("to enculturate against" the "culture of racism") and the ground she maps for engaging the reproduction of racism (the realm of "everyday lives") imply the relevance of culture as a mode of analysis and as a characterization of what it is that really matters in confronting the enduring significance of race.[6] This analytic potential of the culture concept is further demonstrated by the important insights it is used to generate in current ethnographic studies of how racial identities are generated and lived in the United States.

VIEWS FROM THE FIELD

A variety of recent ethnographic projects prompt a broad reconsideration of the fundamental importance of cultural analysis to make sense of race. Set in fast-changing urban contexts, they cover some of the most interesting, dynamic terrains where racial identities are contested and formulated. Findings of these ethnographers support the case that it is exactly the cultural dimensions—distinct from ideological analyses, abstract models of racial consciousness, or sole reliance on racism as an explanatory principle—that are critical to making sense of how racial identities are shaped, experienced, and reproduced within the larger frame of racial dynamics. Strikingly, several of these ethnographies focus on whiteness, that unmarked, normative order that has long maintained its power through a "culture of no culture."[7] If the cultural dimensions of whiteness can be evidenced in a manner that keeps racism in view while also effectively accounting for the dimensions of everyday life where racial identities are reproduced, then it should be evident that some effective uses of culture in relation to race remain.

Leland Saito (1998), in his ethnography of the dynamic racial and ethnic changes in Monterey Park, California, *Race and Politics: Asian Americans, Latinos, and Whites in a Los Angeles Suburb*, makes a strong case for the critical importance of grasping the cultural dimension of white racialness. Saito's findings are notable because he draws on whiteness studies and effectively deploys this concept in framing white interests and responses to the dramatic racial transformations in southern California. In particular, Saito takes issue with Roediger's assertion that whiteness represents "not a culture but precisely the absence of culture," which I discussed in chapter 7. Saito's criticism stems from his recognition that not all facets of whites' social lives are reducible to racism; he asserts, too, that culture offers an important perspective on the way whites create, experience, and reproduce a sense of place, one that varyingly reproduces or exceeds racial identity. Saito asserts that there are "two sides of white culture—racial privilege and hierarchy and an emotional connection to place" (51). The latter relates to dimensions of racial and ethnic identities that "flow from an attachment to a geographic place." In the case of the white minority in Monterrey Park, Saito writes, "The daily routine of leaving the house to engage in conversation with a friendly shopkeeper as one buys thread; dropping by a local restaurant after a city council meeting for a cup of coffee and a rehash of the evening's topics; and a special dinner at a small, neighborhood Chinese restaurant run by a helpful Chinese American family are everyday activities situated in a life enriched by many forms of culture associated with whites" (51). He concludes that "asserting the emptiness of white culture" only deprives analysts of a means to recognize how such racial identities are articulated in daily life and, more important, to critically engage the investments of race such attachments to place implicitly or explicitly entail.

Roger Sanjek further develops both this recognition of the importance of cultural analysis in relation to white racialness and the critical basis this cultural dimension provides to whites as they disinvest themselves from whiteness as an ideology or a mode of racial consciousness. Sanjek (1998) examines "neighborhood New York," in particular, the Elmhurst-Corona community in Queens, and finds that it has much to tell us about the demographic, economic, social, and political transformations occurring in the United States. As suggested by this ethnography's title, *The Future of Us All: Race and Neighborhood Politics in New York City*, Sanjek uses neighborhood New York to closely frame the dramatic processes of immigration, white flight, and economic disinvestments that have drastically reconfigured this country's social landscape. The way these developments have played out in Elmhurst-Corona, he argues, offers a window onto how their effects will unfold in other American cities. In 1970 the population of this working- and middle-class community in New York City was 98 percent white; in 1990 whites composed only 18 percent of Elmhurst-Corona residents. Whites who remain in this neighborhood have firsthand experiences of and insights into the profound demographic transformations that are occurring with increasing frequency across the United States. The reorientations they undergo in their experience of how race matters presents a challenging social situation for analysis and a provocative example of how some whites are rethinking the significance of race.

As does Saito, Sanjek recognizes that the bonds whites share in this community are significant, but he thinks they are grounded more in an experience of place than in an abstract conception of white culture or whiteness as a racial ideology: "What white Elmhurst-Corona residents shared most was local knowledge, common experience, and lifelong memories. They viewed their streets and neighborhood through layers of reminiscence, which surfaced in everyday conversation. . . . These understandings and routines constituted what anthropologists call 'culture'—a way of life that

was reproduced daily along predictable pathways and in ordinary interactions, grew more meaningful over years and decades, and at the same time
was continually adjusted to new circumstance" (1998, 242). This cultural experience of place became a basis by which the whites remaining in Elmhurst-
Corona practically disinvested in whiteness as an ideology, choosing the
integrated social spaces and community institutions of their neighborhood
over the segregated spaces of suburbia. Sanjek relates how white racial solidarity was initially invoked in the battles over integration in this area in
the 1960s and 1970s. But in the wake of those struggles and the devastating impact of white flight, that sense of a shared and imperiled whiteness crumbled. Sanjek observes that the remaining "white population now
understood that local quality of life was affected as much by white business
owners, police, school board members, mayors, absentee landlords, organized crime groups, and developers as by anyone else" (253). Through ongoing battles with city government over diminishing civic resources, whites
in Elmhurst-Corona realized that the threat to their quality of life bore a
white visage and exercised forms of power and privilege based in class distinctions: "The stayers recognized differences between themselves and other
groups of whites: the Manhattan elites who formulated economic and governmental policies affecting the neighborhood; local business proprietors,
police, and school board members who lived outside of [Elmhurst-Corona]
but influenced its quality of life; recent European immigrants, particularly
Italians, Greeks and (by the 1990s) Russians; upper-middle-class 'liberals,'
mainly residents of Manhattan; and 'yuppies,' the beneficiaries of the 1980s
boom" (229). Each of these social collectives, distortingly blurred or col-
lapsed together in generalizations about whiteness and white culture, registers as a distinct and at times threatening entity to whites in Queens rather
than as potential affines with which they must maintain racial solidarity.

The key feature Sanjek's study offers for any critical interest in whiteness
or white cultural identity is his use of culture in an anthropological sense—
not as an abstract notion of commonality, but as a host of nuanced practices
and interpretive repertoires linked to specific locales. Whites make sense of
race via this form of culture, one that presents antiracists with an important
inroad into white racial thinking and analysts of race fundamental insights
into operations of maintaining and reproducing racial identity. I suspect
that antiracists' characterizations of whites as privileged and powerful would
have as little traction in the minds of whites in Elmhurst-Corona as they did
for whites in Warrendale, discussed in the previous chapter. More important, though, these whites in Queens, in their experiences of these dramatic

social transformations, offer real-world glimpses of how race matters that are far more interesting than vanguardist notions about how whiteness should be abolished. Through daily engagement in the give-and-take of local politics rather than through consciousness-raising seminars, "lines of race and ethnicity had become crossable" in Elmhurst-Corona. These lines still significantly score the larger landscapes of New York City and the nation. But this local setting provides a model of how such crossing can be encouraged in other settings.

As the neighborhood became integrated during the 1980s and 1990s, a powerful sense of place operated inclusively to transform immigrants and in-movers into "locals." The means of establishing their belonging ranged from mundane exchanges—forms of courtesy, joking relations, and informal ties—to highly orchestrated rituals of inclusion at community gatherings that mobilized "symbols of ethnic diversity and exhortations of racial harmony" (1998, 330). This was not a simple form of face-to-face encounter, the kind that is often promoted (simplistically) as a means to break down racialized forms of social identity. Rather, these encounters derived from a daily experience of neighborhood life. Sanjek recounts how residents with distinct and often conflicted racial and ethnic backgrounds, through "their common culture of political struggle, began to see each other 'in the round,' as persons who resided in the same place and faced the same threats to their quality of life: crowded schools, crowded subways, crowded streets. Individual characteristics other than race were increasingly recognized as important" (330). Whites in particular moved from categorical perceptions of people of color as threatening outsiders to regarding their Latino, Asian, and black neighbors in personal terms. This transformation of white racial perceptions developed out of changes in the neighborhood and was facilitated by the local political structures that provided both a common meeting ground and a means for articulating shared interests.

Sanjek's findings have bearing on several aspects of current assessments of how race matters. Importantly, his ethnography demonstrates that civic politics and sociality are not strictly a terrain of reproducing racial difference; they are also a means by which projections of difference can be undermined. As well, the changes in Elmhurst-Corona underscore the need to think in terms of place and locale rather than generalized notions of racial community. Sanjek's attention to cultural practices and dynamics helps reveal how white residents in Elmhurst-Corona revamp and revise their understandings of race. This does not derive from targeting attitudes and beliefs, but from engagement in local politics that allowed residents to move from categorical identities to personal relations. As Sanjek observes, "People usually move from categorical to personal relationships not because of mysterious inner changes but because of the changing circumstances around them" (1998, 392). These "changing circumstances," which are increasingly frequent aspects of urban America, need to be tapped for all the potential they offer for critically engaging the enduring significance of race. Yet this is not to suggest that such sites are in any way magical or possess transcendental powers. Sanjek raises this caution himself in discussing white residents' efforts to both recognize racial significance and yet also fashion a "nonracial" political discourse to facilitate assertions of collective local interests.

Whites in Elmhurst-Corona tentatively assembled a means for talking about local concerns and interests using "a vocabulary of race, ethnicity, and nationality that was widely shared but also undergoing change" (1998, 253). That is, whites drew on newcomers' cues and naming practices to develop a means for speaking about the racial dimensions of their common predicaments as residents of this fast-changing neighborhood. Significantly, he notes, "The boundary around 'American' could shift as whites used the term differently in different situations," thus rendering this critical categorical identity increasingly inclusive rather than exclusive. But whites' efforts to disassociate race from categorical relations and well-bounded, distinct interests, however well intentioned, also risked compounding certain racial problems. White residents promoted a nonracial discourse in a political setting because "it dissolved a racial definition of whites that connected them to whites who supported policies they opposed, especially those that a person of color might label 'racist'" (254). Yet, this discourse also undermined the basis for recent immigrants or black in-movers to articulate aspects of their concerns that hinged primarily on racializing practices. Sanjek observes, "Insistence upon a nonracial discourse among residents . . . could thus silence 'minority' expressions of issues affecting persons because they were not white." He cautions that "whites who do treat individual immigrants and African Americans in personal rather than categorical terms must be prepared to admit that others do not. Certainly the white real estate industry, many white employers, and those whites who routinely use ethnic and racial slurs do not" (391). This reminder underscores the need to not treat such spaces or this general attention to place naïvely. In any social situation conflicts arise, and given the enduring significance of race in the United States there will frequently be a racial dimension to such conflicts. But

Sanjek's attention to culture brings into view how whites are able to negotiate and learn to think differently about these racial dimensions based on their experiences in a rapidly changing urban setting.

Pamela Perry (2002) develops yet another take on the crucial role of cultural analysis in relation to white racial identity in *Shades of White: White Kids and Racial Identities in High School*, a comparative ethnographic study of two central California schools, one suburban and vastly white, the other urban and multiracial, where whites compose just 12 percent of the student body. At its most fundamental level, Perry notes, "cultural identity formation involves, above all, a process of investment in and *identification* with the meanings attached to one's social location" (73). Echoing Saito and Sanjek, she argues that this cultural dimension—including attachment to place as well as specific practices and modes of expression—is key to grasping how whites make sense of race. Perry finds that white students develop situated meanings in relation to racial identity and that the distinct social contours of these locations, the urban and suburban high schools, profoundly constrain or facilitate their abilities to think about whiteness and blackness.

Perry observes, "White racial identities were not only multiple across contexts, but within contexts and even individual minds. They were made multiple by the ways race, gender, class, age, and other identities influence one another, and also by the quantity and quality of association with people of different racial ascriptions" (2002, 191). She carefully details how the forms of association and the contours of social status that shape these white kids' racial perceptions and experiences are a function of their specific locale. Rather than focusing on core attitudes and beliefs, she analyzes how students' racial thinking, first, hinged on institutional and local factors and, second, generated nuanced forms of multiple identities. Three key social processes impacted the way whites identified in racial terms. These began with the "different types and proximities of interracial association" that prevailed in each school, which were conditioned, in turn, by the distinct demographics and social location of these institutions. White racial identification was also impacted by "the ways racial-ethnic differences were structured by school practices," which ranged from implicit tracking policies to promotion of ethnic heritage events. Finally, "the ways youths defined their relationships to people of color" (97), whether through direct social ties or via various forms of popular culture, also shaped how whites articulated a sense of racial belonging and difference. Each of these cultural processes open onto far more complicated realms than can be addressed through a singular focus on racism.

Perry's approach to cultural analysis is particularly revealing in relation to the forms of popular culture that youth use to negotiate or enforce boundaries shaping collective and individual identities. She fashions a deft reading of how various instances of "white cultural community" manifest, not from an ideological core of racial values and beliefs, but through a much more complicated interplay and reproduction of tastes, homologies, and constitutive activities. This nexus is shaped by fundamental cultural dynamics: tastes, though pliable to some extent, are assimilated in early socialization; homologies are both perceived and produced based on core cultural orientations; and constitutive activities derive from and reproduce basic cultural dispositions. Through these dynamics, Perry explains, youths comprehend popular cultural traditions and innovations as white or not. She usefully states, "White music is not white because it reflects something or authentically articulates some sort of white tastes or experiences, but because it creates our understanding of what 'whiteness' is, because it places us in the social world in a particular way" (2002, 122). This formulation allows for and acknowledges the plasticity and fluidity of processes of racial identification, while also holding in view the institutional practices and the experiences of place that profoundly amplify or restrict this pliability.

Most profoundly, Perry's reading of the uses of popular cultural media of music, clothing, food, hairstyles, dance, and body art leads to a recognition of what she characterizes as the "multiracial self": a product of the sophisticated, fast-paced revisions, incorporations, and projections youths make in relation to racial collectives. The multiracial self derives partly from the inversions of racial power relations that occur in such settings where whites are a minority, but it also stems from the recognition by youths of "the many ways that racial difference and sameness are interdependent, one and the same, and, in the final analysis, arbitrary" (2002, 132). In both schools, Perry found that "the cultural identities of white, black, and other students of color were dialogically shaped with respect to one another, indirectly in some cases" (127). Through this dialogic process youths craft shifting modes of racial identification that generate a "multiracial self," one reflective of "the interdependent nature of racial-ethnic identities and the many ways that the self and the 'other' are one and the same" (128). Perry delineates four interrelated facets of the multiracial self:

> The first is evident in the us-them dialogue. The self only knows who he/she is because of who the other is; the racial self and other are two sides of the same coin. From another perspective, it might be said that the

self is "populated" by racial others: whites carry the "eyes" of blacks, Asians, Latinos and others in their views of themselves. In the third facet of the multiracial self, the other is the self, projected outward. And, finally, to the extent racial identities are constructed around "cultural" characteristics, individuals will have cross-cultural competencies and fluencies that, in effect, make them bi- or multi-cultural, even if they predominantly identify with only one set of cultural ascriptions. (129)

In placing culture in quotes here, Perry demonstrates that it is possible to maintain awareness of the problematic features of invoking cultural discourse in discussing race, while still pursuing a detailed analysis of the underlying cultural dynamics that fundamentally shape racial matters.

Through this concept of the multiracial self, Perry analyzes how students refashioned and reworked personal and collective dimensions of racial identification. In these two schools, the depth of the multiracial self depends on the demographic, economic, and social contours of these sites: "The closer and more diverse the relational context, the more racially populated, multiple, and complex the self becomes" (130). But in both locations this form of self-identification grounds a host of interpretive and evaluative practices by which students assess and access, revise and inflect their personal competencies in these stylistic and expressive media that were available to all youths in these settings. Similar to my study of how race matters for white Detroiters, Perry also emphasizes the importance of grasping the interpretive work of racial subjects over analyzing ideological structures of thought: "The interdependency and multiracialness also revealed itself in the ways white youth interpreted and *evaluated* their own cultural practices, that is, how they determined the relative heaviness, violence, meaninglessness, and so on of their popular cultural preferences" (129). This focus on the interpretative work of subjects reflects a basic assumption of cultural analysis: that people actively shape and rework meaningful structures and they typically do so in distinct places, where the multiplicity of encounters and the mutability of the landscape often militate against stock ideological reflexes.

In Detroit I found that the meaning of race varies by location and that racial identities are recursively constitutive of and reproduced by place (Hartigan 1999). The conclusions I reached through studying whites in distinct class neighborhoods and the lessons I draw from these ethnographies led me to argue for the importance of cultural analysis in relation to racial matters. A cultural perspective allowed me to recognize that people are often provisional in their racial assessments in a way that typically is either missed by surveys or neutralized by political polarization. I also found that a great deal of interpretive work goes into sounding out and thinking through the significance of race; this work is then either confirmed or challenged by changing circumstances, as in the sites studied by Saito, Sanjek, and Perry. Taken as a whole, these ethnographers depict the fundamental role of space and place, that is, the way neighborhoods and cityscapes reinforce or undermine certain racialized assumptions. These assumptions are not necessarily generated by a core of beliefs, but rather derive from interpretive repertoires that reproduce certain delimited readings of race. These repertoires can be expanded or altered through a growing disjuncture between self and place or even by antiracist interventions to reveal the "racial logic" implicit in these assumptions. The advantage of such an attention to interpretive repertoires is that it highlights the variety of discourses that whites and people of color speak commonly, though often from different positions or with distinct emphases. These commonalities form the basis by which whites in Elmhurst-Corona and Detroit strive to articulate collective interests that cross rather than reproduce the color line.

WHAT IS CULTURAL ANALYSIS?

Cultural analysis, as I construe it here, includes some or all of the following aspects, which each featured in the various approaches I have taken in this book to grasping the significance of white trash and to analyzing whiteness. As stressed above, attention to interpretive repertoires or to narrative structures is crucial, but so is an analysis of what John and Jean Comaroff (1992, 41) refer to as "body work": all the disciplinary forms of naturalizing social orders, identities, and behaviors by inscribing them in individual bodies, particularly through modes of etiquette and decorum. Culture, at its core, is a means for naturalizing social orders or ideological structures, and for this, body work is fundamental, as in the practices examined in chapters 1 through 4. But culture also operates or manifests through various spatializing practices, means of organizing space and localities as meaningful sites. The enduring relevance of ethnography to the pursuit of cultural analysis is predicated on the crucial role of place in human experience, and its relevance to discussions of race should be evident both from the works cited above and the perspectives delineated in chapters 6 and 8 (see also P. Jackson and Penrose 1993; Gupta and Ferguson 1997). Yet another dimension of culture involves the basic cultural process of sorting out belonging and difference. Often, this process is formulated via notions of pollution and requires boundary maintenance, animated by moralizing systems, such as those examined in chapters 2 through 5. But perceptions of belonging and difference also turn on processes of self-construction and the production of categorical identities, as are evidenced keenly in the work of ethnographers featured in this chapter (see also Battaglia 1995). Culture involves means of establishing and maintaining social relations, as through forms of kinship and exchange. Race, perhaps the penultimate example of culturally con-structed biology, certainly influences and is in turn shaped by ideas about kinship, as explored in chapter 8. The reformulation of kinship studies by anthropologists via attention to genetics, new reproductive technologies, and adoption practices certainly has the potential to impact the way we think critically about race (see K. Weston 2001; Marks 2001).[8] Finally, each of these dynamics are interpretively engaged and enacted via expressive me-diums in local contexts that are shaped by national and transnational power structures and flows (Appadurai 1996).

Yet, what of the critique of culture raised in the opening of this chapter? Certainly, the findings of recent field studies arrayed here offer a coherent retort to the position that we jettison "culture" entirely. The valuable per-spectives they compose could not have been shaped without some recourse to the concept of culture. But there is also a more pointed response to the critique of culture. Robert Brightman argues that a "straw culture" concept has been retroactively assembled to privilege and advance recent theoretical posturing (1995, 528). Brightman concludes "that certain contemporary cri-tiques of culture derive their cogency and persuasiveness from a strategic and selective retrospective construction of the meaning of the concept in earlier conditions in anthropology. Reconstituted precisely as the antithesis of theoretical agendas currently in place," Brightman sees culture presented only to be transcended, asserting that the move to get "beyond" culture is "the effect of rhetorical strategies that (re)construct an essentialized culture concept in the antipodes of contemporary theoretical argument." Indeed, "recent arguments that the culture construct is evanescent and dispensable foreground conceptual stability at the expense of liability, presupposing that there existed in the past and into the present *a* culture construct with *a* determinate definition, now discredited" (527). Which of the many versions of culture, Brightman asks, are we to reject? Whatever the basis for such choices, Brightman warns that "anthropologists who self-consciously reject 'culture' in favor of 'discourse,' 'hegemony,' or 'habitus' will traffic partly in old signifieds with new signifiers" (541).

Most important, after reviewing early anthropological works (by Bronislaw Malinowski, Ruth Bendecit, Alfred Kroeber, and Franz Boas) and more recent efforts (by Marshall Sahlins, Roy Rappaport, Roy Wagner, and Renato Rosaldo) and finding that each wrestles with the task of redefining culture, Brightman concludes that the prevailing characteristics then and now are not invocations of "coherence, timelessness, and discreteness." Rather, he finds stress laid on historicity, contested social orders, and flows of exchange between various cultural locales. "Neither in earlier disciplinary history nor as deployed in recent anthropological writings does the culture concept consistently exhibit the attributes of ahistoricism, totalization, holism, legalism, and coherence with which its critics selectively reconstitute it. These are invented images of culture, both arbitrary and partial with respect to a much more diverse and versatile field of definitions and use" (1995, 541). However selectively the works by founding figures can be read to promote a critical vision of culture as static and homogeneous, Brightman asserts that "history, chaos, contestation, and strategy have been anthropological growth stocks since at least 1980, and disciplinary writing reflects this state of affairs, both in theoretical exposition and in the interpretation of ethnographic materials" (540). In the end, culture, as with any concept, bears the features with which we invest it, and it need bear the onerous connotations no more than the favorable ones.

Several points follow from Brightman's reassessment of critiques of the culture concept. First, the critical assertion of discourse as a primary analytical focus for ethnographers may have been developed in contrast to a straw version of culture, but favorable outcomes have resulted. As Brightman notes, ethnographic inquiry has been entirely transformed since the early 1980s, developing accounts that are effective in undercutting an overly homogeneous, static, "timeless" view of peoples, promoting instead an attention to contestation and the pliability of cultural media. The move to discourse, promoted early on by Abu-Lughod, made ethnographers newly attentive to ways social relations and forms exceed the tightly bounded formulation of national or individual cultures; the movements of peoples, objects, and ideas now are primary foci in contemporary ethnographies. The key point is that these developments, though articulated initially through a critique of culture, are not dependent on the erasure of that concept (see also Brumann 1999; Barth 2002; Wade 1999; Sokefeld 1999). Rather than an alternative to culture, discourse serves as a means to critically reinvigorate this irreplaceable perspective on social relations. Discourse, though powerful, is limited, too, particularly by its language-centered perspective. Unlike culture, discourse only sketchily references spatial practices, social relationships, and forms of body work that naturalize cultural systems of action and belief. Thus, the turn to culture I am arguing for builds on and extends critical assessments of ethnographic work rather than refuting entirely the important critiques outlined at the opening of this chapter.

Basically, there can be no question of "returning" to an originary culture concept. Brightman makes clear that such a singular entity never existed, but more important, the cultural perspective I am advocating builds on the postmodernist critiques of the political tendencies and social assumptions that bound anthropology to colonialist projects. This reconstituted use of culture is predicated on self-reflexive attention to issues of representation, is cognizant of global restructurings of national, local, and indigenous forms of identity, and features a critical regard for the serious political and economic impacts of wielding culture. The ethnographic works recounted above deploy culture while also being attentive to processes of objectification and astute about the interested aspects of the observers and their observing context. Such awareness reflects the way cultural anthropologists have learned from critiques of ethnographic authority and representational practices. But these works also underscore that no other concept as effectively systematically links attention to the disparate dynamics of social relations and spatial practices in one overarching perspective as does culture. The value of this perspective gains in importance particularly in relation to issues of race.

The particular version of the critique of culture I have traced here centrally turns on the racial impacts and implications of its invocation. And my efforts to articulate a positive role for culture in response to this critique is in no way a rejection of the claims that there are negative racial effects to invoking this concept. Abu-Lughod and Dominguez are right that we need to be circumspect about the potential for culture to reinscribe racial thinking, and the uses I am advocating here will require continued vigilance. To use culture, then, in relation to race involves also engaging with and disrupting popular uses and imaginings of the term that do equate its subjects with static, "traditional," and unchanging exotic entities. And it is exactly this type of engagement with enduring assumptions that underscores the central reason for making renewed use of culture in relation to race. From my efforts to teach students about race, I realize that without an overarching attention to culture it is very hard, first, to convey the extent of racial thinking and, second, to effectively engage the multiple, overlapping structures of perception and experience that reproduce racial identities and collectives. Many people cannot begin to recognize how thoroughly the significance of race informs social life unless they have the ability to first grasp culture as a field of intelligibility that structures their actions and perceptions. Fundamentally, one needs a cultural vision in order to denaturalize the view of race as a "natural" order of difference.

Concerns about race bring into view past misuses of culture, but the countervailing point is that the culture concept holds perhaps the most powerful counterweight to racial thinking because it depicts, on one hand, the plastic and artificial aspects of racial identification and, on the other, all the forms of commonality that undercut racialized inscriptions of essential orders. Thinking in terms of culture, research in the United States can be more finely honed to ask about racial dynamics but also cross-cutting discursive practices that whites and people of color share in common. Steven Gregory's (1998) study of black middle-class homeowners, discussed in the previous chapter, is an excellent example (see also Hochschild 1995). Gregory's attention to the "construction of black class identities through the political culture of grass-roots activism" (124) opens a view onto social forms that operate across racial lines and yet are also distinctly inflected in the process of racial formation. His account of how these homeowners "interpret, debate, and publicly perform the present meanings of black class divisions and racial identities" (17) provides a most nuanced reading of processes of racial identification and disidentification that would not be possible either by solely relying on the concept of race or without an attention to cultural dynamics. Or consider Michael Moffatt's (1986) study of conflicts in an interracial college dorm. Moffatt found that these conflicts were similarly assessed by black and white students, who all made reference to the crucial American cultural concept of "friendliness." Regardless of race, each of these students traced the origins of conflicts to a perceived lack of friendliness by members of the other racial group. White and black students differed in what they perceived as signs of friendliness, but they were commonly linked in a very American conception that sociality is predicated on demonstration of this cultural characteristic (see Park 1996). The advantage of such a perspective on racial conflicts is suggestive; not predicated on essentializing differences (i.e., whiteness and blackness), nor casting historical forces as unambiguously determinate of current social relations, it focuses discussion instead on the very tangible and fundamentally plastic terrain of social cues and perceptions.

The value of such a cultural perspective is further evident in considering the recent critiques of whiteness studies, where lack of attention to broad cultural dynamics is striking. Historians Eric Arnesen (2001) and

Peter Kolchin (2002) have each formulated thorough assessments of the huge amount of research recently produced on whiteness. Key themes in their critiques of the concept are that it reifies racial identity, is too generally or loosely defined, and is inattentive to the density of social relations in lived, historical situations. Arnesen concludes emphatically, "The category of whiteness has to date proven to be an inadequate tool of historical analysis" (6). He summarizes: "Whiteness is, variously, a metaphor for power, a proxy for racially distributed material benefits, a synonym for 'white supremacy,' an epistemological stance defined by power, a position of invisibility or ignorance, and a set of beliefs about racial 'Others' and oneself that can be rejected through 'treason' to a racial category" (9). From looseness in definition there follows other problems, such as a highly selective approach to sources, vagueness about agency, and inattention to concrete social relations. As a result, "its conceptual imprecision and the creative literary and evidentiary liberties taken in its name render whiteness a problematic category of historical analysis" (23). Barbara Fields (2001), writing in response to Arnesen's assessment, further disparages the analytical emphasis in deployments of whiteness on abstracting out a certain limited set of dynamics rather than depicting and analyzing specific settings and times. Fields finds that, "as an organizing concept, whiteness leads to no conclusion that it does not begin with as assumptions. Whiteness is a racial identity; therefore, white people have a racial identity. Whiteness equals white supremacy; therefore European immigrants become white by adopting white supremacy. Whiteness entails material benefits; therefore, the material benefits white people receive are a reward for whiteness" (53). Fields's critique depicts whiteness as a conceptual perspective that presupposes too much and is not well suited for the task of descriptively rendering and accounting for the nuances of distinct social relations in particular locations.

Kolchin both ratifies and extends this critique of whiteness, though he is also attentive to the great potential of these new studies. He credits this area of inquiry for providing crucial "insights that collectively help us define our interpretation of race in America and at large," also for showing "how assumptions about race and races have changed over time and exploring human agency in the making of race" (2002, 36). But he draws on Fields's work to delineate further within whiteness studies "a set of tricky problems centering on the reality, pervasiveness, and permanence of whiteness and especially its relationship to concrete historical situations" (14). Kolchin discerns a tendency in uses of whiteness to constitute ideological "attitudes" as the object of study, leaving their relation to actual social relations murky. "In viewing whiteness as an independent category, many whiteness studies authors come close to reifying it and thereby losing sight of its constructed nature; in assigning whiteness such all-encompassing power, they tend to ignore other forms of oppression, exploitation, and inequality; and in focusing so heavily on representations of whiteness, they too often ignore the lived experiences—as well as the perceptions—of those perceived as nonwhite or 'not quite' white" (15). Kolchin also asserts that Jacobson and Roediger come "close to portraying race as a ubiquitous and unchanging transhistorical force rather than a shifting and contingent 'construction' " (15).

In this last regard, Kolchin is disturbed by an uncanny alternation in conceptualization of whiteness that undermines the ability of this concept to adequately analyze the settings it is deployed to analyze: "In short, there is a persistent dualism evident in the work of the best whiteness studies authors. At times, race—and more specifically, whiteness—is treated as an artificial construct with no real meaning aside from its particular social setting; at other times it becomes not only real, but omnipresent and unchanging, deserving attention as an independent force. Race appears as real and unreal, transitory and permanent, ubiquitous and invisible, everywhere and nowhere" (16). The emphasis on ideology in conceptualizations of whiteness leaves this line of inquiry prey to such fluctuations and confusions.

At stake in these various critiques of whiteness is the matter of whether this mode of inquiry is a reliable means for depicting the world and its racial inflections; as well, does it provide us with a means of actually learning from situations in the past or current, unfolding cultural moments? In Fields's criticism that "whiteness leads to no conclusion that it does not begin with as assumptions," I hear a concern that this approach presupposes too much, formulating answers in advance that only ratify the initial suspicions of the researcher rather than providing a heuristic means for adequately learning something about how the world works. Kolchin's concern over reifications of whiteness that lead researchers "to ignore other forms of oppression, exploitation, and inequality" strikes me as an important reminder that, rather than simple conveyors of racism or automatons dominated by a racial ideology, whites' racial actions and beliefs involve, as with any cultural dynamic, interpretive work, made more or less precarious depending on the types of reinforcements provided by particular social settings. Racial interpretations are always competing with (and often conflating with) other interpretive repertoires such as class and gender and neighborhood and nation; as well, white attitudes and behavior often are not only about race,

but result from multiple, overlapping, at times mutually reinforcing or contradictory frames of reference that inform social judgments and actions.
When Kolchin raises the concern that whiteness studies is "focusing so
heavily on representations," it is the subsequent inattention to these competing, conflating, and mutable circumstances that undermines the value of
these research projects. In Kolchin's point about "portraying race as a ubiquitous and unchanging transhistorical force rather than a shifting and contingent 'construction,'" I sense a similar uneasiness that the concept of
whiteness will not really advance our abilities to think through the complexities, ambiguities, and nuances of fast-changing racial situations. That is,
formulating problems in terms of whiteness, though importantly compen-
sating for devastating myopia in regard to race, is not adequate to the
dynamism of social relations.

The question of whether social relations are adequately framed and analyzed via racial analytics raises another question, one that Kolchin brought
into view when he addressed the "tricky problems centering on the reality,
pervasiveness, and permanence of whiteness." Simply put, are we getting it
right when we describe the world via abstractions such as whiteness and
blackness? Certainly, these terms are relevant and revealing, but only to a
point. That limit is sketched in another area of recent scholarship, one that
has gained less attention than whiteness studies but that can perhaps be
equally profound in its implications. In the early 1990s, and stemming from
the same intellectual ferment that spawned the critique of culture, Occidentalism was formulated as a related problematic to Said's critique of Orientalism (see Gewertz and Errington 1991; Carrier 1995). Constituting a
similar operation, Occidentalism connotes the process of constructing essentialized, unified, and absolutist depictions of the West or Westerners. The
sources, functions, and effects of Occidentalism can be construed variously
as mirroring, stemming from, or diverging from those of Orientalism, but
the basic formulation suggests that we participate in a similarly delimited
and compromised representational practice when we wield the abstraction
such as the West or whiteness.

Anthropologist James Carrier (1995, vii) describes how he came to use the
term to characterize "the ways that some anthropologists typified the United
States in particular and Western societies in general." In response to the
growing recognition of Orientalizing practice in the discipline, anthropologists further compounded the problem by construing a generic West that
was to blame for such depictions. "These were conscientious scholars who

devoted great effort to uncovering the nuances, complexities, and inter-connection of the societies they studied. Yet they would casually and super-ficially characterize Western society in terms so simplistic that they would not be tolerated of an anthropologist speaking about a village society" (vii–viii). And although such depictions certainly pertain to broadly construed global power dynamics, their relevance to particular, nuanced social set-tings remains questionable (Stewart 1996). Nor was it just Westerners par-ticipating in Occidentalism. Xiaomei Chen (1992, 688) described early on how "the Chinese Orient has produced a new discourse marked by a par-ticular combination of the Western construction of China with the Chinese construction of the West, with both of these components interacting and interpenetrating each other. This seemingly unified discursive practice of Occidentalism exists in a paradoxical relationship to the discursive practices of Orientalism, and in fact shares with it many ideological techniques and strategies." This form of Occidentalism has particularly powerful effects, as Chen observed in relation to its uses by the Chinese government, which studiously invests and mobilizes this discourse: "In this process, the Western Other is constructed by a Chinese imagination, not for purposes of domi-nating it, but in order to discipline, and ultimately to dominate the Chinese self at home" (688). This divergence in the objects of domination in relation to these mirroring and overlapping discourses is significant, but it does not undermine the basic resonance between these two modes of objectification.[9]

In the wake of September 11 in the United States, this incipient focus on Occidentalism received a surge of attention. Occidentalism is now discern-able in a broad range of political reactions, from Shinto-based, Japanese nativism of the 1930s and 1940s to the recent round of Al-Qaeda terrorist attacks against the United States. A common thread of critical disdain for capitalism, humanism, individualism, consumerism, and a host of other ideologies associated with the West links these disparate representations. As Avishai Margalit and Ian Buruma (2002, 2) note, "Occidentalism, which played such a large part in the attacks of September 11, is a cluster of images and ideas of the West in the minds of its haters. Four features of Occidental-ism can be seen in most versions of it; we call them the City, the Bourgeois, Reason, and Feminism. Each contains a set of attributes, such as arrogance, feebleness, greed, depravity, and decadence, which are invoked as typically Western, or even American, characteristics." Whatever basis exists for such characterizations, Margalit and Buruma are quick to note that we must regard these as we have learned to recognize Orientalist depictions: as interested representations that work on multiple levels to operationalize a range of politically charged, power-laden distinctions that quite exceed the simple notion that they are either accurate or not.

Margalit and Buruma (2002, 2) recognize in Occidentalist discourse certain thematics, such as a deep hatred of urban life, with its "commerce, mixed populations, artistic freedom, sexual license, scientific pursuits, leisure, personal safety, wealth, and its usual concomitant, power." In response to such unruly circumstances, championed solutions consistently feature restoring purity of soil and blood, typically at the expense of immigrants and minorities. As well, Occidentalists promote spiritualism over Western materialism: "Occidentalists extol soul or spirit but despise intellectuals and intellectual life." Margalit and Buruma see this as another variant of the "fairly common belief among all peoples that 'others' don't have the same feelings we do" (3). Occidentalism also features "heroic creeds" to sharply contrast with images of "the settled bourgeois," which also turns on gendered ideals of masculinity. In contrast to the forms of discipline promoted as the basis for opposition to the West, "the power of female sexuality will be seen as a direct threat" (4). Each of these themes conflate into a powerful interpretive repertoire that works to reduce the heterogeneity or discrepancies among citizens and nations in the West into a charged, politically useful depiction of Otherness.

The parallels between this critique of Occidentalism and those of whiteness delineated above I hope are apparent. Each stands charged with promoting abstract generalizations, singularly attending to forms of homogeneity, and distortingly depicting static entities in the face of more fluid social relations. Is it surprising that this sketch also covers the broad charges levied against the culture concept? Overstatements of conformity and coherence are a problem for whiteness and Occidentalism, just as the earlier allegations against culture have charged. And whiteness, too, stands accused of being predetermined in its findings. What accounts for the uniformity of these critiques? They each are formulated in terms of representation, its limits and its problematic tendencies. Whiteness and Occidentalism share fundamental dynamics with representations of culture criticized above as too abstract or as interested depictions that tell more about the subjects producing the representations than those being represented. As a critical concept, whiteness offers no better chance of breaking the circular dynamics of representation than any other form of objectification; indeed, it may be even more compromised because it features so little basis for self-reflection about these types of problems.

The overarching focus of the discussion in this chapter is on assessing the limits of research and interventions that either posit race as the most fundamental dimension of social reality or regard racism as the core of all racial matters. I have suggested that cultural analysis allows for a more thoroughgoing approach, one that is perhaps less effective in crafting an unambiguous political message but that does generate examples and analyses that are powerful because they grapple with the opacities of daily life. The approach to racial matters I'm promoting has two key features: first, it delineates a frame of reference that attends broadly to cultural dynamics; second, it engages in analysis and representation via systematic attention to social settings and their nuanced dimensions. Instead of construing whiteness as an ideological construct, I regard it like any other cultural artifact: it is constituted in daily life through symbols, images, discursive logics and interpretive repertoires, narrative genres, various forms of body work and discipline, and all the other arbitrary conventions that characterize cultural constructions. And it is the very arbitrariness or contingency of these forms that offers one of the best openings to deconstruct whiteness. Each mode of reinforcing white privilege is maintained through a tight correspondence of material, economic, and political structures that, in the end, must be meaningfully perceived and experienced by individuals in particular cultural locations. The web of culture makes whiteness a tangible subject of investment, defense, and oppression that is coconstructed with class, gender, regional, and national identities. Painstakingly untangling this web offers an alternative and potentially more effective means of breaking this process of investment than singularly targeting racism, simply because a crucial segment of the white population has tuned out any discussion of this subject.

Cultural analysis offers the potential of revealing racial strands in the textures of daily life in a way that may yet get through to whites who are inured to charges of racism. Culture provides a way to effectively reformulate attention to race by analyzing the "complex social forces" and their overdetermined impact on what Harrison (1998, 611) characterized as the "system of material relations that produces and reproduces taken-for-granted power and privileges, such as those associated with whiteness." It is cultural analysis that precisely accomplishes what Harrison calls for: a sustained attention to "the very cultural logic of the manner in which ordinary people feel, think, speak, and live their everyday lives in this increasingly multiracial and multicultural society and world" (616).

Cultural analysis, as demonstrated by Saito, Sanjek, and Perry, deploys this attention to complex social forces in nuanced settings of everyday life, showing the pervasiveness of racial matters via examples of white subjects who are not simply or only racist but people mired in complicated situations. These views from the field are compelling for their depiction and analysis of daily circumstance, thus providing a greater range of material for thinking through race in all its complexities. Indeed, they are interesting because they frame the ambiguities and confusions of daily life, while also depicting the systematic way that race informs cultural experience. Compare Perry's account of the "multiracial self" that students develop as a means of negotiating material, symbolic, and discursive forms of racial matters with that of the accounts of whiteness critiqued above by Arnesen and Kolchin. The contrast is distinct because of the greater attention to place and the recognition of a wider array of social forces at work in these ethnographies.

The goal of this book has been to argue for and demonstrate an approach to analyzing race that brings to bear a range of methods and analytical dispositions that have been subject to intense critique over the past decade or so. The basis of that critique has been an attention to dynamics of representation and the overdetermined inscriptions of power and dominance that shape such representations into depictions of Otherness. Attention to forms of othering has profoundly transformed the way academics and activists work at representing social relations. Indeed, it provided a basis for the project of analyzing whiteness. But Otherness dynamics do not constitute the entire spectrum of racial matters, nor does an awareness of projections of Otherness constitute a sufficient basis for analyzing the fast-changing ways that race matters today. What is needed additionally is a means for thinking about the discrepant and diverse circumstances in which people are racialized. This approach requires a renewed and revitalized deployment of culture.

Cultural analysis is not an end in itself, and there are still too many reasons to keep racism at the forefront of any analysis of race. But cultural analysis is well suited to presenting interesting examples to use as a basis for thinking through how race matters. These objectifications of social relations and situations will always be interested and partial, as is any representation. But they obtain a broader purchase on both social conditions and our capacity to imagine them than is offered by ideological analyses or critiques of representation alone. Now that whiteness has been added to the analytical tool kit, the study of race must open onto more nuanced and less certain types of situations and problems, where whiteness and blackness as abstract orders of dominance and subordination are not assured. In this regard, this book contributes to a developing shift in the way social scientists think about race, producing knowledge concerning how racial subjects are constituted and racial interpretive repertoires deployed.

David Theo Goldberg (1993; see also H. Moore 1996) critically characterized the practice of anthropology as the production of racial knowledge, the generation of detailed information about the Other that both confirms and produces its existence for "the West." Colonialist and capitalist enterprises require "information about racial nature: about character and culture, history and traditions, that is, about the limits of the Other's possibilities. Information, thus, has two senses: detailed facts about racial natures; and the forming of racial character. . . . Production of social knowledge about the racialized Other, then, establishes a library or archive of information, a set of guiding ideas and principles about Otherness: a mind, a characteristic behavior or habits, and predictions of likely responses" (150). Goldberg's critique, developed as an extension of Edward Said's notion of Orientalism, is probably familiar to most practitioners of cultural studies and fairly certainly stands as a depiction of what ethnographers resist producing now. The shift in anthropological subjects of study to numerous sites within the West and of transnational processes of identity formation and community construction is effecting a dismantling or subversion of this model of racial knowledge production. But I raise Goldberg's characterization here in closing because it helps to frame alternative directions that the new interest in whiteness can take when it is applied in ethnographic settings. One option, certainly, is to systematically compile a comprehensive knowledge about whiteness and its operations, which could be used to deconstruct this hegemonic institution. An alternative course, one that I favor, is to use this attention to the racialness of whites to articulate a new form of racial knowledge, one that does not primarily support global institutions of power and dominance but instead details cultural processes that extend or exceed the Otherness model. Attempted in these pages are studies of the process of racialization generally rather than ethnographic accounts of the cultural construction of one order or another (of whiteness or of blackness), underscoring the fundamental insight that race is not equivalent to essential, natural orders of difference (Barot and Bird 2001).

To seek out and authoritatively compile anthropological knowledge of whiteness risks leaving the model of racial knowledge critiqued by Goldberg fundamentally intact. Reversing its dynamics by objectifying a consistent and reliable knowledge about whites leaves the logic of this model unchallenged. Gayatri Spivak (1999, 1) intones a similar caution in the opening of her recent work, *A Critique of Postcolonial Reason*, which I think can be usefully echoed in relation to studies of whiteness: "Postcolonial studies, unwittingly commemorating a lost object, can become an alibi unless it is placed in a general frame. Colonial Discourse studies, when they concentrate only on the representation of the colonized or the matter of the colonies, can sometimes serve the production of current neocolonial knowledge by placing colonialism/imperialism securely in the past, and/or by suggesting a continuous line from that past to our present." I parse her cautions in relation to whiteness studies as follows: unless the analysis of whiteness is positioned in a more general frame, it will stand as a unique, essentialized object and reveal little about the ongoing, mutable significance of race. To posit whiteness as a continuous operation and identity in countless sites around the world affirms more than challenges current assumptions of racial identity and difference. However, by observing "whites" in the field as a series of discontinuous, nonequivalent objectifications and discursive positions, cultural analysts participate in the painstaking task of assembling a new order of racial knowledge, one that no longer ratifies and reproduces Otherness, but attempts, instead, to detail the process of racialization, whether whites or people of color are its immediate subjects. The key shift is from studies *of* whiteness to a variety of perspectives on how white racialness is projected, manipulated, and deployed in disparate places. The discursive terrains in these various locales bear multiple points of resonance and dissonance with these other sites and with global systems of capital, labor, and power. The emphasis falls on the incommensurate aspects of racial matters and the local relations that are affected but not wholly determined by global orders and historical regimes.

The point of producing racial knowledge is not to assemble it in order to characterize and define a particular group or order—such as whiteness or blackness—but rather to generate it as a basis for comprehending when, how, and if certain dynamics are racial, especially in situations where "race" is not ostensibly present. The perspective I am suggesting for racial knowledge production is oriented toward learning from current moments in their nuanced relation to the onrushing future, when the power relations, expressive forms, and local dynamics shaping race will be increasingly complicated. Such a mode of generating social knowledge concerning racial matters delineates the copious overlapping linkages between race and other key registers for sorting out the cultural matters of belonging and difference— class, gender, and nation. Making racial analysis a form of social knowledge production perhaps will allow studies of race to open onto a broader understanding of how culture and society works and, as well, will help to break "race" out of its fairly ghettoized location in academia.

These chapters, then, should be read as a series of investigations of racialization broadly, linked by an attention to racializing practices and interpretive repetoires generally and not to a shared confidence about what constitutes whiteness. In terms of racial knowledge, or anthropological knowledge about the operation of racial logics and idioms, this book traces how discourses of race are deployed as modes of interpretation in certain situations (according to fluctuating and variable criteria), changing how participants act out or respond to these predicaments.

NOTES

INTRODUCTION

1 The defining features of culture are subject to constant interrogation in a process of continual reevaluation that has followed this key concept throughout its long career. For current overviews of the stakes in defining culture, see Bonnell and Hunt (1999); Clifford (1988); Dirks (1998); R. Fox and King (2002); R. Fox and Lears (1993); Kuper (1999); Ortner (1999).

2 I am interested in the process by which complex cultural phenomena or dynamics are rendered as objects of analysis, either in academic or popular processes. The touchstone for my use of objectification is drawn from Berger and Luckman (1966); Cetina (1999); Haraway (1997).

3 The field of whiteness studies is burgeoning rapidly and is difficult to delineate with a few citations. Key works that survey this field include the symposium "Whither Whiteness?" published in a special edition of *Souls: A Critical Journal of Black Politics, Culture, and Society* titled "Seeing Through the Whiteout" (2002) as well as Brander et al. (2001) and Delgado and Stefancic (1997).

4 "A monolithically normative and therefore invisible Whiteness—effectively assumed even by those critiquing it—overlooks the highly diverse range of degrees of agency, autonomy, status, and social power within White society, and hence assumes, for those residing at its lowest stratum, a degree of implicit benefits from being a member of the dominant race that many underclass individuals have in all likelihood never enjoyed, nor are ever likely to enjoy; concomitantly, it imposes upon them more responsibility for the evil consequent on that same dominance" (J. Wilson 2002, 398).

5 On the enduring but complicated relevance of "tribe," see Strong and Van Winkle (1993), who also discuss a certain leveling effect achieved by applying this vestige of ethnocentrism onto whites.

6 In attempting to navigate "between the Scylla of 'race as illusion' and the Charybdis of racial objectivism," Howard Winant (1994, 18) offers the following

definition of race: "Race provides a key cultural marker, a central signifier, in the reproduction and expression of identity, collectivity, language, and agency itself. Race generates an 'inside' and an 'outside' of society, and mediates the unclear border between these zones; all social space, from the territory of the intra-psychic to that of the U.S. 'national character,' is fair game for racial dilemmas, doubts, fears, and desires" (30). See also Stuart Hall in the film *Race: The Floating Signifier*, produced and directed by Sut Jhally, Media Education Foundation, Northampton, Mass., 1996.

7 On the multiple cultural processes shaping stereotypes, see Bhabha (1983); Herz-feld (1997); Schauer (2003); Van den Berghe (1997).

8 A notable exception is K. Moss (2003).

9 The central works on class and racial formations are Omi and Winant (1986) and E. Wright (1985). Also see Banton (1998); Conley (1999).

10 Stuart Hall's (1992) discussion of the difficult task of analyzing racial dimensions amid competing forms of attention to gender and class in the "profoundly mythic" realm of popular culture helps map the approach to white trash I follow here. The challenge of synthetically treating class, gender, and race simulta-neously is well summarized by Sacks (1989).

11 The two forms of cultural analysis referred to here—the empirical and represen-tational approaches, respectively—are summarized in Bal (1999) and Bonnell and Hunt (1999). For a historical perspective on these approaches in the United States, particularly in regard to race, see Cruz (1999). Also, I echo Vered Amit-Talai and Caroline Knowles (1996, 14) in calling "for a re-energized research project, one that resituates the production of identities in the systematic inves-tigation of power relations, that pays heed to discursive hegemonies but not at the expense of rigorous, empirically grounded analysis and an insistence on concrete social change."

12 Peter Wade (2002, 24) tracks efforts to combine these competing analytical forms of attention to race, parsed as "material" versus "symbolic" approaches, in "social studies as a whole . . . to focus on the notion of embodiment, to look to bodily experience, enactment and performance in order to understand some of the material aspects of the discursive construction of social life." Wade fur-ther sketches a promising line of inquiry that "would focus on ideas about essences, human nature, how racialised bodies are constituted (rather than rep-resented, perceived and experienced—aspects which have been the subject of research)" (35).

13 For an ethnographic example of such an approach, see Uriciuoli (1996).

14 Many cultural critics and social theorists are struggling with the conundrum of how to talk about the social construction of race without reproducing this basis for viewing the world. For an excellent review of these efforts, see Barot and Bird (2001). I agree with Robert Miles and Rudy Torres (1996, 32) that "the idea of 'race' is used to effect a reification within sociological analysis insofar as the outcome of an often complex social process is explained as the consequence of

something named 'race' rather than of the social process itself." But I do not agree that the solution is to stop referring to race, substituting in its place an attention to racism. Colloquial and technical uses of race are far too established to reject this term entirely. Rather, I think it is critical when using race to continually deconstruct it by guiding people's attention to the social processes that shape its impact and significance. Racism involves certain attitudes and beliefs as well as institutional practices and structures that perpetuate and re-produce a particular racial order where life chances are discrepantly shaped by racial identification. See Fredrickson (2002); Memmi (2000); Miles (1989, 1993); Wellman (1993). This approach to racial analysis is best illustrated by critical race theory. See Delgado and Stefancic (2000).

15 For a critique of the perspective that "race is over," see Roediger (2002).

16 Paul Gilroy's (2000) description of the "crisis of raciology" characterizes this predicament well. See also Banton (1998); Miles (1989).

17 Many of these key works are reviewed in chapter 7, but here I mention par-ticularly Massey and Denton (1993) and Twine (1998).

18 See Maharidge (1996); also Winant (1994) on the "crisis of white identity."

19 On these class and regional dynamics, as well as on the contested status of "Latino," see Davila (2001).

20 For developed and varied articulations of this perspective, see Dominguez (1986); Drummond (1980); Lott (1993); Brackette Williams (1989, 1991, 1995).

21 What I mean by a "cultural perspective" here can be usefully sketched in contrast to the centrality of "identity" in cultural studies. Stuart Hall (Hall and Du Gay 1996, 5–6) explains, "I use 'identity' to refer to the meeting point, the point of suture, between on the one hand the discourses and practices which attempt to 'interpellate,' speak to us or hail us into place as the social subjects of particular discourses, and on the other hand, which produce subjectivities, which con-struct us as subjects which can be 'spoken.' " Without dismissing the importance of this perspective on subjects and discourse, "culture" posits social collectives broadly as objects of description and analysis.

22 A number of cultural critics focus on liberalism, with its stress on individualism, as a cultural logic that undergirds racial exclusions. See Goldberg (1993); Mehta (1999); Delgado and Stefancic (2000).

23 Banton (1987, ix) pursued such a shift by taking "racial typology" instead of "race" as an analytical focus: "This meant I could dispense with using the word 'racism' and disentangle myself from the confusions that spread after the late 1960s when this word came to be used in diverse ways."

24 For a compilation of such perspectives, see Gregory and Sanjek (1994).

25 As Sherry Ortner (2003, 51) explains, at least in terms of race and class, "The trick . . . is to keep both dimensions in focus, to neither reduce race/ethnicity to class or lose sight of the class implications of racial and ethnic categories."

26 Pushing whiteness studies to develop or draw on a more international perspec-tive on race was the subject of a special issue of the journal *Identities: Global*

Studies in Power and Culture in 2001. See Hartigan (2000). Also see Levine-Rasky (2002). The work on race in Latin America alone is both relevant and massive. Among other works cited below, see Sansone (2003); Sheriff (2001); Twine (1998); Wade (1993, 1997); Warren (2001); Whitten and Torres (1998).

27 Anthropologists distinguish two senses of "culture," one particular (e.g., American culture) and the other generic, referring to a common dimension of human behavior and belief. The lack of a cultural perspective on race today stems from the overemphasis on the former, as is evident in the debates from the 1960s to the 1990s over the "culture of poverty" and the "pathology" of "black culture." Regarding race today, I suggest the latter connotations of culture can provide great insight when paired with an understanding of the institutional and historical dimensions of race.

28 As in my critique of Bonilla-Silva's homogenizing generalizations about whites, the problem I see with ideological analyses of racial dynamics is that they tend to depict fairly monolithic subjects, regarding their statements as revealing a particular mental conditioning rather than an effort to interpretively make sense of shifting cultural situations. On ideological analysis, see J. Thompson (1984).

29 In addition to works cited in chapter 7, see Lamont (2000).

30 The fusion I am attempting here draws on the work of W. E. B. Du Bois. The application of social science methods and theories to the problem of race stems from his pioneering efforts in *Philadelphia Negro* (1899/1996), which empirically analyzed the facts of racial inequality and the role of racial prejudice in shaping the landscape of racial disadvantage. But Du Bois found the ability of social scientific methods and theories to objectify the nuanced dynamics of racial matters limited. His classic work, *The Souls of Black Folk* (1903/2000), strikingly moves beyond literal objectifications of race as a "problem" into the subjective and expressive dimensions of black racial experience. Du Bois extended his analytic repertoire further in *Dusk of Dawn* (1940/1980), when he speculatively tried to personify and analyze the cultural logic of "the white world" to lay bare the subjective dynamics that animate and perpetuate racial thinking. The analytic tactics Du Bois deployed in the latter works are today largely the purview of cultural studies approaches and are clearly critical to the task of understanding racial dynamics today.

In *The Souls of Black Folk*, Du Bois drew on rich but actively suppressed traditions and expressive forms that responded to oppressive conditions of racial segregation and terror. That is, "the Negro" Du Bois studied was a "positive" object, in an empirical sense. White trash, though its roots are historically deep, has largely been a negative form of identity, produced by and generating a play of projections and ascriptions of difference that have always been volatile and unstable, reflecting shifting landscapes of racial, class, and gender configurations of social inequality. This dimension of cultural studies approaches, that of analyzing expressive forms derived from distinct cultural traditions, is inadequate to the task of making sense of the degrading and debasing uses that have long defined white trash. And the cultural studies approach reflected in whiteness studies, which seeks to analyze the subjective process of self-formation via notions of projected forms of Otherness, is also insufficient in that it posits a fairly uniform and homogeneous form of racial consciousness. White trash makes evident that whatever whiteness may be, it is a far more riven, conflicted, and heterogeneous social position than so far postulated. Such a complicated and nuanced cultural identity can hardly be adequately analyzed via a critical assessment of representations of racial identity and difference. Rather, as the critics of whiteness studies cited in chapter 10 have stressed, we need instead to analyze the correspondence of such representations to concrete situations and to broad collective processes; this is where I turn to social science approaches that posit empirical engagement with the field as a basis for learning from what people actually do with charged cultural matters like race.

31 Elizabeth Chin (2001, 46) criticizes ethnographers working in the inner city and attempting to write against stereotypes of the urban underclass: "These empirical responses have been tremendously important, but because few have chosen to attack the images themselves head on social science has to some degree allowed these portrayals to continue their circulation unabated."

32 A closely related, or perhaps overlapping concept is that of "hygiene," which Judith Farquhar and Marta Hanson (1998, 507) define as "an effort to discipline the unruly forces of the nature and culture in the pathways of the—presumed to be—proper, orderly, and normative." As Mary Douglas (1966, 7) succinctly explains, "Our idea of dirt is compounded of two things, care for hygiene and respect for conventions." See also Grimson (2002).

33 On the crucial role etiquette continues to play as charged register for making sense of race, see Omi and Winant (1986, 62); Jacobs (1999); L. Williams (2000).

34 As Mark Caldwell (1999, 6–7) observes, "Civility and rudeness play themselves out just where the academic hesitates to go, among the unmeasurables of daily life, in anecdotes, in random events and imperfectly recorded human exchanges that may often seem unreadable, too eccentric and evanescent for systematic analysis."

35 I examine this dynamic from a historical perspective in Hartigan (1999).

36 Richard Delgado and Jean Stefancic (2000, xvii) offer the following characterization of culture in their introduction to *Critical Race Theory: The Cutting Edge*: "Because racism is an ingrained feature of our landscape, it looks ordinary and natural to persons in the culture." They promote a "storytelling" strategy to construct a different cultural reality rather than trying to comprehend the forms and media of the one that makes racial identities seem natural. "Starting from the premise that a culture constructs its own social reality in ways that promote its own self-interest, these scholars set out to construct a different reality."

1 This relational dimension of class formation involves the cultural work of developing and maintaining morally charged, symbolic boundaries, while articulating contrasting cultural stylistics. See Bourdieu (1984) and also Michele Lamont's (1992) revision of Bourdieu's theories.

2 On the cultural constructedness of class, see Ortner (2003, 11–12).

3 The basis for an attention to construction of middle-class self-identity is articulated in Frykman and Lofgren (1987); Stallybras and White (1986); Lowe (1982).

4 Judith Walkowitz (1992, 10–11) analyzes "the tradition of urban male spectatorship and the creation of a bifurcated imaginary urban landscape as a backdrop for personal adventure and self-creation." This tradition was eroded in London in the 1880s as the boundaries shaping this imaginary landscape of London were increasingly transgressed by emergent public subjects, including journalists, women activists, and workingmen. Dorian Gray's story bears vestiges of this imaginative transformation.

5 On the enduring fascination with these two stories, see Mank (1994).

6 I draw my use of classed imaginaries from Jameson (1981).

7 As O'Day (1989, 30) notes, "Underlying his famous 'Poverty Map' was a considerable understanding of the urban area as a unit of analysis, which prefigured much of our current concern with social geography of industrial cities." Booth's work also profoundly influenced the first work of urban sociology in the United States, W. E. B. Du Bois's *The Philadelphia Negro* (1899/1996).

8 David Cannadine (2001, 8) argues in *Ornamentalism* that when Britons "came to apply their conventionally hierarchical tools of observation, their prime grid of analysis was individual status rather than collective race." Cannadine makes the case bluntly "that these attitudes, whereby social ranking was as important as (perhaps more important than?) colour of skin in contemplating the extrametropolitan world, remained important for the English, and latterly, for the British long after it has been generally supposed they ceased to matter."

9 The emphasis on behavior both reflects and contributes to, in circular fashion, an effort to characterize the underclass as alien to the mainstream. The other failing, as Robin Kelley (1997, 23) notes, is that "social scientists do not treat behavior as situational, an individual response to a specific set of circumstances; rather, inner city residents act according to their own unique cultural norms."

10 As John Marriott (1999, 82) relates, "In the first half of the nineteenth century, the metropolitan poor were constructed as a race apart. Urban explorers and evangelical journalists, claiming distinct access to their object of inquiry, abandoned iconographies of the criminal, bizarre and grotesque to develop perspectives deeply embedded in theorisations of the Anglo-Saxon subject over both poor and colonial others."

11 Marriott (1999, 94) further comments: "The Booth survey was situated uneasily—in some respects it defined the moment—between past racialisations of

the poor and moderninst impulses to see them as part of the metropolitan totality."

12 The impression of filth and dirt was central both to characterizations of the poor and to the ambivalent equivalence that was projected between these bottom dwellers of the metropolis and colonial others. As Marriott (1999, 82) observes, "Dirt featured prominently in the imaginative universe constructed around the nineteenth-century metropolitan and colonial poor." This symbolic feature grounded discourses on "contagion" and "contamination," "tropes through which the imperial formation appropriated the metropolis and the colonies, and expressed fears that dismantling boundaries between suburb and slum, public and private would threaten class distinctions" (84).

13 "Despite its innovations, Booth's seventeen-volume *Life and Labor of the People of London* by no means represents an imaginative break with the tradition of urban exploration pioneered forty years earlier by Engels and Mayhew, and adapted and continued in the mid-Victorian period by Greenwood, Sims, and Mearns. On the contrary, Booth reproduced many key features of the literary genre; he recreated himself as a male spectator and flaneur within an imaginary landscape of the metropolis." Most notably, "he did not obliterate the psychological opposition that distinguished and distanced Self from low-Other. Despite his scientific pretensions, his study relied heavily on moralized impressions of social customs and conditions that reproduced familiar tropes of degeneration, contagion, and gender disorder, in order to mark off the dangerous from the respectable working class" (J. Walkowitz 1992, 33).

14 As Bales (1999, 154–155) relates, "Booth was one of the first to realise how atomised the East End working class truly was, and how little they were able to organise any form of action, much less threaten the social order. This finding alone was seen as a breakthrough by many commentators when Booth announced his results. The social and political climate shaped the nature of Booth's research questions, and in turn, his results were to shape social and political responses to poverty."

15 Stevenson's tale is multidimensional and warrants many distinct, even contrary emphases. In addition to works cited below, my reading of this text is particularly informed by Veeder and Hirsch (1988); Aratta (1996); Dowling (2001); E. Smith and Haas (1999).

16 Accounts by various urban explorers, journalists as well as sociologists, played a crucial role in the construction of middle-class self-identity. As Judith Walkowitz (1992, 16) explains, "The fact and fantasy of urban exploration had long been an informing feature of nineteenth-century bourgeois male subjectivity." Furthermore, "The crisis of the 1880s, experienced as a turning point by so many late Victorian reformers, and shifting in some important ways the prevailing imaginary landscape of London from one that was geographically bounded to one whose boundaries were indiscriminately and dangerously transgressed, was not only a response to the material crisis of London employment and housing: it was

also very much a product of bourgeois self-doubt and journalistic intervention"
(29). Along these lines, Marriott (1999, 91) comments that the urban crisis
emerging in central London "fostered in the bourgeois consciousness a sense of
fragmentation, self-doubt and loss of confidence in inexorable progress at a time
of imperial expansion."

17 On the role of monsters in processes of self formation, see White (1978).

18 On the multiple dimensions of racial discourses in *Dr. Jekyll and Mr. Hyde* and
The Picture of Dorian Gray, see Malchow (1996).

19 The "irregularities" in Jekyll's character, as in those of the subsequent "monsters"
discussed in this chapter, include sexual as well as class and racial transgressions.
This dimension is not examined in detail but is acknowledged via a range of
secondary sources discussed below.

20 An argument running throughout this work is that the conjuncture of racial and
class distinctions in whiteness mandates and depends on rigorous forms of
etiquette and bodily control, often manifest through attention to hygiene. One
source of support for this view is Ann Stoler's (1995, 95–137) account of the
reverberation of racial discourses "between metropole and colony." Surveying
the slew of British books on conduct, health manuals, and housekeeping guides
in this period, Stoler discerns a common attention to "management of life" by
which "middle-class distinctions were made not only in contrast to a European-
based working class, but through a racialized notion of civility that brought the
colonial convergence of—and conflict between—class and racial membership in
sharp relief. My starting point is not the hegemony of imperial systems of
control, but their precarious vulnerabilities" (97). This aspect of vulnerability is
developed further in chapter 2.

21 Robert Nye (1985, 67) explains that "sociologists throughout the nineteenth
century found degeneration theory indispensable in their work. It effectively
accounted for the terrible human costs of modernization, expressed in the perceived growth of 'urban' diseases, of alcoholism, crime, insanity, suicide, and
various sexual perversions. Integrated into sociological theory, the idea of degeneration was able to resolve the apparent paradox of misery amidst growing
plenty, of individual pathologies in a vigorous and highly integrated social or-
ganism. But, displaying its debt to its medical and biological origins, degeneration theory ordained that there were certain natural limits in the ability of social
organisms to withstand the spread of infected individuals. . . . Progress was
most tenuous and most vulnerable at its moments of greatest triumph, an irony
that haunts us still in our century." Additionally, Nancy Stepan (1985, 113) analyzes how the "medical-racial style of degeneracy theory" permeated sociology
around the end of the nineteenth century. Stepan makes clear the fluidity of
"racial" markings for inscribing and recording perceptions of intraracial difference: "Since degeneracy was a 'semiotic' science par excellence, it borrowed
many of its signs from racial biology, as well as the techniques of measurement.
The small head shape, the narrow skull, the prognathous jaw, the prematurely

closed sutures were all signs of lower races and the stigmata of degeneracy in higher races—indications that an individual from a higher race had deviated from the ideal standard."

22 Though I have stressed class connotations of this drama, another key tension in this tale is the predicament posed by homoeroticism. See particularly Showalter (1999); Malchow (1996); Self (2002).

23 For more on this genre, see Schocket (1998).

24 This conflation can be read as a form of "abjecting whiteness," which Kelly Hurley (1996) discerns in H. G. Wells's *The Time Machine.*

25 Simian features were used to symbolize multivalent class and racial distinctions, particularly in relation to the Irish. Marriott (1999, 86) notes, "Even the brutal stereotypes of African 'savages' at the time did not come close in terms of monstrousness to the Irish and Irish American gorillas of the Fenian era." See also Curtis (1971).

26 For a thorough assessment of how competing claims to the priority of either class or racial distinctions in founding and articulating bourgeois self-identity can be resolved via an attention to their mutually constitutive role in colonialist discourse, see Comaroff and Comaroff (1992); Shaw (1995); Stoler (1995). Stoler analyzes "how the distinctions defining bourgeois sexuality were played out against not only the bodies of an immoral European working class and native Other, but against those of destitute whites in the colonies and in dubious contrast to an ambiguous population of mixed-blood origin. If we accept that 'whiteness' was part of the moral rearmament of bourgeois society, then we need to investigate the nature of that contingent relationship between European racial and class anxieties in the colonies and bourgeois cultivation of self in England, Holland, and France" (100). Stoler bases her assessment on an examination of the pervasive anxiety about white degeneration in the colonies and the "subterranean colonial discourse that anxiously debated who was truly European and whether those who were both poor and white should be included among them?" (103). This anxiety and discourse manifest keenly in contests over middle-class identity constructions. As Stoler observes: "The self-affirmation of white, middle-class colonials thus embodied a set of fundamental tensions between a culture of whiteness that cordoned itself off from the native world and a set of domestic arrangements and class distinctions among Europeans that produced cultural hybridities and sympathies that repeatedly transgressed these distinctions" (112). These dimensions of self-construction, which turned on uncertain or unstable perceptions of sameness rather than singularly on projections of Otherness, are raised in Cannadine (2001).

27 Mr. Hyde neatly encapsulates William Miller's (1997, 21) argument on how "key shifts in the styles of contempt had a constitutive role in the formation of democracy as we know it. I see democracy as based less on mutual respect for persons than on a ready availability of certain styles of contempt to the low that once were the prerogatives of the high." Hyde disturbs the well-to-do because,

though knowledgeable of the conventions of proper social life, he snarls at the dictates of decorum; he evidences the contempt that Miller recognizes influencing the progress of democracy in the eighteenth and nineteenth centuries. "Once the high find themselves the objects of the same styles of contempt that they felt were their prerogative alone, we not only have a different emotional terrain, but a different political one as well. The high's serene and secure contempt either gives way to a more anxious contempt that tries to efface itself in acts of charity or in various attempts at mingling with the low, or it takes the opposite course and adopts a more visceral contempt that traffics with disgust and is openly aversive and hostile" (237). Responses to Mr. Hyde evidence the latter course; he provokes horror rather than simple contempt. Miller relates the following, supporting the mode of argument made in this chapter: "When the conventional contempt of the upper classes becomes less certain of its warrant, when the lower classes are no longer invisible or safely disattendable, when they constitute rather intrusive sources of concern and anxiety, then, as I have just indicated, contempt reconstitutes itself in a different form. No longer quite capable of complacent indifference, *it moves towards horror, loathing, fear, hatred and disgust*" (237; emphasis added).

28 For other comparisons of these two tales, see Dollar (1994); Kabel (1996).

29 The racial codings of class divisions in *Dorian Gray* are complicated by Wilde's racialized status as Anglo-Irish and by his depictions of the dynamics of homo-erotic desire across class lines through the practices of "slumming." As he gazes on the portrait that records his occulted degeneration, Dorian takes "pleasure at the misshapen shadow that had to bear the burden that should have been his own" (1891/1974, 144). See Marez (1997). On slumming, see G. Jones (1984, 284–285) and Chauncey (1994).

30 Such a dream also consumed Charles Booth, who took rooms in rooming houses in order to pass unnoticed among the poor.

31 For an example of coffee-table-style aestheticizing of such settings in the United States, see Vergara (1995).

32 Philippe Bourgois (1995) tries to disrupt such spectatorship by composing his ethnography of Spanish Harlem as a critique of the "pornography of violence" related to the inner city; unfortunately, though, he reproduces this mode of spectatorship more than he deconstructs it. For more developed critiques of his approach, see Lassalle and O'Dougherty (1997); Torres (1998).

33 The film is based on one of Clive Barker's (1985) short stories, "The Forbidden." Interestingly, race does not figure at all in the short story, though it is fundamental to the film. Both versions frame the aestheticization of inner-city violence via academic study.

34 The fact of class segregation is so naturalized an aspect of urban life that it receives scant attention from social researchers. See Zunz (1982).

35 Gary Fine and Patricia Turner (2001) open their excellent discussion of racial

rumors in the United States with a detailed discussion of *Candyman*, as the film so effectively dramatizes the muddled realm of urban legends.

36 The housing project of Cabrini-Green was razed in 2000 and redeveloped to feed the real estate boom along Chicago's "Gold Coast." For a view of the social history of Cabrini-Green and other Chicago housing projects, see Popkin et al. (2000); Venkatesh (2000).

37 Fine and Turner (2001, 3) comment on the film: "In spite of the racial identity of the bogeyman, the young folklorists seem unaware that this narrative's vigor is largely the result of its reflection of the racial disharmony that has long marked Chicago and its environs. As their understanding of the racial politics of their world increases, so, too, does the graduate students' comprehension of the power of folklore."

38 This is a striking departure from the short story version, which features white residents of the housing project and no racial subtext.

39 Judith Halberstam (1995, 5) is dubious on this score, insisting that "no amount of elaborate framing within this film can prevent it from confirming racist assumptions about black male aggression towards female bodies." But it seems that the interrogation of Helen as to her responsibility for these crimes and her active agency, ranging from self-sacrifice to return the stolen baby to the vengeful murder of her husband, suggests a more nuanced reading of the film.

40 See also Thomas Laqueur's (1989) critical historical account of the origin and implicit limitations of the humanitarian narrative.

CHAPTER 2 BLOOD WILL TELL

1 In narrating the nationalization of white trash, I draw on Alexander Saxton's (1990, 187–195, 321–344) discussion of "the Western Hero" and the cultural figure of "bad whites" in nineteenth-century U.S. literature of the frontier. On the origins of white trash, see Wray (2000).

2 For a more detailed history of the cultural figure of white trash from the colonial era to the 1930s, see McIlwaine (1939).

3 There is several decades' worth of impressive and insightful scholarship on eugenics. In addition to the works cited below, I draw primarily on the following: Carlson (2001); Nye (1993); Lewontin, Rose, and Kamin (1984); Tylor (1977); G. Allen (1975); Rosenberg (1974); Haller (1963).

4 This label captures some of the "dirty" work of class identification—the active forms of disparagement, of insult, condemnation, and stigmatization (i.e., techniques of distancing and boundary maintenance) that comprise key relational aspects of class.

5 See McIlwaine (1939). The title of this section quotes Cairnes (1862, 54).

6 Maximilian Schele de Vere in *Americanism: The English of the New World* (1872, 617): "*Mean whites* were, in the days of slavery, the white citizens of the South

who had no slaves to work for them, and yet deemed themselves too good to work themselves. Ignorant and intemperate as a class, and imbued with that pride which is the greatest hindrance to culture, they were a cancer in the body politic of many of the Southern States, and are now (1871) a serious obstacle to their regeneration. A more contemptuous term is *poor white folks*, or even *poor white trash.*"

7 On the origins of this moral perception, see Himmelfarb (1983); M. Katz (1986).

8 Eric Foner (1995, 48) explains, "In the eyes of many Republicans, slavery's impact upon labor was visible not only in the South but in the areas of the free states settled by southern migrants. The southern parts of the states of the lower West— Ohio, Indiana, and Iowa—were inhabited by migrants from the slave states, while the northern areas were settled by easterners."

9 See *Breaking the Land: The Transformation of Cotton, Tobacco, and Rice Cultures since 1880* (Daniel 1985). This policy endured despite efforts by the Federal Emergency Relief Agency to encourage planters to hire poor whites. When planters were asked what they intended to do about such whites, "invariably the answer is 'Starve them out. They are not worth feeding. We do not want them in our county" (89). Additionally, see Foley (1997).

10 See Bulah Brinton's novel about Missouri during the Civil War, *Man Is Love* (1873), and Isaac Kelso's memoir, *The Stars and Bars, or, The Reign of Terror in Missouri* (1863).

11 For a further discussion of the regional and class dynamics in *Poor White*, see Hegeman (1999, 120–125).

12 Matthew Guterl (2001, 19, 37) notes that distinct languages of racial classification operated in the New South and the urban North from the 1880s through the 1920s, with each region changeably framing distinct "race problems." In particular, he points to Madison Grant's "reluctance to consider 'the Negro' in Africa or in the American South as a threat" as evidence of a "continued disjunction between the symbolic economy of racial classification in the Northeast and that in the South." See also Rabinowitz (1992).

13 Jackson Lears (1994, 75) analyzes a similarly intense investment in "an ideal of unified, controlled selfhood—a bourgeois self—as a counterweight to the centrifugal tendencies unleashed by the market economy" in the antebellum era. For more on class forms of self-construction in this period, see Kasson (1990) and Levine (1998).

14 Dugdale (1877, 4; emphasis added). The quote is from Elisha Harris, in the introduction. There were no actual photographs taken of the Jukes.

15 Nicole Rafter (1988) argues that these poor white families played a critical role in various efforts of the emerging tier of social control professionals to establish their social position and class formation. See also G. Allen (1975). For further dimensions of the dynamics of class formation that played out via such objectifications of poor whites, see Brechin (1996); Meehan (1997); Tylor (1997). More

broadly, on the relational dynamics of class formation as it pertains to the uses professionals made of the poor, see M. Larson (1977); D. Walkowitz (1999).

16 More than sixty thousand Americans were surgically sterilized between 1907 and 1963, as a host of states passed laws permitting such involuntary interventions on institutionalized persons. See Reilly (1991).

17 Rafter details the heavy-handed representational practices deployed in constructing "objective" or "scientific" depictions of these families, as fieldworkers wielded concepts like feeblemindedness without concern for verifiability; indeed, their assessments were consistently made "at a glance," ensuring that researchers and readers alike found what they were looking for no matter what situations they confronted. Rafter (1988, 26) also delineates the numerous rhetorical techniques employed in these depictions of poor whites: "By carefully selecting descriptions, using bumpkin pseudonyms, and sending covert signals to readers, the authors constructed a symbolic world."

18 Marouf Arif Hasian (1996, 37) remarks on the utter ubiquity of eugenical discourse in this era: "Growing up in the Anglo-American world in the first few decades of the twentieth century meant being constantly bombarded with lectures on eugenics from ethical, debating, and philosophical societies; health, women's, and medical associations—sometimes even the YMCA." The class dimensions of this rhetoric were clear: "For the middle classes, the eugenic concentration on the intellectual, emotional, and genetic character of the young meant that someone was finally recognizing that merit, hard work, and clean living were more important than primogeniture" (31). See the chapter "From Cradle to Grave: The Popularization of Eugenics within the Rhetorical Sphere, 1900–1940."

19 On the role of etiquette in processes of class formation, see Wouters (1995).

20 On the continuing role of "stupidity" in policing class identities, see Kadi (1996).

21 For a grounding in anthropological attention to etiquette, see Beidelman (1993, 60–63).

22 For a detailed analysis of the various efforts to popularize eugenics via newspapers, magazines, popular and educational writings, college textbooks, and teacher training manuals, see Selden (1999).

23 Two additional dimensions of etiquette need to be stressed. First is that this era saw an enormous increase in interest in etiquette manuals and advice of all kinds, as middle-class whites strove to solidify their developing social status. See Kasson (1990); Schlesinger (1946). The second point is that etiquette has long been and continues to operate as a critical means by which racial identities are both maintained and contested. See Doyle (1937); Lasch-Quinn (2001).

24 Jennifer Scanlon (1995) observes that magazines like the *Ladies' Home Journal* studiously avoided direct acknowledgment of the color line, even as they featured eugenics discourse on improving the race. In an era (1900–1930) when the number of black domestics increased by 43 percent as white employment in this

field dropped in concert, the magazine "overwhelmingly presented domestic help as white." Scanlon concludes: "In a changing and volatile world, the whiteness offered by the *Ladies' Home Journal* and other popular magazines may have been as therapeutic to readers as were the individual advertisements the magazines housed" (34–39). On the class dimension of this readership, see also Kammen (1999).

25 Eugenicists used "race" as both a specific and a general referent. Davenport alternately invoked "the human race" or "advancement of the race" interchangeably with reference to particular "racial traits" that "if bad they curse the race or strains which carries them, and in time they tend to disseminate throughout the whole population." The power of this rhetorical tactic lay in allowing race to be alternately inclusive and exclusive as a referent (C. Davenport and Laughlin 1915, 32, 33, 3; Dikotter 1998).

26 In detailing how interest in "public hygiene" functioned in the process of bourgeois self-constitution, Michel Foucault (1990, 122–124) observes that the "deployment of sexuality was not established as a principle of limitation of the pleasures of others by what have traditionally been called the 'ruling classes.' Rather it appears to me that they first tried it on themselves." The policing, disciplining, and medicalization of sexuality in this era "has to be seen as the self-affirmation of one class rather than the enslavement of another. . . . With this investment of its own sex by a technology of power and knowledge which it had itself invented, the bourgeois underscored the high political price of its body, sensations, and pleasures, its well-being and survival." In this regard, Foucault concludes, "this class must be seen rather as being occupied, from the mid-eighteenth century on, with creating its own sexuality and forming a specific body based on it, a 'class' body with its health, hygiene, descent, and race."

27 One of the most profound and enduring impacts of the eugenics movement was on marriage restrictions, though this critical development has received scant attention. See Lindsay (1998).

28 On the class connotations associated with tuberculosis, see Ott (1996).

29 The registers for reading race in this era far exceeded observations concerning skin color. Madison Grant (1916, 26) noted that the "four unit characters, skull shape, eye color, hair color, and stature, are sufficient for us to differentiate clearly between the three main races of Europe." Stature, as were the matters of comportment listed by Davenport, was keyed to class, as Grant made clear: "No one can question the race value of stature who observes on the streets of London the contrast between the Piccadilly gentleman of Nordic race and the cockney costermonger of the old Neolithic type."

30 Noted eugenicist Samuel J. Holmes (1921, 129–130) made the class dimension of this racial concern explicit in his book, *The Trend of the Race*: "The most serious menace to racial welfare, not only in America, but in most civilized lands, is the relative sterility of superior types of humanity. On the other hand, those who are

mentally defective or subnormal tend, through their lack of restraint and foresight, to be unusually prolific. The records of the Jukes, Kallikaks, Nams, Hill Folk, Tribe of Ishmael and other notorious defective strains show that these degenerates are distinguished for unusual fecundity which more than offsets their high infant mortality." This point is further underscored: "If their productiveness suffers from crime and vice, the celibate careers, late marriages and restricted birth rate of the classes in the higher social strata apparently reduce fecundity still more" (140).

31 This emphasis on self-examination and objectifying one's own family was even more widely pursued through the fitter family contests held at fairs across the country. At eugenics exhibits, visitors were encouraged to provide detailed objectification of the eugenical qualities of themselves and family members. The objective of the fitter family movement, according to Dr. Florence Sherborn, was "the stimulation of family and racial consciousness and responsibility." Through her work, Robert Rydell (1993, 48–49) argues, "an essentially upper-class ideology" was made "acceptable to a broader audience."

32 Rydell (1993, 38–39) asks, "Why, despite the critique of eugenics mounted after the First World War by anthropologists, geneticists, and literary intellectuals, were eugenicists so successful in appealing to the American public?" The answer lies in the variety of modes of dissemination eugenicists deployed: "printed propaganda, consisting of pamphlets, periodicals, and books." But perhaps their greatest influence lay in eugenicists' recognition of "the exhibition medium as ideally suited to popularizing the race-betterment agenda." Eugenics exhibits "became fixtures at state and county fairs around the country during the 1920s."

33 The breadth of registers of social conditioning that were perceived racially is conveyed in Knight Dunlap's (1920) book on racial betterment and beauty. Under "signs of race," he explains: "There are certain negative details of stature, feature, color, and movement and habits which are important because they indicate in the first instance a race or species of the human family against which, for reasons which may be instinctive or due to education, there may be a prejudice" (18).

34 The imagery in Stoddard's work resonates powerfully with that found in the novels and memoirs of the German Freikorps mercenaries, analyzed by Kalus Theweleit (1987, 1989).

35 But when H. L. Mencken (1920) penned his screed characterizing life in the South "as sterile, artistically, intellectually, culturally, as the Sahara Desert" ("Sahara of the Bozart"), he surely referenced nationally held connotations of the term. "The old aristocracy went down the red gullet of war; the poor white trash are now in the saddle. . . . Virginia is the best of the south to-day, and Georgia is perhaps the worst. The one is simply senile; the other is crass, gross, vulgar and obnoxious" (Mencken 1920, 142).

An earlier version of this chapter appeared in *Cultural Studies* 11, no. 2 (1997): 316–343.

1 This history of social contempt for white trash draws, in part, on aspects of the regional Otherness that Appalachia has served for white Americans at least since the previous century. The region's general "backwardness" has been objectified and represented in multiple genres: travelogues, scientific studies, novelistic settings and characters, and industrial rampages. See Batteau (1990). This sense of cultural Otherness has hardly dimmed today. See Stewart (1996).

2 One bellwether of this change was an episode of the *Oprah Winfrey Show*, titled "Tired of Being Labeled 'White Trash,'" where poor whites related their experiences of being stigmatized by this epithet. "Tired of Being Labeled 'White Trash'" aired on February 3, 1992 and was rebroadcast on June 12, 1992. White women who had been called white trash as children discussed the "contagious" nature of the shame felt by their parents for their social shortcomings.

3 One notable, pre-1980 exception is Stone and Grey's (1976) collection, *White Trash: An Anthology of Contemporary Southern Poets*. In the work's introduction, George Garrett noted: "Some southern writers would rather die slowly and badly than admit to a touch of trash. They will go to great lengths to deny there's any such (of a) thing as a Cracker in their gene pool or a Redneck in the woodpile. But the truth is every Southerner has a streak of trash just as every selfsame Southerner has a drop (just a tad) of Plantagenet blood. Some have the strength of character and well-developed mixed feelings (what editors fairly enough call 'irony') to admit it and even enjoy it" (xi). Stone and Grey add, "If the news media, the philosophers of the instantaneous, continue to tout the Sun Belt, the South can expect a tsunami of tourists, retirees, and industry. White trash may then be in for the kind of attention that invites sayings from a lot of fake trash, so that anybody who can imitate William Faulkner or Tennessee Williams will be put in a book" (xiv).

4 In the earliest attempt that I know of to treat poor whites as a real cultural group, A. N. J. Den Hollander (1934, 414) defines them by noting that the term is used only on a subgroup of poor whites: "The 'poor-whites' were those who were both poor and conspicuously lacking in the common social virtues and especially fell short of the standard in certain economic qualities. Laziness, carelessness, unreliability, lack of foresight and ambition, habitual failure and general incompetency characterized them."

5 Some literary critics have tracked the development of images of the poor white in fiction as a cultural figure used to ground certain shifting moral orders and social mores. This approach has been less extensively pursued than the social historical study of poor whites, but the primary works, Shirley McIlwaine's (1939) *The Southern Poor-White: From Lubberland to Tobacco Road* and Sylvia Cook's (1976) *From Tobacco Road to Route 66: The Southern Poor White in Fiction*, are quite

excellent. However, these critics treat images of the poor white generically, rather than concentrating on specific uses of white trash.

6 I use this phrase following Kathleen Stewart's (1991, 396) call for "contaminated cultural critique," which deconstructively "disrupts the distance between observing subject and the 'real' world of objects."

7 The *Oxford English Dictionary* credits the first derogatory usage of "trash" to Shakespeare in *Othello* (1604). Other early instances of the term in Britain all bear a distinctly gendered edge: "Prostitutes, actresses, dancing women and that sort of trash." In the United States, the term has always been racially based. Eugene Genovese (1976, 22–25) and many commentators attribute the origins of white trash to black slaves.

8 "Trash" demonstrates remarkable versatility; it is applied in a host of novel contexts, such as the band Cracker's song about a "Eurotrash girl." The term has also found use in computer hacker subcultures. See Kroker (1994).

9 I am suggesting that certain conflations of racial and class identities occur, such that whiteness is most identified with the lifestyles and behaviors of upper-class whites; working- and lower-class whites have their connection to a racial collective often challenged in subtle and implicit ways. This point is partly illustrated in David Roediger's (1992) *The Wages of Whiteness*.

10 I piece together the notion of an unpopular culture from the efforts of Stuart Hall (1981, 1994), Fredric Jameson (1990), and Renato Rosaldo (1994) to problematize readings of the "popular" as a largely undifferentiated, homogeneous cultural realm. Each of these theorists has revised understandings of the popular by emphasizing both the heterogeneous groupings of classes under the signs of elite and subordinate cultures and the relational basis of key categories and identities. It is tempting to read the figure of white trash as a carnivalesque expression of the "proletarian body." John Fiske (1992, 97–99) demonstrates the theoretical grounds for such a reading by describing the "working-class body" as a "dirty and threatening" figure that challenges the "bourgeois sterilized body." But taking white trash as an expression of an undifferentiated people would miss the stigmatizing use of the name which also operates among the white working and lower classes. In the United States, even just among whites, there are a host of disturbing cultural orders that disrupt an easy assertion of purely popular cultures. Susan Harding's (1991) work on fundamentalists in the United States is an excellent example of such internal cultural others.

11 Among its many uses, "white trash" names that strange conflation of disgust and desire that lower-class bodies hold for members of the upper classes. *Penthouse Forum* (September 1988) devoted a special issue to this body, *How to Wallow in White Trash Lust*. This issue, with feature stories such as "The Welfare Mama" and "My First Gang Bang," offers a "field guide" perspective on the distinct types of white trash: Backwater Trash, Trailer Trash, Welfare Trash, and Nouveau Trash. The delineation of these types rests on the sexual proclivities and perversities characteristic of each subtype of trash, and the guide offers such authorita-

tive assertions as "Welfare mamas love to give head, priding themselves on their technique and willingness to do it anytime, anyplace" (44). (Quotation from Kitty Pedone, "The Great White Lay," 42–48).

12 "Trash" here emerges as a mapping of what Peter Stallybras and Allon White (1986, 25) referred to as those "discursive sites where social classification and psychological processes are generated as conflictual complexes. It is precisely here where the realms of ideology and fantasy conjoin. . . . Thus, the logic of identity-formation involves distinctive associations and switching between location, class and the body, and these are not imposed on a subject-identity from the outside. They are the core terms of an exchange network, an economy of signs, in which individuals, writers and authors are sometimes but perplexed agencies." See also Frykman and Lofgren (1987).

13 Another major source of imagery of poor whites is Erskine Caldwell's *Tobacco Road* (1932). Though this novel provides one of the central storehouses for popular imagery of poor whites, I do not examine this work in depth here because, to my knowledge, he does not use the label white trash in this novel.

14 Williamson tracks how the grits thesis first "sank into the academic mind" and has continued to be reproduced in media interpretations of the civil rights movement in the 1960s. "But in recent years the thesis has shown a capacity for life anew. The resurgence is dangerous because it is no more true today than it was true then. Upper-class Southern whites are still no more specially sympathetic to black people than are lower-class whites. There is and there has been a difference between the racism of upper-class Southern whites and that of the lower orders. But the difference is not one of essential assumptions and consequent attitudes" (1984, 294).

15 Mickler's initial effort was followed by *White Trash Cooking II: Recipes for Gatherin's* (1997), *More White Trash Cooking* (1998), and *Ruby Ann's Down Home Trailer Park Cookbook* (2002).

16 See a review of this book in *People Weekly*, "Cookbook Author Shows True Grit," 26, no. 21 (November 24, 1986): 73–78.

17 Reprinted in Hunter Thompson (1988). Thompson's attention to white trash goes back to his first book, *Hell's Angels* (1967); drawing the lineage of these bikers through the migratory waves of Okies, Arkies, and hillbillies that made their way to California in the Depression era—citing Nelson Algren's A *Walk on the Wild Side* as "one of the best historical descriptions of American white trash ever" (199)—he suggests that "nobody who has ever spent time among the inbred Anglo-Saxon tribes of Appalachia would need more than a few hours with the Hell's Angels to work up a very strong sense of deja vu. There is the same sulking hostility towards 'outsiders,' the same extremes of temper and action, and even the same names, sharp faces and long-boned bodies that never look quite natural unless they are leaning on something" (202).

18 Tom Arnold's quote about the status of himself and his now ex-wife, Roseanne, is most apropos: "We're America's worst nightmare—white trash with money."

See "By Any Name, Roseanne Is Roseanne Is Roseanne," in the *New York Times* Art and Leisure section, August 18, 1991.

19 The discussion that follows was written roughly ten years ago. In the intervening years there has been a wealth of excellent scholarship that, if I had time and space to rewrite this analysis, would bring greater resonance to this perspective. Instead, I'll only direct you to Ching (2001); Jensen (1998); Malone (2002); R. Peterson (1997).

20 Jeff Foxworthy is the penultimate example of how "redneck" has been publicly valorized. Certainly, in his routines the term retains the ambivalence that accompanies white trash. But with his sitcom on ABC, his double-platinum comedy album *"You Might Be a Redneck If . . . ,"* and his selling more than six million books, it is clear that Foxworthy has tapped an identity that millions of whites are willing to wallow in gladly.

21 It should not be assumed that hillbilly operates unequivocally as a positive, identifying term. Bill Malone (1985, 40), in *Country Music, U.S.A.*, points out, "Country music fans have always reacted ambivalently to the term, sometimes resenting it as a presumed denigration of their music and the way of life it supposedly represents, but often proclaiming it proudly as an accurate description of their musical and cultural tastes. Many country entertainers, such as Waylon Jennings, Loretta Lynn, and Tammy Wynette, still privately describe themselves as hillbillies, but respond bitterly if someone else calls them that."

22 Aside from whether or not the term has been featured in many songs, Aaron Fox (2004) observes that country music itself is widely regarded as trashy: "For many cosmopolitan Americans, especially, country is 'bad' music precisely because it is widely understood to signify an explicit claim to whiteness, not as an unmarked, neutral condition of lacking (or trying to shed) 'race,' but as a marked, foregrounded claim of cultural identity—a bad whiteness." The characteristic early usage of "white trash" in country music is reflected in the Charlie Daniels Band's song "The Legend of Wooley Swamp" on *Full Moon* (1980). "The Cable boys was white trash. . . . They were mean as a snake, sneaky as a cat, and belligerent when they'd speak." They kill an old man for his money but then meet a bad ending deep in the swamp.

23 James Branscome (1978) points out that West Virginia led the nation in per capita deaths in Vietnam with 25 per 100,000 being killed while the national average was 17 per 100,000 soldiers. More bleak, though, fatalities from mining accidents in the region were more than double the number of U.S. fatalities in Vietnam over the course of the conflict.

24 In addition to those bands whose self-naming claims white trash, there are Korn, the Screaming Trees, the Melvins, and I'm sure a few more. See reviews of these bands in *Melody Maker* (August 10, 1991): 62; (June 27, 1992): 13; (October 2, 1993): 12–13.

25 A perfect example of the proliferation of references to white trash is the *Phonolog Record Catalogue*. When I first checked listings under "white trash" in 1988 there

were four references. Checking again in 1994 I found only ten titles, which included ZuZu Petals' "White Trash in Love" (Twintone) and Southgang's "White Trash with Cash" (Charisma Music). But a notably less celebratory use of the term appears with the band Southern Culture on the Skids. In their song "White Trash," the constant refrain is "Don't call me that." By 2004, songs about or referencing white trash are so numerous that they warrant an article-length treatment in their own right.

26 Another author that could be considered here, if space allowed, is Harry Crews. In addition to his works, such as *Feast of Snakes* (1986) and *Body* (1990), see Frank Shelton's (1988) overview of Crews's class position.

27 The overlap between social and moral/sexual transgressions under the sign of white trash repeats for other gay artists who are at a great remove from the economic conditions traditionally associated with the term. Ronald Kraft (1993), in an article on architect Brian Murphy, whose designs have been called "white-trash modern," conveys a debate over whether or not Murphy's style is only possible to maintain because he is an openly gay man. The sign of white trash is hardly an oddity in gay aesthetics. See the travel essay by Lane and Crotty (1991).

28 The other key distinction is that Chute's first novel, *The Beans of Egypt, Maine*, appeared in 1985, several years ahead of Allison's collection of short stories. Critics were apparently not ready to accept voices of poor whites as literature. Chute also was accused of being a "class traitor" because she took the profits from her book and moved out of her tiny trailer. To my knowledge, Allison's success has not led to charges that she has thereby become inauthentic.

29 For interesting parallels across the color line, see my discussion of poor white uses of "nigger" in Detroit (Hartigan 1999).

30 This reference to minority discourse is cautiously drawn from Abdul R. Jan-Mohamed and David Lloyd's (1987) introduction to an issue of *Cultural Critique*. The purpose of this connection is not to make a claim that certain whites are damaged and truncated by hegemonic forces in the United States, even though white trash, too, is characterized "as inauthentic, perverse, criminal, and underdeveloped in relation to the white middle class" (7). Rather, I want to note that their call for "double vigilance" needs to include the troubling body of white trash. This insulting term is susceptible to the strategic recuperations that minority discourses in general must contest. In Florida in 1991, the first prosecution proposed under the state's harsh Hate Crimes Act was of a black man who called a white police office a "cracker" while the officer was trying to arrest him. Under the Act, the charge was an extension of the assault charge based on the black man's threat to shoot the officer: "I'll shoot you, white cracker" (reported in the *New York Times*, August 28, 1991). The assault charge was later dropped, so the prosecution for the use of this racial epithet was also abandoned. Yet the ease with which a legal apparatus designed to protect minorities was recuperated by a certain white power structure in the process of invoking a concern for working-class whites is a disturbing and complicated event.

31 Films are a key example of the profusion of white trash, though tracking when the term is actually used or simply critically applied is complicated. Eugenia Bone (1994) notes: "The white trash oeuvre has a long and venerable history in Hollywood. From class trash like Tennessee William's 'Babydoll' to the mosaic of mangy characters in 'Short Cuts,' stars just can't say no to playing trigger-happy ignoramuses with voracious appetites for carnal pleasure. Alarmed by the recent plethora of trailer-park dramas and jalopy adventurers, we have conducted a study of the genre—the greasy incurable romantics, the synthetic fabrics, the inexplicably good dental work." Bone lists the following films as examples: *Kalifornia, Guncrazy, True Romance, Short Cuts, Flesh and Bone, A Perfect World*. These movies are only the most recent in a tradition that arguably begins with *Poor White Trash* (1957), Peter Graves's screen debut. Like *Deliverance*, it gained notoriety for a rape scene that exceeded the "bounds of decency" in the 1950s. Originally, it was released under the title *Bayou*, but it did poorly and was rereleased as *Poor White Trash* in 1961.

32 Roseanne has used the term white trash several times in her show. The first time I am aware of was in the 1992–1993 season. In an episode after Dan was arrested, she announced, "Well, people have been saying it for years . . . and this proves it: we are white trash!" In the 1994–1995 season, in an episode dealing with how racism is passed from parent to child, Roseanne refers to real racists as "those barefoot, banjo-playing, cousin-dating, embarrassments to respectable white trash like us."

33 As well, "white trash" is not used in *True Romance*. In the beginning of *Kalifornia*, Brian Kessler (David Duchovny) says, "If you looked in the dictionary under 'poor white trash,' a picture of Adele and Early would be there."

CHAPTER 4   READING TRASH

An earlier version of this essay appeared in *Visual Anthropology Review* 6, no, 2 (1992): 8–15.

1 For a recent assessment of the relevance of Douglas's work, see Culler (1985), which is also a review of Michael Thompson's (1979) book *Rubbish Theory: The Creation and Destruction of Value*.

2 In particular, see Hawkins (1990). Reviews of *Deliverance* were divided as to its status. While Stephen Faber (*New York Times*, August 19, 1972) praised the serious dramatic quality of the film and the cinemagraphic excellence of its images, *Variety* (July 19, 1972) considered *Deliverance* as further proof of pandering to unwholesome lusts.

3 The first approach is noticeable in ethnographies of black communities, from Stack (1974) to D. Rose (1987). The best example of the second type of analysis is Gilroy (1987).

4 The general notion of poetics here is derived from Todorov (1981); Stallybras and White (1981). The most succinct working definition, though, comes from James

Clifford's (Clifford and Marcus 1986, 24) introduction to *Writing Culture: The Poetics and Politics of Ethnography*: "Cultural poesis—and politics—is the constant reconstitution of selves and others through specific exclusions, conventions, and discursive practices."

5 For an erudite discussion of this "critical double bind" over the realness or agency of the Other in such a situation, see the essay by Gates (1991).

6 *Deliverance* stays current through continual allusions and references to the movie in comedy routines. An example is the film *City Slickers*, which in important ways can be seen as a humorous revision of *Deliverance*'s drama of male bonding by city dwellers on an adventure in the wild, uncivilized portions of the United States. When the "dangerous" cowboy, Jack Palance, informs Billy Crystal that he must accompany him alone overnight into a desolate canyon, the worried Crystal whispers to his buddies, "This is just like *Deliverance*."

7 For an excellent discussion of these productions, see Branscome (1978).

8 The history of this narrative form is quite long. See Cook (1976).

9 Johannes Fabian (1983, 18) states: "Primitive being essentially a temporal concept, is a category, not an object, of Western thought." For an account of the figurative forms of the primitive in Western thought, see White (1978).

10 For a chronicle of the historical types of Otherness from the middle class in the United States that Appalachians have been used to dramatize, see Batteau (1990).

11 My use of the notion of the grotesque as a bodily form and poetics is drawn from Bakhtin (1984), who examines the class relations that structure the contours of this body image.

12 Fred Pfeil (1990) gives a condensed history of bourgeois narrative form in *Another Tale to Tell*.

13 Hortense Powdermaker (1939/1968) stressed the symbolic importance of poor whites as a buffer community between whites and blacks in Mississippi, but did not feel the need to devote ethnographic attention to them.

14 This point has been demonstrated most thoroughly by Pierre Bourdieu (1984) in *Distinction* and anthropologist Charles Valentine (1968) in *Culture and Poverty*.

CHAPTER 5   TALKING TRASH

1 "I know I'm a pathetic White Guy," writes Rick Riley in self-effacing fashion, while lamenting a perceived double standard allowing black athletes to talk openly about race ("White Like Me," *Sports Illustrated*, February 4, 2002, p. 152). Also see Leonard Pitts's commentary, "Who Can Say What to Whom," *Miami Herald*, February 9, 2002.

2 Lucy Jarosz and Victoria Lawson (2002, 10) "theorize that, in the contemporary U.S., 'redneck' discourse serves to obscure materialist processes of economic restructuring that are producing class polarization in three ways. First, rural working-class whites are discursively constructed as obsolescent. Second, class

status is understood and defined as lifestyle. Third, white racism is constructed as redneck discourse."

3 For instance, Los Angeles Lakers' coach Phil Jackson makes running disparagements of basketball fans in Sacramento with the term "redneck." Such connotations are apparently behind the decision of NASCAR officials to reject advertisements by RedneckJunk.com "because it does not project a proper image" (Whitley 2004).

4 A similar gesture, though in relation to a past form of poor white culture, is made by McWhiney in *Cracker Culture* (1988).

5 This quote is from a promotional flyer for "The Ozarks: Just That Much Hillbilly in Me," Southwest Missouri State University, 1999.

6 Burkhard Bilger's (2000) article in the New Yorker, "Squirrel and Man: Is a Local Custom Worth Dying For?" generated a host of criticisms in Kentucky (Fierson 2000), as did a *New York Times* crossword puzzle titled "Words Hillbilly-Style" (Ferenchick 2000; see also Morrin 1997).

7 This performative stance is best embodied in the movie *8 Mile*, which opens with a scene of white debasement before a black audience—a nervous Eminem vomits on himself before he goes on stage and then ingloriously chokes at the mike, to the hoots and hollers of the all-black crowd—unparalleled since the novel *Tobacco Road* (1932). In the film's climatic performance, Eminem preemptively lists all the degrading classed elements of his impoverished roots—"I am white trash / I am a fucking bum," and "I do live in a trailer with my mom"—before his primary competition in the rap contest can use these against him.

8 Eminem objectifies his whiteness here as both a form of privilege and of threat, acknowledging, "Look at my sales / let's do the math / If I was black I would've sold half," but also underscoring that "I could be one of your kids," based on his blue eyes and his bleached hair. "White America," on *The Eminem Show*, Aftermath Records, 2002.

9 Following the release of the movie *8 Mile*, Frank Rich (2002, 52) asked, "Could it be that in just two years the scourge of bourgeois values is now entering the American mainstream?" Rich suggests, "When you are the No. 1 act in music, no matter how provocative your songs or how ugly your rap sheet, the culture industry has a vested interest not merely in protecting the franchise but also in expanding it." He also speculates that Eminem's lyrics resonate widely "in a country in which broken homes, absentee parents and latchkey kids are endemic to every social class."

CHAPTER 6 GREEN GHETTOS AND THE WHITE UNDERCLASS

An earlier version of this essay was published in *Social Research* 64, no. 2 (1997): 339–365.

1 For an analysis of the rise and decline of research on the urban underclass, see O'Connor (2001). The soaring economy and the accompanying rise in gen-

trification during the 1990s profoundly affected the scope and significance of concentrated urban poverty. But the extent to which these developments were either halted or reversed by the downturn in the early 2000s is yet to be discerned. See Jargowsky (2003).

2 The symbolic aspects of the inner city are linked to a host of cultural reconfigurations. See Vergara (1992); Virilio (1991).

3 Researchers who discern a distinct behavioral component to the urban underclass, from Erol Ricketts and Isabel Sawhill (1988) to William Julius Wilson (1987), assert that inner-city neighborhoods and census tracts are generative environments for socially disadvantageous or disruptive lifestyles.

4 This is demonstrated by *Confronting Poverty: Prescriptions for Change* (Danziger, Sandefur, and Weinburg 1994). Although this work admirably deploys current social science research to counter some of the more conservative policy proposals, not a single ethnographic study is included.

5 There are, however, two notable exceptions: Terry Williams (1989) focused on a white man who primarily kept a New York crackhouse operating; Jay MacLeod (1987) made a group of poor whites in a northeastern urban housing project the center of his ethnographic research on leveled aspirations.

6 According to the Census Bureau, in 1990 Detroit's population fell below 1 million residents. The city filed suit and successfully demanded a recount, which brought the population count to 1,027,974.

7 Reported in Holly (1993). The *Free Press* ran follow-up stories on April 29, 1993, as did the *Detroit News* on April 30, 1993. Both papers featured op-ed pieces on the downsizing plan. See also Guyette (2001).

8 This poll was reported in the *Detroit Free Press*, April 29, 1993.

9 These figures were reported in a three-part series by the *Detroit News*, beginning with "City Caught in Trash Avalanche," July 4, 1993.

10 These figures are compiled from 1930 census data reported in Detroit Bureau of Governmental Research, Inc. (1937).

11 The area that now comprises Briggs was tabulated through five census tracts in 1930 and 1940. Due to the drastic drop in population, only one census tract is now required to cover approximately the same area. Because the remaining tract inexactly matches either the terrain covered in the previous five tracts or the current, lived boundaries of Briggs, the figures that I cite here represent an approximation of the demographic shift rather than an exact count.

12 These approaches are by no means exclusive. Sawhill (1989), who finds that "what is most distinctive, most interesting, and most troubling about the underclass [is] its behavior," relies on both behavior-based and location-based means of measuring the size of the underclass. See also Mincy, Sawhill, and Wolf (1990). On overlapping aspects of such approaches, see Littman (1991); P. Peterson (1991). Attention to geographic factors predominated in Jencks and Peterson (1991). Locational measures tend to involve an attention to structural considerations that can be lacking in behavior-based models; see Greene (1991b); C. Wilson (1992).

13 But whether or not these behavioral indicators are exclusively linked to the underclass is a matter of debate. See H. Rose and Deskin (1991). There is also some question of the geographic extension of the characterizations that Wilson makes concerning concentrated poverty (Greene 1991a). Also, Yvette Alex-Assensoh (1995) argues persuasively that these specified behaviors are hardly confined to African American communities. In a study of Columbus, Ohio, she establishes the fact that there are concentrated poverty areas where "whites and African Americans exhibit statistically indistinguishable and substantively similar levels of such behaviors" (3).

14 Poor whites are also concentrated on the city's southwest side. In areas like Delray/Springwells (63 percent white) and Chadsey (67 percent white), the poverty rate stands at 37 percent and 38 percent, respectively. See Southeast Michigan Census Council (1993).

15 Gunnar Myrdal (1963), writing for a general audience, may have been the first social scientist to use the term "under-class"; he depicted it as a function of the emerging displacement of unskilled and even some skilled workers from the labor force, with scant emphasis on race. Indeed, he included "the white hillbillies not far south of Washington, D.C., and similar groups of poor whites elsewhere in the country" as part of the host of people who "had no possibility of sharing in the American image of liberty and opportunity of rising economically and socially" (36). But as the term gained greater coherence in the 1980s, primarily through Douglas Glasgow's (1980) *The Black Underclass*, the racial connotations became well established.

16 Anthropologists entering this debate have problematized the resonances between the concept of the underclass and the dubious notion of a "culture of poverty." See Maxwell (1993); Bourgois (1995); Vincent (1993).

17 Social Science Research Council's (SSRC) Urban Underclass Database, 1994.

18 These terms are drawn from the SSRC's Urban Underclass Database.

19 Greene (1991b) examined how concentrated poverty has emerged unevenly in urban areas across the United States in relation to broad demographic and economic changes.

20 Wilson's emphasis on the role of race in generating an underclass receives further stress and elaboration by Massey and Denton (1993), who stress the role that racial segregation plays in producing and maintaining concentrations of urban poverty.

21 In 2000, as in 1990, non-Hispanic whites make up about one quarter of the residents in high-poverty areas. The profound shift in concentrated urban poverty that resulted from the strong economy in the 1990s impressively reduced the numbers of blacks and Hispanics living in such neighborhoods by roughly 12 percent and 7 percent, respectively. But the decrease for whites in high-poverty areas was a minuscule 1 percent (Jargowsky 2003).

22 In this inscription of "stupidity," Murray was laying the groundwork for his later insistence that intelligence is the primary marker of class position, as is articulated in *The Bell Curve*, which is examined in some detail below.

23 Herrnstein and Murray's (1994) register of "civility," which includes "mowing the lawn in the summer, or keeping the sidewalks shovelled in the winter, maintaining a tolerable level of personal hygiene" (254), *naturally* demarcates the civilized and the primitive within the national order, whiteness.

24 The literature on Appalachian migration is quite extensive. See Obermiller and Philiber (1987); Philiber and McCoy (1981). The subject of this movement, part of the Great Migration of southern blacks, has been debated in relation to the origins of the urban underclass. See Lemann (1991); J. Jones (1993).

25 For a more detailed discussion on the viewing habits of the urban poor, see Brett Williams's (1988) chapter "Tele-visions of Urban Life."

26 These remarks were reported in the *Detroit Free Press*, December 12, 1993.

CHAPTER 7   ESTABLISHING THE FACT OF WHITENESS

An earlier version of this essay appeared in *American Anthropologist* 99, no. 3 (1997): 495–505.

1 Jennifer Lee's (2002) ethnographic account of merchant-customer relations in Los Angeles reveals that, despite copious grounds for conflict, interethnic relations are largely characterized by civility.

2 Recent studies of whiteness have been the subject of several reviews. See Fishkin (1995); Hyde (1995); Brody (1996).

3 Quoted on ABC's *Nightline* special, "America in Black and White," June 1996.

4 The notion of marked and unmarked terms derives from linguistic theories. See Waugh (1982).

5 For more on this usage of "white culture," see Hitchcock (2001).

6 Roediger asserts this position very strongly. He argues that "the central political implication arising from the insight that race is socially constructed is the specific need to attack whiteness as a destructive ideology rather than to attack the concept of race abstractly" (1994, 3). His purposes is to counter whites' claims to victimization by "reverse racism" and to undermine their interests in responding in kind to the overt politicization of blackness. While the political importance of this stance should be clear, it is exactly these confused efforts by whites to make sense of the changing significance of race that we need to analyze and understand.

7 An exception is Jane Hill's (1993, 150) analysis of "the ambivalent project of Anglo domination, that attempts simultaneously to reduce Hispanics to economic dependence and marginality, yet adopts many of their practices and exploits their presence in the region as a source of 'color' and 'romance' that will attract tourists and investors."

8 Whatever the state of race relations in Detroit, whiteness remains hegemonic nationally. The interplay of racial formations at the national, regional, city, and neighborhood level can be usefully figured through the model of "partial connections" that Marilyn Strathern (1991) has described.

9 See, "Whiteness in the Field," a special edition of *Identities: Global Studies in Culture and Power* 7, no. 3 (2000).

CHAPTER 8 LOCATING WHITE DETROIT

1 The notion of regions for ethnography is hardly an objectively given unit. As Richard Fardon (1990, 22) notes, "The inscription of locality has been one of the more complex results of the history of ethnography." On the one hand, regions are political and economic constructs, following administrative delineations and academic divisions of labor. On the other hand, regions are areas that cohere according to "the terms on which members of a host culture allowed the ethnographer to know them" (22). Fardon argues that anthropological research has consisted not of an encounter between a fieldworker and "the Other," but of "the nuanced continuation and modification of a relation between an approach delineating a region and the people who live within it" (25).

2 My stress on the uneven reproduction and experience of whiteness echoes that of Eric Lott (1993), who found in blackface minstrelsy a fractious white racial subjectivity that varied by region and was particularly animated and confused by transgressions of the color line in the urban centers of the North in the previous century.

3 Strathern follows James Glick by invoking the model of Cantor's dust to describe scaling phenomena.

4 This notion of bringing greater regional specificity to racial analytics is not exactly novel, and it precedes social construction of race models. Anthropologist Stanley Garn (1961) distinguishes between "geographical," "local," and "micro" races.

5 I examine the demographic basis of these transformations in urban settings in more detail in Hartigan (1997d, 103–115).

6 Although Omi and Winant's demarcation of micro- and macrolevels of racial orders are meant to be generally inclusive, and though the authors do not specifically exclude family from their definition of collectivity, I feel that family marks a level of phenomena between those they list that needs to be specified in this analysis.

7 Families have been a key analytical site for arguing about the significance of race in American culture at least since the Moynihan Report (see Rainwater and Yancey 1967). Following criticisms of ethnographic studies of this topic and critiques of notions such as the culture of poverty, anthropologists broke off their engagement with policy discussions concerning the "Negro family." But there are still important insights to be gained from fieldworkers' accounts of this critical site. David Schneider and Raymond Smith (1973), in their study of poor African American, southern white, and Spanish American families living in Chicago, make the case that kinship patterns are identical across these ethnoracial groupings. The fundamental aspect of their commonality as a lower-class culture emerges in contrast with kinship patterns of middle-class culture.

8 Additionally, the location of the family in the home brings into focus another fundamental ground on which racial orders are constructed. One of the critical material inscriptions of race in the post–World War II era has been real estate. Though ostensibly geographic in nature, real estate conflates several distinct domains, such as family and economy. See the chapter "Homegrown Revolution" in Davis (1992).

9 Because my work is concentrated on the underclass, I tend to follow William Julius Wilson (1978, 1987) in laying primary stress on class and the increasing intraracial polarization along economic lines. I address the political and theoretical issues of including whites in the urban underclass in chapter 6.

10 Anthropologists are highlighting the heterogeneity of racial constructs from a number of critical perspectives. See Stoler (1989); W. Wright (1990); Brackette Williams (1991); Streicker (1995).

11 I use the term racialness to indicate how race operates as a form of cultural materiality that is read in shifting contexts and against varying backgrounds of significance. In relation to both whiteness and blackness, racialness is a means of drawing attention to the possibilities of racially reading individuals when the collective character of distinct races in certain locales is mutable and unstable.

12 The title of this section is from the front of a T-shirt one of the white men I lived with wore occasionally. On the back, the shirt read: "now get yo' ass out of here."

13 My use of "black" here follows the local, preferred means of self-identification. A survey conducted by the *Detroit Free Press* (October 12, 1992) suggests a clear, emerging generational divide concerning preferences for "African American" over "black": 46 percent of blacks in Detroit under age thirty-five preferred African American, and 37 percent chose black. Those over age thirty-five preferred black by a 2 to 1 margin (48 percent to 24 percent).

14 Though blackness is hegemonic in Detroit, its significance to or extension over all blacks is hardly a given. This was clear in the city's most recent mayoral election. The contest pitted two black opponents, Dennis Archer and Sharon McPhail, vying to replace the long-time, also black, mayor, Coleman Young. When Archer's blackness was called into question, first by Young and subsequently by McPhail and other civic leaders who tried to suggest that he was a pawn of white suburban interests, the local media referred to this tactic as "injecting race into the campaign," as if, before these comments, the unitary color of the campaigners precluded the presence or significance of race. McPhail's apparent strategy of trying to establish herself as "the black candidate" seemed to follow the contours of the mayoral race in Cleveland in 1989, when George Forbes tried to "out-black" his black opponent, Michael White, who was a state senator at the time. Like McPhail, Forbes lost that race.

15 This figure was reported in "City Caught in Trash Avalanche," *Detroit Free Press*, July 4, 1993.

16 *Detroit Free Press*, June 12, 1993, and June 14, 1993. In a related event, promoters of the Detroit Grand Prix held the following week on the island drew a storm of

protests over a poster produced to announce the event. The poster was based on a painting by Georges Seurat that features a crowd of people taking in a sunny afternoon at a park. Over the image was a picture of the Detroit skyline, and in the foreground, a strip of roadway and several Formula One cars had been added. The *Detroit Free Press* for June 27, 1993 reported that "the creators of the poster were stunned when some black Detroiters objected to the poster for the Belle Isle event because it showed only white people."

17 The per capita income for white families ($57,132) was slightly less than for black families ($57,193) in this census tract, though the percentage of whites with incomes below the poverty line (39.5) was not as large as for blacks (52.1), according to the 1990 Census.

18 Reported by News Service, March 22, 1996.

19 The charged stigma of being both poor and white in the inner city is treated in detail by Jay MacLeod (1987). MacLeod studied two groups of youths in a low-income urban housing development, one white and the other black. The white group (the Hallway Hangers) was the central focus of his study because they so consistently expressed and enacted a near-total sense of being forever mired at the bottom of this country's economic order. Just as consistently, the black teenagers (the Brothers) were animated by the achievement ideology operating broadly in the United States. Race played a multifaceted, critical role in these groups' divergent views and experiences. MacLeod summarizes this role as follows: "The Hallway Hangers reject the achievement ideology because most of them are white. Whereas poor blacks have racial discrimination to which they can point as a cause of their family's poverty, for the Hallway Hangers to accept the achievement ideology is to admit that their parents are lazy or stupid or both. Thus, the achievement ideology not only runs counter to the experiences of the Hallway Hangers, but is also a more serious assault on their self-esteem. Acceptance of the ideology on the part of the Brothers does not necessarily involve such harsh implications, for they can point to racial prejudice to explain their parents' defeats. The severe emotional toll that belief in the achievement ideology exacts on poor whites relative to poor blacks explains why the Hallway Hangers dismiss the ideology while the Brothers validate it" (129–130).

  While the Brothers, too, are burdened with the "abnegations of the dominant society," "the achievement ideology represents a more potent assault on the Hallway Hangers because as white youths, they can point to no extenuating circumstances to account for their poverty. The subculture of the Hallway Hangers is in part a response to the stigma they feel as poor, white Americans" (133–134).

20 The term "poor whites" derives from the confusion among researchers over whether class or race is more important for identifying these whites. As Michael Maloney (1987) asks, "What conceptual framework do we use in studying urban Appalachians: ethnicity, race, or class? The concept of 'poor white' implies both race and class, while the concept of 'working class' could imply an approach

across racial and ethnic lines. The concept of 'Appalachian' ethnicity has been used for a combination of pragmatic and philosophical reasons too complex to discuss here, and the concept of 'minority group' has also been used by Appalachian advocates." Maloney's ambivalence regarding the suitability of all these terms is something we share.

21 These modes of interest are linked to distinct traditions of name-calling. I deal with this range of attentions toward this stratum of whites in Hartigan (1997c).

22 The Irish are a key group through which the foundations and contours of developing constructions of whiteness can be traced historically. Irish parades in the United States are key sites for the performance and objectification of racial and ethnic consciousness. See Kenneth Moss (1985, 1995); Marston (1989).

23 Urban Appalachians complicate a number of scholarly models and popular stereotypes of inner-city poverty. See Philiber and McCoy (1981); Philiber (1981); Obermiller and Philiber (1987); Borman and Obermiller (1994).

24 Between 1950 and 1990, Detroit's white population declined by approximately 1.3 million people.

25 I detail the complex usages of "hillbilly" in Hartigan (1996).

26 They seemed to be pointing to class differences as much as to being out of place in terms of race. In their later comments they stressed the occupational role, "researcher."

27 Other whites in the area who still walked past the projects while going toward Woodward, Detroit's central avenue, had many stories of being assaulted, verbally or physically, by blacks who lived there.

28 The term "hood" was used by young blacks and some whites in this area. Whites like Jerry used it with playfully ironic inflections in referring to their neighborhood.

29 The distinctness of their class position in relation to whiteness is underscored by contrasting their sense of place with that of working-class whites. Sam and David talked about what would happen if they went "over there." They did not talk about blacks coming "over here," which is what sets off the defensive response that characterizes racial conflicts in cities like New York and Boston. This neighborhood in Detroit does not ground a sense of defensive racial community because it is too racially heterogeneous. The contrast is best demonstrated by drawing on Rieder (1985).

30 I arrived in Detroit after the riots in Los Angeles, so I asked people why they thought there had been no outburst in Detroit, even though other cities around the nation had seen sympathetic outbursts of rage and frustration. People in this neighborhood consistently replied that it wasn't hot enough. Michigan experienced its coldest summer on record that year, and whether true or not, the local estimation was that the weather had defused any potential upsurge in violence. Most of the whites in this area had lived through the 1967 riot, which devastated this neighborhood.

31 Though the popular narrative regarding Detroit's history is that the city was

drained by white flight, reasons for leaving Detroit were not exclusively racial. The trend of moving factories out of the city began during World War II. After Detroit's population peaked in 1952, the outflow of people followed jobs; this was years before the 1967 riot, which looms large in explanations of the city's depopulation. In 1948 Detroiters held 60.3 percent of the metropolitan area's manufacturing jobs, 72.6 percent of the area's retailing jobs, and 60.3 percent of the employment in the wholesale industry. By 1954, the percentage of these jobs held by Detroiters had already begun to decline noticeably. By 1982, the city had lost more than 185,000 jobs in these three sectors. The depopulation of Detroit and other postindustrial cities is as much a reflection of the mobility of capital as it is a function of racial flight. The statistics are from Darden et al. (1987).

32 A key register through which the significance of racial categories materializes is the use of statistics that reveal racial discrepancies in matters such as infant mortality rates, access to institutions, and the availability of mortgages. Opinion surveys generally produce an interesting version of racialness, in that the opinions of the races on particular issues evidence a fundamental heterogeneity along with whatever significant attitudes are demonstrated overall. In this regard, I want to call attention to a survey conducted by the University of Michigan in 1992 as part of the Detroit Area Study. One of the questions posed to white respondents involved a series of four residential scenarios. Each scenario presented a fifteen-house block with varying degrees of racial integration. The first scenario had only one of the fifteen houses occupied by a black family, the fourth had eight of the fifteen inhabited by blacks (which fairly closely resembles the demographics of this part of Detroit). White respondents were asked if they would feel comfortable in each block, whether they would move in, or, if they lived there already, would they move out? Seventy percent of the whites said that they would not move into the area represented in the fourth scenario, and 52 percent responded that if they lived there already, they would move out. If whiteness is exemplified in the sentiments of the 70 percent of whites who were anxious about such living arrangements, then Jerry and the other whites in this neighborhood cannot be said to be participating in the same ideological construct or discursive order in any absolute manner.

33 Since the 1980s, Detroit has received national attention for the huge number of houses that arsonists burned on Devil's Night. See Chafets (1990).

34 I follow Omi and Winant's usage of "site" as "a region of social life with a coherent set of constitutive relations" (1986, 67).

35 One day after I had apparently been ripped off by a friend of his, Jerry explained to me that I had to watch out for everybody. I replied, "I thought he was a friend of yours." And Jerry responded, "He is. But see, I only been knowing him five years now. You never know with people."

36 The class contempt of Esther's reflections on her daughters and her grandchildren emerges more clearly in Ruth Frankenberg's (1993) analysis of white women's discourses on interracial marriages. Frankenberg identifies a key aspect

of middle- and working-class people's discourse on interracial couples: instead of openly expressing concern over the union, they articulate an anxiety about the social acceptance of the children's "mixed" racial identities. Esther, however, did not fret that her grandchildren would be "an affront to cultural belonging"; rather, she was distressed primarily by the bureaucratic challenges to her familial connections with the children. Also, she did not deploy the virulent images of black men as "primitive," uncivilized, animalistic predators that Frankenberg found so common among middle-class white women. Another sense of the class difference entailed in this contrast involves the desire for attention. Frankenberg points to the overwhelming dread on the part of her working-class informant, Sandy Alvarez, of drawing social attention by being part of an interracial couple. If Esther is right about her daughters' desire for attention, a desire perhaps linked to the numerous lacks endured daily by members of the underclass, then they seem even further removed from the social conditions of working-class white women.

37 Esther's sense of racialness is distinct from that of Jerry and his brothers. Although a gendered reading of this difference seems apparent, there are many complexities that would require extensive elaboration for that difference to be established accurately.

38 Eighty-eight percent of Detroit public school students are black (*Detroit Free Press*, January 19, 1992).

39 This history of Detroit is recounted in many works; see, for example, Meirer and Ruwick (1979); Capeci (1984); Jefferies (1989).

40 It was, of course, Nathan Glazer and Daniel Moynihan in *Beyond the Melting Pot* (1963) who first called attention to the end of this mythic image. They pointed to the stubborn maintenance of ethnic interests and identities in New York as proof that a homogeneous population was an elusive dream. My reading of the end of this myth differs by focusing on the irreducible basis of racialness as a continuing order of cultural significance in the United States, interpreted distinctly in changing and emergent social contexts. For an excellent account of how ethnic identities complicate the formation of a self-identified working class in this city, see Zunz (1982). For accounts of the crucial transformation of class divisions in the black community in Detroit, see Levine (1976); Katzman (1973); Thomas (1992).

41 I thank Roger Rouse for drawing my attention to the distinct futures that the two cities are used to envision in popular cultural productions in the United States today.

42 Rather than simply declare one myth dead and offer nothing in its stead, I turn to the real/fictional figure of the cyborg, particularly as elaborated by Donna Haraway (1991). This figure is compelling and irresistible in this context because, regarding race, it is important to rethink replication away from holistic models and more in synch with the new economic environment of biotechnical politics. "In relation to objects like biotic components, one must think not in terms of

essential properties, but in terms of design, boundary constraints, rates of flow, systems logics, costs of lowering constraints" (162).

Marilyn Strathern (1991) turns to the cyborg, as well, to help figure the future of ethnographic writing. In the disjointed realms of culture(s), she finds its figure useful, in part because "it is a whole image, but not an image of a whole" (162). Like the racial formations I have sketched, "its internal connections comprise an integrated circuit, but not a single unit" (162). But the segue from the melting pot to the cyborg occurs to Haraway also: "Our best machines are made of sunshine; they are all light and clean because they are nothing but signals, electromagnetic waves, a section of the spectrum, and these machines are eminently portable, mobile—a matter of immense human pain in Detroit and Singapore" (153).

CHAPTER 9 OBJECT LESSONS IN WHITENESS

An earlier version of this essay appeared in *Identities: Global Studies in Culture and Power* 7, no. 3 (2000): 373–406.

1 The role of antiracism in the teaching and scholarly pursuit of anthropology was the focus of a session at the 1998 American Anthropological Association's annual meeting, "Subverting Racism: Is There an Anthropological Consensus?" This subject is most actively discussed in relation to the pedagogical roles of anthropology in Parry (1984); Searle-Chatterjee (1987); Street (1987); Feuchtwang (1987); Walcott (1990); Askin (1991); Casey (1991): McCaskell (1995); Spears (1991); C. Martin (1996); Solomon and Levine-Rasky (1996). See Eugenia Shanklin (1999, 669) for a detailed list of suggestions covering "what the profession needs to do next to cope with racism and its consequences."

2 Whiteness is the subject of an intense amount of current research on the social dynamics and assumptions that serve to maintain white identity as normative and white people as dominant in Western societies. With more than seventy books published on this topic, I find summarizing them difficult in a single footnote. Please see the superb collection of reviews of this research in "The White Issue," *Minnesota Review*, 47 (1996), guest editor, Mike Hill. Other reviews include Brody (1996); Fishkin (1995): Hyde (1995).

3 The case for the "abolition" of whiteness is made strongly by contributors to the journal *Race Traitor* and by Roediger (1994).

4 Gilroy uses a range of posters and promotional materials to discern fundamental problems in this version of antiracism: "The concept of racism required no elaboration, but would be recognized immediately as a negative and unwholesome political trait" (1987, 139); "This vague, semi-religious language conveys a complete inability to locate what is specific to racial oppression and therefore to anti-racism" (144); "This municipal anti-racism allows the concept of racism to ascend to rarified heights where, like a lost balloon, it becomes impossible to retrieve" (144); "Racism covers all society's institution's like a thick blanket of

snow. Deprived of any overall direction and purpose anti-racists are invited to dig away into its frosty crust anywhere that tickles their fancy" (145). Gilroy frames his critical commentary by emphasizing the distinctions and distances between these movements and black struggles against oppression, which are less abstract in their formulation of "the problem." "People do not encounter racism in general or in the abstract, they feel the effects of its particular expressions: poor housing, unemployment, repatriation, violence or aggressive indifference. . . . It is not that the people who are actually affected by racism are incapable of thinking abstractly about the character of the oppression which determines their lives, but rather that the understanding of it, revealed in their expressive culture at least, is both too sophisticated and too practical to be diverted into the belief that 'race' is a simple cause rather than a complex effect of the underlying problems they face" (116).

5 For a review of what may be broadly construed as the historical extent of anti-racist politics in the United States, see Aptheker (1995). In terms of the 1970s movement, Judy Katz's (1978) book *White Awareness: Handbook for Anti-racism Training* is a fundamental text.

6 For a critical discussion of Racism Awareness Training, see Sivanandan (1985). For an example of more current manuals in this vein, see American Counseling Association (1998).

7 Afrocentrism was never a fixed and ratified object in this controversy. When opponents made reference to it, and when they suggested readings for me, they stressed a panoply of authors: Maulana Karenga, Asa Hilliard, Molefi Asante, Cheikh Diop.

8 Bonnett (1997, 177) asserts that antiracists must "become aware of, and escape from, the practice of treating Whiteness as a static, ahistorical, aspatial, objective 'thing': something set outside social change, something central and permanent, something that defines the 'other' but is not itself subject to others' definitions . . . a category which is not subject to the constant process of challenge and change that [has] characterised the history of other 'racial' names."

9 I think this perspective can travel to and be adopted in other disciplinary settings, just as many methodological elements of fieldwork have been appropriated by scholars outside of anthropology. See Clifford (1997).

10 This critical characterization of antiracism echoes the developed critiques of antiracist thinking in Britain from Michael Banton and Robert Miles. Each of these theorists challenges the circular logic that animates most critical discussions of race: race is asserted to be a false "social construction," but it is also posited as a characteristic of distinct populations with differential historical experiences and contrasting positions in relation to social dominance. Banton (1991, 118) has argued that the concept of racism should be rejected because of the way it reifies the complex problems that it targets and homogenizes practices that have to be analyzed separately if the mechanisms for the reproduction of racial inequality are to be assailed effectively. Miles has developed a sustained and

sophisticated critique of the lack of analytical clarity of antiracist scholars' efforts to objectify racism. A point he stresses vehemently, one that resonates with the frustration of Warrendale whites over their positioning in the antiracist workshop in relation to the controversy at the Academy, is that racism cannot be regarded as simply a "white ideology" developed exclusively to dominate blacks. Miles articulates this critique via his extensive historical research on patterns of migration in Europe and on a variety of other social researchers who suggest we need to comprehend that there are multiple racisms rather than a unique white ideology of racial dominance. Miles (1993, 23) thus asserts, "The nation states of the European Community are not confronted with a 'race problem,' but rather with the problem of racism, a problem which requires us to map and explain a particular instance of exclusion, simultaneously, in its specificity and in its articulation with a multiplicity of other forms of exclusion."

11 Audrey Smedley articulately states this position: "Accepting the fact that race is a cultural construct invented by human beings, it is easy to understand that it emerged out of a set of definable historical circumstances and is thus as amenable to analysis as are other elements of culture. *No amount of comparative definitions and synchronic explorations of modern race relations will lead us to more refined definitions and understandings of race.* On the contrary, it is a complex of elements whose signficance and meanings lie in historical settings in which attitudes and values were formed. We should be able to analytically isolate the central components, investigate their probable genesis, and determine how they evolved over time" (1993, 16; emphasis added).

12 For a compendium of such examples, see L. Williams (2000).

13 Gergory (1998, 144) elaborates: "This bureaucratization of the community's service infrastructure increased the social, political, and ideological distance between low- and middle-income [black] residents by differentiating the institutional settings in which the needs and interests of the two groups were defined and addressed. This sense of difference was heightened by the discourse of urban blight which, by locating the origins of complex neighborhood problems in the behavioral traits of residents of the 'strip,' exaggerated spatial and ontological distinctions between 'blighted' areas of the poor and the stable environs of the middle class."

14 I raise this matter because of the resonances I hear in these statements with the comments made by whites in Corktown, another of the three neighborhoods where I worked in Detroit, an area that was undergoing gentrification (Hartigan 1999). Gregory (1998, 149) argues that "the associations' resistance to the foster care facility illustrates how the state's harnessing of the discourse and politics of urban poverty has sharpened the perception and impact of class divisions within Corona-East Elmhurst by framing poverty and its related social issues as bureaucratic problems imposed on the neighborhood by *outside* agencies." This was also the case in Corktown, where white residents opposed the expansion of a local homeless shelter, one of many poverty-relief programs in the area. Indeed,

they argued that their neighborhood had one of the highest concentrations of social service agencies in the city; this was partly due to their location within a mile of the city's downtown. They could as surely make the case that their "backyard is already full," as did the black middle-class residents Gregory describes. Hence, I did not rely on their resistance to the shelter's expansion to demonstrate how race mattered in this class setting. Although it was certainly a possible reading, the textures of race played a more critical role in a more subtle terrain concerning aesthetics and technical interests that were expressed in their promotion of "historic designation" for the neighborhood. White racialness mattered, but not in terms of actively defending a white neighborhood from encroachment by the black poor, who already coursed through Corktown; rather, its significance showed most sharply in their debates over which whites fit the (historic) character of the neighborhood, which fundamentally turned on relative degrees of class advantage.

CHAPTER 10 CULTURAL ANALYSIS

1   Some of the best work on whiteness features class and gender analyses, but in each case, these crucial dimensions of social distinctions are seen singularly in terms of race. See Frankenberg (1993); Bederman (1995).

2   A similar assertion is made by Walter Benn Michaels (1992): "Our sense of culture is characteristically meant to displace race, but . . . culture has turned out to be a way of continuing rather than repudiating racial thought."

3   Dominguez (1992, 38–39) further notes, "Interlocking patterns of global and societal culturalism . . . continue to be used by populations in power to dominate, persuade, control, and justify—taking advantage of the simultaneous communicative inefficiency and community valorization of the cultural."

4   "It isn't just the alleged content of the culture that differentiates; it is the concept of culture itself that carries in its continued discursive usage a huge social, economic, and political value" (Dominguez 1992, 35).

5   For another critique of Visweswaran's position, see Bauer (2000) and Stassinos (1998).

6   Paul Gilroy (2000, 282) observes that in addition to its racial connotations, "culture retains yet another set of meanings that underpin but also resist the political conflicts that emerged with its pluralization, racialization, and ethnification. In English at least, though strongly inflected by class and its hierarchies, the concept helped to signpost the wholesome and attractive alternatives to anarchy, barbarization, nihilism, and anomie. . . . It can still bring to mind the promotion of mutuality and creativity in an imaginative regime that reaches towards the realization of collective truth, beauty, and right." Gilroy mobilizes these later connotations in the practice of cultural criticism to depict the conditions of "ethnic and racialized countercultures" (284).

7 I take this provocative phrase from Sharon Traweek's (1998) description of scientists.

8 Like kinship, each element of this list was originally formulated in a modernist framework that emphasized these as discrete, autonomous spheres. Thus, as with kinship, they each need to be reformulated via postmodernist critiques to reflect changing global and social circumstances.

9 See also the study of Japanese in Carrier (1995).

REFERENCES

Abbott, John. 1860. *South and North; or, Impressions Received During a Trip to Cuba and the South*. New York: Abbey and Abbot.

Abu-Lughod, Lila. 1991. "Writing against Culture." In *Recapturing Anthropology*, ed. Richard Fox, 137–162. Santa Fe: School of American Research.

——. 1999. "Comments." *Current Anthropology* 40 supplement: S13–S15.

Alba, Richard. 1990. *Ethnic Identity: The Transformation of White America*. New Haven: Yale University Press.

Alexander, Jack. 1977. "The Culture of Race in Middle-Class Kingston, Jamaica." *American Ethnologist* 4, no. 3: 413–435.

Alex-Assensoh, Yvette. 1995. "Myths about Race and the Underclass: Concentrated Poverty and 'Underclass' Behviors." *Urban Affairs Review* 31, no. 1: 3–19.

Allen, Garland E. 1975. "Genetics, Eugenics and Class Struggle." *Genetics* 79: 29–45.

Allen, Theodore. 1994. *The Invention of the White Race: Racial Oppression and Social Control*. Vol. 1. New York: Verso.

——. 1997. *The Invention of the White Race: The Origin of Racial Oppression in Anglo-America*. London: Verso.

Allison, Dorothy. 1988. *Trash*. New York: Firebrand Books.

——. 1992. *Bastard Out of Carolina*. New York: Dutton.

American Counseling Association. 1998. *Confronting Prejudice and Racism During Multicultural Training*. Washington, D.C.: ACA.

Amit-Talai, Vered, and Caroline Knowles, eds. 1996. *Re-Situating Identities: The Politics of Race, Ethnicity, Culture*. Peterborough, Ontario: Broadview Press.

Anderson, Elijah. 1990. *Streetwise: Race, Class, and Change in an Urban Community*. Chicago: University of Chicago Press.

Anderson, Sherwood. 1920/1966. *Poor White*. New York: Viking Press.

Appadurai, Arjun. 1996. *Modernity at Large: The Cultural Dimensions of Globalization*. Minneapolis: University of Minnesota Press.

Appel, R. W. 2000. "Polishing Nashville's Twang." *New York Times*, July 28, p. 1.

Aptheker, Herbert. 1995. "Anti-racism in the United States: 1865–1900." In *Racism and Anti-Racism in World Perspective.* Thousand Oaks, Calif.: Sage.

Aratta, Stephen. 1996. *Fictions of Loss in the Victorian Fin de siecle.* Cambridge, England: Cambridge University Press.

Arnesen, Eric. 2001. "Whiteness and the Historians' Imagination." *International Labor and Working-Class History* 60: 3–32.

Arnold, Gina. 1992. "Wholly Greil: Two Rock Critics Seek the Truth on Jesus, Madonna, Elvis, and Nirvarna." *Metro Guide,* April 30–May 6, 1992, 19–25.

Askin, William. 1991, "Teaching within an Anti-Racist Framework: Unwrapping the American Museum of Natural History." *Transforming Anthropology* 2, no. 1: 28–30.

Auletta, Ken. 1982. *The Underclass.* New York: Vintage.

Bakhtin, Mikhail. 1984. *Rabelais and His World.* Cambridge, Mass.: MIT Press.

Bal, Mike, ed. 1999. *The Practice of Cultural Analysis: Exposing Interdisciplinary Interpretation.* Stanford: Stanford University Press.

Bales, Kevin. 1999. "Popular Reactions to Sociological Research: The Case of Charles Booth." *Sociology* 33, no. 1: 153–168.

Balibar, Etienne. 1991. "Is There a 'Neo-Racism'?" In *Race, Nation, Class: Ambiguous Identities,* ed. Etienne Balibar and Immanuel Wallerstein. London: Verso.

Banton, Michael. *Racial Theories.* 1987. Cambridge, England: Cambridge University Press.

——. 1991. "The Race Relations Problematic." *British Journal of Sociology* 42, no. 1: 115–130.

——. *Racial Theories.* 1998. Cambridge, England: Cambridge University Press.

Barker, Clive. 1985. *Books of Blood, Volume 5.* London: Weidenfeld and Nicolson.

Barker-Benfield, G. J. 1976. *The Horrors of the Half-Known Life: Male Attitudes towards Women and Sexuality in Nineteenth-Century America.* New York: Harper Colophon.

Barot, Rohit, and John Bird. 2001. "Racialization: The Genealogy and Critique of a Concept." *Ethnic and Racial Studies* 24, no. 4: 601–618.

Barth, Frederick. 2002. "Toward a Richer Description and Analysis of Cultural Phenomena." In *Anthropology Beyond Culture,* ed. Richard Fox and Barbara King. Oxford: Berg.

Basso, Keith. 1979. *Portraits of "The Whiteman": Linguistic Play and Cultural Symbols among the Western Apache.* New York: Cambridge University Press.

Battaglia, Debbora, ed. 1995. *Rhetorics of Self-Making.* Berkeley: University of California Press.

Batteau, Allen. 1990. *The Invention of Appalachia.* Tucson: University of Arizona Press.

Bauer, Janet. 2000. "Genealogies of Race and Culture in Anthropology: The Marginalized Ethnographers." In *Race and Racism in Theory and Practice,* ed. Berel Lang. New York: Rowman and Littlefield.

Bederman, Gail. 1995. *Manliness and Civilization: A Cultural History of Gender and Race in the United States, 1880–1917.* Chicago: University of Chicago Press.

Beidelman, T. O. 1986. *Moral Imagination in Kaguru Modes of Thought.* Washington, D.C.: Smithsonian Institution Press.

Berger, Peter, and Thomas Luckman. 1966. *The Social Construction of Reality: A Treatise in the Sociology of Knowledge.* New York: Anchor.

Bhabha, Homi. 1983. "The Other Question: The Stereotype and Colonial Discourse." *Screen* 24, no. 6: 18–29.

Bilger, Burkhard. 2000. "Squirrel and Man." *The New Yorker*, July 17, 59–67.

Bolton, Charles. 1994. *Poor Whites of the Antebellum South: Tenants and Laborers in Central North Carolina and Northeast Mississippi.* Durham: Duke University Press.

Bone, Eugenia. 1994. "Trailer-Made." *Premiere*, 36.

Bonilla-Silva, Eduardo. 2001. *White Supremacy and Racism in the Post–Civil Rights Era.* Boulder, Colo.: Lynne Rienner.

Bonnell, Victoria, and Lynn Hunt, eds. 1999. *Beyond the Cultural Turn.* Berkeley: University of California Press.

Booth, Charles. 1902. *Life and Labour of the People in London, First Series: Poverty.* London: Macmillan.

Borman, Kathryn, and Phillip Obermiller, eds. 1994. *From Mountain to Metropolis: Appalachian Migrants in American Cities.* Westport, Conn.: Bergin and Garvey.

Bourdieu, Pierre. 1984. *Distinction: A Social Critique of the Judgement of Taste.* Cambridge, Mass.: Harvard University Press.

Bourgois, Philippe. 1995. *In Search of Respect: Selling Crack in El Barrio.* Cambridge, England: Cambridge University Press.

Bowser, Benjamin. 1995. *Racism and Anti-Racism in World Perspective.* Thousand Oaks: Sage Publications.

Brander, Brigit, et al., eds. 2001. *The Making and Unmaking of Whiteness Studies.* Durham, N.C.: Duke University Press.

Branscome, James. 1978. "Annihilating the Hillbilly: Appalachians' Struggle with America's Institutions." In *Colonialism in Modern America: The Appalachian Case*, ed. Helen Lewis et al. Boone, N.C.: Appalachian Consortium Press.

Brechin, Gray. 1996. "Conserving the Race: Natural Aristocracies, Eugenics, and the U.S. Conservation Movement." *Antipode* 28, no. 3: 229–245.

Brightman, Robert. 1995. "Forget Culture: Replacement, Transcendence, Relexification." *Cultural Anthropology* 10, no. 4: 509–46.

Brinton, Bulah. 1873. *Man Is Love: An American Story*. Philadelphia: J. B. Lippincott.

Brody, Jennifer. 1996. "Reading Race and Gender: When White Women Matter." *American Quarterly* 48, no. 1: 153–159.

Brogan, Kathleen. 1998. *Cultural Haunting: Ghosts and Ethnicity in Recent American Literature.* Charlottesville: University Press of Virginia.

Brumann, Christoph. 1999. "Writing for Culture: Why a Successful Concept Should Not Be Discarded." *Current Anthropology* 40, supplement: S1–S28.

Bultman, Bethany. 1996. *Redneck Heaven: Portrait of a Vanishing Culture.* New York: Bantam.

Bushman, Richard. 1992. *The Refinement of America: Persons, Houses, Cities.* New York: Knopf.

Byrne, Bridget. Forthcoming. *White Lives: Gender, Race, and Class in Contemporary London,* Durham, N.C.: Duke University Press.

Cairnes, John Elliott. 1862. *The Slave Power: Its Character, Career, and Probably Design: Being an Attempt to Explain the Real Issues Involved in the American Contest.* New York: Carleton.

Caldwell, Erskin. 1932. *Tobacco Road.* New York: Duell, Sloan, and Pearce.

Caldwell, Mark. 1999. *A Short History of Rudeness: Manners, Morals, and Misbehavior in Modern America.* New York: Picador.

Cannadine, David. 2001. *Ornamentalism: How the British Saw Their Empire.* Oxford: Oxford University Press.

Capeci, Dominic, Jr. 1984. *Race Relations in Wartime Detroit: The Sojourner Truth Housing Controversy.* Philadelphia: Temple University Press.

Carlson, Elof. 2001. *The Unfit: A History of a Bad Idea.* Cold Spring Harbor, N.Y.: Cold Spring Harbor Laboratory Press.

Carr, Howie. 2001. "Clinton Departure Removes Trash from the White House." *Boston Herald,* January 21, p. A14.

Carrier, James. 1995. *Occidentalism: Images of the West.* Oxford: Clarendon Press.

Casey, Geraldine. 1991. "Racism, Anger, and Empowerment: Teaching Anthropology in a Multi-Racial Working-Class Environment." *Transforming Anthropology* 2, no. 1: 9–15.

Cecil-Fronsman, Bill. 1992. *Common Whites: Class and Culture in Antebellum North Carolina.* Lexington: University of Kentucky Press.

Cell, John. 1982. *The Highest Stage of White Supremacy: The Origins of Segregation in South Africa and the American South.* Cambridge, England: Cambridge University Press.

Cetina, Karin Knorr. 1999. *Epistemic Cultures: How the Sciences Make Knowledge.* Cambridge, Mass.: Harvard University Press.

Chafets, Ze'ev. 1990. *Devil's Night and Other True Tales of Detroit.* New York: Vintage.

Chauncey, George. 1994. *Gay New York: Gender, Urban Culture, and the Making of the Gay World, 1890–1940.* New York: Basic Books.

Chen, Xiaomei. 1992. "Occidentalism as Counterdiscourse: 'He Shang' in Post-Mao China." *Critical Inquiry* 18 (summer): 686–712.

Chin, Elizabeth. 2001. *Purchasing Power: Black Kids and American Consumer Culture.* Minneapolis: University of Minnesota Press.

Ching, Barbara. 2001. *Wrong's What I Do Best: Hard Country Music and Contemporary Culture.* New York: Oxford University Press.

Chock, Phyllis. 1987. "The Irony of Stereotypes: Toward an Anthropology of Ethnicity." *Cultural Anthropology* 2, no. 3: 347–368.

Christopher, Renny. 1993. "Lower Class Voices and the Establishment: The Reception of Carolyn Chute." Unpublished manuscript.

Chute, Carolyn. 1985. *The Beans of Egypt, Maine.* New York: Warner Brothers.

——. 1988. *Letourneau's Used Auto Parts*. New York: Harper and Row.

Clifford, James. 1988. *The Predicament of Culture: Twentieth-Century Ethnography, Literature, and Art*. Cambridge, Mass: Harvard University Press.

——. 1997. *Routes: Travel and Translation in the Twentieth Century*. Cambridge, Mass.: Harvard University Press.

Clifford, James, and Marcus, George, eds. 1986. *Writing Culture: The Poetics and Politics of Ethnography*. Berkeley: University of California Press.

Cohen, Nancy. 2002. *The Reconstruction of American Liberalism, 1865–1914*. Chapel Hill: University of North Carolina Press.

Comaroff, John, and Jean Comaroff. 1992. *Ethnography and the Historical Imagination*. Boulder, Colo.: Westview.

Conley, Dalton. 1999. *Being Black, Living in the Red: Race, Wealth, and Social Policy in America*. Berkeley: University of California Press.

Cook, Sylvia. 1976. *From Tobacco Road to Route 66: The Southern Poor White in Fiction*. Chapel Hill: University of North Carolina Press.

Crapanzano, Vincent. 1986. *Waiting: The Whites of South Africa*. New York: Random House.

Cruz, Jon. 1999. *Culture on the Margins: The Black Spiritual and the Rise of American Cultural Interpretation*. Princeton: Princeton University Press.

Culler, Jonathan. 1985. "Junk and Rubbish: A Semiotic Approach." *Diacritics* 15, no. 3: 2–12.

Curtis, Perry. 1971. *Apes and Angels: The Irishman in Victorian Caricature*. Washington, D.C.: Smithsonian Institution Press.

Daniel, Pete. 1985. *Breaking the Land: The Transformation of Cotton, Tobacco, and Rice Cultures since 1880*. Urbana: University of Illinois Press.

Danzinger, Sheldon, Gary Sandefur, and Daniel Weinburg, eds. 1994. *Confronting Poverty: Prescriptions for Change*. Cambridge, Mass.: Harvard University Press.

Darden, Joe, et al. 1987. *Detroit: Race and Uneven Development*. Philadelphia: Temple University Press.

Davenport, Charles B. 1911. "Euthenics and Eugenics." *Popular Science Monthly*, January, 16–20.

——. 1913. *The Family History Book*. Cold Spring Harbor, N.Y.: Eugenics Record Office.

Davenport, Charles B., and Harry H. Laughlin. 1915. *How to Make a Eugenical Family Study*. Cold Spring Harbor, N.Y.: Eugenics Record Office.

Davenport, Gertrude C. 1914. "Society and the Feebleminded." *The Independent* (Boston), April 27, 170.

Davila, Arlene. 2001. *Latinos Inc.: The Marketing and Making of a People*. Berkeley: University of California Press.

Davis, Mike. 1992. *City of Quartz: Excavating the Future in Los Angeles*. New York: Vintage.

Delgado, Richard, and Jean Stefancic, eds. 1997. *Critical White Studies*. Philadelphia: Temple University Press.

——, eds. 2000. *Critical Race Theory: The Cutting Edge.* 2nd ed. Philadelphia: Temple University Press.

Detroit Bureau of Governmental Research, Inc. 1937. *Population (1930 Census) and Other Social Data for Detroit by Census Tracts.* Report no. 143. Detroit Public Library.

Dikotter, Frank. 1998. "Race Culture: Recent Perspectives on the History of Eugenics." *American Historical Review* 103, no. 2: 467–78.

Di Leonardo, Micaela. 1998. *Exotics at Home: Anthropologies, Others, American Modernity.* Chicago: University of Chicago Press.

Dirks, Nicholas, ed. 1998. *In Near Ruins: Cultural Theory at the End of the Century.* Minneapolis: University of Minnesota Press.

Dollar, Gerard. 1994. "Addiction and the 'Other Self' in Three Late Victorian Novels." In *Beyond the Pleasure Dome: Writing and Addiction from the Romantics,* ed. Sue Vice, Matthew Campbell, and Tim Armstrong. Sheffield, England: Sheffield Academic Press.

Dominguez, Virginia. 1986. *White by Definition: Social Classification in Creole Louisiana.* New Brunswick, N.J.: Rutgers University Press.

——. 1992. "The Messy Side of 'Cultural Politics.' " *South Atlantic Quarterly* 91, no. 1: 19–42.

Douglas, Mary. 1966. *Purity and Danger: An Analysis of Pollution and Taboo.* London: Pelican.

Douglas, Mary, and Aaron Wildavsky. 1982. *Risk and Culture.* Berkeley: University of California Press.

Douglass, Frederick. 1857. *My Bondage and My Freedom.* New York: Miller, Orton.

Douglass, Lisa. 1992. *The Power of Sentiment: Love, Hierarchy, and the Jamaican Family Elite.* Boulder, Colo.: Westview.

Dowling, Andrew. 2001. *Manliness and the Male Novelist in Victorian Literature.* Burlington, Vt.: Ashgate.

Doyle, Bertram Wilbur. 1937. *The Etiquette of Race Relation in the South.* Port Washington, N.Y.: Kennikat.

Drummond, Lee. 1980. "The Cultural Continuum: A Theory of Intersystems." *Man* 15, no. 2: 352–374.

Du Bois, W. E. B. 1899/1996. *The Philadelphia Negro: A Social Study.* Philadelphia: University of Pennsylvania Press.

——. 1903/2000. *The Souls of Black Folks.* Bensenville, Ill.: Lushena.

——. 1940/1980. *Dusk of Dawn: An Essay towards an Autobiography of a Race Concept.* Franklin Center, Pa.: Franklin Library.

Dugdale, Richard. 1877. *"The Jukes": A Study in Crime, Pauperism, Disease, and Heredity.* New York: G.P. Putnam's Sons.

Dunlap, Knight. 1920. *Personal Beauty and Racial Betterment.* St. Louis: C.V. Mosby.

Dyer, Richard. 1988. "White." *Screen* (fall), 44–64.

Echlin, Hobey. 2002. "The Real Slim Shady." *Metro Times Detroit,* October 30, 11–14.

Eckardt, Wolf von. 1987. *Oscar Wilde's London: A Scrapbook of Vices and Virtues, 1880–1900.* Garden City, N.Y.: Anchor.

Eddy, Chuck. 2000. "Motor Suburb Madhouse." *Village Voice,* July 11, 69–70.

Elias, Norbert. 1994. *The Civilizing Process.* Oxford: Blackwell.

Ellis, Havelock. 1911. *The Problem of Race-Regeneration.* New York: Moffat, Yard.

Ellsworth, Elizabeth. 1989. "Why Doesn't This Feel Empowering? Working through Repressive Myths of Critical Pedagogy." *Harvard Educational Review* 59, no. 3: 297–324.

Estabrook, Arthur. 1916. *The Jukes in 1915.* Washington, D.C.: Carnegie Institute.

Fabian, Johannes. 1983. *Time and Other: How Anthropology Makes Its Object.* New York: Columbia University Press.

Fardon, Richard. 1990. *Localizing Strategies: The Regional Traditions of Ethnographic Writing.* Edinburgh: Scottish Academic Press.

Farley, Reynolds, Charlotte Steeh, Tara Jackson, Maria Krysan, and Keith Reeves. 1993. "Continued Racial Segregation in Detroit: 'Chocolate City, Vanilla Suburbs' Revisited." *Journal of Housing Research* 4, no. 1: 1–38.

Farquhar, Judith, and Marta Hanson. 1998. "Guest Editors' Introduction." *Positions: East Asia Cultures Critique* 6: 507–513.

Ferenchik, Mark. 2000. "Appalachian Officials: Puzzle Unfit to Print." *Columbus Dispatch,* March 5, 2c.

Ferguson, Andrew. 1996. "Who Is This Sex-Crazed Hillbilly?" *Wall Street Journal,* January 26, p. A9.

Feuchtwang, Stephan. 1987. "The Anti-Racist Challenge to Anthropology in the U.K." *Anthropology Today* 3, no. 5: 7–9.

Fields, Barbara. 2001. "Whiteness, Racism, and Identity." *International Labor and Working-Class History* 60: 48–56.

Fine, Gary, and Patricia Turner. 2001. *Whispers on the Color Line: Rumor and Race in America.* Berkeley: University of California Press.

Fishkin, Shelly. 1995. "Interrogating 'Whiteness,' Complicating 'Blackness': Remapping American Culture." *American Quarterly* (September): 428–466.

Fiske, John. 1992. *Understanding Popular Culture.* Boston: Unwin Hyman.

Flynt, J. Wayne. 1989. *Poor but Proud: Alabama's Poor Whites.* Tuscaloosa: University of Alabama Press.

Foley, Douglas. 1990. *Learning Capitalist Culture.* Philadelphia: University of Pennsylvania Press.

Foley, Neil. 1997. *The White Scourge: Mexicans, Blacks, and Poor Whites in Texas Cotton Culture.* Berkeley: University of California Press.

Foner, Eric. 1995. *Free Soil, Free Labor, Free Men: The Ideology of the Republican Party before the Civil War.* Oxford: Oxford University Press.

Fordham, Signithia. 1996. *Blacked Out: Dilemmas of Race, Identity, and Success at Capital High.* Chicago: University of Chicago Press.

Foucault, Michel. 1990. *The History of Sexuality.* Vol. 1. New York: Vintage.

Fox, Aaron. 2004. "White Trash Alchemies of the Abject Sublime: Country as 'Bad' Music." In *Bad Music: The Music That We Love to Hate*, ed. Christopher J. Washburne and Maiken Durno. New York: Routledge.

Fox, Richard, and Barbara King, eds. 2002. *Anthropology beyond Culture*. Oxford: Berg.

Fox, Richard, and T. J. Jackson Lears, eds. 1993. *The Power of Culture: Critical Essays in American History*. Chicago: University of Chicago Press.

Frankenberg, Ruth. 1993. *White Women, Race Matters: The Social Construction of Whiteness*. Minneapolis: University of Minnesota Press.

Fredrickson, George. 1981. *A Comparative Study of American and South African History*. New York: Oxford University Press.

———. 2002. *Racism: A Short History*. Princeton: Princeton University Press.

Frei, Hans. 1974. *The Eclipse of Biblical Narrative: A Study in Eighteenth and Nineteenth Century Hermeneutics*. New Haven: Yale University Press.

Friend, Tad. 1994. "The White Trashing of America." *New York*, August 22, 22–30.

Frierson, Chaundra. 2000. "New Yorker Article Gets Unfavorable Reviews from Featured Residents." *Messenger-Inquirer*, March 5, 1A.

Frykman, Jonas, and Ovar Lofgren. 1987. *Culture Builders: A Historical Anthropology of Middle Class Life*. New Brunswick, N.J.: Rutgers University Press.

———. 1999. *Culture Builders: A Historical Anthropology of Middle-Class Life*. New Brunswick, N.J.: Rutgers University Press.

Gadamer, Hans-Georg. 1984. "The Hermeneutics of Suspicion." In *Hermeneutics: Questions and Prospects*, ed. Gary Shapiro and Alan Sica. Amherst: University of Massachusetts Press.

Gans, Herbert. 1993. "From 'Underclass' to 'Undercaste': Some Observations about the Future of the Postindustrial Economy and Its Major Victims." *International Journal of Urban and Regional Research* 17, no. 3: 327–335.

Garn, Stanley. 1961. *Human Race*. Springfield, Ill.: Charles Thomas.

Gates, Henry Louis, Jr. 1991. "Critical Fanonism." *Cultural Inquiry* 17 (spring).

Genovese, Eugene. 1971. *The World the Slaveholders Made: Two Essays in Interpretation*. New York: Vintage Books.

———. 1976. *Roll, Jordan, Roll*. New York: Vintage.

Gerstel, Gary. 2001. *American Crucible: Race and Nation in the Twentieth Century*. Princeton: Princeton University Press.

Gewertz, D., and F. Errington. 1991. "We Think, Therefore They Are? On Occidentalizing the World." *Anthroplogical Quarterly* 64, no. 2: 80–92.

Gilroy, Paul. 1987. *There Ain't No Black in the Union Jack*. Chicago: University of Chicago Press.

———. 2000. *Against Race: Imagining Political Culture Beyond the Color Line*. Cambridge, Mass.: Harvard University Press.

Girard, Rene. 1977. *Violence and the Sacred*. Trans. Patrick Gregory. Baltimore: Johns Hopkins University Press.

Gitlin, Todd, and Nanci Hollander. 1970. *Uptown: Poor Whites in Chicago*. New York: Harper and Row.

Glasgow, Douglas. 1980. *The Black Underclass: Poverty, Underemployment, and the Entrapment of Ghetto Youth*. San Fransisco: Jossey-Brass.

Glazer, Nathan, and Daniel Patrick Moynihan. 1963. *Beyond the Melting Pot*. Cambridge, Mass.: MIT Press.

Goad, Jim. 1997. *The Redneck Manifesto: America's Scapegoats. How We Got That Way and Why We're Not Going to Take It Anymore*. New York: Simon and Schuster.

Goddard, Henry. 1913. *The Kallikak Family: A Study in the Heredity of Feeble-Mindedness*. New York: Macmillan.

Goldberg, David Theo. 1993. *Racist Culture: Philosophy and the Politics of Meaning*. Oxford: Blackwell.

Gordon, Avery. 1997. *Ghostly Matters: Haunting and the Sociological Imagination*. Minneapolis: University of Minnesota Press.

Goster, Gary, and Richard Hummel. 1997. "Wham, Bam, Thank You, SAM: Critical Dimensions of the Persistence of Hillbilly Caricatures." *Sociological Spectrum* 17, no. 2: 157–177.

Grant, Madison. 1916. *The Passing of the Great Race, or The Racial Basis of European History*. New York: Charles Scribner's Sons.

——. 1933. *Conquest of a Continent, or The Expansion of Races in America*. New York: Scribner.

Green, Archie. 1965. "Hillbilly Music: Source and Symbol." *Journal of American Folklore* 78, no. 309 (1965): 204–28.

Green, Vera. 1970. "The Confrontation of Diversity within the Black Community." *Human Organization* 29, no. 4: 267–272.

Greenblatt, Stephen. 1987. "Towards a Poetics of Culture." *Southern Review* 20 (March).

Greene, Richard. 1991a. "Poverty Area Diffusion: The Depopulation Hypothesis Examined." *Urban Geography* 12, no. 6: 536–541.

——. 1991b. "Poverty Concentration Measures and the Urban Underclass." *Economic Geography* 67, no. 3: 240–252.

Gregory, Steven. 1998. *Black Corona: Race and the Politics of Place in an Urban Community*. Princeton: Princeton University Press.

Gregory, Steven, and Roger Sanjek, eds. 1994. *Race*. New Brunswick, N.J.: Rutgers University Press.

Grimson, Alejandro. 2002. "Hygiene Wars on the Mercosur Border: Local and National Agency in Uruguaiana (Brazil) and Paso de los Libres." *Identities: Global Studies in Power and Culture* 9, no. 2: 151–172.

Guimares, Antonio Sergio Alfredo. 1995. "Racism and Anti-Racism in Brazil: A Postmodern Perspective." In *Racism and Anti-Racism in World Perspective*, ed. Benjamin Browser, 208–225. Thousand Oaks, Calif.: Sage.

Gupta, Akhil, and Ferguson, James. 1997. *Anthropological Locations: Boundaries and Grounds of a Field Science*. Berkeley: University of California Press.

Gurnah, Ahmed. 1984. "The Politics of Racism Awareness Training." *Critical Social Policy*, no. 10 (summer): 6–20.

Guterl, Matthew. 2001. *The Color of Race in America, 1900–1940.* Cambridge, Mass.: Harvard University Press.

Guyette, Curt. 2001. "Down a Green Path: An Alternative Vision Takes Shape for a Section of East Detroit." *Metro Times Detroit,* October 31–November 6, 10–13.

Halberstam, Judith. 1995. *Skin Shows: Gothic Horror and the Technology of Monsters.* Durham, N.C.: Duke University Press.

Hale, Grace Elizabeth. 1998. *Making Whiteness: The Culture of Segregation in the South, 1890–1940.* New York: Vintage.

Hall, Stuart. 1981. "Notes on Deconstructing the 'Popular.'" In *People's History and Socialist Theory,* ed. R. Samuel. London: Routledge.

——. 1992. "What Is This 'Black' in Black Popular Culture?" In *Black Popular Culture,* ed. Gina Dent. Seattle: Bay Press.

——. 1994. "Cultural Studies: Two Paradigms." In *Culture/Power/History,* ed. Geoff Eley, Nick Dirks, and Sherry Ortner. Princeton: Princeton University Press.

Hall, Stuart, and Paul Du Gay, eds. 1996. *Questions of Cultural Identity.* London: Sage.

Haller, Mark H. 1963. *Eugenics: Hereditarian Attitudes in American Thought.* New Brunswick, N.J.: Rutgers University Press.

Hancock, Carl. 2003. "Eminem: The New White Negro." In *Everything but the Burden: What White People Are Taking from Black Culture,* ed. Greg Tate. New York: Harlem Moon.

Haraway, Donna. 1991. "A Cyborg Manifesto: Science, Technology, and Socialist-Feminism in the Late Twentieth Century." In *Simians, Cyborgs, and Women: The Reinvention of Nature.* New York: Routledge.

——. 1992. "The Promise of Monsters: A Regenerative Politics for Inappropriate/d Others." In *Cultural Studies,* ed. Lawrence Grossberg, Cary Nelson, and Paula Treichler. New York: Routledge.

——. 1997. *Modest_Witness@second_Millennium. FemaleMan_Meets_OncoMouse.* New York: Routledge.

Harding, Susan. 1991. "Representing Fundamentalism: The Problem of the Repugnant Cultural Other." *Social Research* 58, no. 2: 373–393.

Harrison, Faye. 1988. "Introduction: An African Diaspora Perspective for Urban Anthropology." *Urban Anthropology* 17, nos. 2–3: 111–140.

——. 1991. *Decolonizing Anthropology: Moving Further toward an Anthropology for Liberation.* Washington, D.C.: American Anthropological Association.

——. 1992. "The Du Boisian Legacy in Anthropology." *Critique of Anthropology* 12, no. 3: 239–260.

——. 1995. "The Persistent Power of 'Race' in the Cultural and Political Economy of Racism." *Annual Review of Anthropology* 24: 47–74.

——. 1998. "Expanding the Discourse on 'Race.'" *American Anthropologist* 100, no. 3: 609–631.

Hartigan, John, Jr. 1996a. "Disgrace to the Race: 'Hillbillies' and the Color-Line in Detroit." In *Downtown: Urban Appalachians Today*, ed. Phillip Obermiller. Dubuque, Iowa: Kendall/Hunt.

——. 1996b. "Name Calling and Objectifying 'Poor Whites' and 'White Trash.' " In *White Trash: Class, Race and the Construction of American Identity*, ed. Matt Wray and Annalee Newitz. London: Routledge.

——. 1997a. "Establishing the Fact of Whiteness." *American Anthropologist* 99, no. 2: 495–505.

——. 1997b. "When Whites Are a Minority." In *Cultural Diversity in the United States*, ed. Larry Naylor. Westport, Conn.: Bergin and Garvey.

——. 1997c. "When White Americans Are a Minority." In *Cultural Diversity in the United States*, ed. Larry Naylor. Westport, Conn.: Bergin and Garvey.

——. 1999. *Racial Situations: Class Predicaments of Whiteness in Detroit*. Princeton: Princeton University Press.

——. 2000. "Whiteness in the Field: Introduction to a Special Issue of *Identities*." *Identities* 7, no. 3: 269–279.

Hasian, Marouf. 1996. *The Rhetoric of Eugenics in Anglo-American Thought*. Athens: University of Georgia Press.

Hawkins, Harriette. 1990. *Classics and Trash: Traditions and Taboos in High Literature and Popular Modern Genres*. London: Harvester Wheatsheaf.

Heath, Shirley Brice. 1983. *Ways with Words: Language, Life, and Work in Communities and Classrooms*. Cambridge, England: Cambridge University Press.

Hegeman, Susan. 1999. *Patterns for America: Modernism and the Concept of Culture*. Princeton: Princeton University Press.

Heller, Zoe. 2001. "When All Else Fails, Tell Her She Has Got Lumpy Thighs." *Daily Telegraph*, August 4, p. 23.

Helper, Hinton Rowan. 1860. *The Impending Crisis of the South: How to Meet It*. New York: A. B. Burdick.

Henwood, Doug. 1997. "Trash-O-Nomics." In *White Trash: Race and Class in America*, ed. Matt Wray and Annalee Newitz. New York: Routledge.

Heringer, Rosana. 1995. "Introduction to the Analysis of Racism and Anti-Racism in Brazil." In *Anti-Racism in World Perspective*, ed. Benjamin Browser. Thousand Oaks, Calif.: Sage.

Herrnstein, Richard, and Charles Murray. 1994. *The Bell Curve: Intelligence and Class Structure in American Life*.

Herron, Jerry. 1993. *After Culture: Detroit and the Humiliation of History*. Detroit, Mich.: Wayne State University Press.

Herzfeld, Michael. 1997. *Cultural Intimacy: Social Poetics in the Nation-State*. New York: Routledge.

Hewitt, Roger. 1986. *White Talk, Black Talk: Inter-racial Friendship and Communication amongst Adolescents*. Cambridge, England: Cambridge University Press.

Hill, Jane. 1993. "Hasta La Vista, Baby: Anglo Spanish in the American Southwest." *Critique of Anthropology* 13, no. 2: 145–76.

Himmelfarb, Gertrude. 1983. *The Idea of Poverty: England in the Early Industrial Age*. New York: Random House.

Hitchcock, Jeff. 2001. *Unraveling the White Cocoon*. New York: Kendall/Hunt.

Hochschild, Jennifer. 1995. *Facing Up to the American Dream: Race, Class, and the Soul of the Nation*. Princeton: Princeton University Press.

Hoetnik, H. 1985. " 'Race' and Color in the Caribbean." In *Caribbean Contours*, ed. Sidney Mintz and Sally Price. Baltimore: Johns Hopkins University Press.

Holden, Madronna. 1976. "Making All the Crooked Ways Straight." *Journal of American Folklore* 89, no. 353: 271–293.

Hollander, A. N. J. Den. 1934. "The Tradition of 'Poor Whites.'" In *Culture in the South*, ed. W. T Couch. Chapel Hill: University of North Carolina Press.

Holloway, Jonathan. 1990. *Africanisms in American Culture*. Bloomington: University of Indiana Press.

Holloway, Lynette. 2002. "The Angry Appeal of Eminem Is Cutting across Racial Lines." *New York Times*, October 28, p. 1.

Holly, Dan. 1993. "Move These People Out." *Detroit Free Press*, April 27, p. A3.

Holmes, Samuel. 1921. *The Trend of the Race: A Study of the Present Tendencies in the Biological Development of Civilized Mankind*. New York: Harcourt, Brace.

Holt, Thomas. 2000. *The Problem of Race in the Twenty-First Century*. Cambridge, Mass.: Harvard University Press.

hooks, bell. 1992. "Representing Whiteness in the Black Imagination." In *Cultural Studies*, ed. Lawrence Grossberg, Cary Nelson, and Paula Treichler. New York: Routledge.

Howell, Joseph. 1973. *Hard Living on Clay Street: Portraits of Blue Collar Families*. Garden City, N.Y.: Anchor.

Hughes, Mark Allen. "Misspeaking Truth to Power: A Geographical Perspective on the 'Underclass' Fallacy." *Economic Geography* 65, no. 3: 187–207.

Humphreys, Seth. 1913. "Parenthood and the Social Conscience: Who Shouldn't Be a Parent." *Forum*, April, pp. 457–64.

Hundley, D. R., Esq. 1860. *Social Relations in Our Southern States*. New York: Henry B. Price.

Hurley, Kelly. 1996. *The Gothic Body: Sexuality, Materialism, and Degeneration at the Fin de siecle*. Cambridge, England: Cambridge University Press.

Hyde, Cheryl. 1995. "The Meaning of Whiteness." *Qualitative Sociology* 18, no. 1: 87–95.

Jackson, Eileen. 1993. "Whiting-Out Difference: Why U.S. Nursing Research Fails Black Families." *Medical Anthropology Quarterly* 7, no. 4: 363–385.

Jackson, Peter, and Jan Penrose. 1993. *Constructions of Race, Place, and Nation*. Minneapolis: University of Minnesota Press.

Jacobs, Bruce. 1999. *Race Manners: Navigating the Minefield between Blacks and White Americans*. New York: Arcade.

Jacobson, Matthew. 1998. *Whiteness of a Different Color: European Immigrants and the Alchemy of Race*. Cambridge, Mass.: Harvard University Press.

Jameson, Fredric. 1981. *The Political Unconscious: Narrative as a Socially Symbolic Act.* Ithaca, N.Y.: Cornell University Press.

——. 1990. *Signatures of the Visible.* New York: Routledge.

Jamieson, Kathleen Hall. 1992. *Dirty Politics: Deception, Distraction, and Democracy.* New York: Oxford University Press.

Janis, Pam. 2001. "Of Gratitude and Platitudes: In Search of Civility in an Age of Indifference." *Washington Post*, August 12, p. B5.

JanMohamed, Abdul R., and David Lloyd. 1987. "Introduction: Minority Discourse—What Is to Be Done?" *Cultural Critique*, no. 7: 5–18.

Jargowsky, Paul. 2003. *Stunning Progress, Hidden Problems: The Dramatic Decline of Concentrated Poverty in the 1990s.* Washington, D.C.: Brookings Institution.

Jarosz, Lucy, and Victoria Lawson. 2002. "'Sophisticated People versus Rednecks': Economic Restructuring and Class Difference in America's West." *Antipode* 34, no. 1: 8–27.

Jefferies, Steve. 1989. "Matters of Mutual Interest: The Unionization Process at Dodge Main, 1930–1939." In *On the Line: Essays in the History of Artwork*, ed. Nelson Lichtenstein and Stephen Meyer. Urbana: University of Illinois Press.

Jefferson, Margo. 1988. "Slumming: Ain't We Got Fun." *Vogue*, March, 344–47.

Jencks, Christopher, and Paul Peterson, eds. 1991. *The Urban Underclass.* Washington, D.C.: Brookings Institution.

Jensen, Joli. 1998. *The Nashville Sound: Authenticity, Commercialization, and Country Music.* Nashville, Tenn.: Country Music Foundation and Vanderbilt University Press.

Jessen, Wade. 2000. "Country Corner." *Billboard* 112, no. 30: 60.

Jones, Gareth Stedman. 1984. *Outcast London: A Study in the Relationship between Classes in Victorian Society.* New York: Pantheon.

Jones, Jacqueline. 1993. *The Dispossessed: America's Underclass from the Civil War to the Present.* New York: Basic Books.

Kabel, Ans. 1996. "The Influence of Walter Pater in *Dr. Jekyll and Mr. Hyde* and *The Picture of Dorian Gray*." In *Beauty and the Beast: Christina Rossetti, Walter Pater, R. L. Stevenson and Their Contemporaries*, ed. Peter Tigges and Wim Liebregts. Amsterdam: Rodopi.

Kadi, Joanna. 1996. *Thinking Class: Sketches from a Cultural Worker.* Boston: South End.

Kammen, Michael. 1999. *American Culture, American Tastes: Social Change and the 20th Century.* New York: Knopf.

Kasson, John F. 1990. *Rudeness and Civility: Manners in Nineteenth-Century Urban America.* New York: Hill and Wang.

Katz, Judy. 1978. *White Awareness: Handbook for Anti-racism Training.* Norman: University of Oklahoma Press.

Katz, Michael. 1986. *In the Shadow of the Poorhouse: A Social History of Welfare in America.* New York: Basic Books.

———. 1993. *The "Underclass" Debate: Views from History.* Princeton: Princeton University Press.

Katzman, David. 1973. *Before the Ghetto: Black Detroit in the Nineteenth Century.* Urbana: University of Illinois Press.

Kefalas, Maria. 2003. *Working Class Heroes: Protecting Home, Community, and Nation in a Chicago Neighborhood.* Berkeley: University of California Press.

Kelley, Robin. 1997. *Yo' Mama's Disfunktional! Fighting the Culture Wars in Urban America.* Boston: Beacon.

Kelly, Michael. 2001. "Not-Us? Tough Luck." *Washington Post,* July 25, p. A21.

Kelso, Isaac. 1863. *The Stars and Bars, or, The Reign of Terror in Missouri.*

Kenny, Lorraine. 2000. *Daughters of Suburbia: Growing Up White, Middle Class, and Female.* New Brunswick, N.J.: Rutgers University Press.

Kevels, Daniel. 1985. *In the Name of Eugenics: Genetics and the Uses of Human Heredity.* Cambridge, Mass: Harvard University Press.

Kirke, Edmund [James Gilmore]. 1864. *Down in Tennessee, and Back by Way of Richmond.* New York: Carleton.

Kirkendall, Rebecca. 1995. "Who's a Hillbilly?" *Newsweek,* November 27, p. 22.

Kite, Elizabeth S. 1913. "The 'Pineys.'" *The Survey,* October 4, pp. 7–13, 31–33.

Kochman, Thomas. 1981. *Black and White Styles in Conflict.* Chicago: University of Chicago Press.

Kolchin, Peter. 2002. "Whiteness Studies: The New History of Race in America." *The Journal of American History* 89, no. 1: 154–173.

Kolker, Claudia. 2000. "Scrutiny Yielding a Clouded Picture, Texans Say." *Los Angeles Times,* October 25.

Kraft, Ronald. 1993. "This Gay House." *The Advocate,* August 24, pp. 56–59.

Kristeva, Julia. 1984. *The Revolution in Poetic Language.* Trans. Margaret Waller. New York: Columbia University Press.

Kroker, Arthur. 1994. *Data Trash: The Theory of the Virtual Class.* New York: St. Martin's.

Kuper, Adam. 1999. *Culture: The Anthropologists' Account.* Cambridge, Mass.: Harvard University Press.

Kushnick, Louis. 1995. "Racism and Anti-Racism in Western Europe." In *Racism and Anti-Racism,* ed. Benjamin Bowser. Thousand Oaks, Calif.: Sage.

Labov, Teresa. 1990. "Ideological Themes in Reports of Interracial Conflict." In *Conflict Talk: Sociolinguistic Investigations of Arguments in Conversations,* ed. Allen Grimshaw. Cambridge, England: Cambridge University Press.

Lamont, Michele. 1992. *Money, Morals, Manners: The Culture of the French and the American Upper-Middle Class.* Chicago: University of Chicago Press.

———. 2000. *The Dignity of Working Men.* Cambridge, Mass.: Harvard University Press.

Lane, Michael, and Jim Crotty. 1991. "Westwego Is Our Kind of Place: Pure White Trash." *The Advocate,* February 26, p. 79.

Laqueur, Thomas. 1989. "Bodies, Details, and the Humanitarian Narrative." In *The New Cultural History*, ed. Lynn Hunt. Berkeley: University of California Press.

Larson, Edward. 1995. *Sex, Race, and Science: Eugenics in the Deep South*. Baltimore: Johns Hopkins University Press.

Larson, Magali. 1977. *The Rise of Professionalism: A Sociological Analysis*. Berkeley: University of California Press.

Lasch-Quinn, Elisabeth. 2001. *Race Experts: How Racial Etiquette, Sensitivity Training, and New Age Therapy Hijacked the Civil Rights Revolution*. New York: Norton.

Lassalle, Yvonne, and Maureen O'Dougherty. 1997. "In Search of Weeping Worlds: Economies of Agency and Politics of Representation in the Ethnography of Inequality." *Radical History Review* 69: 243–260.

Lears, Jackson. 1994. *Fables of Abundance: A Cultural History of Advertising in America*. New York: Basic Books.

Lee, Harper. 1960. *To Kill a Mockingbird*. New York: Popular Library.

Lee, Jennifer. 2002. *Civility in the City: Blacks, Jews, and Koreans in Urban America*. Cambridge, Mass.: Harvard University Press.

Lemann, Nicholas. 1991. *The Promise Land: The Great Black Migration and How It Changed America*. New York: Vintage.

Levine, David Alan. 1976. *Internal Combustion: The Races in Detroit, 1915–1926*. Westwood, Conn.: Greenwood.

Levine-Rasky, Cynthia, ed. 2002. *Working Through Whiteness: International Perspectives*. Albany: State University of New York Press.

Lewis, Herbert. 1998. "Anthropology and Race, Then and Now." *American Anthropologist* 100, no. 4: 979–981.

Lewontin, Richard C., Steven Rose, and Leon J. Kamin. 1984. *Not in Our Genes*. New York: Parthenon.

Lieberman, Leonard. 1995. "An Attempted Revival of the Race Concept." *American Anthropologist* 97, no. 3: 590–592.

Lieberson, Stanley. 1985. "Unhyphenated Whites in the United States." In *Ethnicity and Race in the USA: Towards the Twenty-first Century*, ed. Richard Alba. Boston: Routledge and Kegan Paul.

Limon, Jose. 1998. *American Encounters: Greater Mexico, the United States, and the Erotics of Culture*. Boston: Beacon.

Lindsay, Matthew. 1998. "Reproducing a Fit Citizenry: Dependency, Eugenics, and the Law of Marriage in the United States, 1860–1920." *Law and Social Inquiry* 23, no. 3: 541–585.

Lipsitz, George. 1995. "The Progressive Investment in Whiteness: Racialized Social Democracy and the 'White' Problem in American Studies." *American Quarterly* 47, no. 3: 369–387.

Littman, Mark. 1991. "Poverty Areas and the 'Underclass': Untangling the Web." *Monthly Labor Review* 114, no. 3: 19–32.

Lopez, Steve. 2000. "A Visit to Bush Country." *Time* 155, no. 8: 36–38.

Lott, Eric. 1993. *Love and Theft: Blackface Minstrelsy and the American Working Class.* Oxford: Oxford University Press.

Lowe, Donald. 1982. *The History of Bourgeois Perception.* Chicago: University of Chicago Press.

Macleod, Jay. 1995. *Ain't No Making It: Leveled Aspirations in a Low-Income Neighborhood.* Boulder, Colo.: Westview.

Maharidge, Dale. 1996. *The Coming White Minority: California's Eruptions and America's Future.* New York: Times Books.

Malchow, H. L. 1996. *Gothic Images of Race in Nineteenth-Century Britain.* Stanford: Stanford University Press.

Malone. 1985. *Country Music, U.S.A.* Austin: University of Texas Press.

Malone, Bill. 2002. *Don't Get above Your Raisin': Country Music and the Southern Working Class.* Urbana: University of Illinois Press.

Maloney, Michael. 1987. "A Decade in Review: The Development of the Ethnic Model in Urban Appalachian Studies." In *Too Few Tomorrows: Urban Appalachians in the 1980s*, ed. Phillip Obermiller and William Philliber. Boone, N.C.: Appalachian Consortium Press.

Mank, Gregory. 1994. *Hollywood Cauldron: Thirteen Horror Films from the Genre's Golden Age.* Jefferson, N.C.: McFarland.

Marable, Manning. 2002. "Whither Whiteness." *Souls: A Critical Journal of Black Politics, Culture, and Society* 4, no. 4: 45–73.

Marchand, Nolan. 1997. "American Redneck Society." *Outdoor Life* 199, no. 1: 12.

Marcus, Greil. 1992. "Wholly Greil." Interview. *Metro* (April 30–May 6): 19–25.

Marez, Curtis. 1997. "The Other Addict: Reflections on Colonialism and Oscar Wilde's Opium Smoke Screen." *English Literary History* 64, no. 1: 257–287.

Margalit, Avishai, and Iam Buruma. 2002. "Occidentalism." *New York Review of Books*, January 17.

Marks, Jonathan. 2001. " 'We're Going to Tell These People Who They Really Are': Science and Relatedness." In *Relative Values: Reconfiguring Kinship Studies*, ed. Sarah Franklin and Susan McKinnon. Durham, N.C.: Duke University Press.

Marriott, John. 1999. "In the Darkest England: The Poor, the Crowd, and Race in the Nineteenth-Century Metropolis." In *New Ethnicities, Old Racisms?*, ed. Phil Cohen. London: Zed.

Marston, Sallie. 1989. "Public Rituals and Community Power: St. Patrick's Day Parade in Lowell, Massachusetts, 1841–1874." *Political Geography Quarterly* 8, no. 3 (July): 255–269.

Martin, Catherine. 1996. "Educating to Combat Racism: The Civic Pole of Anthropology." *Anthropology and Education Quarterly* 27, no. 2: 253–269.

Martin, Emily. 1987. *The Woman in the Body: A Cultural Analysis of Reproduction.* Boston: Beacon Press.

Marty, Debian. 1999. "White Antiracist Rhetoric as Apologia: Wendell Berry's *The*

Hidden Wound." In *Whiteness: The Communication of Social Identity*, ed. Thomas Nakayama and Judith Martin. Thousand Oaks, Calif.: Sage.

Massey, Douglas, and Nancy Denton. 1993. *American Apartheid: Segregation and the Making of the Underclass.* Cambridge, Mass.: Harvard University Press.

Masters, Edgar Lee. 1915/1962. *Spoon River Anthology.* New York: Macmillan.

Matthews, Glenna. 1987. *"Just a Housewife": The Rise and Fall of Domesticity in America.* New York: Oxford University Press.

Maxwell, Andrew. 1993. "The Underclass, 'Social Isolation' and 'Concentration Effects.'" *Critique of Anthropology* 13, no. 3: 231–245.

McCaskell, Tim. 1995. "Anti-Racist Education and Practice in the Public School System." In *Beyond Political Correctness: Towards the Inclusive University*, ed. Stephen Richer and Lorna Weir. Toronto: University of Toronto Press.

McClellan, Catharine. 1970. "Indian Stories about the First Whites in Northwestern America." In *Ethnohistory in Southwestern Alaska and the Southern Yukon: Methods and Content*, ed. Margaret Lantis et al. Lexington: University of Kentucky Press.

McCulloch, Oscar. 1888. "The Tribe of Ishmael: A Study in Social Degradation." In *White Trash: The Eugenics Family Study, 1877–1919*, ed. Nicole Rafter. Boston: Northeastern University Press.

McIlwaine, Shirley. 1939. *The Southern Poor-White: From Lubberland to Tobacco Road.* Norman: University of Oklahoma Press.

McIntosh, Peggy. 1989. "White Privilege: Unpacking the Invisible Knapsack." *Peace and Freedom* (July–August): 10–12.

McIntyre, Alice. 1997. *Making Meaning of Whiteness: Exploring Racial Identity with White Teachers.* Albany: State University of New York Press.

McPherson, Tara. 2000. "I'll Take My Stand in Dixie-Net: White Guys, the South, and Cyberspace." In *Race in Cyberspace*, ed. Lisa Nakamura, Beth Kolko, and Gilbert Rodman. London: Routledge.

McWhiney, Grady. 1988. *Cracker Culture: Celtic Ways in the Old South.* Tuscaloosa: University of Alabama Press.

Mead, Andy. 1995. "An Invisible Minority: Appalachians Find Prejudice Awaiting in Urban Settings." *Dallas Morning News*, March 13, p. A11.

Mears, J. E. 1910. *The Problem of Race Betterment.* Philadelphia: William J. Dornan.

Meehan, Mary. 1997. "Eugenics and the Power Elite." *Social Justice Review* 88, no. 11/12: 167–170.

Mehta, Uday. 1999. *Liberalism and Empire: A Study in Nineteenth-Century British Liberal Thought.* Chicago: University of Chicago Press.

Meirer, August, and Elliot Ruwick. 1979. *Black Detroit and the Rise of the UAW.* New York: Oxford University Press.

Memmi, Albert. 2000. *Racism.* Minneapolis: University of Minnesota Press.

Mencken, H. L. 1919/2000. *The American Language: An Inquiry into the Development of English in the United States.* New York: Knopf.

——. 1920. *Prejudices: Second Series.* New York: Knopf.

Merrill, Maud A. 1918. "Minnesota's Heritage: From the Mountaineers of the South." *The Survey*, August 17, pp. 562–564.

Merry, Sally. 1981. *Urban Danger: Life in a Neighborhood of Strangers*. Philadelphia: Temple University Press.

Michaels, Walter Benn. 1992. "Race into Culture: A Critical Genealogy of Cultural Identity." *Critical Inquiry* 18 (summer): 655–685.

Miles, Robert. 1989. *Racism*. London: Routledge.

———. 1993. *Racism after "Race Relations."* London: Routledge.

Miles, Robert, and Rudy Torres. 1996. "Does 'Race' Matter? Transatlantic Perspectives on Racism after 'Race Relations.' " In *Re-Situating Identities: The Politics of Race, Ethnicity, Culture*, ed. Vered Amit-Talai and Caroline Knowles. Petersborough, Ontario: Broadview.

Millard, Bailey. "Are You Fit to Marry?" *Technical World Magazine*, no. 20: 329–37.

Miller, Herbert Adolphus. 1914. "The Psychological Limit of Eugenics." *Popular Science Monthly*, April, pp. 390–396.

Miller, William Ian. 1997. *The Anatomy of Disgust*. Cambridge, Mass.: Harvard University Press.

Mincy, Roland, Isabel Sawhill, and Douglas Wolf. 1990. "The Underclass: Definition and Measures." *Science* (April): 450–453.

Mitchell, Margaret. 1936/1973. *Gone With the Wind*. New York: Avon.

Moffatt, Michael. 1986. "The Discourse of the Dorm." In *Symbolizing America*, ed. Herve Varenne. Lincoln: University of Nebraska Press.

Mohanty, Chandra. 1989–90. "On Race and Voice: Challenges for Liberal Education in the 1990s." *Cultural Critique* 14 (winter): 179–208.

Montgomery, David. 1993. *Citizen Worker: The Experience of Workers in the United States with Democracy and the Free Market during the Nineteenth Century*. Cambridge, England: Cambridge University Press.

Moore, Henrietta. 1996. *The Future of Anthropological Knowledge*. London: Routledge.

Moore, Solomon, and Robin Fields. 2002. "The Great 'White' Influx." *Los Angeles Times*, July 31, pp. 1A.

Morago, Greg. 2001. "Summer of Shame." *Hartford Courant*, August 2, p. D1.

Morrison, Toni. 1992. *Playing in the Dark: Whiteness and the Literary Imagination*. Cambridge, Mass.: Harvard University Press.

Moss, Kenneth. 1985. "Why Should We Care for a Little Trouble or a Walk through Mud: St. Patrick's and Columbus Day Parades in Worcester, Massachusetts." *New England Quarterly* 58, no. 1 (March): 5–26.

———. 1995. "St. Patrick's Day Celebrations and the Formation of Irish-American Identity, 1845–1875." *Journal of Social History* 29, no. 1: 125–148.

Moss, Kirby. 2003. *The Color of Class: Poor Whites and the Paradox of Privilege*. Philadelphia: University of Pennsylvania Press.

Murray, Charles. 1986. "White Welfare, White Families, 'White Trash.' " *National Review* 38, no. 5: 5–10.

——. 1993. "The Coming White Underclass." *Wall Street Journal*, October 29, p. A14.

Myrdal, Gunnar. 1963. *Challenge to Affluence.* New York: Pantheon.

Nader, Laura. 1969. "Up the Anthropologist—Perspectives Gained from Studying Up." In *Reinventing Anthropology*, ed. Dell Hymes. New York: Pantheon.

Nearing, Nellie, and M. L. Scott. 1912. "When a Girl Is Asked to Marry." *Ladies' Home Journal*, March, n.p.

Nelson, Dana. 1992. *The Word in Black and White: Reading "Race" in American Literature 1638–1867.* New York: Oxford University Press.

Newby, Idus A. 1989. *Plain Folk in the New South: Social Change and Cultural Persistence, 1880–1915.* Baton Rouge: Louisiana State University Press.

Nixon, Mojo. 1990. "Mojo Nixon: Rock's Joker with a Social Conscience." Interview. *San Jose Mercury News*, October 12, pp. 1E, 16E.

Nobles, Melissa. 2000. *Shades of Citizenship: Race and the Census in Modern Politics.* Stanford: Stanford University Press.

Nowicka, Ewa. 1984. "Through American Indian Eyes: The Image of the White Man and White Culture among North American Indians." *North American Indian Studies* 2: 190–203.

Nye, Robert A. 1993. "The Rise and Fall of the Eugenics Empire." *Historical Journal* 36, no. 3: 687–700.

Obermiller, Philip, and William Philiber. 1987. *Too Few Tomorrows: Urban Appalachians in the 1980's.* Boone, N.C.: Appalachian Consortium Press.

O'Connor, Alice. 2001. *Poverty Knowledge: Social Science, Social Policy, and the Poor in Twentieth-Century U.S. History.* Princeton: Princeton University Press.

O'Day, Rosemary. 1989. "Retrieved Riches: Charles Booth's Life and Labor of the People in London." *History Today* (April): 29–35.

"Oklahoma Governor Criticized: Keating's 'Trash' Talk Labeled as Offensive." 1999. *Dallas Morning News*, November 13, p. A32.

Olmsted, Frederick Law. 1857. *A Journey through Texas: Or, A Saddle-trip on the Southwestern Frontier.* London: S. Low.

Omi, Michael, and Howard Winant. 1986. *Racial Formations in the United States: From the 1960's to the 1980's.* New York: Routledge.

O'Nell, Theresa. 1994. "Telling About Whites, Talking About Indians: Oppression, Resistance, and Contemporary American Indian Identity." *Cultural Anthropology* 9, no. 1: 94–126.

O'Rourke, P. J. 2001. "Who the Heck Are These People?" *Forbes*, March 5, 90.

Ortner, Sherry, ed. 1999. *The Fate of "Culture": Geertz and Beyond.* Berkeley: University of California Press.

——. 2003. *New Jersey Dreaming: Capital, Culture, and the Class of '58.* Durham, N.C.: Duke University Press.

Ott, Katherine. 1996. *Fevered Lives: Tuberculosis in American Culture since 1870.* Cambridge, Mass.: Harvard University Press.

Page, Clarence. 1993. "The Growth of a White Underclass May Finally Move America to Act." *Detroit Free Press*, November 1, 13A.

Page, Helan. 1995. "North American Dialogue [Interview]." *Anthropology Newletter* (January): 21.

Page, Helan, and R. Brooke Thomas. 1994. "White Public Space and the Construction of White Privilege in U.S. Health Care: Fresh Concepts and a New Model of Analysis." *Medical Anthropology Quarterly* 8, no. 1: 109–116.

Pappas, Ben. 1999. "Transparent Eyeball." *Forbes* 164, no. 1: 45.

Park, Kyeyoung. 1996. "Use and Abuse of Race and Culture: Black-Korean Tensions in America." *American Anthropologist* 98, no. 3: 492–505.

Parry, Gareth. 1984: "Anti-Racist Anthropology." *Royal Anthropological Institute Newsletter (RAIN)*, 3–4.

Pasternak, Judy. 1994. "Bias Blights Life outside of Appalachia." *Los Angeles Times*, March 29, p. A1.

Pearlman, Jeff. 1999. "At Full Blast." *Sports Illustrated*, December 27, p. 60.

Perry, Pamela. 2002. *Shades of White: White Kids and Racial Identities in High School.* Durham, N.C.: Duke University Press.

Peterson, Paul. 1991. "The Urban Underclass and the Poverty Paradox." *Political Science Quarterly* 106, no. 4: 617–637.

Peterson, Richard. 1992. "Class Unconscious in Country Music." In *You Wrote My Life: Lyrical Themes in Country Music*, ed. Melton A. McLaurin and Richard A. Peterson. Philadelphia: Gordon and Breach.

———. 1997. *Creating Country Music: Fabricating Authenticity.* Chicago: University of Chicago Press.

Pfeil, Fred. 1990. *Another Tale to Tell. Politics and Narrative in Postmodern Culture.* London: Verso.

Philliber, William. 1981. *Appalachian Migrants in Urban America: Cultural Group or Ethnic Group Formation?* New York: Praeger.

Philliber, William, and Clyde McCoy, eds. 1981. *The Invisible Minority: Urban Appalachians.* Lewisville: University Press of Kentucky.

Piersen, William. 1993. *Black Legacy: America's Hidden Heritage.* Amherst: University of Massachusetts Press.

Plotnikoff, David. 1990. "Mojo Nixon: Rock's Joker with a Social Conscience." *San Jose Mercury News*, October 12, 1E.

Polk, William. 1912. "The Practical Application of Eugenics." *Good Housekeeping* 55, 131–33.

Popkin, Susan, et al. 2000. *The Hidden War: Crime and the Tragedy of Public Housing in Chicago.* New Brunswick, N.J.: Rutgers University Press.

Powdermaker, Hortense. 1939/1968. *After Freedom: A Cultural Study in the Deep South.* New York: Russell and Russell.

Premdas, Ralph. 1995. "Racism and Anti-Racism in the Caribbean." In *Racism and Anti-Racism in World Perspective*, ed. Benjamin Browser. Thousand Oaks, Calif.: Sage.

Rabinowitz, Howard. 1992. *The First New South, 1865–1920.* Arlington Heights, Ill.: Harlan Davidson.

———. 1994. *Race, Ethnicity, and Urbanization*. Coumbia: University of Missouri Press.

Rafter, Nicole, ed. 1988. *White Trash: The Eugenics Family Studies, 1877–1919*. Boston: Northeastern University Press.

Rahier, Jean Muteba, ed. 1999. *Representations of Blackness and the Performance of Identities*. Westport, Conn..: Bergin and Garvey.

Rainwater, Lee, and William Yancey. 1967. *The Moynihan Report and the Politics of Controversy*. Cambridge, Mass.: MIT Press.

Rapp, Rayna. 1999. *Testing Women, Testing the Fetus: The Social Impact of Amniocentesis in America*. New York: Routledge.

Rebel, Hermann. 1989a. "Cultural Hegemony and Class Experience: A Critical Reading of Recent Ethnological-historical Approaches. Part 1." *American Ethnologist* 16, no. 1: 117–136.

———. 1989b. "Cultural Hegemony and Class Experience: A Critical Reading of Recent Ethnological-historical Approaches. Part 2." *American Ethnologist* 16, no. 2: 350–365.

Reed, Adolph, Jr. 2000a. *Class Notes: Posing as Politics and Other Thoughts on the American Scene*. New York: New Press.

———. 2000b *Stirrings in the Jug: Black Politics in the Post-segregation Era*. Minneapolis: University of Minnesota Press.

Reilly, Philip. 1991. *The Surgical Solution: A History of Involuntary Sterilization in the United States*. Baltimore: Johns Hopkins University Press.

Rich, Frank. 2002. "Mr. Ambassador." *New York Times*, November 3, p. 52.

Ricketts, Erol, and Isabel Sawhill. 1988. "Defining and Measuring the Underclass." *Journal of Policy Analysis and Management* 7, no. 2: 316–325.

Rieder, Jonathan. 1985. *Canarsie: The Jews and Italians of Brooklyn against Liberalism*. Cambridge, Mass.: Harvard University Press.

Rodriguez, Clara. 2000. *Changing Race: Latinos, the Census, and the History of Ethnicity in the United States*. New York: New York University Press.

Roediger, David. 1992. *The Wages of Whiteness: Race and the Making of the American Working Class*. New York: Verso.

———. 1994. *Towards the Abolition of Whiteness*.

———, ed. 1998. *Black on White: Black Writers on What It Means to Be White*. New York: Schocken.

———. 2002. *Colored White: Transcending the Racial Past*. Berkeley: University of California Press.

Rosaldo, Renato. 1994. "Whose Cultural Studies?" *American Anthropologist* 96: 524–529.

Rose, Dan. 1987. *Black American Street Life*. Philadelphia: University of Pennsylvania Press.

Rose, Harold, and Donald Deskin. 1991. "The Link between Black Teen Pregnancy and Economic Restucturing in Detroit: A Neighborhood Scale Analysis." *Urban Geography* 12, no. 6: 508–525.

Rosenberg, Charles. 1974. "The Bitter Fruit: Heredity, Disease, and Social Thought in Nineteenth-century America." *Perspectives in American History* 3: 189–235.

Rushton, J. Phillippe. 1995. *Race, Evolution, and Behavior: A Life History in Perspective.* New Brunswick, N.J.: Transaction.

Ryan, Patrick J. 1997. "Unnatural Selection: Intelligence Testing, Eugenics, and American Political Cultures." *Journal of Social History* 30: 669–685.

Rydell, Robert. 1993. *World of Fairs: The Century of Progress Expositions.* Chicago: University of Chicago Press.

Sacks, Karen. 1989. "Towards a Unified Theory of Class, Race, Politics, and the Working Class." *American Ethnologist* 16: 534–550.

Said, Edward. 1978. *Orientalism.* New York: Vintage.

Saito, Leland. 1998. *Race and Politics: Asian Americans, Latinos, and Whites in a Los Angeles Suburb.*

Sanjeck, Roger. 1998. *The Future of Us All: Race and Neighborhood Politics in New York City.* Ithaca, N.Y.: Cornell University Press.

Sanlon, Jennifer. 1995. *Inarticulate Longings: The* Ladies Home Journal, *Gender, and the Promises of Consumer Culture.* New York: Routledge.

Sansone, Livio. 1994. "The Making of Black Culture: The New Subculture of Lower-class Young Black Males of Surinamese Origin in Amsterdam." *Critique of Anthropology* 14, no. 2: 173–198.

———. 2003. *Blackness without Ethnicity: Constructing Race in Brazil.* New York: Palgrave Macmillan.

Santiago, Roberto. 2001. "Lizzie's Trash Talk Offends." *Daily News,* July 28, p. 17.

Sawhill, Isabel. 1989. "The Underclass: An Overview." *Public Interest* 96: 3–15.

Saxton, Alexander. 1990. *The Rise and Fall of the White Republic: Class Politics and Mass Culture in Nineteenth-Century America.* London: Verso.

Schauer, Frederick. 2003. *Profiles, Probabilities, and Stereotypes.* Cambridge, Mass.: Belknap.

Schele De Vere, Maximillian. 1872. *Americanisms: The English of the New World.* New York: Scribner.

Scherman, Tony. 1994. "Country." *American Heritage* 45, no. 7: 38–52.

Schlesinger, Arthur. 1946. *Learning How to Behave: A Historical Study of American Etiquette Books.* New York: Macmillan.

Schneider, David, and Raymond Smith. 1973. *Class Differences and Sex Roles in American Kinship and Family Structure.* Englewood Cliffs, N.J.: Prentice-Hall.

Schocket, Eric. 1998. "Undercover Explorations of the 'Other Half,' Or, The Writer as Class Transvestite." *Representations* 64: 109–133.

Searle-Chatterjee, Mary. 1987. "The Anthropologist Exposed: Anthropologists in Multi-Cultural and Anti-Racist Work." *Anthropology Today* 3, no. 4: 16–18.

Seeger, Charles. 1946. "Conference on Folklore." *Journal of American Folklore,* no. 59: 512–21.

Sefa Dei, George. 1996. "Critical Perspectives in Antiracism: An Introduction." *The Canadian Review of Sociology and Anthropology* 33: 247–67.

Segal, Daniel. 1993. " 'Race' and 'Color' in Pre-Independence Trinidad and Tobago." In *Trinidad Ethnicity*, ed. Kevin Yelvington. Knoxville: University of Tennessee Press.

Selden, Steve. 1999. *Inheriting Shame: The Story of Eugenics and Racism in America.* Advances in Contemporary Educational Thought Series, vol. 23. New York: Teachers College Press.

Self, Will. 2002. *Dorian: An Imitation.* New York: Grove.

Shanklin, Eugenia. 1999. "The Profession of the Color Blind: Sociocultural Anthropology and Racism in the 21st Century." *American Anthropologist* 100, no. 3: 669–679.

Sharff, Jagna. 1998. *King Kong on 4th Street: Families and the Violence of Poverty on the Lower East Side.* Boulder, Colo.: Westview Press.

Shaw, Carolyn Martin. 1995. *Race, Sex, and Class in Kenya.* Minneapolis: University of Minnesota Press.

Shelton, Frank. 1988. "The Poor Whites' Perspective: Harry Crews among Georgia Writers." *Journal of American Culture* 11, no. 3: 47–50.

Sheriff, Robin. 2001. *Dreaming Equality: Color, Race, and Racism in Urban Brazil.* New Brunswick, N.J.: Rutgers University Press.

Showalter, Elaine. 1999. "Dr Jekyll's Closet." In *The Haunted Mind*, ed. Elton Smith and Robert Haas. Lanham, Md.: Scarecrow.

Simon, Stephanie. 2001. "It May Be Hillbilly, but These Kids Love Their Mountain Music." *Los Angeles Times*, March 29, A5.

Sivanandan, A. 1985. "RAT and the Degradation of Black Struggle." *Race and Class* 26, no. 4: 1–33.

Skerry, Peter. 2000. *Counting on the Census? Race, Group Identity, and the Evasion of Politics.* Washington, D.C.: Brookings Institution.

Smedley, Audrey. 1993. *Race in North America: Origins and Evolution of a World View.* Boulder, Colo.: Westview Press.

Smith, Elton, and Robert Haas, eds. 1999. *The Haunted Mind: The Supernatural in Victorian Literature.* Lanham, Md.: Scarecrow.

Smith, J. David. 1985. *Minds Made Feeble: The Myth and Legacy of the Kallikaks.* Rockville, Md.: Aspen.

Sokefeld, Martin. 1999. "Debating Self, Identity, and Culture in Anthropology." *Current Anthropology* 40, no. 4: 417–447.

Sollors, Werner. 1986. *Beyond Ethnicity: Consent and Descent in American Culture.* New York: Oxford University Press.

Solomon, Patrick, and Cynthia Levine-Rasky. 1996. "Transfroming Teacher Education for an Antiracism Pedagogy." *Canadian Review of Sociology and Anthropology* 33: 337–359.

Southeast Michigan Census Council. 1993. 1990 Census Subcommunity Profiles for the City of Detroit. October. Available at: Detroit Public Library.

Spears, Arthur. 1991. "Teaching Race, Racism, and Ideology." *Transforming Anthropology* 2, no. 1: 16–21.

Spindler, Amy. 1993. "Trash Fash." *New York Times*, September 12, 10.

Spivak, Gayatri. 1988. "Can the Subaltern Speak?" In *Marxism and the Interpretation of Culture*, ed. Lawrence Grossberg and Cary Nelson. Urbana: University of Illinois Press.

——. 1999. *A Critique of Postcolonial Reason: Toward a History of the Vanishing Present*. Cambridge, Mass.: Harvard University Press.

Srivasta, Sarita. 1994. "Voyeurism and Vulnerability: Critiquing the Power Relations of Anti-Racist Education." *Canadian Woman Studies* 14, no. 2: 105–109.

Stack, Carol. 1974. *All Our Kin*. New York: Harper and Row.

Stallybras, Peter, and Allon White. 1981. *The Politics and Poetics of Transgression*. Ithaca, N.Y.: Cornell University Press.

——. 1986. *The Politics and Poetics of Transgression*. London: Methuen.

Stanley, Amy Dru. 1998. *From Bondage to Contract: Wage Labor, Marriage, and the Market in the Age of Slave Emancipation*. Cambridge, England: Cambridge University Press.

Stassinos, Elizabeth. "Response to K. Visweswaran, 'Race and the Culture of Anthropology.'" *American Anthropologist* 100, no. 4 (1998): 981–983.

Stepan, Nancy. 1985. "Medicine and Degeneration." In *Degeneration: The Dark Side of Progress*, ed. Edward Chamberlin. New York: Columbia University Press.

Stevenson, Robert Louis. 1886/1985. *Dr. Jekyll and Mr. Hyde*. New York: Bantam.

Stewart, Kathleen. 1991. "On the Politics of Cultural Critique: A Case for 'Contaminated' Critique." *Social Research* 58, no. 2: 395–412.

——. 1996. *A Space on the Side of the Road: Cultural Politics in an "Other" America*. Princeton: Princeton University Press.

Stirling, James. 1857. *Letters from the Slave States*. London: J. W. Parker.

Stoddard, Lothrop. 1920. *The Rising Tide of Color*. New York: Scribner.

——. 1922. *Revolt against Civilization: The Menace of the Under Man*. New York: Scribner.

——. 1925. "Worthwhile Americans." *Saturday Evening Post*, January 17, p. 23.

Stoler, Ann. 1995. *Race and the Education of Desire: Foucault's History of Sexuality and the Colonial Order of Things*. Durham, N.C.: Duke University Press.

Stone, Nancy, and Roberts Grey. 1976. *White Trash: An Anthology of Contemporary Southern Poets*. Charlotte, N.C.: New South.

Storrs, Debbie. 1999. "Whiteness as Stigma: Essentialist Identity Work by Mixed-Race Women." *Symbolic Interaction* 22, no. 3: 187–212.

Strathern, Marilyn. 1991. *Partial Connections*. Savage, Md.: Rowman and Littlefield.

Street, Brian. 1987. "Anti-Racist Education and Anthropology." *Anthropology Today* 3, no. 6: 13–15.

Streicker, Joel. 1995. "Policing Boundaries: Race, Class, and Gender in Cartagena, Colombia." *American Ethnologist* 22, no. 1: 54–74.

Strong, Pauline Turner, and Barrik Van Winkle. 1993. "Tribe and Nation: American Indians and American Nationalism." *Social Analysis: Journal of Cultural and Social Practice*, no. 33: 9–26.

Sugrue, Thomas. 1994. "Origins of Urban Crisis: Housing and Development in Detroit, 1940–1960." Ph.D. diss., Princeton University.

Tapper, Melbourne. 1999. *In the Blood: Sickle Cell Anemia and the Politics of Race, Philadelphia*. Philadelphia: University of Pennsylvania Press, 1999.

Theweliet, Klaus. 1987. *Male Fantasies: Women, Floods, Bodies, History*. Vol. 1. Minneapolis: University of Minnesota Press.

———. 1989. *Male Fantasies: Male Bodies. Psychoanalyzing the White Terror*. Vol. 2. Minneapolis: University of Minnesota Press.

Thomas, Richard. 1992. *Life for Us Is What We Make It: Building Black Community in Detroit, 1915–1945*. Bloomington: Indiana University Press.

Thompson, Hunter S. 1967. *Hell's Angels*. New York: Ballantine.

Thompson, John. 1984. *Studies in the Theory of Ideology*. Berkeley: University of California Press.

———. 1988. *Generation of Swine: Tales of Shame and Degradation in the '80s*. New York: Vintage.

Thompson, Michael. 1979. *Rubbish Theory: The Creation and Destruction of Value*. Oxford: Oxford University Press.

Todorov, Tzvetan. 1981. *Introduction to Poetics*. Minneapolis: University of Minnesota Press.

———. 1984. *The Conquest of America: The Question of the Other*. New York: Harper and Row.

Torres, Arlene. 1998. "From Jibara to Anthropologist: Puerto Rican Ethnography and the Politics of Representation." *Identities* 5, no. 1: 107–122.

Traweek, Sharon. 1988. *Beamtimes and Lifetimes: The World of High-Energy Particle Physics*. Cambridge: Harvard University Press.

Trouillot, Michel-Rolph. 2002. "Adieu, Culture: A New Duty Arises." In *Anthropology beyond Culture*, ed. Richard Fox. Oxford: Berg.

Twine, Frances Winddance. 1998. *Racism in a Racial Democracy: The Maintenance of White Supremacy in Brazil*. New Brunswick, N.J.: Rutgers University Press.

Tylor, Peter. 1977. "'Denied the Power to Choose the Good': Sexuality and Mental Defect in American Medical Practice." *Journal of Social History* 4: 474–490.

Uriciuoli, Bonnie. 1996. *Exposing Prejudice: Puerto Rican Experiences of Language, Race, and Class*. Boulder, Colo.: Westview.

Valentine, Charles. 1968. *Culture and Poverty: Critique and Counter-Proposals*. Chicago: University of Chicago Press.

Van den Berghe, Pierre. 1997. "Rehabilitating Stereotypes." *Ethnic and Racial Studies* 20: 1–16.

Varenne, Herve. 1986. *Symbolizing America*. Lincoln: University of Nebraska Press.

Veeder, William, and Gordon Hirsch, eds. 1988. *Dr. Jekyll and Mr. Hyde after One Hundred Years*. Chicago: University of Chicago Press.

Venkatesh, Sudhir. 2000. *American Project: The Rise and Fall of a Modern Ghetto*. Cambridge, Mass.: Harvard University Press.

Vergara, Camilo Jose. 1992. "Detriot Waits for the Millennium." *The Nation*, May 18, pp. 660–664.

——. 1995. *The New American Ghetto*. New Brunswick, N.J.: Rutgers University Press.

Vincent, Joan. 1993. "Framing the Underclass." *Critique of Anthropology* 13, no. 3: 215–230.

Virilio, Paul. 1991. *Lost Dimension*. New York: Semiotext(e).

Visweswaran, Kamala. 1998. "Race and the Culture of Anthropology." *American Anthropologist* 100, no. 1: 70–83.

Wade, Peter. 1993. *Blackness and Race Mixture: The Dynamics of Racial Identity in Columbia*. Baltimore: Johns Hopkins University Press.

——. 1997. *Race and Ethnicity in Latin America*. London: Pluto.

——. 1999. "Working Culture: Making Cultural Identities in Cali, Colombia." *Current Anthropology* 40, no. 4: 449–71.

——. 2002. *Race, Nature and Culture: An Anthropological Perspective*. London: Pluto.

Walcott, Rinaldo. 1990. "Theorizing Anti-Racist Education: Decentering White Supremacy in Education." *Western Canadian Anthropologist* 7, nos. 1–2: 109–120.

Walkowitz, Daniel. 1999. *Working with Class: Social Workers and the Politics of Middle-Class Identity*. Chapel Hill: University of North Carolina Press.

Walkowitz, Judith R. 1992. *City of Dreadful Delight: Narratives of Sexual Danger in Late-Victorian London*. Chicago: University of Chicago Press.

Walters, Ronald. 1974. *Primers for Prudery: Sexual Advice to Victorian Americans*. Englewood Cliffs, N.J.: Prentice-Hall.

Ward, David. 1989. *Poverty, Ethnicity, and the American City, 1840–1925: Changing Conceptions of the Slum and the Ghetto*. Cambridge, England: Cambridge University Press.

Ware, Vron, and Les Black. 2002. *Out of Whiteness: Color, Politics, and Culture*. Chicago: University of Chicago Press.

Warren, Jonathan. 2001. *Racial Revolutions: Antiracism and Indian Resurgence in Brazil*. Durham, N.C.: Duke University Press.

Wartofsky, Alona. 1999. "Eminem's Hard Shell." *Washington Post*, July 27, p. C1.

Waugh, Linda. 1982. "Marked and Unmarked: A Choice between Unequals in Semiotic Structure." *Semiotica* 38, nos. 3–4: 299–318.

Weismantel, Mary. 2001. *Cholas and Pishtacos: Stories of Race and Sex in the Andes*. Chicago: University of Chicago Press.

Wellman, David. 1993. *Portraits of White Racism*. 2nd ed. Cambridge, England: Cambridge University Press.

Weston, George. 1856. *The Poor Whites of the South*. Washington, D.C.: Buell and Blanchard, printers.

Weston, Kath. 2001. "Kinship, Controversy, and the Sharing of Substance: The Race/Class Politics of Blood Transfusion." In *Relative Values: Reconfiguring Kinship Studies*, ed. Sarah Franklin and Susan McKinnon. Durham, N.C.: Duke University Press.

White, Hayden. 1978. "The Forms of Wildness: Archeology of an Idea." In *Tropics of Discourse: Essays in Cultural Criticism*. Baltimore: Johns Hopkins University Press.

———. 1999. *Figural Realism: Studies in the Mimesis Effect.* Baltimore: Johns Hopkins University Press.

Whitley, David. 2004. "Anti-Redneck PR Puts NASCAR in Alternate Universe." *Austin American-Statesman,* March 31, p. D2.

Whitten, Norman, and Arlene Torres, eds. 1998. *Blackness in Latin America and the Carribbean: Social Dynamics and Cultural Transformations.* Bloomington: Indiana University Press.

Wilde, Oscar. 1891/1974. *The Picture of Dorian Gray.* New York: Dell.

Will, George. 1993. "America Must Get Much Tougher to Discourage Illegitimate Births." *Detroit Free Press,* November 18, p. 15A.

Williams, Brackette. 1989. "A Class Act: Anthropology and the Race to Nation across Ethnic Terrain." *Annual Review of Anthropology* 18: 401–444.

———. 1991. *Stains on My Name, War in My Veins: Guyana and the Politics of Cultural Struggle.* Durham, N.C.: Duke University Press.

———. 1995. "Classification Systems Revisited: Kinship, Caste, Race, and Nationality as the Flow of Blood and the Spread of Rights." In *Naturalizing Power: Essays in Feminist Cultural Analysis,* ed. Carol Delaney. London: Routledge.

Williams, Brett. 1988. *Upscaling Downtown: Stalled Gentrification in Washington, D.C.* Ithaca, N.Y.: Cornell University Press.

Williams, Lena. 2000. *It's the Little Things: Everyday Interactions That Anger, Annoy, and Divide the Races.* New York: Harcourt.

Williams, Terry. 1989. *The Cocaine Kids: The Inside Story of a Teenage Drug Ring.* Reading, Mass.: Addison-Wesley.

Williamson, Joel. 1984. *Crucible of Race: Black and White Relations in the American South Since the End of Emancipation.* New York: Oxford University Press.

Wilson, Carter. 1992. "Restructuring and the Growth of Concentrated Poverty in Detroit." *Urban Affairs Quartely* 28, no. 2: 187–205.

Wilson, Jacqueline. 2002. "Invisible Racism: The Language and Ontology of 'White Trash.'" *Critique of Anthropology* 22, no. 4: 387–401.

Wilson, William Julius. 1978. *The Declining Significance of Race: Blacks and Changing American Institutions.* Chicago: University of Chicago.

———. 1987. *The Truly Disadvantaged: The Inner City, the Underclass, and Public Policy.* Chicago: University of Chicago Press.

Winant, Howard. 1994. *Racial Conditions: Politics, Theory, Comparisons.* Minneapolis: University of Minnesota Press.

Winship, A. E. 1900. *Jukes-Edwards: A Study in Education and Heredity.* Harrisburg, Pa.: R. L. Myers.

Wouters, Cas. 1995. "Etiquette Books and Emotion Management in the 20th Century: Part One—Integration of Social Classes." *Journal of Social History* 29, no. 1: 107–124.

Wray, Matt. 2000. "Not Quite White: Poor Rural Whites in the Southern United States, 1877–1927." Ph.D. diss., University of California, Berkeley.

Wray, Matt, and Annalee Newitz, eds. 1997. *White Trash: Race and Class in America.* New York: Routledge.

Wright, Erik Olin. 1985. *Classes.* London: Verso.

Wright, Winthrop. 1990. *Cafe Con Leche: Race, Class, and National Image in Venezuela.* Austin: University of Texas Press.

Zenderland, Leila. 1998. *Measuring Minds: Henry Herbert Goddard and the Origins of American Intelligence Testing.* Cambridge, England: Cambridge University Press.

Zunz, Oliver. 1982. *The Changing Face of Inequality: Urbanization, Industrial Development, and Immigrants in Detroit, 1880–1920.* Chicago: University of Chicago Press.

INDEX

Abbott, John, 64, 68–69
Abu-Lughod, Lila, 259, 261, 276
Activists, 1, 4, 8, 13
Adoption, 222–223
Aesthetics, 121, 161, 323–324 n.14
Afrocentrism, 239
Alexander, Jack, 192
Allison, Dorothy, 126–127, 132
Ambiguity, 7, 144, 227, 232, 241, 247–249, 252, 255
American culture, 14, 56, 109, 162, 171, 258, 277
Anderson, Elijah, 201
Anderson, Sherwood, 74–75, 78
Anglo-Saxon, 76, 78, 80, 103
Antiracism, 28, 164, 231–256, 267
Appalachia, 157, 304 n.1, 314 n.24
Arnesen, Eric, 277–278

Bakhtin, Mikhail, 133
Bales, Kevin, 41
Banton, Michael, 322 n.10
Barr/Arnold, Roseanne, 25, 121, 306–307 n.18
Bashkow, Ira, 198
Behavior, 35–36, 39–40, 81, 99, 120–121, 167, 170, 181, 257
Beidelman, T. O., 18
Bellamy Brothers, 125

Belonging, 21–22, 59–60, 90, 107, 110, 149, 165, 199, 257, 268, 274
Black middle-class, 254–255, 277
Blackness, 10, 26–27, 40, 132, 149, 184, 189, 200, 316 n.14
Bodies, 16, 18, 23–24, 141, 273
Bonilla-Silva, Eduardo, 5–6
Bonnet, Alastair, 238, 241
Booth, Charles, 37, 39–40, 42–43, 63, 169
Boundary work, 15, 20–22, 36, 68
Bourdieu, Pierre, 20
Brightman, Robert, 274–278
Bultman, Bethany, 151–152, 159
Buruma, Ian, 281–282

Cairnes, John 65–67
California: northern, central, 270–273; Monterey Park, 265–266
Candyman, 52–56
Cannadine, David, 12–13
Cape Fear, 130–131
Carrier, James, 280–281
Cell, John, 195
Charlie Daniels Band, 307 n.22
Chen, Xiaomei, 281
Chicago, 52–54
Chute, Carolyn, 126–129, 132
Class: 1, 7, 24, 72, 165, 254–255; bodily dimensions, 20, 35, 40, 46, 129, 182;

Class (*continued*)
"class racism," 47; conflicts, 89, 127–129; cultural construction, 36–37; decorums, 24, 121; formations, 20; forms of otherness, 80, 129; relational dynamics, 20, 24–25, 34–35, 42, 294 nn.1–2; self-construction, 52; social distance, 44, 49, 110, 122, 219–220

Clinton, Bill, 121, 156–157, 183

Collective identities, 2–3, 8, 11–12, 18, 60, 63, 80, 88, 188

Concentration effects, 38

Conflation of race and class, 23, 40, 168, 189

Cracker, 61, 84, 143–144, 308 n.30

Crapanzano, Vincent, 196–197

Critical race theory, 29, 291 n.14, 293 n.36

Culler, Jonathan, 115

Cultural analysis, 9–12, 136, 257–258, 272–274, 283, 290 n.11

Cultural dynamics, 10, 13, 257–258, 272, 285

Cultural objects, 18, 59

Cultural poetics, 24, 135–136, 138, 148, 161

Cultural representations, 7, 20, 25

Cultural studies, 15, 20, 292–293 n.30

Culture: the concept of, 11, 28–29, 137, 258, 273–274, 276, 282, 292 n.27; deploying the concept, 57, 146, 191, 265, 267–268; processes of classification and categorization, 2, 10, 41, 47

"Dangerous classes," 37

Davenport, Charles, 89–90, 96–98, 100

Davenport, Gertrude, 101

Deconstruction, 3, 283

Degeneration, 38, 51, 66, 77, 296 n.21

Dei, George Sefa, 233

Deindustrialization, 172

Detroit, 165–166, 169, 197, 202, 209–229, 272–273

Discourse, 20–21, 257, 275–276

Disgust, 47, 68, 95

Dominguez, Virginia, 259–262, 276

Douglas, Mary, 114–115, 118, 210, 293 n.32

Douglass, Frederick, 62

Douglass, Lisa, 191–192

Dr. Jekyll and Mr. Hyde, 43–48

Du Bois, W. E. B., 201–202, 292–293 n.30, 294 n.7

Dugdale, Richard, 79–80

Earle, Steve, 125

Eminem, 25, 161–162, 165, 311 nn.7–9

Empirical analysis, 3, 39, 57, 165, 189

Ethnicity, 63, 110, 213, 228, 267–269

Ethnography, 14, 26, 56, 188–189, 198–201, 232–237; ethnographic objects, 135; urban ethnography, 56, 170–171

Etiquette, 11, 18–20, 43, 46, 79, 88–90, 119, 149, 273

Eugenics, 44, 70; family field studies, 71–72, 78–79; movement, 78, 84, 89, 104–105; popular writings, 88, 90–99

Eugenics Records Office, 84

Everyday life, 8, 26, 248, 255, 283

Expressive culture, 135–136

Feeblemindedness, 92, 103

Fiction, 33, 56

Fields, Barbara, 278–279

Figuration, 15–18, 24

Fiske, John, 305 n.10

Foner, Eric, 300 n.8

Foucault, Michel, 302 n.26

Fox, Aaron, 307 n.22

Frankenberg, Ruth, 188, 190–192, 227, 242, 249–252, 319–320 n.36

Fredrickson, George, 195–196

"Free labor" ideology, 62

Gadamer, Hans-Georg, 246

Gender, 4, 9, 16–18, 20, 28, 75, 257, 270; homoerotic, 140, 298 n.29; masculinity, 81, 137–138, 140; sexuality, 17,

Narrative, 17, 78, 144–146, 244–245, 273, 283, 299 n.1
New England, 71, 78
New Jack City, 130
New York, 266–267
Nixon, Mojo, 121

Objectification, 2, 9, 41, 106, 289 n.2
Occidentalism, 280–282
Omi, Michael, 207–209
Orientalism, 12–13, 259, 280–281, 285
Ortner, Sherry, 291 n.25
Otherness, 3, 11–14, 107, 228, 257, 285

Page, Helan, 188, 202
Parenting, 93–94
Performance, 11
Perry, Pamela, 270–272, 283
Peterson, Richard, 124
Picture of Dorian Gray, 48–52
Place, 14–15, 28, 268–269, 273
Pollution, 18, 62, 91, 99–103, 104, 114–115, 211, 273
Poor White, 74–75
Poor whites, 3–4, 22–23, 64, 96, 103, 317 n.19, 317–318 n.20; white underclass, 25, 120, 158, 176, 181–182
Popular culture, 148–149, 168–169, 187, 271–272
Poverty, 23, 25, 34, 62, 147, 214, 226; poverty line, 39; urban forms, 23, 25, 33–57, 167–184
Professionalism, 43–46, 80, 202
Psychoanalytic analysis, 13
Public discourse, 3, 160, 187

Race, 1, 4, 8, 43, 148, 171, 190, 223, 227, 289–290 n.6
Racial: 103–104, 256; active and passive forms of identity, 212–214, 248; consciousness, 88, 91–92, 98, 100; dynamics, 5, 10, 21; epithets, 16, 21; formations, 14–15, 207–209, 290 n.9;

identity politics, 240–241; idioms, 194; interpretations, 279–280; plasticity, 194; subjects, 15–16, 285; violence, 218, 227
Racialization, 40, 148, 155, 225, 246, 284–286
"Racial poisons," 70, 88
Racism, 6, 20–22, 150, 168, 237, 247, 249–250, 253–255, 261, 263–264, 270, 283, 291 n.7; new forms of, 5–6, 21
Racism Awareness Training, 233
Rafter, Nicole, 83, 300–301 n.150
Rattansi, Ali, 241
Redneck, 25, 123, 148–155
Reed, Adolph, Jr., 33, 40
Representation, 4, 9, 20, 33–34, 37, 42, 66–67, 81, 115, 120, 123, 165, 282, 284; economies of, 52
Rhetorical identity, 24, 132, 159
Roediger, David, 193, 279, 305 n.9
Rosaldo, Renato, 275, 305 n.10

Saito, Leland, 265, 273, 283
Sameness, 12–13, 22, 69, 78, 102, 136
Sanjek, Roger, 266–268, 273, 283
Sawyer Brown, 125
Scale, 27, 183, 205–208, 226
Scientific discourse, 78, 89, 93, 105
Seeger, Charles, 124
Segal, Dan, 191
Segregation: class forms of, 50, 52, 56, 298 n.34; conceptual forms of, 182; eugenical forms of, 92, 106; of moral orders, 43–45, 48, 51; racial forms of, 52–53, 56, 196, 202, 252
Self, 35–36, 55, 78, 90, 93, 136, 143, 146
Shame, 142
Silence of the Lambs, 130–131
Smedley, Audrey, 192–193
Social conditions, 147–148
Social isolation, 181–182
Socialization, 9, 13, 22, 109, 245
Social problems, 85, 87

JOHN HARTIGAN JR. IS AN ASSOCIATE PROFESSOR OF

ANTHROPOLOGY IN THE AMÉRICO PAREDES CENTER FOR

CULTURAL STUDIES AT THE UNIVERSITY OF TEXAS, AUSTIN.

HE IS THE AUTHOR OF *RACIAL SITUATIONS: CLASS*

PREDICAMENTS OF WHITENESS IN DETROIT.

LIBRARY OF CONGRESS CATALOGING-IN-PUBLICATION DATA

HARTIGAN, JOHN.

ODD TRIBES : TOWARDS A CULTURAL ANALYSIS OF WHITE PEOPLE /

JOHN HARTIGAN JR.

P. CM.

INCLUDES BIBLIOGRAPHICAL REFERENCES AND INDEX.

ISBN 0-8223-3584-0 (CLOTH : ALK. PAPER)

ISBN 0-8223-3597-2 (PBK. : ALK. PAPER)

1. WHITES—RACE IDENTITY—UNITED STATES. 2. WHITES—UNITED

STATES—SOCIAL CONDITIONS. 3. WHITES—UNITED STATES—

ECONOMIC CONDITIONS. 4. WHITES IN POPULAR CULTURE—UNITED

STATES. 5. WORKING CLASS WHITES—UNITED STATES. 6. REDNECKS—

UNITED STATES. 7. POOR—UNITED STATES. 8. POVERTY—SOCIAL

ASPECTS—UNITED STATES. 9. UNITED STATES—RACE RELATIONS.

10. UNITED STATES—SOCIAL CONDITIONS—1980–   I. TITLE.

E184.A1H344 2005   305.8'00973—DC22   2005010059